PAULO COELHO

A WARRIOR'S LIFE

THE AUTHORIZED BIOGRAPHY

FERNANDO MORAIS

HarperOne
An Imprint of HarperCollins*Publishers*

HarperOne

HarperCollins books may be purchased for educational, business, or sales promotional use. For information please write: Special Markets Department, HarperCollins Publishers, 10 East 53rd Street, New York, NY 10022.

HarperCollins Web site: http://www.harpercollins.com

HarperCollins®, 📖®, and HarperOne™ are trademarks of HarperCollins Publishers.

FIRST INTERNATIONAL EDITION

Library of Congress Cataloging-in-Publication Data is available upon request.

ISBN 978–0–06–193468–1

09 10 11 12 13 RRD(H) 10 9 8 7 6 5 4 3 2 1

*For Marina, my companion on yet another crossing
of the Rubicon*

When the world fails to end in the year 2000, perhaps what *will* end is this fascination with the work of Paulo Coelho.

Wilson Martins, literary critic, April 1998, O Globo

Brazil is Rui Barbosa, it's Euclides da Cunha, but it's also Paulo Coelho. I'm not a reader of his books, nor am I an admirer, but he has to be accepted as a fact of contemporary Brazilian life.

Martins again, July 2005, O Globo

CONTENTS

CHAPTER 1

Paulo today: Budapest–Prague– Hamburg–Cairo

IT'S A DREARY, GREY EVENING in May 2005 as the enormous white Air France Airbus A600 touches down gently on the wet runway of Budapest's Ferihegy airport. It is the end of a two-hour flight from Lyons in the south of France. In the cabin, the stewardess informs the passengers that it's 6.00 p.m. in Hungary's capital city and that the local temperature is 8°C. Seated beside the window in the front row of business class, his seat belt still fastened, a man in a black T-shirt looks up and stares at some invisible point beyond the plastic wall in front of him. Unaware of the other passengers' curious looks, and keeping his eyes fixed on the same spot, he raises the forefinger and middle finger of his right hand as though in blessing and remains still for a moment.

After the plane stops, he gets up to take his bag from the overhead locker. He is dressed entirely in black – canvas boots, jeans and T-shirt. (Someone once remarked that, were it not for the wicked gleam in his eye, he could be mistaken for a priest.) A small detail on his woollen jacket, which is also black, tells the other passengers – at least those who are French – that their fellow traveller is no ordinary mortal, since on his lapel is a tiny gold pin embossed in red, a little larger than a computer chip, indicating to those around him that he is a Chevalier of the Legion of Honour. This is the most coveted of French decorations, created in

1802 by Napoleon Bonaparte and granted only at the personal wish of the President of the Republic. The award, which was given to the traveller at the behest of Jacques Chirac, is not, however, the only thing that marks him out. His thinning, close-cropped white hair ends in a tuft above the nape of his neck, a small white ponytail some 10 centimetres long. This is a *sikha*, the lock of hair worn by Brahmans, orthodox Hindus and Hare Krishna monks. His neat white moustache and goatee beard are the final touch on a lean, strong, tanned face. At 1.69 metres he's fairly short, but muscular and with not an ounce of fat on his body.

With his rucksack on his back and dying for a cigarette, he joins the queue of passengers in the airport corridor, with an unlit, Brazilian-made Galaxy Light between his lips. In his hand is a lighter ready to be flicked on as soon as it's allowed, which will not, it seems, be soon. Even for someone with no Hungarian, the meaning of the words '*Tilos adohanyzas*' is clear, since it appears on signs everywhere, alongside the image of a lighted cigarette with a red line running through it. Standing beside the baggage carousel, the man in black looks anxiously over at the glass wall separating international passengers from the main concourse. His black case with a white heart chalked on it is, in fact, small enough for him to have taken it on board as hand luggage, but its owner hates carrying anything.

After going through customs and passing beyond the glass wall, the man in black is visibly upset to find that his name does not appear on any of the boards held up by the drivers and tour reps waiting for passengers on his flight. Worse still, there are no photographers, reporters or television cameras waiting for him. There is no one. He walks out on to the pavement, looking around, and even before lifting the collar of his jacket against the cold wind sweeping across Budapest, he lights his cigarette and consumes almost half of it in one puff. The other Air France passengers go their separate ways in buses, taxis and private cars, leaving the pavement deserted. The man's disappointment gives way to anger. He lights another cigarette, makes an international call on his mobile phone and complains in Portuguese and in a slightly nasal voice: 'There's no one waiting for me in Budapest! Yes! That's what I said!' He repeats this, hammering each word into the head of the person at the other end:

'That's right – *there's no one waiting for me here in Budapest.* No one. I said *no one!*'

He rings off without saying goodbye, stubs out his cigarette and starts to smoke a third, pacing disconsolately up and down. Fifteen interminable minutes after disembarking he hears a familiar sound. He turns towards it, and his eyes light up. An enormous smile appears on his face. The reason for his joy is only a few metres away: a crowd of reporters, photographers, cameramen and paparazzi are running towards him calling his name, nearly all of them holding a microphone and a recorder. Behind them is a still larger group – his fans.

'Mister Cole-ro! Mister Paulo Cole-ro!'

This is how Hungarians pronounce the surname of the Brazilian author Paulo Coelho, the man in black who has just arrived in Budapest as guest of honour at the International Book Festival. The invitation was a Russian initiative, rather than a Brazilian one (Brazil doesn't even have a stand), Russia being the guest country at the 2005 festival. Coelho is the most widely read author in Russia, which, with 143 million inhabitants, is one of the most populous countries in the world. Along with the reporters come people bearing copies of his most recent success, *The Zahir*, all open at the title page, as they step over the tangle of cables on the ground and face the hostility of the journalists, simply to get his autograph. The flashbulbs and the bluish glow from the reflectors cast a strange light on the shaven head of the author, who looks as if he were on the strobe-lit dance floor of a 1970s disco. Despite the crowd and the discomfort, he wears a permanent, angelic smile and, even though he's drowning in a welter of questions in English, French and Hungarian, he appears to be savouring an incomparable pleasure: world fame. He is in his element. Mister Cole-ro with his sparkling eyes and the sincerest possible smile is once again Paulo Coelho, superstar and a member of the Brazilian Academy of Letters, whose books have been translated into 66 languages and dialects across 160 countries. He is a man accustomed to receiving a pop star's welcome from his readers. He tells the journalists that he has been to Hungary only once, more than twenty years before. 'I'm just afraid that fifteen years of capitalist tourism may have done Budapest more harm than the Russians did in half a century,' he says provocatively, referring to the period when the country was part of the former Soviet Union.

That same day, the author had another opportunity to savour public recognition. While waiting for the plane at Lyons airport he was approached by a fellow Brazilian, who told him that he had read and admired his work. On being called to take the bus to the plane, they walked together to the gate, but the other Brazilian, when asked to produce his boarding pass, couldn't find it. Anxious that the other passengers would grow impatient as the man searched clumsily through his things, the Air France employee moved him to one side, and the queue moved on.

Out of kindness, Paulo Coelho stood beside his fellow countryman, but was told: 'Really, you don't need to wait. I'll find it in a minute.'

All the other passengers were now seated in the bus, and the Air France employee was threatening to close the door. 'I'm sorry, but if you haven't got a boarding pass, you can't board the plane.'

The Brazilian began to see his holiday plans falling apart, but he wasn't going to give up that easily. 'But I know I've got it. Only a few minutes ago I showed it to the author Paulo Coelho, who was with me, because I wanted to know if we were going to be sitting next to each other.'

The Frenchman stared at him. 'Paulo Coelho? Do you mean that man is Paulo Coelho?' On being assured that this was so, he ran over to the bus, where the passengers were waiting for the problem to be resolved, and shouted, 'Monsieur Paulo Coelho!' Once the author had stood up and confirmed that he had indeed seen his fellow Brazilian's boarding pass, the Frenchman, suddenly all politeness and cordiality, beckoned to the cause of the hold-up and allowed him to board the bus.

Night has fallen in Budapest when a tall, thin young man announces that there are to be no more photos or questions. To the protests of both journalists and fans, Paulo Coelho is now seated in the back of a Mercedes, its age and impressive size suggesting that it may once have carried Hungary's Communist leaders. Also in the car are the men who are to be his companions for the next three days: the driver and bodyguard, Pal Szabados, a very tall young man with a crew cut; and Gergely

Huszti, who freed him from the reporters' clutches and who is to be his guide. Both men were appointed by the author's publisher in Hungary, Athenäum.

When the car sets off, and even before Gergely has introduced himself, Paulo asks for a moment's silence and, as he did in the plane, he gazes into the distance, raises his forefinger and middle finger, and for a few seconds prays. He performs this solitary ceremony at least three times a day – when he wakes, at six in the evening and at midnight – and repeats it in planes when taking off and landing and in cars when driving off, regardless of whether he is on a long-haul flight or a short trip in a cab.

On the way to the hotel, Gergely reads out the planned programme: a debate followed by a signing session at the book festival; a visit to the Budapest underground with the prefect, Gabor Demszky; five individual interviews for various television programmes and major publications; a press conference; a photo shoot with Miss Peru, one of his readers (who is in Hungary for the Miss Universe contest); two dinners; a show at an open-air disco …

Coelho interrupts Gergely in English. 'Stop there, please. You can cut out the visit to the underground, the show and Miss Peru. None of that was on the programme.'

The guide insists: 'I think we should at least keep the visit to the underground, as it's the third oldest in the world … And the prefect's wife is a fan of yours and has read all your books.'

'Forget it. I'll sign a book especially for her, but I'm not going to the underground.'

With the underground, the disco and Miss Peru scrapped, the author approves the schedule, showing no signs of fatigue in spite of the fact that he has had an exhausting week. With the launch of *The Zahir* he has given interviews to reporters from the Chilean newspaper *El Mercurio*, the French magazine *Paris Match*, the Dutch daily *De Telegraaf*, the magazine produced by Maison Cartier, the Polish newspaper *Fakt* and the Norwegian women's magazine *Kvinner og Klær*. At the request of a friend, an aide to the Saudi royal family, he also gave a long statement to Nigel Dudley and Sarah MacInnes from the magazine *Think*, a British business publication.

Half an hour after leaving the airport, the Mercedes stops in front of the Gellert, an imposing four-star establishment on the banks of the Danube, one of the oldest spa hotels in Central Europe. Before signing in, Paulo embraces a beautiful dark-haired woman who has just arrived from Barcelona and has been waiting for him in the hotel lobby. Holding her hand is a chubby, blue-eyed little boy. She is Mônica Antunes and the boy is her son. Although she acts as Paulo Coelho's literary agent, it would be a mistake to consider her, as people often do, as merely that, because it accounts for only a small part of the work she has been doing since the end of the 1980s.

Some people in the literary jet set say that behind her beautiful face, soft voice and shy smile lies a ferocious guard dog, for she is known and feared for the ruthlessness with which she treats anyone who threatens her author's interests. Many publishers refer to her – behind her back of course – as 'the witch of Barcelona', a reference to the city where she lives and from where she controls everything to do with the professional life of her one client. Mônica has become the link between the author and the publishing world. Anything and everything to do with his literary work has to pass through the modern, seventh-storey office that is home to Sant Jordi Asociados, named in Catalan after the patron saint of books, St George.

While her Peruvian nanny keeps an eye on her son in the hotel lobby, Mônica sits down with the author at a corner table and opens her briefcase, full of computer printouts produced by Sant Jordi. Today, it's all good news: in three weeks *The Zahir* has sold 106,000 copies in Hungary. In Italy, over the same period, the figure was 420,000. In the Italian bestseller lists the book has even overtaken the memoirs of the recently deceased John Paul II. The author, however, doesn't appear to be pleased.

'That's all very well, Mônica, but I want to know how *The Zahir* has done in comparison with the previous book in the same period.'

She produces another document. 'In the same period, *Eleven Minutes* sold 328,000 copies in Italy. So *The Zahir* is selling almost 30 per cent more. *Now* are you happy?'

'Yes, of course. And what about Germany?'

'There *The Zahir* is in second place on *Der Spiegel*'s best-seller list, after *The Da Vinci Code*.'

As well as Hungary, Italy and Germany, the author asks for information about sales in Russia and wants to know whether Arash Hejazi, his Iranian publisher, has resolved the problems of censorship, and what is happening regarding pirate copies being sold in Egypt. According to Mônica's figures, the author is beating his own records in every country where the book has come out. A week after its launch in France, *The Zahir* topped all lists, including the most prized, that of the weekly news magazine *L'Express*. In Russia, sales have passed the 530,000 mark, while in Portugal, they stand at 130,000 (whereas *Eleven Minutes* had sold only 80,000 copies six months after its launch). In Brazil, *The Zahir* has sold 160,000 copies in less than a month (60 per cent more than *Eleven Minutes* in the same period). And while Coelho is appearing in Hungary, 500,000 copies of the Spanish translation of *The Zahir* are being distributed throughout the southern states of America – to reach the Spanish-speaking communities there – and throughout eighteen Latin-American countries. The only surprise is the last piece of news: the previous day, an armed gang stopped a lorry in a Buenos Aires suburb and stole the entire precious cargo – 2,000 copies of *The Zahir* that had just left the printer's and were on their way to bookshops in the city. Some days later, a literary critic in the *Diario de Navarra* in Spain suggested that the robbery had been a publicity stunt dreamed up by the author as a way of selling more copies.

All this stress and anxiety is repeated every two years, each time Paulo Coelho publishes a new book. On these occasions, he shows himself to be as insecure as a novice. This has always been the case. When he wrote his first book, *O Diário de um Mago* [*The Pilgrimage*], he shared the task of distributing publicity leaflets outside Rio's theatres and cinemas with his partner, the artist Christina Oiticica, and then went round the bookshops to find out how many copies they had sold. After twenty years, his methods and strategies may have changed, but he has not: wherever he is, be it in Tierra del Fuego or Greenland, in Alaska or

Australia, he uses his mobile phone or his laptop to keep abreast of everything to do with publication, distribution, media attention and where his books are on the best-seller lists.

He has still not yet filled out the inevitable hotel form or gone up to his room, when Lea arrives. A pleasant woman in her fifties, married to the Swiss Minister of the Interior, she is a devoted reader of Coelho's books, having first met him at the World Economic Forum in Davos. When she learned that he was visiting Budapest, Lea took the train from Geneva, travelling over 4,000 kilometres through Switzerland, Austria and half of Hungary in order to spend a few hours in Budapest with her idol. It is almost eight o'clock when Coelho finally goes up to the suite reserved for him at the Gellert.

The room seems palatial in comparison with his modest luggage, the contents of which never vary: four black T-shirts, four pairs of coloured silk boxer shorts, five pairs of socks, a pair of black Levi's, a pair of denim Bermudas and a pack of Galaxy cigarettes (his stock of the latter is regularly topped up by his office in Rio or by kind visitors from Brazil). For formal occasions he adds to his luggage the coat he was wearing when he flew in from France, a shirt with a collar, a tie and his 'society shoes' – a pair of cowboy boots – again all in black. Contrary to what one might think on first seeing him, his choice of colour has nothing to do with luck, mysticism or spirituality. As someone who often spends two-thirds of the year away from home, he has learned that black clothes are more resistant to the effects of hotel laundries, although on most occasions he washes his own socks, shirts and underpants. In one corner of his case is a small wash bag containing toothbrush and toothpaste, a razor, dental floss, eau de cologne, shaving foam and a tube of Psorex, a cream he uses for the psoriasis he sometimes gets between his fingers and on his elbows. In another corner, wrapped in socks and underpants, are a small image of Nhá Chica, a holy woman from Minas Gerais in Brazil, and a small bottle of holy water from Lourdes.

Half an hour later, he returns to the hotel lobby freshly shaved and smelling of lavender, and looking as refreshed as if he has just woken from a good night's sleep; his overcoat, slung over his shoulders, allows a glimpse of a small blue butterfly with open wings tattooed on his left forearm. His last engagement for the day is dinner at the home of an artist in the Buda hills above the city on the right bank of the Danube, with a wonderful view of the old capital, on which, this evening, a fine drizzle is falling.

In a candlelit room some fifty people are waiting for him, among them artists, writers and diplomats, mostly young people in their thirties. And, as usual, there are a lot of women. Everyone is sitting around on sofas or on the floor, talking or, rather, trying to talk above the noise of heavy rock blasting out from loudspeakers. A circle of people gathers round the author, who is talking non-stop. They soon become aware of two curious habits: every now and then, he makes a gesture with his right hand as if brushing away an invisible fly from in front of his eyes. Minutes later, he makes the same gesture, but this time the invisible fly appears to be buzzing next to his right ear. At dinner, he thanks everyone in fluent English for their kindness and goes on to praise Hungarian cooks, who can transform a modest beef stew into an unforgettable delicacy – goulash. At two in the morning, after coffee and a few rounds of Tokaji wine, everyone leaves.

At a quarter to ten the following morning, the first journalists invited to the press conference have already taken their places on the thirty upholstered chairs in the Hotel Gellert's small meeting room. Anyone arriving punctually at ten will have to stand. The person the reporters are interested in woke at 8.30. Had it not been raining he would have taken his usual hour-long morning walk. Since he dislikes room service ('Only sick people eat in their bedrooms'), he has breakfasted in the hotel's coffee bar, gone back to his room to take a shower, and is now reading newspapers and surfing the Internet. He usually reads a Rio newspaper and one from São Paulo, as well as the Paris edition of the *International Herald Tribune*. The remainder of his daily reading will arrive later in the form of cuttings and synopses focusing on the author and his books.

At exactly ten o'clock he enters the room, which is lit by reflectors and full of journalists, and sits down behind the small table provided, on which stand a bottle of mineral water, a glass, an ashtray and a vase of red roses. His guide, Gergely, takes the microphone, explains the reason for the author's visit to the country and announces the presence in the front row of his agent, Mônica Antunes. She stands shyly and acknowledges the applause.

Coelho speaks in English for forty minutes, which includes the time it takes for Gergely to translate each sentence into Hungarian. He recalls his visit to Budapest in 1982, and talks a little about his personal life and his career as a writer. He reveals, for example, that, following the success of *The Pilgrimage*, the number of pilgrims to Santiago de Compostela rose from 400 a year to 400 a day. In recognition of this, the Galician government has named one of the streets of Santiago 'Rua Paulo Coelho'. When the meeting is opened up for questions, it becomes clear that the journalists present are fans of his work. Some mention a particular book as 'my favourite'. The meeting passes without any indiscreet or hostile questions being asked; the friendly atmosphere is more like a gathering of the Budapest branch of his fan club. When Gergely brings the meeting to an end, the reporters reward the author with a round of applause. A small queue forms in front of the table and an improvised signing session exclusive to Hungarian journalists begins. Only then does it become apparent that nearly all of them have copies of his books in their bags.

The writer, who rarely lunches, has a quick snack in the hotel restaurant – toast with liver pâté, a glass of orange juice and an espresso. He makes use of a free half-hour before his next appointment to glance at the international news in *Le Monde* and *El País*. He's always interested in what's going on in the world and he's always well informed about any wars and crises that hit the headlines. It's quite usual to hear him speaking confidently (but without ever appearing to be dictatorial or superior) on matters as various as the growing crisis in Lebanon or the nationalization of oil and gas in Bolivia. He publicly defended the exchange of hostages held by Marxist guerrillas in Colombia for political prisoners being held by the Colombian government, and his protest letter in 2003 entitled 'Thank you, President Bush', in which he castigated the American leader for the imminent invasion of Iraq, was read by 400 million people and caused much debate.

Once he has read the newspapers, he gets back to work. Now it is time for Marsi Aniko, the presenter of RTL Club's *Fokusz2*, which regularly tops the Sunday evening ratings. The unusual thing about *Fokusz2* is that, at the end of each programme, the interviewee is given a Hungarian dish prepared by Marsi Aniko herself. In a small, improvised studio in the hotel, the face-to-face interview again holds no surprises, apart from the way she blushes when a cheerful Coelho decides to start talking about penetrative sex. At the end, he receives a kiss on each cheek, a tray of *almásrétes* – a traditional Hungarian tart filled with poppy petals that Aniko swears she has made with her own fair hand – and a bottle of Pálinka, a very strong local brandy. Within minutes, the set has been removed to make way for another jollier, more colourful one, for an interview with András Simon from Hungarian MTV. An hour later, once the recording is over, the journalist hands the author a stack of seven books to sign.

With a few minutes' break between each interview – time enough for the author to drink an espresso and smoke a cigarette – these interviews continue into the late afternoon. When the last reporter leaves the hotel, it is dark.

Coelho declares that he is not in the least tired. 'On the contrary. Talking about so many different things in such a short space of time only increases the adrenalin. I'm just getting warmed up ...'

Whether it is professionalism, vanity or some other source of energy, the fact is that the author, who is about to turn sixty, is on enviably good form. A shower and another espresso are all it takes for him to reappear at 8.30 in the hotel lobby, gleefully rubbing his hands. Mônica, Lea (who has managed to attach herself to the group), the silent bodyguard Szabados and Gergely are waiting for him. There is one more engagement before the end of the day: a dinner with writers, publishers and journalists at the home of Tamás Kolosi, who owns the publishing house Athenäum and is one of the people behind Coelho's visit to Hungary. When Gergely asks Coelho if he's tired after all the day's activities, the author roars with laughter.

'Certainly not! Today was just the aperitif. The real work begins tomorrow.'

After dinner with the publisher, Mônica uses the ten minutes in the car journey back to the hotel to tell him what she has organized with Gergely for the following day.

'The opening of the book festival is at two in the afternoon. You've got interviews at the hotel in the morning, so there'll be no time for lunch, but I've booked a restaurant on the way to the book festival so that we can grab a sandwich and some salad.'

Coelho's mind is elsewhere. 'I'm worried about the Israeli publisher. He doesn't like the title *The Zahir* and wants to change it. Call him tomorrow, will you, and tell him I won't allow it. Either he keeps the title or he doesn't get to publish the book. It was bad enough them changing the name of the shepherd Santiago in *The Pilgrimage* to Jakobi.'

He was equally stubborn before he became famous. Mônica recalls that the US publisher of *The Alchemist* wanted to re-name it *The Shepherd and His Dreams*, but the author refused to sanction the change.

Listening to her now, he says, smiling: 'I was a complete nobody and they were HarperCollins, but I stuck to my guns and said "No way," and they respected me for that.'

The following morning it is sunny enough to encourage the author to take his usual hour-long walk – this time along the banks of the Danube. Then after a shower, a quick glance at the Internet, breakfast and two interviews, he's ready for the second part of the day: the opening of the book festival. On the way there, they stop at the place reserved by Mônica, a snack bar, where all the other customers seem to have been driven away by the incredibly loud music coming from an ancient jukebox.

Coelho walks over, turns down the volume, puts 200 florins into the machine and selects a 1950s hit, 'Love Me Tender' by Elvis. He goes back to the table smiling as he imitates the rock star's melodious tones: '"Love me tender, love me true …" I adore the Beatles, but this man is the greatest and will be around for ever …'

Gergely wants to know why he's so happy, and Coelho flings wide his arms.

'Today is the feast of St George, the patron saint of books. Everything's going to be just fine!'

The International Book Festival in Budapest takes place every year at a convention centre located in a park – which, today, is still powdered with winter snow – and brings in hundreds of thousands of visitors.

Coelho is welcomed at a private entrance by three burly bodyguards and ushered into the VIP lounge. When he learns that there are almost five hundred people waiting at the publisher's stand to have their books signed, he says:

'We said that only 150 vouchers were to be handed out.'

The manager of the publishing house explains that they have no means of getting rid of the readers and fans. 'I'm sorry, but when the vouchers ran out, the other people in the queue simply refused to leave. There were even more people originally, but some of them have gone over to the auditorium where you're due to speak. The problem is that it only seats 350, and there are now 800 waiting to get in. We've had to erect screens outside for them.'

Mônica goes quietly out of the room to the Athenäum stand and returns five minutes later, shaking her head and looking worried. 'It's just not going to work. It's going to be bedlam.'

The security people say there's no danger, but suggest that Mônica's son and the nanny remain in the VIP lounge until the end of the programme.

Now, however, the news that the festival is crammed with fans and readers appears to have dispelled Coelho's initial feelings of irritation. He gets up smiling, claps his hands and makes a decision: 'So there are too many people? The more the merrier! Let's go and meet the readers. Just give me five minutes alone.'

He goes to the toilet as if for a pee, but once there he stands and stares into space, praying silently. Then he asks God to make sure that everything goes well during the day. 'Now it's up to You.'

God appears to have listened. Protected by the three bodyguards, and by Szabados, who has orders never to let him out of his sight, Paulo Coelho arrives in the Béla Bártok room lit by the lights of television crews and the flashlights of photographers. All the seats are taken and even the passageways, aisles and galleries are filled to capacity. The audience is equally divided between men and women, but most are young. He is escorted to the stage by the security guards and he acknowledges the applause, his hands pressed to his chest. The harsh lights and the crush of people mean that the heat is unbearable. The author speaks for half an hour in fluent French, talking about his life, his beliefs and the struggle to realize his dream to become a writer, all of which is then translated into Hungarian by a young woman. After this a small number of people are selected to ask questions, at the end of which the writer stands up to thank everyone for their welcome.

The audience doesn't want him to leave. Waving their books in the air, they yell: '*Ne! Ne! Ne!*'

In the midst of the uproar, the interpreter explains that '*ne*' means 'no' – those present do not want the author to leave without signing their books. The problem is that the security people are also saying '*ne*'. There are simply too many people. The cries of '*Ne! Ne!*' continue unabated. Coelho pretends not to have understood what the security people are saying, takes a pen out of his pocket and returns, smiling, to the microphone. 'If you can get yourselves in some kind of order, I'll try and sign a few.'

Dozens of people immediately start pushing forward, climbing on to the stage and surrounding the author. Fearing a stampede, the security guards decide to step in. They lift Coelho bodily off the floor and carry him through the curtains and from there to a secure room. He bursts out laughing.

'You could have left me there. I'm not frightened of my readers. What I fear is creating panic. In 1998, in Zagreb, a security man with a pistol at his waist tried to break up the queue and you can imagine how dangerous that was! My readers would never harm me.'

With two bodyguards in front of him and two behind, and under the curious gaze of onlookers, the author is accompanied down the corridors of the convention centre to the Athenäum stand, where copies of *The Zahir* await him. The queue of 500 people has become a crowd too large to organize. The 150 voucher holders wave their numbered cards in the air, surrounded by the majority, who have only copies of Paulo Coelho's books as their passport to an autograph. He is, however, used to such situations and immediately takes command. Speaking in French with an interpreter on hand, he raises his arms to address the multitude – and yes, this really is a multitude: 1,500? 2,000? It's impossible to know who is there to get his autograph or to get a glimpse of their idol and who has simply been attracted by the crowd. Finding it hard to be heard, he shouts: 'Thank you for coming. I know lots of you have been here since midday and I've asked the publisher to provide water for you all. We're going to have two queues, one for those who've got a voucher and the other for those who haven't. I'm going to try to deal with everyone. Thank you!'

Now comes the hard work. While waiters circulate with trays of cold mineral water, the author tries to create some order out of the chaos. He signs thirty books for those in the queue and then another thirty for those who have had to wait outside. Every fifty or sixty minutes he pauses briefly to go to the toilet or to a small area outside, the only place in the entire conference centre where he can smoke, and which he has named 'bad boy's corner'. On his third visit, he comes across a non-smoker, book in hand, waiting out of line for an autograph. He is Jacques Gil, a twenty-year-old Brazilian from Rio who has moved to Hungary to play for the oldest football club there, Újpest. Coelho quickly signs the book and takes four or five drags on his cigarette. He then hurries back to the stand, where the crowd is waiting patiently.

By the time the last of the fans reach the table, it is dark, and with the official programme at an end, it is time to relax. The original group – with the addition of half-a-dozen young men and women who refuse to leave – agree to meet after dinner in the hotel foyer for an evening's entertainment. At ten, everyone goes to a karaoke bar in Mammut, a popular shopping centre. The young Hungarians accompanying the author are disappointed when they learn that the sound system isn't working.

'That's too bad,' one complains to the manager. 'We managed to persuade Paulo Coelho to sing for us ...'

The mention of Coelho's name again opens doors, and the manager whispers something to a shaven-headed man, who immediately picks up a motorcycle helmet from the table and rushes off. The manager returns to the group, smiling. 'There's no way we're going to miss a performance by Paulo Coelho just because we've no karaoke equipment. My partner has gone to borrow some from another club. Please, take a seat.'

The motorcyclist takes so long to come back that the much-hoped-for performance becomes what musicians might call an 'impromptu' and a fairly modest one at that. Coelho sings Frank Sinatra's 'My Way' with

Andrew, a young American student on holiday in Hungary. He follows this up with a solo version of 'Love Me Tender', but declines to give an encore.

Everyone returns to the hotel at midnight, and the following morning, the members of the group go their separate ways. Mônica returns with her son and Juana to Barcelona, Lea goes back to Switzerland, and the author, after an hour's walk through the centre of Budapest, is once again sitting in the back of the Mercedes driven by Szabados. Next to him is a cardboard box full of his books. He opens one at the first page, signs it and hands it to Gergely, who is in the front seat. In the last two books, he writes a personal dedication to his driver and his guide. An hour later, he is sitting in business class in another Air France plane, this time bound for Paris, and again he is saying his silent prayer.

When the plane has taken off, a beautiful young black woman with her hair arranged in dozens of tiny plaits approaches him with a copy of *The Pilgrimage* in Portuguese. Her name is Patrícia and she is secretary to the famous Cape Verdean singer Cesária Évora. She asks him to sign the book. 'It's not for me, it's for Cesária, who's sitting back there. She's a big fan of yours, but she's really shy.'

Two hours later in Paris, at Charles de Gaulle airport, Coelho has yet another short but unexpected signing and photo session, when he's recognized by a group of Cape Verdean Rastafarians who are waiting for the singer. Their excitement attracts the attention of other people, who immediately recognize the author and ask to be allowed to take some photos as well. Although he's clearly tired, he cheerfully deals with all of them. At the exit, a chauffeur is waiting with a Mercedes provided by Coelho's French publisher. Although a suite costing 1,300 euros a day has been reserved for him at the Hotel Bristol, one of the most luxurious hotels in the French capital, he prefers to stay at his own place, a four-bedroom apartment in the smart 16th *arrondissement* with a wonderful view of the Seine. The problem is getting there. Today marks the anniversary of the massacre of the Armenians by the authorities of the Ottoman Empire, and a noisy demonstration is being held outside the Turkish Embassy, which is right near the apartment building. On the way, the Mercedes passes newspaper stands and kiosks displaying a full-page advertisement for *Feminina*, the weekly women's supplement with a circulation of 4 million, which is offering its readers an advance chapter from *The Zahir*. An enormous photo of the author fills the front page of the *Journal du Dimanche*, advertising an exclusive interview with him.

By dint of driving on the pavement and going the wrong way down one-way streets, Georges, the chauffeur, finally manages to park outside the apartment block. Despite having bought the place more than four years ago, Coelho is so unfamiliar with it that he still hasn't managed to learn the six-digit code needed to open the main door. Christina is upstairs waiting for him, but she has no mobile with her and, besides, he can't remember the phone number of the apartment. There are two alternatives: he can wait until a neighbour arrives or shout up to Christina for her to throw down the key. It's drizzling, and the wait is becoming uncomfortable. In a six-storey building with just one apartment per floor he might have to wait hours for a Good Samaritan to come in or out. The only thing to do is to shout and hope that Christina is awake.

He stands in the middle of the street and yells, 'Chris!'

No response. He tries again. 'Christina!'

He looks round, fearing that he might be recognized, and yells one more time, 'Chris-tiii-naaaaaa!'

Like a mother looking down at a naughty child, she appears, smiling, in jeans and woollen jumper, on the small balcony on the third floor and throws the bunch of keys to Coelho (who really does look tired now).

The couple spend only one night there. The following day they are both installed in suite 722 of the Hotel Bristol. The choice of hotel is deliberate: it is a temple to luxury in the Faubourg St Honoré and it is here that Coelho set parts of *The Zahir*, among the Louis XV sofas in the hotel lobby. In the book, the main character meets his wife, the journalist Esther, in the hotel café to drink a cup of hot chocolate decorated with a slice of crystallized orange. In recognition of this, the Bristol has decided to name the drink '*Le chocolat chaud de Paulo Coelho*' and the name is now written in gold letters on tiny bars of chocolate served to guests at 10 euros a go.

On this particular afternoon, the hotel has become a meeting place for journalists, celebrities and various foreign guests, all of whom have been invited to a dinner where Flammarion will announce the scoop of the year in the European publishing world: it has signed a contract to publish Paulo Coelho. Since 1994, the author has remained faithful to the small publisher Éditions Anne Carrière, which has achieved sales that have been the envy of even the most well-established publishing houses: in a little more than ten years it has sold 8 million copies of his books. After years of turning down ever-more enticing and hard-to-refuse offers, the author has decided to give way to what is reputed to be a 1.2 million-euro deposit in his bank account by Flammarion, although both parties refuse to confirm this sum.

Paulo and Christina appear in the hotel lobby. She is an attractive fifty-five-year-old, slightly shorter than Paulo, with whom she has been living since 1980. She is discreet and elegant, with fair skin, brown eyes and a delicate nose. On the inside of her left arm, she bears a tattoo of a small blue butterfly identical to Paulo's. Her glossy hair is cut just below her ears, and over her long black dress she's wearing a bright red shawl. But it is the two rings on her fingers ('blessed by a tribal leader', she explains) that attract most attention. They are a gift brought by Paulo from Kazakhstan. He, as ever, is dressed entirely in black – trousers, jacket, cowboy boots. The only slight change is that he is wearing a collar and tie.

The first friend to arrive is also a guest at the hotel and has come a long way. He is the Russian journalist Dmitry Voskoboynikov, a large, good-natured man who still bears the scars from the injuries he suffered during the 2004 tsunami in Indonesia, where he and his wife Evgenia were spending Christmas and New Year. A former London correspondent for TASS and the son of a member of the KGB, he is the owner of Interfax, a news agency with its headquarters in Moscow and which covers the world from Portugal to the farthest-flung regions of eastern Asia. The four sit round one of the small tables in the marble lobby and Evgenia, a magnificent blonde Kazak, gives the author a special present – a richly bound edition of *The Zahir* translated into her mother tongue. Four glasses of champagne appear on the table along with crystal bowls full of shelled pistachios. The subject changes immediately to gastronomy and Evgenia says that she has eaten a '*couscous à Paulo Coelho*' in Marrakesh, and Dmitry recalls dining in a Restaurant Paulo Coelho at Gstaad. The

conversation is interrupted by the arrival of another well-known journalist, the Brazilian Caco Barcellos, the head of the European offices of Rede
Globo de Televisão. He has arrived recently from their London office,
having been sent to Paris solely to report on the Flammarion dinner. At
seven in the evening, Georges arrives with the Mercedes to take Paulo
and Christina to the ceremony. The choice of venue for this banquet for
250 guests leaves no doubt as to the importance of the evening: it is the
restaurant Le Chalet des Îles, a mansion that Napoleon III ordered to be
dismantled and brought over from Switzerland to be rebuilt, brick by
brick, on one of the islands on the lake of the Bois de Boulogne as proof
of his love for his wife, the Spanish Countess Eugenia de Montijo. The
guests are checked by security guards on the boat that takes them across
to the Île Supérieure. On disembarking, they are taken by receptionists to
the main door, where the directors of Flammarion take turns greeting the
new arrivals. Publishers, literary critics, artists, diplomats and well-known
representatives of the arts in Europe are surrounded by paparazzi and
teams from gossip magazines wanting photos and interviews. There are
at least two ambassadors present, Sergio Amaral from Brazil and
Kuansych Sultanov from Kazakhstan, where *The Zahir* is partly set. The
only notable absentee is Frédéric Beigbeder, a former advertising executive, writer and provocative literary critic, who has worked as a publisher
at Flammarion since 2003. Some years ago, when he was a critic for the
controversial French weekly *Voici*, he wrote a very negative review of
Paulo Coelho's *Manual of the Warrior of Light*. When everyone is seated,
the author goes from table to table, greeting the other guests. Before the
first course is served, there is a short speech from Frédéric Morel, managing director of Flammarion, who declares the new contract with Paulo
Coelho to be a matter of pride for the publisher, which has launched so
many great French writers. The author appears genuinely moved and
gives a short address, thanking everyone for their good wishes and saying
how pleased he is that so many people have come. After dessert, champagne toasts and dancing to a live band, the evening comes to an end.
The following morning an hour-long flight takes the author and Christina
to Pau in the south of France. There they take the car Coelho left in the
car park some days earlier – a modest rented Renault Scénic identical to

Chris's. His obvious lack of interest in consumer goods, even a certain stinginess, means that although he's very rich, he didn't own his first luxury car until 2006, and even that was obtained without any money changing hands. The German car-makers Audi asked him to produce a short text – about two typed pages – to accompany their annual share-holders report. When asked how much he wanted for the work he joked: 'A car!' He wrote the article and sent it off by e-mail. A few days later, a truck from Germany delivered a brand-new, gleaming black Audi Avant. When he heard that the car cost 100,000 euros, a Brazilian journalist worked out that the author had earned 16 euros per character. 'Not bad,' Coelho remarked when he read this. 'Apparently Hemingway got paid 5 dollars a word.'

Half an hour after leaving Pau, Coelho and Christina are in Tarbes, a small, rather dismal town of 50,000 inhabitants on the edge of the French Basque country, a few kilometres from the Spanish border. Four kilometres out towards the south on a near-deserted road, they finally reach their house in Saint-Martin, a tiny community of 316 inhabitants and a few dozen houses set among wheatfields and pasturelands grazed by Holstein cows. The couple took the unusual decision to move here in 2001, when they made a pilgrimage to the sanctuary in Lourdes, 16 kilometres away. There wasn't a bed to be had in Lourdes, and they ended up staying in the Henri IV, a modest three-star hotel in Tarbes. It was the peacefulness of the region, its proximity to Lourdes and the incredible view of the Pyrenees that made them decide to settle there. While looking for a suitable house to buy and being in no hurry, Paulo and Christina spent almost two years in the only suite in the Henri IV, a rambling old house lacking any of the comforts they were accustomed to in large hotels. The absence of any luxury – which meant no Internet connection either – was more than made up for by the care lavished on them by the owner, Madame Geneviève Phalipou, and by her son, Serge, who, depending on the time of day, was manager, waiter or hotel porter. The so-called suite the couple occupied was, in fact, nothing more than a room with ensuite bath like all the others, plus a second room which served as a sitting room.

During their long stay in that small town, Coelho soon became a famil-iar figure. Since he has never employed secretaries or assistants, he was always the one who went to the post office, the chemist's or the butcher's, and shopped at the local supermarket, just like any other inhabitant. At first, he was regarded as a celebrity (particularly when foreign journalists started hanging around outside the Henri IV), but fame counts for little when one is standing in the queue at the baker's or barber's, and within a matter of months he had become a member of the Tarbes community. Even after he left the hotel and moved to his own house in Saint-Martin, the inhabitants of Tarbes continued to consider him one of their own – a compliment that Coelho is always eager to repay. He demonstrated his gratitude during an interview for *Tout le Monde en Parle*, a live programme on the French station France 2, whose presenter, Thierry Ardisson, is known for asking embarrassing questions. On this occasion, the singer Donovan and the designer Paco Rabanne were also on the programme.

Ardisson went straight to the point: 'Paulo Coelho, there's something I've been wanting to ask you for a long time. You're rich, world-famous, and yet you live in Tarbes! Isn't that rather stupid?'

The author refused to rise to the bait. He merely laughed and replied: 'Even the inhabitants were surprised, but it was love at first sight. Love is the only explanation.'

The presenter went on: 'Be serious now. What was the real reason you chose to live in Tarbes?'

'As I said, it was love.'

'I don't believe you. Admit it – you lost some bet and had to move to Tarbes.'

'No, I didn't!'

'Are they holding your wife hostage in order to force you to live there?'

'No, absolutely not!'

'But doesn't anyone who lives in Tarbes have to go to Laloubère or Ibos to do their shopping?'

'Yes, that's where I do all my shopping.'

'And does anyone there know you and know that you're Paulo Coelho?'

'Of course, everyone knows me.'

'Well, since you like it so much there, would you like to send a message to the inhabitant – sorry, the inhabitants – of Tarbes?'

'Absolutely. Tarbes people, I love you. Thank you for welcoming me as a son of your town.'

This was music to the ears of his new fellow citizens. A few days later, the newspaper *La Dépêche*, which covers the entire region of the Hautes-Pyrénées, praised Coelho's actions and stated: 'On Saturday night, Tarbes had its moment of national glory.'

Contrary to what one might read in the press, he doesn't live in a castle. The couple live in the old Moulin Jeanpoc, a disused mill that they have converted into a home. The living area is less than 300 square metres and is on two storeys. It's very comfortable but certainly not luxurious. On the ground floor are a sitting room with fireplace (beside which he has his work table), a small kitchen, a dining room and a toilet. While renovating the place the couple had an extension added, made entirely of strengthened glass, including the roof, where they can dine under the stars. They also converted an old barn into a comfortable studio, where Christina spends her days painting. On the first floor is the couple's bedroom, a guest room and another room, where Maria de Oliveira sleeps. She is the excellent cook whom Christina brought over from Brazil.

The most delightful part of the house, though, is not inside but outside, where there is a magnificent view of the Pyrenees. The view is even more beautiful between November and March, when the mountains are covered in snow. In order to enjoy this view, the author had to buy his neighbour's house and knock it down. He cannot remember exactly how much he paid for either his own house or the neighbour's, but agents in the area value the house alone, without the surrounding land, at about 900,000 euros. The author's property portfolio – which includes the house in Tarbes, the apartment in Paris and another in Copacabana – was substantially increased when His Highness Sheikh Mohammed bin Rashid Al Maktoum, Emir of Dubai and Prime Minister of the United Arab Emirates, gave him a fully furnished mansion worth US$4.5 million in one of the most exclusive condominiums in Dubai. The sheikh made similar gifts to the German racing driver Michael Schumacher, the English midfielder David Beckham and the Brazilian footballer Pelé.

Since they have no other help but Maria, not even a chauffeur, it is Coelho who is responsible for all the routine tasks: sawing wood for the fire, tending the roses, cutting the grass and sweeping up dead leaves. He is very organized and tries to keep some kind of discipline in the domestic timetable with a regime he laughingly calls 'monastic rules'. Apart from when he is involved in the launch of a new book or attending debates and talks around the world, his daily routine doesn't change much. Although he's no bohemian, he rarely goes to bed before midnight; he drinks wine in moderation and usually wakes in a good mood at about eight in the morning. He breakfasts on coffee, bread, butter and cheese, and, regardless of the weather, he goes out for an hour's walk every day, either in the wheat fields surrounding the house or, on a fine day, in the steep, stony hills near by, at the foot of the Pyrenees. Christina almost always goes with him on these walks, but if she's away or unwell, he goes alone. Any friends who stay at the house know that they will have to accompany their host – this is one of the monastic rules. One of his favourite walks takes him to the chapel of Notre Dame de Piétat in the *commune* of Barbazan-Debat, next to Saint-Martin and Tarbes. Here he kneels, makes the sign of the cross, says a brief prayer, puts a coin in the tin box and lights a candle in front of the small painted wooden image of the Virgin Mary holding the body of her dead son.

Back at the house, Coelho does some odd jobs in the garden, deadheads the plants and clears any weeds blocking the little stream that runs across the land. Only then does he go and take a shower and, afterwards, turn on his computer for the first time in the day. He reads online versions of at least two Brazilian newspapers and then takes a look at the electronic clippings agency that picks up on anything published about him and his books the previous day. Before pressing the enter key that will open up a site showing the best-seller lists, he places his outspread hands over the screen as though warming himself in front of a fire, closes his eyes and meditates for a moment, seeking, he says, to attract positive energy.

Today, he hits the key and smiles as the screen shows that, in the countries that matter most, he has only been beaten to number one in Germany and Brazil. In both these countries it is Dan Brown's *The Da Vinci Code* that heads the list. His e-mails also hold no great surprises. There are messages from no fewer than 111 countries, listed in alphabetical order from Andorra to Venezuela, passing through Burkina Faso, in Africa, to Niue off the coast of New Zealand and Tuvalu in Polynesia.

He says to Christina, who is sitting beside him: 'What do you make of that, Christina? When we got back from our walk it was 11.11 and the thermometer was showing 11°C. I've just opened my mailbox and there are messages from 111 countries. I wonder what that means.'

It's not uncommon to hear him say such things: while the majority of people would put something like that down to mere coincidence, Coelho sees such things as signs that require interpretation. Like the invisible fly he's always trying to drive away with his hand, his preoccupation with names, places, dates, colours, objects and numbers that might, in his view, cause problems, leads one to suspect that he suffers from a mild form of obsessive compulsive disorder. Coelho never mentions Paraguay or the ex-president Fernando Collor (or his Minister of Finance, Zélia Cardoso de Mello), and he felt able to mention the name of Adalgisa Rios, one of his three long-term partners, only after her death in June 2007. Indeed, if anyone says one of the forbidden names in his presence he immediately knocks three times on wood in order to drive away any negative energy. He crosses the road whenever he sees a pigeon feather on the pavement, and will never tread on one. In April 2007, in an eight-page article about him in *The New Yorker* magazine, he candidly confessed to the reporter Dana Goodyear that he refuses to dine at tables where thirteen people are seated. Christina not only understands this eccentric side of Coelho but shares his fears and interpretations and is often the one to warn him of potential risks when deciding whether or not to do something.

One afternoon a week is set aside for reading correspondence that arrives via ordinary mail. Once a week, he receives packages in the post from his Rio office and from Sant Jordi in Barcelona. These are stacked up on a table on the lawn and opened with a bone-handled penknife, and the letters arranged in piles according to size. From time to time, the silence is broken by a cow mooing or by the distant sound of a tractor. Any manuscripts or disks from aspiring authors go straight into the waste-paper bin, precisely as his various websites say will happen. At a time when letter bombs and envelopes containing poisonous substances have become lethal weapons, Coelho has begun to fear that some madman might decide to blow him up or contaminate him, but in fact he has never yet received any suspect package. However, because of his concern, he now meditates briefly over any parcels arriving from Rio or Barcelona, even when they're expected, in order to imbue them with positive vibes before they are opened. One cardboard package, the size of a shirt box, from his Rio office, contains replies to readers' letters that require his signature. The longer ones are printed on the official headed notepaper of the Brazilian Academy of Letters, of which Coelho has been a member since 2002. Shorter replies are written on postcards printed with his name. The session ends with the signing of 100 photos requested by readers, in which the author appears, as usual, in black trousers, shirt and jacket.

After a few telephone calls, he relaxes for an hour in an area in the garden (or in the woods around the house), where he practises kyudo, the Japanese martial art of archery, which requires both physical strength and mental discipline. Halfway through the afternoon, he sits down in front of his computer to write the short weekly column of 120 words that is published in thirty newspapers around the world, from Lebanon (*Al Bayan*) to South Africa (*Odyssey*), from Venezuela (*El Nacional*) to India (*The Asian Age*), and from Brazil (*O Globo*) to Poland (*Zwierciadlo*).

In other respects, the couple's day-to-day life differs little from that of the 300 other inhabitants of the village. They have a small circle of friends, none of whom are intellectuals or celebrities or likely to appear in the gossip columns. 'I can access 500 television channels,' Coelho declared years ago in an interview with the *New York Times*, 'but I live in a village where there's no baker.' There's no baker, no bar, no supermarket and no petrol station. As is the case in the majority of France's 35,000 *communes*, there isn't a single commercial establishment in sleepy Saint-Martin. Tarbes is the nearest place for shops, as long as you get there before five in the afternoon, when the small town starts to shut down. Coelho's evening programme often consists of a visit to one of the three good restaurants there.

Eventually, it is time for Coelho to return to work. An e-mail from Sant Jordi contains a packed programme for the following three weeks, which, if he agrees to it, will mean a round-the-world trip. On the programme are invitations to the launch of *The Zahir* in Argentina, Mexico, Colombia, Puerto Rico and Paris. He is also to receive the Goldene Feder prize in Hamburg, and there are signings as well in Egypt, Syria and Lebanon, plus a trip to Warsaw for the birthday of Jolanda, the wife of the President of Poland at the time, Aleksander Kwaśniewski. Then on to London to take part with Boris Becker, Cat Stevens and former secretary general of the UN Boutros Boutros Ghali in a fund-raising dinner for the campaign against the use of land-mines. The following day he will return to France for dinner with Lily Marinho, widow of Roberto Marinho, the owner of Organizações Globo. Four days later, he is supposed to attend the launch of *The Zahir* in Japan and South Korea. On his return to Europe he will stop off in Astana, the capital of Kazakhstan, for the sixty-fifth birthday of the President, Nursultan Nazarhayev. The last engagement on the list cannot be missed: an invitation from Klaus Schwab, creator and president of the World Economic Forum held annually in Davos, for the author to speak at the opening of another of Schwab's enterprises, the Cultural Festival in Verbier, where young classical musicians from all over the world meet.

Coelho brushes away the invisible fly two or three times and mutters something along the lines of: 'No human being could possibly do all that.'

Christina hears the complaint and teases him gently: 'Look, you were the one who chose to be a Formula 1 champion, so get in your Ferrari and drive!'

The remark soothes him. He laughs and agrees that not only did he make that choice but he fought his whole life to become what he is now, and so has no right to complain. 'But I still can't take on the whole programme. Some of the events are too close together and on three different continents!'

Usually, the stress of travel is caused not by the engagements themselves, but by the misery of modern air travel, especially since 9/11, when the consequent increase in vigilance and bureaucracy has created even longer delays for passengers. He faces the same queues, delays and overbookings as his millions of readers, and one of the problems with the programme suggested by Sant Jordi is that it will have to be undertaken entirely on commercial flights. Coelho prints out the list and, pen

in hand, starts by cutting out any engagements that entail intercontinen-
tal flights, which means putting off Latin America, Japan and South
Korea, and the birthday party in Kazakhstan. Syria and Lebanon also go,
but Egypt remains. Warsaw is replaced by Prague, where he wants to fulfil
a promise made twenty years earlier. Finally, he decides that his first stop,
in the Czech Republic, will be followed by Hamburg, where he will receive
his prize and from where he will fly on to Cairo. However, the problem,
once again, is flights. There are no connections that will allow him to stick
to the timetables for Germany and Egypt. The Germans refuse to change
the programme, which has already been printed and distributed, but they
suggest an alternative: the private plane of Klaus Bauer, president of the
media giant Bauer Verlagsgruppe, which sponsors the Goldene Feder
prize, will take him and those in his party from Hamburg to Cairo as soon
as the ceremony is over.

Hours later, when the programme has been agreed by all concerned,
he telephones Mônica and jokes: 'Since we're going to Prague, what about
putting on a "blitzkrieg" there?'

'Blitzkrieg' is the name Coelho gives to book signings that take place
unannounced and with no previous publicity. He simply walks into a
bookshop chosen at random, greets those present with 'Hi, I'm Paulo
Coelho' and offers to sign copies of his books for anyone who wants him
to. Some people say that these blitzkriegs are basically a form of exhibi-
tionism, and that the author loves to put them on for the benefit of journalists. This certainly appeared to be the case when the reporter Dana
Goodyear was travelling with him in Italy, where a blitzkrieg in Milan bore
all the marks of having been deliberately staged for her benefit. In Prague,
in fact, he is suggesting a middle way: to tell the publisher only the night
before so that while there is no time for interviews, discussions or chat
shows to be set up, there is time to make sure, at least, that there are
enough books for everyone should the bookshop be crowded.

However, the objective of this trip to the Czech Republic has nothing
to do with selling books. When he set out on the road back to Catholicism
in 1982, after a period in which he had entirely rejected the faith and
become involved in Satanic sects, Coelho was in Prague with Christina
during a long hippie-style trip across Europe. They visited the church of

Our Lady Victorious in order to make a promise to the Infant Jesus of Prague. For some inexplicable reason, Brazilian Christians have always shown a particular devotion to this image of the child, which has been in Prague since the seventeenth century. The extent of this devotion can be judged by the enormous number of notices that have been published over the years in newspapers throughout Brazil, containing a simple sentence, followed by the initial of the individual: 'To the Infant Jesus of Prague, for the grace received. D.' Like millions of his compatriots, Coelho also came to make a request, and by no means a small one. He knelt at the small side altar where the image is displayed, said a prayer and murmured so quietly that even Christina, who was beside him, could not hear: 'I want to be a writer who is read and respected worldwide.'

He realized that this was quite a request, and that he would need to find a comparable gift to give in return. As he was praying, he noticed the moth-eaten clothes worn by the image, which were copies of the tunic and cloak made by Princess Policena Loblowitz in 1620 for the first known image of the Infant Jesus of Prague. Still in a whisper, he made a promise which, at the time, seemed somewhat grandiose: 'When I'm a well-known author, respected worldwide, I will return and bring with me a gold-embroidered cloak to cover your body.'

Three decades later the idea of the blitzkrieg is really an excuse to revisit Prague and repay the grace he has been granted. Made exactly to fit the image, which is about half a metre high, the red velvet cloak, embroidered with fine gold thread, is the result of weeks of work by Paula Oiticica, Christina's mother.

Packed in an acrylic box so that it can be transported safely, the gift creates a small incident at Charles de Gaulle airport, when the police demand that the package be passed through an X-ray machine in order to prove that it doesn't conceal drugs or explosives; unfortunately, it's too big for the machine. Coelho refuses to board without the cloak, while the police maintain that, if it can't be X-rayed, it can't travel. A superior officer notices the small crowd gathering, recognizes M. Coelho and resolves the deadlock: the cloak is taken on to the plane without being scanned.

When the couple arrive at the church in Prague, some two dozen faithful are there, all apparently foreigners. Since he speaks only Czech and

Italian, the Carmelite priest, Anastasio Roggero, appears not to understand quite who this person is and what he is doing in his church holding a red cloak. He listens to what Coelho is saying to him in English, smiles, thanks him and is preparing to stow the box away behind a cupboard in the sacristy when an old French woman recognizes the author.

In an inappropriately loud voice, she tells the members of her group: 'Look, it's the writer Paulo Coelho!'

All the tourist groups converge on him, clamouring for his autograph and to have their photo taken with him. Father Anastasio turns, looks again at the cloak he is holding and begins to realize his mistake. He apologizes to Coelho for not having recognized him or the significance of the gift the Infant Jesus has just received. He returns to the sacristy and comes back armed with a digital camera to take photos of the cloak, the tourists and, of course, himself with his famous visitor, whose work he claims to know well.

Once Coelho has settled his account with the Infant Child, the couple spend their free time revisiting the capital and seeing Leonardo Oiticica, Christina's brother, who is married to Tatiana, a diplomat at the Brazilian embassy in Prague. Two newspapers – *Pravó* and *Komsomólskaia* – have now publicized Paulo Coelho's presence in the city, and so the intended blitzkrieg cannot be a genuinely spontaneous event. By three in the afternoon, an hour before the agreed time, hundreds of people are lined up outside the Empik Megastore, the enormous modern bookshop chosen by Coelho's Czech publisher, Argo. He arrives at the agreed hour and finds things much as they were in Budapest. This time only 150 readers have managed to get vouchers, but hundreds of people are filling the aisles of the shop and spilling out into Wenceslas Square. They all want an autograph. The author does what he did in Hungary: he asks the bookshop to provide everyone with water, and divides the waiting crowd into those with vouchers and those without. At six in the evening, he looks at his watch and asks to be allowed a toilet break. Instead, he goes behind a screen only a few metres away in order to say his silent prayer. It's dark by the time he has signed the last book. He ends the evening enjoying Czech *nouvelle cuisine* in a smart restaurant in the old part of the city with a small group of friends.

The following day he is back in Paris for yet another signing, this time at the Fnac bookshop in the Place des Thermes. Although the shop is expecting only about a hundred people, the news has spread and about three hundred are packed into the small auditorium. Outside, people are trying to get to the display of CDs and DVDs, part of a small exhibition, not only of his books but also of his own literary, musical and cinematographic favourites. Among the books are Albert Camus' *The Outsider*, Henry Miller's *Tropic of Cancer*, Jorge Luis Borges' *Fictions*, Jorge Amado's *Gabriela, Clove and Cinnamon* and the biography of the matador El Cordobés, *I'll Dress You in Mourning*, by Dominique Lapierre and Larry Collins. The films on display include *Blade Runner* (Ridley Scott), *Once Upon a Time in the West* (Sergio Leone), *2001: A Space Odyssey* (Stanley Kubrick), *Lawrence of Arabia* (David Lean) and *The Promise* (Anselmo Duarte), while the selection of CDs is even more eclectic: from The Beatles' *Abbey Road* to Beethoven's Ninth Symphony, from Pink Floyd's *Atom Heart Mother* to Chopin's First Piano Concerto. The French fans are as patient as the Hungarians and Czechs. After giving a half-hour talk and answering questions, the author signs books for all those present before leaving the shop.

In marked contrast to this relaxed atmosphere, the Goldene Feder award ceremony, the following day, is organized with almost military precision. Hamburg has been in a permanent state of alert (and tension) since the discovery that the people behind the 9/11 attacks in the United States had been part of an Al Qaeda terrorist cell active there. Of the twenty men directly involved in the attack, nine lived in an apartment on the edge of the city, among them the leader of the group, the Egyptian Mohammed Atta. Judging by the number of private security guards present, the ceremony is clearly considered a prime target. Bankers, industrialists, businessmen, publishers and the famous have arrived from all corners of Europe to be here. In order to avoid any problems, the organizers of the event have allowed only five minutes for the press to photograph the guests and prize-winners (prizes are also being given to a scientist, a professor, a businesswoman and a priest). During the presentation ceremony, the reporters, along with the security guards and chauffeurs, are relegated to a canteen where they can watch everything on TV monitors.

Five hours later, the writer and his rucksack are in the VIP lounge at Hamburg airport, ready to take a Falcon jet to Cairo. His arrival in Egypt coincides with a visit to Cairo by the First Lady of the United States, Laura Bush, which means that security measures are even tighter. Friends have expressed their concern for Coelho's safety, given the frequency with which tourists in Egypt have been the victims of terrorist attacks by radical Islamic groups. 'What if some group of religious fanatics kidnapped you and demanded the release of 100 political prisoners in exchange?' they ask. He, however, appears unconcerned. This is not only because he has previously consulted the oracles but because he knows that during his visit he will be protected by Hebba Raouf Ezzar, the woman who invited him to speak at Cairo University. This forty-year-old Muslim mother of three, and visiting professor at Westminster University in London, is a charismatic political scientist who has overcome the prejudices of a society wedded to machismo and has become a major influence in the battle for human rights and the promotion of dialogue between Islam and other faiths. Being in Egypt at her invitation means being able to circulate freely – and safely – among a wide variety of political and religious groups.

There are other reasons, too, for Coelho to visit Egypt. The country is possibly the world champion when it comes to producing pirate editions of his books. Even though almost half the population is illiterate, it has been estimated that more than four hundred thousand illegal copies of his books – some 5 per cent of all pirate copies of his work worldwide – are available here. You can find Arabic translations of everything from *The Pilgrimage* to *The Zahir* in the windows of smart bookshops and on the pavements of Cairo, Alexandria and Luxor. And there are pirated editions for every pocket, from crude home-made versions to hardback editions printed on good-quality paper and produced by established publishers, some of them state-run. The author receives almost nothing in royalties from Egypt, but the real loser is the reader, who ends up buying copies either with chapters missing or in the wrong order, or that are translations intended for other Arab-speaking countries and not necessarily comprehensible to Egyptians. The pirate producers enjoy total immunity from prosecution; indeed, at the last International Book Fair in Cairo,

Paulo Coelho's works topped the best-seller lists, as if they had been produced by publishers complying with internationally agreed laws.

Keen to put a stop to the problem, Coelho lands in Cairo, accompanied by Mônica Antunes and Ana Zendrera, the proprietor of Sirpus in Spain, which specializes in Arabic publications destined for the Middle East and North Africa. Since May 2005, only two companies, All Prints in Lebanon and Sirpus, have been legally authorized to publish his books in Egypt.

At the airport, which is full of soldiers carrying sub-machine guns, the three are greeted by Hebba and her husband, the activist Ahmed Mohammed. He is dressed in Western clothes, but she is wearing a beige hijab. They all speak English, which is Egypt's second language. The small group goes straight to the Four Seasons Hotel, where a suite has been reserved for the author on the top floor with a view of Giza at the edge of the Sahara.

Hebba has drawn up a packed programme of events: interviews and TV appearances, visits to the famous (among them the Nobel Laureate Naguib Mahfouz, who is ninety and losing his sight, but determined to receive the author in his apartment for a cup of tea), a seminar at Cairo University and two talks, one at the Egyptian Association of Authors and the other at its rival, the Union of Egyptian Authors. At Paulo's request, Hebba has arranged a lunch in one of the dining rooms of the Four Seasons to which the principal publishers and booksellers in the country have been invited, along with representatives of the Ministry of Culture. It is here that the author is hoping to ram home his point about defending the rights of the author. He tells Hebba: 'You know perfectly well, Hebba, that when a warrior takes out his sword, he has to use it. He can't put it back in its sheath unbloodied.'

The following morning, the lobby of the Four Seasons Hotel is invaded by TV network people waiting for the interviews Mônica has organized. Cameras, tripods, reflectors, cables and batteries are stacked in corners and spread out on tables and sofas. Individual interviews are the privilege of the television reporters; newspaper and magazine journalists have to make do with a press conference. The only exception is *Al Ahram*, the main Egyptian newspaper – state-run as, it seems, most are –

which also has the privilege of being first in line. Once the interview is over, the reporter, Ali Sayed, opens his briefcase and asks the author to sign three books, *The Alchemist*, *Maktub* and *Eleven Minutes* – all of them pirate copies, bought in the street for US$7 each. In the early afternoon, the five go to a restaurant for a quick lunch washed down with Fanta, Coca Cola, tea and mineral water. Although there is wine and beer available, the meal is going to be paid for by Ahmed, a Muslim, and good manners require that no alcohol be drunk.

Once the engagements with the press are over Coelho takes part in hurried debates at the two writers' associations. At both, the number of members of the public is two or three times greater than the venues' capacity and he attends kindly and good-naturedly to the inevitable requests for signings at the end. Before returning to the hotel, he is taken to Mohamed Heikal's apartment. Heikal is a veteran politician who started his career alongside President Nasser, who governed from 1954 to 1970, and he has so far managed to weather the political upheavals in Egypt. Surrounded by bodyguards, Heikal receives his visitor in a small apartment. The walls are covered in photos of him with great international leaders of the twentieth century, such as the Soviet leader Nikita Khrushchev, Chou En-Lai of China, Jawalarhal Nehru of India and Chancellor Willy Brandt, as well as Leonid Brezhnev and, of course, Nasser himself. Coelho's meeting with the Nobel Laureate Naguib Mahfouz is also subject to intense vigilance by security guards (years ago Mahfouz narrowly escaped death at his door when he was knifed in the neck by a Muslim fundamentalist who accused him of blaspheming against the Koran). The two speak rapidly in English, exchange signed copies of their books and that's it. With the day's agenda over, the evening is reserved for a boat trip on the Nile.

The following day the morning is free, allowing Coelho to wake later than usual, take his walk without hindrance and give some time to looking at news online. At one o'clock, he goes down to the hotel dining room for the lunch that he has suggested. In spite of the smiles and salaams during the presentations, it is clear that the idea is to set things to rights. Before the food is served and once all the guests are seated, one of the publishers stands up to greet the visitor and makes a point of stating that this is a meeting of friends.

'The author Coelho has proved his commitment to the Arab peoples not only in his work but in brave public statements such as in his letter "Thank you, President Bush", which clearly condemned the invasion of Iraq by the United States.'

Someone else speaks, and then it is Coelho's turn. Beside him at the table are three pirate copies of his books, deliberately placed there in order to provoke unease among the publishers – the elegant men in jackets and ties who are seated before him. He begins gently, recalling that some of his books have found inspiration in both Egyptian and Arabic culture. Then, face-to-face with the pirates themselves, he broaches the thorny topic of piracy, saying: 'Any author would, of course, love to see his books published in Egypt. My problem is precisely the opposite: I have too many publishers in Egypt.'

No one finds the joke funny, but he is unperturbed. He glances upwards, as if asking St George for the strength to defend his books, and then adopts a blunter approach.

He picks up a pirate copy of *The Alchemist* and waves it in the air. 'I am here as a guest of Dr Hebba, that is, of the Egyptian people. But I have come here on my own account as well because I want to sort out, once and for all, the problem of the pirate copies of my books being published here.'

The guests shift uncomfortably in their seats. Some, embarrassed, are doodling on their napkins.

Coelho knows full well that some are important figures in the Ministry of Culture (which has shares in many of the publishing houses he is accusing of piracy) and he makes the most of this opportunity: 'The government neither punishes nor condemns piracy, but Egypt is a signatory to international treaties on royalties and must conform to them. I could get the best lawyer money can buy and win the case in international courts, but I'm not here merely to defend material values, I'm defending a principle. My readers here buy books at a cheap price and get cheap editions, and it's got to stop.'

Coelho's suggestion that they call an armistice doesn't seem to please anyone.

'I'm not interested in the past. Let's forget what's happened up to now. I'm not going to claim royalties on the 400,000 books published in a country where I've never even had a publisher. But from now on, any book of mine published in Egypt that is not produced by Sirpus or by All Prints will be considered illegal and therefore the subject of legal action.'

To prove that he's not bluffing, he announces that there will be a special blitzkrieg in the Dar El Shorouk bookshop, next to the hotel: he will sign the first book produced under the new regime (a pocket version of *The Alchemist* in Arabic with the Sirpus stamp on it) as well as copies of the English translation of *The Zahir*. This awkward meeting ends without applause and with the majority of those present looking stony-faced.

Everything seems to be going as he predicted. The signing is a success and he says to any journalist who hunts him out: 'I think the publishers have accepted my proposal. From now on, my Egyptian readers will read my books only in official translations published by Sirpus.' His confidence, however, will prove short-lived, because the only real change in the situation is that now the pirates have another competitor in the market – Sirpus.

The conference at Cairo University, the following day, the last engagement of his trip to Egypt, goes smoothly. The conference takes place in a 300-seat auditorium and there are exactly 300 people present. The majority are young women who, unlike Hebba, are wearing Western dress – tight jeans and tops revealing bare shoulders and midriffs. After his talk, idolatry gets the better of discipline, and they crowd around him, wanting him to sign copies of his books.

On the way back to the hotel, Hebba suggests doing something not on the schedule. Readers belonging to the Official Paulo Coelho Fan Club in Egypt who did not manage to get to any of his public appearances want to meet him at the end of the afternoon for a chat. Cheered by what he believes to have been the success of his lunch with the publishers, he agrees without asking for any further details. His response means that Hebba has to go off at once to mobilize the public. The place she has chosen is an improvised open-air auditorium under one of the bridges that cross the Nile. No one knows quite what methods she has used to gather so many people together, but there is general astonishment among the Brazilian contingent when they arrive and find a crowd of more than two thousand people. The venue appears to be a building that has been left half-finished with concrete slabs and bits of iron still visible. The place is packed, with people sitting in between the seats and in the side aisles. It seems quite incredible that so many could have been gathered together on a weekday without any prior announcement in the newspapers, on the radio or television. There are even people perched on the walls and in the trees surrounding the auditorium.

In the infernal heat, Hebba leads Coelho to a small dais in one corner of the area, where a coffee table and three armchairs await them. When he says his first words in English – 'Good afternoon, thank you all for being here' – a hush descends. He talks for half an hour about his life, his struggle to become a recognized author, his drug-taking, his involvement in witchcraft, the time he spent in mental institutions, about political repression and the critics, and how he finally rediscovered his faith and realized his dream. Everyone watches him entranced, as if they were in the presence not of the author of their favourite books but of someone who has lessons in life to teach them. Many are unable to hide their feelings and their eyes are filled with tears.

When he says his final 'Thank you' Coelho is crying too. The applause looks set to continue, and, making no attempt to conceal his tears now, Paulo thanks the audience again and again, folding his arms over his chest and bowing slightly. The people remain standing and applauding. A young girl in a dark hijab goes up on to the dais and presents him with a bouquet of roses. Although he is quite used to such situations, the author appears genuinely moved and is at a loss how to react. The audience is still applauding. He turns rapidly, slips behind the curtains for a moment, glances upwards, makes the sign of the cross and repeats for the umpteenth time a prayer of gratitude to St Joseph, the saint who, almost sixty years earlier, watched over his rebirth – because, but for a miracle, Paulo Coelho would have died at birth.

CHAPTER 2

Childhood

PAULO COELHO DE SOUZA was born on a rainy night on 24 August 1947, the feast of St Bartholomew, in the hospital of São José in Humaitá, a middle-class area of Rio de Janeiro. The doctors had foreseen that there might be problems with the birth, the first for twenty-three-year-old Lygia Araripe Coelho de Souza, married to a thirty-three-year-old engineer, Pedro Queima Coelho de Souza. The baby would be not only their first child but a first grandchild for the four grandparents and a first nephew for uncles and aunts on both sides. Initial examination had shown that the child had swallowed a fatal mixture of meconium – that is, his own faeces – and amniotic fluid. He was not moving in the womb and showed no inclination to be born, and finally had to be delivered by forceps. As Paulo was pulled into the world, at exactly 12.05 a.m., the doctor must have heard a slight crack, like a pencil snapping. This was the baby's collarbone, which had failed to resist the pressure of the forceps. Since the baby, a boy, was dead, this was hardly a problem.

Lygia was a devout Catholic and, in a moment of despair, the first name that came to her lips was that of the patron saint of the maternity hospital: 'Please bring back my son! Save him, St Joseph! My baby's life is in your hands!'

The sobbing parents asked for someone to come and give the last rites to their dead child. Only a nun could be found, but just as she was about to administer the sacrament, there was a faint mewing sound. The child was, in fact, alive, but in a deep coma. He had faced his first challenge and survived it.

He spent his first three days in an incubator. During those decisive seventy-two hours, his father, Pedro, remained with him all the time. On the fourth day, when Paulo was taken out of the incubator, Pedro finally managed to get some sleep, and was replaced in his vigil by his mother-in-law, Maria Elisa or Lilisa, as she was known. Six decades later, Paulo would state without hesitation that his earliest memory was of seeing a woman come into the room and knowing that she was his grandmother. In spite of weighing only 3.33 kilos at birth and measuring 49 centimetres, the child seemed healthy. According to Lygia's notes in her baby album, he had dark hair, brown eyes and fair skin, and looked like his father. He was named after an uncle who had died young from a heart attack.

Apart from a bout of whooping cough, Paulo had a normal, healthy childhood. At eight months, he said his first word, at ten months, his first teeth appeared and at eleven months, he began to walk without ever having crawled. According to Lygia, he was 'gentle, obedient, extremely lively and intelligent'. When he was two, his only sister, Sônia Maria, was born; he was always fond of her and, apparently, never jealous. At three, he learned to make the sign of the cross, a gesture that was later accompanied by requests to God for the good health of his parents, grandparents, cousins, uncles and aunts.

Until he was thirteen, he and his family lived on an eleven-house estate built by his father in Botafogo, a pleasant middle-class area of Rio. The best of the houses – the only one with a garden – was reserved for Pedro's in-laws, Lilisa and Tuca, who owned the land. Another of the houses, a modest, two-storey affair, was given to Pedro in payment for his work and the remaining nine were let, sold or occupied by relatives. The Coelhos were so concerned about security that, although the estate was protected by high gates, all the windows and doors in the house were kept shut. Paulo and the other children could play freely as long as they did so within the confines of the estate; although it was only a few blocks from Botafogo beach, they knew nothing of life beyond its walls. Friendship with children from 'outside' was unthinkable.

From a very young age, Paulo showed that he had an original way of thinking. When, at the age of three, Lygia caught him behaving badly, he said: 'Do you know why I'm being naughty today, Mama? It's because my guardian angel isn't working. He's been working very hard and his battery has run out.'

One of his greatest pleasures was helping his grandfather Tuca repair his enormous Packard car. His father felt that this was clear proof that his son would turn out to be an engineer like him. Pedro also had a car – a Vanguard – but it rarely left the garage. As far as Pedro Coelho was concerned, if the family could take the bus into the city, there was no reason to spend money on petrol.

One of Coelho's earliest memories is of his father's tight grip on domestic finances. Engineer Pedro Queima Coelho de Souza's dream was to build not just a modest house for his family, like those on the estate, but a really large house with drawing rooms, a conservatory, verandahs and several bathrooms. The first step towards building this cathedral was a present from his father-in-law, Tuca: a 400-square-metre plot in Rua Padre Leonel Franca in the smart district of Gávea. From then on all non-essential expenditure for the family was cut in favour of the house in Gávea. 'If we're going to build a house for everyone,' declared Dr Pedro, as he was known, 'then everyone is going to have to cut back on spending.' No new clothes, no birthday parties, no presents, no unnecessary trips in the car. 'At the time,' the author recalls, 'we had nothing, but we didn't lack for anything either.' Christmas was saved for the children by the German electric trains and French dolls that their maternal grandparents gave them.

The dream house in Gávea caused the family a further problem. Instead of placing his savings in a bank, Pedro preferred to invest it in building materials and, since he had no shed in which to store these treasures, he kept everything in the house until he had enough capital to begin the construction work. As a result, both Coelho and his sister recall spending their childhood among lavatory bowls, taps, bags of cement and tiles.

The cutbacks did not, however, impoverish Coelho's intellectual life. Although his father no longer bought any new records, he nevertheless listened to classical music every night. And anyone pressing his ear to the front door of No. 11 would have heard Bach and Tchaikovsky being played by Lygia on the piano that had been with her since before she was married. The house was also full of books, mainly collected by Lygia.

At the beginning of 1952, when he was four and a half, Coelho's parents enrolled him in kindergarten, where he spent two years. Then, in 1954, intending eventually to send their son to a Jesuit secondary school, St Ignatius College, his parents moved him to Our Lady Victorious School, which was seen as the best route to St Ignatius – the most traditional school of its kind in Rio, and one of the most respected educational establishments for boys in the city. St Ignatius was expensive, but it guaranteed the one thing that the Coelhos regarded as essential: strict discipline.

It was certainly true that, at least in Paulo's case, the *cordon sanitaire* placed around the estate to protect the children from the evil world outside had no effect. At five, he was already viewed by his adult neighbours as a bad influence on their children. As there were two other children on the estate called Paulo (his cousins, Paulo Arraes and Paulo Araripe), he was simply called 'Coelho'. To Lygia and Pedro's horror, suspicions that it was 'Coelho' who was responsible for many of the odd things that were happening in the small community began to be confirmed. First, there was the discovery of a small girl bound hand and foot to a tree so that she appeared to be hugging it and who was too afraid to tell on the culprit. Then came the information that, at dead of night, the boys were organizing chicken races, which ended with all the competitors, apart from the winner, having their necks wrung. One day, someone replaced the contents of all the cans of hair lacquer belonging to the young girls on the estate with water. It was one of the victims of this last jape – Cecília Arraes, an older cousin – who worked out who the culprit was. She found a satchel in one of the boys' hiding places containing papers that revealed the existence of a 'secret organization' complete with statutes, the names of the leaders and the minutes of meetings. This was the Arco Organization, its name being taken from the first two letters of the surnames of the chief perpetrators, Paulo Araripe and Paulo Coelho.

Cecília collared the future author and said: 'So what's this Arco business? What does the organization do? If you don't tell me, I'm going to your parents.'

He was terrified. 'It's a secret organization, so I'm forbidden to tell you anything.' When his cousin continued to threaten him, he said: 'No, really, I can't tell you. The only thing I can say is that Arco is an organization specializing in sabotage.' He went on to explain that both the water in the girls' hair lacquer and the girl being tied to the tree were punishments for their having crossed the chalk frontier scratched on the ground to mark the borders of Arco territory, beyond which lay an area 'forbidden to girls'.

When evidence of Paulo's involvement in the matter reached his parents, they were in no doubt that, when he was old enough, the boy should definitely be placed in the stern, wise hands of the Jesuits. While at Our Lady Victorious, he became accustomed to the regime that he would find at St Ignatius, for, unlike at other schools, the pupils had classes on Saturdays and were free on Wednesdays. This meant that Paulo only had Sunday to play with his friends on the estate. On Saturdays, when they were all off, he had to spend the day at school. On Wednesdays, when he was free but had no companions, he had no alternative but to stay at home reading and studying.

The children at Our Lady Victorious ranged in age from seven to eleven, and the school made a point of inculcating the pupils with a belief in the values of hard work and of respect for one's fellows. The children had to learn by heart the school rules, one of which was: 'It shows a lack of politeness, Christian charity and fellowship to wound less talented or less intelligent colleagues by words or laughter.' Coelho loathed all the subjects he was taught, without exception. The only reason he put up with the torment of spending his days bent over his books was that he had to get good marks in order to move up to the next year. In the first two years he spent at Our Lady Victorious, he managed to achieve well-above-average marks. However, from the third year on, things began to slip, as can be seen in a letter he sent to Pedro on Father's Day in 1956:

Papa,

I only got one in my maths test, so I'm going to have to study with you every night. My averages in the other subjects improved though. In religion I went from zero to six, in Portuguese from zero to six and a half, but in maths I went from four and a half to two and a half. My overall place in the class was still pretty bad, but I improved a bit, moving from twenty-fifth to sixteenth.

Love,

Paulo

Twenty-fifth was, in fact, bottom of the class, given that the classes at Our Lady Victorious had a maximum of twenty-five boys in them. However, the fact that he was bottom of the class didn't mean that the Coelhos were bringing up a fool. On the contrary. Their son may have hated studying, but he loved reading. He would read anything and everything, from fairy tales to Tarzan, and whatever his parents bought him or his friends lent him. Little by little, Coelho became the estate's resident storyteller. Years later, his aunt, Cecília Dantas Arraes, would recall the 'boy with skinny legs and baggy, wide-legged trousers': 'When he wasn't thinking up some mischief, he would be sitting on the pavement with his friends around him while he told stories.'

One night, he was with his parents and grandparents watching a quiz programme, *The Sky's the Limit*. A professor was answering questions about the Roman Empire and when the quiz master asked the professor who had succeeded Julius Caesar, Paulo jumped up and, to everyone's astonishment, said: 'Octavius Augustus', adding: 'I've always liked Octavius Augustus. He was the one August was named after, and that's the month I was born in.'

Knowing more than his friends was one way of compensating for his physical weakness. He was very thin, frail and short, and both on the estate and at school he was known as 'Pele' – 'skin' – a Rio term used at the time for boys who were always getting beaten up by their classmates. He may have been his peers' favourite victim, but he soon learned that knowing things no one else knew and reading stories none of his peers had read was one way of gaining their respect.

He realized that he would never come top in anything at school, but when he learned that there was to be a writing competition for all the boys in the third year, he decided to enter. The subject was 'The Father of Aviation', Alberto Santos Dumont. This is what Coelho wrote:

Once upon a time, there was a boy named Alberto Santos Dumont. Every day, early in the morning, Alberto would watch the birds flying and sometimes he would think: 'If eagles can fly, why can't I, after all, I'm more intelligent than the eagles.' Santos Dumont then decided to study hard, and his father and his mother, Francisca Dumont, sent him to an aeromodelling school.

Other people, such as Father Bartholomew and Augusto Severo, had tried to fly before. Augusto Severo flew in a balloon that he had built, but it fell to earth and he died. But Santos Dumont did not give up. He built a balloon that was a tube filled with gas and he flew, went round the Jefel [sic] Tower in Paris and landed in the same place he had taken off from.

Then he decided to invent an aeroplane that was heavier than air. Its shell was made of bamboo and silk. In 1906, in Champs de Bagatelle, he tried out the aeroplane. Lots of people laughed, convinced he would never fly. But Santos Dumont with his 14-bis travelled along for more than 220 metres and suddenly the wheels left the ground. When the crowd saw it there was a cry of 'Ah!' And that was it, aviation had been invented.

The best composition was to be chosen by a vote among the pupils. Paulo was so lacking in confidence that when it came to voting, he ended up choosing the work of another pupil. When the votes were counted, though, he was astonished to find that he was the winner. The pupil for whom he had voted came second, but was later disqualified when it was discovered that he had copied the text from a newspaper article.

However, Paulo's performance in the competition was not reflected in other subjects. When the time came for him to take the entrance exam for St Ignatius, the strict discipline and sacrifices imposed by the harsh regime at Our Lady Victorious proved useless and he failed. As punishment, in order to prepare for the retake, he was forced to stay in Rio having private lessons. This meant he had to forgo the annual family holiday in Araruama, where one of his uncles lived. To make sure that he had no spare time, his mother, who was also concerned by his lack of physical strength, decided that in the mornings he would attend PE classes at a holiday camp in Fortaleza de São João, an army unit in the peaceful, romantic area of Urca in the central region of Rio. Forced to do the two things he most hated – physical exercise in the morning and studying in the afternoon – Paulo felt as if he were spending two months in hell.

Every morning, Lygia took a bus with her son that went directly from Botafogo to Urca, where she handed him over to his tormentors. The climax of the nightmare was the dreaded jump into the river, which the boys – about fifty of them – were forced to do every day at the end of a seemingly endless session of bending, running and bar work. The boys, who were always accompanied by adult instructors, were placed in line and forced to jump from a bridge into the icy water of the river that cuts through the woods around the fortress. Even though he knew there was no chance of drowning or being hurt, the mere thought of doing this made Paulo panic. Initially, he was always last in line. His heart would pound, the palms of his hands would sweat and he felt like crying, calling for his mother, even peeing his pants: he would have done anything to avoid making that leap were it not for the fact that he was even more afraid of looking like a coward. Then he discovered the solution: 'If I was first in line, I would suffer for less time.' Problem solved. 'Not that I got over my fear of jumping,' he recalled years later, 'but the suffering ended and I learned my first lesson in life: if it's going to hurt, confront the problem straight away because at least then the pain will stop.'

These were, in fact, wasted days, in terms of both money and suffering, since he again failed the entrance exam. After spending the whole of 1958 preparing, however, he finally passed and did so with the excellent average mark of 8.3. High marks not only guaranteed admission to the school but also meant being given the title of 'Count'. If his performance improved still more he could become a 'Marquis' or even, as all parents dreamed of their children becoming, a 'Duke', a title reserved for those who ended the year with an average of 10 in all subjects.

But he never fulfilled his parents' dream. The entrance exam was the one moment of glory in his educational career. A graph based on his school reports for 1959 onwards shows a descending curve that would only end when he completed his science course in 1965 at one of the worst colleges in Rio de Janeiro. It was as though he were saying to his parents: 'Your dream of having a son at St Ignatius has come true, now leave me in peace.' As he himself remarked many years later, that mark of 8.3 was his final act in the world of the normal.

CHAPTER 3

Schooldays

I F THE DEVIL WAS HIDING in the hallowed walls of St Ignatius, paradise was 100 kilometres from Rio in Araruama, where Paulo Coelho usually spent the school holidays, almost always with his sister, Sônia Maria, who was two years younger. When family finances allowed, which was rare, they would go to Belém do Pará, where their paternal grandparents lived. Araruama, famous for its long beaches, was chosen by the Coelhos not for its natural beauty but because they had a guaranteed welcome at the home of Paulo's great-uncle, the eccentric José Braz Araripe. He had graduated in mechanical engineering and, in the 1920s, had been employed by the state-owned navigation company Lóide Brasileiro to run the ship repair yard owned by the company in the United States. With the help of another Brazilian engineer, Fernando Iehly de Lemos, Araripe spent all his free time in the Lóide laboratories working on the development of an invention that would change his life, as well as that of millions of consumers world-wide: the automatic gear box. Araripe based his invention on a prototype created in 1904 by the Sturtevant brothers in Boston, which was never taken up because it had only two speeds and would only work when the engine was on full power. It was not until 1932, after countless hours of tests, that Araripe's and Lemos's revolutionary invention was finally patented. That year, General Motors bought the rights from them for mass production, which began in 1938 when GM announced that the Oldsmobile had as an option the greatest thing since the invention of the automobile itself: the Hydra-Matic system, a luxury for which the consumer would pay an additional US$70, about a tenth of the total price of the car. Some say that the two Brazilians each pocketed a small fortune in cash at the time, and nothing else; others say that both opted to receive a percentage of each gearbox sold during their lifetime. Whatever the truth of the matter, from then on, money was never a problem for Araripe, or 'Uncle José', as he was known to his great-nephew and -niece.

With no worries about the future, Uncle José left Lóide and returned to Brazil. It might have been expected that he would live in Rio, close to his family; however, during his time in the United States, he had suffered a slight accident at work, which caused him to lose some movement in his left arm, and someone told him that the black sands of Araruama would be an infallible remedy. He moved there, bought a large piece of land on one of the main streets in the city, and built a six-bedroom house in which all the walls and furniture were retractable. At the command of their owner, walls, beds and tables would disappear, turning the residence into a large workshop where Uncle José worked and built his inventions.

In summer, walls and furniture would be restored in readiness to receive the children. One night a week during the holidays, the walls would disappear again in order to create an area for watching 35mm films on a professional film projector and the workshop would become a cinema. Some summers, Uncle José would have more than twenty guests, among them his great-nephews and -nieces, friends, and the few adults who had the impossible job of keeping an eye on the children. The children's parents were appalled by the man's unconventional behaviour, but the comfort he offered them outweighed their concerns. Anxious mothers whispered that, as well as being an atheist, José held closed sessions of pornographic films when there were only boys in the house – which was, indeed, true – and he took off his oil-stained dungarees (under which he never wore underpants) only on special occasions; but he was open and generous and shared the eccentricities of his house with his neighbours. When he learned that the television he had bought was the only one in town, he immediately turned the screen to face the street and thus improvised a small auditorium where, from seven to ten at night, everyone could enjoy the new phenomenon.

Michele Conte and Jorge Luiz Ramos, two of Coelho's friends in Araruama, recall that, every year, Coelho would arrive from Rio bearing some new 'toy'. Once, it was a Diana airgun with which he shot his first bird, a grassquit whose black wings he carefully plucked and stuck to a piece of paper with the date and a note of the bird's characteristics (a trophy that was to remain among his childhood mementoes in his house in Rio). The following year, he appeared with a diving mask and flippers, which prompted Uncle José to make him a submarine harpoon, its shafts propelled by a wire spring like a medieval man-of-war.

Like the other children, visitors and locals, Paulo woke every day when it was still dark. The town's residents recall a boy with skinny legs, knee-length socks and baggy shorts. The group would disappear off into the woods, explore the lakes, steal boats and go fishing, invade orchards or explore grottoes and caves. On returning home at the end of the day, they would hand over the spoils of their expedition – doves brought down with shot or fish spiked with Uncle José's harpoon – to Rosa, the cook, who would clean and prepare them for dinner. They would often return bruised or scratched or, as was the case once with Paulo, having been arrested by the forest rangers for hunting wild animals.

When Lygia arrived at the weekend to see her children, she would find herself in a party atmosphere. She would take up her guitar and spend the nights playing songs by Trini Lopez and by the rising star Roberto Carlos, accompanied by the children. The only thing Paulo did not enjoy was dancing. He found the parades in Rio fun, but hated dancing, and felt ridiculous when forced by his friends to jump around at Carnival dances in Araruama. To avoid humiliation, he would go straight to the toilets when he arrived at the club, hold his shirt under the tap and put it on again, soaking wet. If anyone invited him to dance he had his excuse ready: 'I've just been dancing. Look how sweaty I am. I'm going to take a break – I'll be back soon.'

Araruama was the place where he made various adolescent discoveries, like getting drunk for the first time. He and two friends went to one of the town's deserted beaches and swiftly downed two bottles of rum he had bought secretly in Rio and concealed among his clothes at the bottom of his suitcase. As a result, he fell asleep on the beach and woke with his body all swollen with sunburn. He was ill for several days. So bad was the hangover that, unlike most boys of his generation, he never became a serious drinker.

He also experienced his first kiss on one of these holidays. Although he liked to boast theatrically to his friends that destiny had reserved something rather different for his first kiss, namely a prostitute, that kiss in fact took place in the innocent atmosphere of Araruama and was shared with the eldest sister of his friend Michele, Élide – or Dedê – who was a little younger than he. It was in Araruama, too, that he experienced his first sexual impulses. When he discovered that his uncle had made the walls of the rooms of very light, thin wood so that they could easily be raised, Paulo managed secretly to bore a hole in one wall large enough for him to enjoy the solitary privilege, before falling asleep, of spying on his female cousins, who were sleeping naked in the next room. He was shocked to see that girls had curly hair covering their private parts. In his amazement, he grew breathless, his heart pounded and his legs shook, so much so that he feared that he might have an asthma attack and be caught in flagrante.

The respiratory problems he had suffered from since birth had developed, with puberty, into a debilitating asthma. The attacks, which were caused by a variety of things – changes in the weather, dust, mould, smoke – were unpredictable. They began with breathlessness, a cough and a whistling in his chest, and culminated in terrible feelings of asphyxia, when his lungs felt as if they were about to burst. He had to make sure that he always had his bag full of cough syrups, medication to dilate the bronchial tubes (usually in the form of cortisone tablets) and a 'puffer' to alleviate the symptoms.

Quite often his parents would take it in turns to sit by his bed at night in order to be there during an emergency and once, in despair, Lygia took him to a faith healer who had been recommended by friends. When they arrived at the consulting room, the man gazed fixedly into Paulo's eyes and said just five words: 'I can see Dr Fritz.'* This was enough for Lygia to take her son by the hand and leave, muttering: 'This is no place for a Christian.' When the asthma manifested itself in Araruama, far from his mother's care, the exchange of letters between Paulo and his mother became more frequent and, at times, worrying: 'Could you come with Aunt Elisa to look after me?' he asked, tearfully. Such requests would provoke anxious telegrams from Lygia to the aunt who looked after the children on holiday, one saying: 'I'm really worried about Paulo's asthma. The doctor said he should be given one ampoule of Reductil for three days and two Meticorten tablets a day. Let me know how things are.'

Although he said that he loved receiving letters, but hated writing them, as soon as he could read and write, and when he was away from home, Paulo would fill page after page, mostly addressed to his parents. Their content reveals a mature, delicate child concerned with his reputation as a bad, ill-behaved student. His letters to Lygia were mawkish and full of senti-mentality, like this one, sent on Mother's Day 1957, when he was nine:

> Dear Mama: No, no, we don't need May 8th to remember all the good things we've received from you. Your constant love and dedication, even though we're, very often, bad, disobedient children.
> [...] The truth is, it's your love that forgives us. That resilient love that never snaps like chewing gum. May God keep you, darling Mama, and forgive my errors because I'm still only small and I prom-ise to improve very very soon.
> Lots of love,
> Paulinho

The letters he sent to his father were more formal, even down to the signature, and written in a rather complaining tone.

---

* Adolf Fritz, generally called Dr Fritz, was a hypothetical German surgeon whose spirit was said to have been channelled by various psychic surgeons in Brazil, starting with Zé Arigo in the 1950s and continuing up to the present. There is no proof that he actually existed.

Papa,

Have you sent my leaflets to be printed? And how is the new house going? When are we going to move in?

I'm counting on your presence here the next time you come.

Love,

Paulo Coelho

As time went by, letter-writing became a regular thing for him. He would write to his parents, uncles and aunts, grandparents and friends. If he had no one to write to, he would simply jot down his ideas on small pieces of paper and then hide his scribbled thoughts in a secret place away from prying eyes. When he was about twelve he bought a pocket diary in which he began to make daily entries. He would always write in ink, in a slightly wobbly hand, but with few grammatical errors. He began by recording typical adolescent tasks – 'tidy my desk', 'Fred's birthday' and 'send a telegram to Grandpa Cazuza' – and gradually he also began to record things he had done, seen or merely thought. Sometimes these were short notes to himself, such as 'swap s. with Zeca', 'papa: equations' and 'do part E of the plan'. This was also the first time he sketched a self-portrait:

I was born on 24 August 1947 in the São José Hospital. I have lived on this estate since I was small. I have attended three schools and in all three I was regarded as a prince because of the way I dressed. I've always had good marks in all the schools I've been to.

I really like studying, but I also like playing. I've never been interested in opera or romantic music. I hate rock-and-roll, but I really like popular Brazilian music. I only like carnival when I'm taken to fancy-dress balls.

I really like adventures, but I'm scared of dangerous things [...] I've had several girlfriends already. I love sport. I want to be a chemist when I grow up because I like working with flasks and medicines. I love the cinema, fishing and making model aeroplanes.

I like reading comics and doing crosswords. I hate picnics and outings or anything that's boring.

This regular exercise of writing about himself or things that happened during the day attracted him so much that he began to record everything – either in a diary kept in a spiral notebook or by dictating into a cassette recorder and keeping the tapes. Later, with the arrival of computers he put together the entire set of records covering the four decades of confessions that he had accumulated up until then and stored them in a trunk, which he padlocked. In those 170 handwritten notebooks and 94 cassettes lay hidden the minutiae of his life and soul from 1959, when he was twelve years old, up to 1995, when he was forty-eight and began to write directly on to a computer. He was famous by then, and had stated in his will that immediately following his death, the trunk and its entire contents should be burned. However, for reasons that will be explained later, he changed his mind and allowed the writer of this biography free access to this material. Diaries are records produced almost simultaneously with the emotion or action described, and are often cathartic exercises for the person writing them. This is clear from Coelho's diaries, where he often speaks of the more perverse sides of his personality, often to the detriment of his more generous and sensitive side.

The diary gave the author the freedom to fantasize at will. Contrary to what he wrote in the self-portrait quoted above, Coelho rarely dressed smartly, he loathed studying just as he loathed sport and his love life was not always happy. According to his diary, his cousin Cecília, his neighbour Mónica, who lived on the estate, Dedê, with whom he shared his first kiss in Araruama, and Ana Maria, or Tatá, a pretty dark-haired girl with braces, were all girlfriends. Young love is often a troubling business, and the appearance of the last of these girls in his life was the subject of dramatically embroidered reports. 'For the first time, I cried because of a woman,' he wrote. At night, unable to sleep, he saw himself as a character in a tragedy: as he cycled past his lover's house, he was run over by a car and fell to the ground covered in blood. Somehow, Tatá was there at his side and knelt sobbing beside his body in time to hear him utter his last words: 'This is my blood. It was shed for you. Remember me ...'

Although the relationship was purely platonic, Tatá's parents took an immediate dislike to Coelho. Forbidden to continue her relationship with that 'strange boy', she nevertheless stood up to her family. She told Paulo that her mother had even hit her, but still she wouldn't give him up. However, when he was holidaying in Araruama, he received a two-line note from Chico, a friend who lived on the estate: 'Tatá has told me to tell you it's all over. She's in love with someone else.' It was as though the walls in Uncle José's house had fallen in on him. It wasn't just the loss of his girlfriend but the loss of face before his friends for having been so betrayed, cuckolded by a woman. He could take anything but that. He therefore invented an extraordinary story, which he described in a letter to his friend the following day. Chico was told to tell everyone that he had lied about his relationship with Tatá; he had never actually felt anything for her, but as a secret agent of the CIC – the Central Intelligence Center, a US spy agency – he had received instructions to draw up a dossier on her. This was the only reason he had got close to her. A week later, after receiving a second letter from Chico, he noted in his diary: 'He believed my story, but from now on, I have a whole string of lies to live up to. Appearances have been saved, but my heart is aching.'

Lygia and Pedro also had aching hearts, although not because of love. The first months their son had spent at St Ignatius had been disastrous. The days when he brought back his monthly grades were a nightmare. While his sister, Sônia Maria, was getting top marks at her school, Paulo's marks got steadily worse. With only rare exceptions – usually in unimportant subjects such as choral singing or craftwork – he hardly ever achieved the necessary average of 5 if he was to stay on at the school. It was only when he was forced to study for hours on end at home and given extra tuition in various subjects that he managed to complete the first year, but even then his average was only a poor 6.3. In the second year, things deteriorated still further. He continued to get high marks in choral singing, but couldn't achieve even the minimum average grade in the subjects that mattered – maths, Portuguese, history, geography, Latin and English. However, his parents were sure that the iron hand of the Jesuits would bring their essentially good-natured son back to the straight and narrow.

As time went by, he became more and more timid, retiring and insecure. He began to lose interest even in the favourite sport of his schoolmates, which was to stand at the gates of the Colégio Jacobina, where his sister was a pupil, to watch the girls coming out. This was a delight they would all remember for the rest of their lives, as the author and scriptwriter Ricardo Hofstetter, who was also a pupil at the Jesuit college, was to recall:

> It was pure magic to walk those two or three blocks to see them coming out. I still have the image in my mind: the girls' slim, exquisite legs, half on view, half hidden by their pleated skirts. They came out in groups, groups of legs and pleated skirts that the wind would make even more exciting. Anyone who experienced this knows that there was nothing more sublime in the world, although I never went out with a girl at the Jacobina.

Nor did Paulo, not at the Jacobina or anywhere else. Apart from innocent flirtations and notes exchanged with the girls on the estate or in Araruama, he reached young adulthood without ever having had a real girlfriend. When his friends got together to brag about their conquests – never anything more than holding hands or a quick kiss or a squeeze – he was the only one who had no adventure to talk of. Fate had not made him handsome. His head was too big for his skinny body and his shoulders narrow. He had fleshy lips, like his father's, and his nose, too, seemed over-large for the face of a boy of his age.

He became more solitary with each day that passed and buried himself in books – not those the Jesuits had them read at school, which he loathed, but adventure stories and novels. However, while he may have become a voracious reader, this still did not improve his performance at school. At the end of every year, in the public prize-giving ceremonies, he had become used to seeing his colleagues – some of whom went on to become leading figures in Brazilian public life – receiving diplomas and medals, while he was never once called to go up to the dais. He only narrowly avoided being kept down a year and thus forced to find another school, since at St Ignatius, staying down was synonymous with being thrown out.

While their son proved himself to be a resounding failure, his parents at least lived in hope that he would become a good Christian and, indeed, he appeared to be well on the way to this. While averse to study, he felt comfortable in the heavily religious atmosphere of the college. He would don his best clothes and happily attend the obligatory Sunday mass, which was celebrated entirely in Latin, and he became familiar with the mysterious rituals such as covering the images of the saints during Lent with purple cloths. Even the dark underground catacombs where the mortal remains of the Jesuits lay aroused his curiosity, although he never had the courage to visit them.

His parents' hopes were re-awakened during his fourth year, when he decided to go on a retreat held by the school. These retreats lasted three or four days, and took place during the week so that they would not seem like a holiday camp or mere recreation. They were always held at the Padre Anchieta Retreat House, or the Casa da Gávea, as it was known – a country house high up in the then remote district of São Conrado, 15 kilometres from the centre of Rio. Built in 1935 and surrounded by woods, it was a large three-storey building with thirty blue-framed windows in the front. These were the windows of the bedrooms where the guests stayed, each with a magnificent view of the deserted beach of São Conrado. The Jesuits never tired of repeating that the silence in the house was so complete that at any hour of the day or night and in any corner of the building you could hear the waves breaking on the beach below.

It was on a hot October morning in 1962 that Paulo left for his encounter with God. In a small suitcase packed by his mother, he took, as well as his clothes and personal belongings, his new, inseparable companions: a notebook and a fountain pen with which to make the notes that were more and more taking on the form of a diary. At eight in the morning, all the boys were standing in the college courtyard and as they waited for the bus to take them to the retreat house, Coelho was suddenly filled with courage. With two friends he went into the chapel in the dark, and walked round the altar and down the stairs towards the catacombs. Lit only by candles, the crypt, which was full of coffins, looked even gloomier. To his surprise, though, instead of being filled with terror, as he had always imagined he would be, he had an indescribable feeling of well-being. He seemed inspired to search for an explanation for his unexpected bravery. 'Perhaps I wasn't seeing death in all its terror,' he wrote in his notebook, 'but the eternal rest of those who had lived and suffered for Jesus.'

Half an hour later, they were all at the Casa da Gávea. During the days that followed, Paulo shared with another young boy a bare cubicle provided with two beds, a wardrobe, a table, two chairs and a little altar attached to the wall. In a corner was a china wash basin and above it a mirror. Once they had unpacked, both boys went down to the refectory, where they were given tea and biscuits. The spiritual guide for the group was Father João Batista Ruffier, who announced the rules of the retreat, the first of which would come into force in the next ten minutes: a vow of silence. From then on, until they left at the end of the retreat, no one was allowed to say a single word. Father Ruffier, who was a stickler for the rules, was about to give one of his famous sermons, one that would remain in the memory of generations of those who attended St Ignatius.

'You are here like machines going into the workshop for a service. You can expect to be taken apart piece by piece. Don't be afraid of the amount of dirt that will come out. The most important thing is that you put back each piece in its right place with total honesty.'

The sermon lasted almost an hour, but it was those opening words that went round and round in Paulo's head all afternoon, as he walked alone in the woods surrounding the house. That night he wrote in his diary, 'I have reviewed all my thoughts of the last few days and I'm ready to put things right.' He said a Hail Mary and an Our Father, and fell asleep.

Although Father Ruffier had made it clear what the retreat was for – 'Here you will drive away the temptations of life and consecrate your-selves to meditation and prayer' – not everyone was there for Christian reflection. Everyone knew that once dinner was over and after the final prayer of the day had been said, shadows would creep along the dark corridors of the house to meet secretly in small groups for whispered games of poker and pontoon. If one of the boys had managed to smug-gle in a transistor radio – something that was expressly forbidden – some-one would immediately suggest placing a bet on the races at the Jockey Club. From midnight to dawn the religious atmosphere was profaned by betting, smoking and even drinking contraband whisky concealed in shampoo bottles. Whenever a light in a cubicle warned of suspicious activities, one of the more attentive priests would immediately turn off the electricity. This, however, didn't always resolve the problem, since the heretical game would continue in the light from candles purloined from the chapel during the day.

On the second day, Paulo woke at five in the morning, his mind confused, although his spirits improved a little when he opened the bedroom window and saw the sun coming up over the sea. At six on the dot, still not having eaten, he met his colleagues in the chapel for the daily mass, prepared to put things right with God and do something he had been putting off for almost a year: taking communion. The problem was not communion itself but the horror of confession, with which all the boys were familiar. They would arrive at the confessional prepared to reveal only the most banal of sins, but they knew that, in the end, the priest would always ask the inevitable question: 'Have you sinned against chastity, my son?' Should the reply be in the affirmative, the questions that followed were more probing: 'Alone or with someone else?' If it was with someone else, the priest would continue, to the mortification of the more timid boys: 'With a person or an animal?' If the response was 'with a person', the sinner was not required to reveal the name of the partner, only the sex: 'With a boy or with a girl?'

Paulo found this an extremely difficult topic to deal with and he didn't understand how it could be a sin. He was so convinced that masturbation was not a shameful activity that he wrote in his notebook: 'No one on this earth can throw the first stone at me, because no one has avoided this temptation.' In spite of this, he had never had the courage to confess to a priest that he masturbated, and living in a permanent state of sin troubled him deeply. With his soul divided, he preferred merely to say the act of contrition and to receive communion without going to confession.

Following mass, Father Ruffier returned to the charge with a particularly harsh sermon. Before a terrified audience, he painted a terrifying picture of the place intended for all sinners: 'We are in hell! The fire is burning mercilessly! Here one sees only tears and hears only the grinding of teeth in mutual loathing. I come across a colleague and curse him for being the cause of my condemnation. And while we weep in pain and remorse, the Devil smiles a smile that makes our suffering still greater.

But the worst punishment, the worst pain, the worst suffering is that we have no hope. We are here for ever.'

Paulo was in no doubt: Father Ruffier was talking about him. After twelve months without going to confession – so as not to have to touch on the taboo subject of masturbation – he realized that if he were to die suddenly, his final destiny would be hell. He imagined the Devil looking into his eyes and snickering: 'My dear boy, your suffering hasn't even begun yet.' He felt helpless, powerless and confused. He had no one to turn to, but he knew that a Jesuit retreat was a place of certainties, not of doubts. Faced with a choice between suffering in the flames for all eternity as described by the priest and giving up his solitary pleasure, he chose faith. Deeply moved and kneeling alone on the stone floor of the mirador, he turned to God and made a solemn promise never to masturbate again.

His decision gave him courage and calmed him, but that feeling of calm was short-lived. The following day, the Devil counter-attacked with such force that he could not resist the temptation and, defeated, he masturbated. He left the bathroom as though his hands were covered in blood, knelt in front of the altar and implored: 'Lord! I want to change, but I can't stop myself! I've said endless acts of contrition, but I can't stop sinning. I sin in thought, word and deed. Give me strength! Please! Please! Please!' Full of despair, he only felt relief when, in a whispered conversation in the woods, he found that he had a companion in eternal suffering: a fellow pupil who had also been masturbating during the retreat.

Ashamed of his own weakness, Paulo was subjected to two more sermons from Father Ruffier, which seemed to have been chosen especially to instil fear into the minds of the boys. Once again, the priest deployed dramatic and terrifying images, this time to alert the boys to the perils of clinging on to material values. From the pulpit Father Ruffier gesticulated like an actor, shaking his short, muscular arms and saying: 'Truly, truly I say unto you, my children: the time will come when we shall all be laid low. Imagine yourselves dying. In the hospital room, your relatives white with fear. The bedside table is crammed with different medicines, all useless now. It is then that you see how powerless you are. You humbly recognize that you are powerless. What good will fame, money, cars, luxuries be at the fatal hour? What use are those things if your death lies in the hands of the Creator?' With his fists clenched, and as though possessed by divine fury, he declared vehemently: 'We must give up everything, my sons! We must give up everything!'

These words should not be confused with an exhortation to embrace socialism or anything of the sort. Not only were the sons of some of the wealthiest families in Rio de Janeiro in the congregation, but the college was politically conservative and was always showing films of executions by firing squads in Fidel Castro's Cuba in order to show the boys 'the bloodthirsty nature of communism'. And Father Ruffier himself was proud of the fact that he had had to leave Colombia in a hurry 'to flee communism' (he was referring to the popular uprising in Bogotá in 1948, known as the Bogotazo).

While the boys stared at each other in astonishment, the priest spoke again. The subject was, once again, hell. Just in case he had not made himself clear in the first part of his sermon, he once more described the eternal state of suffering to which sinners would be condemned: 'Hell is like the sea that is there before us. Imagine a swallow coming along every hundred years and taking a drop of water each time. That swallow is you and that is your penance. You will suffer for millions and millions of years, but one day the sea will be empty. And you will say: at last, it's over and I can rest in peace.' He paused, then concluded: 'But then the Creator will smile from the heights and will say: "That was just the beginning. Now you will see other seas and that is how it will be for all eternity. The swallow empties the sea and I fill it up again."'

Paulo spent the rest of the day with these words echoing in his head. He went into the woods that surrounded the retreat house and tried to distract himself with the beauty of the view, but Father Ruffier's words only resonated inside him more loudly. That night, he set down his thoughts before finally falling asleep, and the notes he made appear to demonstrate the efficacy of the spiritual retreat.

Here, I've completely forgotten the world. I've forgotten that I'm going to fail maths, I've forgotten that Botafogo is top of the league and I've forgotten that I'm going to spend next week on the island of Itaipu. But I feel that with every moment spent forgetting, I'm learning to understand the world better. I'm going back to a world that I didn't understand before and which I hated, but which the retreat has taught me to love and understand. I've learnt here to see the beauty that lies in a piece of grass and in a stone. In short, I've learnt how to live.

Most important was the fact that he returned home certain that he had acquired the virtue which – through all the highs and lows of his life – would prove to be the connecting thread: faith. Even his parents, who appeared to have lost all hope of getting him back on the straight and narrow, were thrilled with the new Paulo. 'We're very happy to see that you finally appear to have got back on the right track,' Lygia declared when he returned. Her son's conversion had been all that was missing to complete domestic bliss, for a few months earlier, the family had finally moved into the large pink house built by Pedro Coelho with his own hands.

In fact, the move to Gávea happened before the building was completed, which meant that they still had to live for some time among tins of paint, sinks and baths piled up in corners. However, the house astonished everyone, with its dining room, sitting room and drawing room, its ensuite bathrooms in every bedroom, its marble staircase and its verandah. There was also an inner courtyard so large that Paulo later thought of using it as a rehearsal space for his plays. The move was a shock to Paulo. Moving from the estate in Botafogo, where he was born and where he was the unchallenged leader, to Gávea, which, at the time, was a vast wasteland with few houses and buildings, was a painful business. The change of district did nothing to lessen his parents' earlier fears, or, rather, his father's, and, obsessively preoccupied with the harm that the 'outside world' might do to his son's character and education, Pedro thought it best to ban him from going out at night. Suddenly, Paulo no longer had any friends and his life was reduced to three activities: sleeping, going to classes at St Ignatius and reading at home.

Reading was nothing new. He had even managed to introduce a clause concerning books in the Arco statutes, stating that, 'besides other activities, every day must include some recreational reading'. He had begun reading the children's classics that Brazilian parents liked to give their children; then he moved on to Conan Doyle and had soon read all of Sherlock Holmes. When he was told to read the annotated edition of *The Slum* by Aluísio Azevedo at school, he began by ridiculing it: 'I'm not enjoying the book. I don't know why Aluísio Azevedo brings sex into it so much.' Some chapters later, however, he radically changed his mind and praised the work highly: 'At last I'm beginning to understand the book: life without ideals, full of betrayal and remorse. The lesson I took from it is that life is long and disappointing. *The Slum* is a sublime book. It makes us think of the sufferings of others.' What had initially been a scholastic exercise had become a pleasure. From then on, he wrote reviews of all the books he read. His reports might be short and sharp, such as 'weak plot' when writing about *Aimez-vous Brahms?* by Françoise Sagan, or, in the case of *Vuzz* by P.A. Hourey, endless paragraphs saying how magnificent it was.

He read anything and everything, from Michel Quoist's lyrical poems to Jean-Paul Sartre. He would read best-sellers by Leon Uris, Ellery Queen's detective stories and pseudo-scientific works such as *O Homem no Cosmos* by Helio Jaguaribe, which he classed in his notes as 'pure, poorly disguised red propaganda'. Such condensed reviews give the impression that he read with one eye on the aesthetic and the other on good behaviour. Remarks such as 'His poetry contains the more degrading and entirely unnecessary aspects of human morality' (on *Para Viver um Grande Amor* by Vinicius de Moraes) or 'Brazilians aren't yet ready for this kind of book' (referring to the play *Bonitinha, mas Ordinária* by Nelson Rodrigues) were frequent in his listings. He had even more to say on Nelson Rodrigues: 'It's said that he's a slave to the public, but I don't agree. He was born for this type of literature, and it's not the people who are making him write it.'

Politically his reactions were no less full of preconceptions. When he saw the film *Seara Vermelha*, which was based on the book of the same name by Jorge Amado, he regretted that it was a work that was 'clearly communist in outlook, showing man's exploitation of man'. He was pleasantly surprised, however, when he read Amado's best-seller *Gabriela,*

Clove and Cinnamon; indeed, he was positively intoxicated: 'It's so natural ... There's not a trace of communism in its pages. I really liked it.' He felt that Manuel Bandeira was the greatest Brazilian poet ('because he leaves aside unhealthy aspects of life, and because of his simple, economical style'); he loathed João Cabral de Melo Neto ('I read some of his verses and I shut the book immediately'); and he confessed that he didn't understand Carlos Drummond de Andrade ('He has a confused, abstract style, which makes it hard to interpret his poetry').

It was apparently at this time, when he was thirteen or fourteen, that Paulo showed the first signs of an undying *idée fixe*, a real obsession that he would never lose – to be a writer. Almost half a century later, as one of the most widely read authors of all time, he wrote in *The Zahir*:

> I write because when I was an adolescent, I was useless at football, I didn't have a car or much of an allowance, and I was pretty much of a weed ... I didn't wear trendy clothes either. That's all the girls in my class were interested in, and so they just ignored me. At night, when my friends were out with their girlfriends, I spent my free time creating a world in which I could be happy: my companions were writers and their books.

In fact, he saw himself as a writer well before he said as much. Besides being the winner of the writing competition at Our Lady Victorious, from the time he could read he had become a full-time poet. He would write short verses and poems for his parents, grandparents, friends, cousins, girlfriends and even the saints revered by his family. Compositions such as 'Our Lady, on this febrile adolescent night/I offer you my pure childhood/That the fire is now devouring/And transforming into smoke so that it may rise up to you/And may the fire also free me from the past', which was inspired by the Virgin Mary; or four-line verses written for his parents: 'If the greatest good in the world/Is given to those who are parents/Then it is also a certain truth/That it is they who suffer most.' If there was no one to whom he could dedicate his verses, he would write to himself: 'The past is over/And the future has not yet arrived/I wander through the impossible present/Full of love, ideals and unbelief/As if I were simply/Passing through life.'

When, at a later age, he grew to know more about books and libraries, he came across a quote attributed to Émile Zola, in which the author of *J'Accuse* said something along the lines of 'My poetic muse has turned out to be a very dull creature; from now on, I shall write prose'. Whether or not these words were true of Zola, Paulo believed that the words were written precisely for him. He wrote in his diary: 'Today I ended my poetic phase in order to devote myself solely to the theatre and the novel.' He made a bonfire in the garden of everything he had written up to then – vast quantities of poems, sonnets and verses.

Such a promise, if meant seriously, would have been a proof of great ingratitude to the art of verse, for it was a poem he wrote – 'Mulher de Treze Anos' ['Thirteen-year-old Woman'] – that rescued him from anonymity among the 1,200 students at St Ignatius. One of the Jesuit traditions was the Academy of Letters of St Ignatius (ALSI), which had been created in 1941 and was responsible for cultural development of the students. Great names in Brazilian culture attended the events held by the ALSI. At the age of fourteen, Paulo appeared for the first time in the pages of the magazine *Vitória Colegial*, the official publication of the ALSI, with a small text entitled 'Why I Like Books'. It was an unequivocal defence of writers, whom he portrayed dramatically as people who spent sleepless nights, 'without eating, exploited by publishers', only to die forgotten:

What does a book represent? A book represents an unequalled wealth of culture. It is the book that opens windows on to the world for us. Through a book we experience the great adventures of Don Quixote and Tarzan as though we ourselves were the characters; we laugh at the hilarious tales of Don Camilo, we suffer as the characters in other great works of world literature suffer. For this reason, I like to read books in my free time. Through books we prepare ourselves for the future. We learn, just by reading them, theories that meant sacrifice and even death for those who discovered them.

Every didactic book is a step in the direction of the country's glorious horizon. This is why I like books when I'm studying. But what did it take for that book to arrive in our hands? Great sacrifice on the part of the author, whole nights spent starving and forgotten, their room sometimes lit only by the spluttering flame of a candle. And then, exploited by their publishers, they died forgotten, unjustly forgotten. What willpower on the part of others was needed for them to achieve a little fame! This is why I like books.

Months later, the ALSI announced the date for entries for its traditional annual poetry prize. Paulo had just seen the Franco-Italian film *Two Women*, directed by Vittorio de Sica, and left the cinema inspired. Based on the novel *La Ciociara*, by Alberto Moravia, the film tells the story of Cesira (Sophia Loren) and her thirteen-year-old daughter Rosetta (Eleanora Brown), both of whom have been raped by Allied soldiers during the Second World War. Paulo based his poem 'Thirteen-year-old Woman' on the character of Rosetta, and it was that poem which he then entered for the competition.

The day the poems were to be judged was one of endless agony. Paulo could think of nothing else. That evening, before the meeting when the three prize-winners were to be announced, he overcame his shyness and asked a member of the jury, a Portuguese teacher, whom he had voted for. He blushed at the response: 'I voted for you, Átila and Chame.'

Twenty poems were selected for the final. Paulo knew at least one of the chosen poems, 'Introduce', by José Átila Ramos, which, in his opinion, was the favourite. If his friend won, that would be fine, and if he himself managed at least third place, that would be wonderful. At nine in the evening, the auditorium was full of nervous boys soliciting votes and calculating their chances of winning. There was total silence as the jury, comprising two teachers and a pupil, began to announce in ascending order the three winners. When he heard that in third place was 'Serpentina and Columbina' and in second 'Introduce', he felt sure he hadn't been placed at all. So he almost fell off his chair when it was announced: 'The winner, by unanimous vote, is the poem … "Thirteen-year-old Woman", by Paulo Coelho de Souza!'

First place! He couldn't believe what he was hearing. Heart pounding and legs shaking, the slight young boy crossed the room and stepped up on to the stage to receive the certificate and the prize, a cheque for 1,000 cruzeiros – about US$47. Once the ceremony was over, he was one of the first to leave the college, desperate to go straight home and for once give his parents some good news. On the tram on the way back to Gávea, he began to choose his words and work out the best way to tell his father that he had discovered his one and only vocation – to be a writer.

He was therefore somewhat surprised on reaching the house to find his father standing outside on the pavement, angrily tapping his watch and saying: 'It's almost eleven o'clock and you know perfectly well that in this house the doors are closed at ten, no argument.'

This time, though, Paulo had up his sleeve a trump card that would surely move his father's cold heart. Smiling, he brandished the trophy he had just won – the cheque for 1,000 cruzeiros – and told his father every-thing: the prize, the unanimous vote, the dozens of contestants, the discovery of his vocation.

But even this failed to win over his grim father. Apparently ignoring everything his son had said, Pedro poured cold water on the boy's excite-ment, saying: 'I'd prefer it if you got good marks at school and didn't come home so late.'

The thought that at least his mother would be thrilled by his win was dispelled in an instant. When he saw her waiting at the front door, he told her, eyes shining, what he had just told his father. To her son's dismay, Lygia quietly gave him the same lecture: 'My boy, there's no point dreaming about becoming a writer. It's wonderful that you write all these things, but life is different. Just think: Brazil is a country of seventy million inhabitants, it has thousands of writers, but Jorge Amado is the only one who can make a living by writing. And there's only one Jorge Amado.'

Desperately unhappy, depressed and close to tears, Paulo did not get to sleep until dawn. He wrote just one line in his diary: 'Mama is stupid. Papa is a fool.' When he woke, he had no doubt that his family was determined to bury for ever what he dramatically called 'my only reason for living' – being a writer. For the first time, he seemed to recognize that he was prepared to pay dearly to realize his dream, even if this meant clashing with his parents. Lygia and Pedro Queima Coelho were not going to have long to wait.

CHAPTER 4

First play, first love

AT THE END OF 1962, at his father's insistence, Paulo was forced to enrol in the science stream rather than the arts as he had hoped. His scholastic performance in the fourth year had been disastrous, and he had finished the year having to re-sit maths, the subject at which his father so excelled. In the end, he passed with a 5 – not a decimal point more than the mark required to move on to the next year and remain at St Ignatius. In spite of this and Paulo's declared intention to study the arts, his parents insisted that he study engineering and, following his appalling scholastic performance, he was in no position to insist.

However, from his point of view, the practical Pedro Coelho had reasons for hoping that his son might yet be saved and become an engineer. These hopes lay not only in the interest Paulo had shown in his grandfather's success as a mechanic – professional and amateur. As a boy, Paulo had frequently asked his parents to buy him copies of the magazine *Mecânica Popular*, a publication dating from the 1950s that taught readers how to do everything from fixing floor polishers to building boats and houses. When he was ten or eleven he was so passionate about aeroplane modelling that any father would have seen in this a promising future as an aeronautical engineer. The difference was that, while lots of children play with model aeroplanes, Paulo set up the Clube Sunday, of which he and his cousin Fred, who lived in Belém, were sole members. Since a distance of 3,000 kilometres separated them and their aeroplanes, the club's activities ended up being a chronological list of the models each had acquired. At the end of each month, Paulo would record all this information in a notebook – the names and characteristics of the small planes they had acquired, the serial number, wing span, date and place of purchase, general construction expenses, the date, place and reason for the loss of the plane whenever this occurred. Not one of these pieces of information served any purpose, but 'It was best to keep things organized,' Paulo said. When the glider Chiquita smashed into a wall in Gávea, it was thought worthy of special mention: 'It only flew once, but since it was destroyed heroically, I award this plane the Combat Cross. Paulo Coelho de Souza, Director.'

This fascination for model aeroplanes rapidly disappeared, but it gave way to another mania, even more auspicious for anyone wanting his son to be an engineer: making rockets. For some months Paulo and Renato Dias, a classmate at St Ignatius, spent all their spare time on this new activity. No one can say how or when it began – not even Paulo can remember – but the two spent any free time during the week in the National Library reading books about such matters as 'explosive propulsion', 'solid fuels' and 'metallic combustibles'. On Sundays and holidays, the small square in front of the Coelho house became a launch pad. As was almost always the case with Paulo, everything had to be set down on paper first. In his usual meticulous way, he started a small notebook entitled 'Astronautics – Activities to be Completed by the Programme for the Construction of Space Rockets'. Timetables stated the time taken on research in books, the specifications of materials used in the construction and the type of fuel. On the day of the launch, he produced a typewritten document with blank spaces to be filled in by hand at the time of the test, noting date, place, time, temperature, humidity and visibility.

The rockets were made of aluminium tubing about 20 centimetres in length and weighing 200 grams and had wooden nose cones. They were propelled by a fuel the boys had concocted out of 'sugar, gunpowder, magnesium and nitric acid'. This concentrated mixture was placed in a container at the base of the rocket, and the explosive cocktail was detonated using a wick soaked in kerosene. The rockets were given illustrious names: Goddard I, II and III, and Von Braun I, II and III, in homage, respectively, to the American aeronautics pioneer Robert H. Goddard and the creator of the German flying bombs that devastated London during the Second World War, Werner von Braun. However, although the rockets were intended to rise up to 17 metres, they never did. On launch days, Paulo would take over a part of the pavement outside their house 'for the public' and convert a hole that the telephone company had forgotten to close up into a trench where he and his friend could shelter. He then invited his father, the servants and passers-by to sign the flight reports as 'representatives of the government'. The rockets failed to live up to the preparations. Not one ever rose more than a few centimetres into the air and the majority exploded before they had even got off the ground. Paulo's astronautical phase disappeared as fast as it had arrived and in less than six months the space programme was abandoned before a seventh rocket could be constructed.

Apart from these fleeting fancies – stamp-collecting was another – Paulo continued to nurture his one constant dream – to become a writer. When he was sixteen, his father, in a conciliatory gesture, offered him a flight to Belém, which, to Paulo, was a paradise on a par with Araruama. Nevertheless, he turned it down, saying that he would rather have a typewriter. His father agreed and gave him a Smith Corona, which would stay with him until it was replaced, first, by an electric Olivetti and, then, decades later, by a laptop computer.

His total lack of interest in education meant that he was among the least successful students in his class in the first year of his science studies and at the end of the year he once again scraped through with a modest 5.2 average. His report arrived on Christmas Eve. Paulo never quite knew whether it was because of his dreadful marks or an argument over the length of his hair, but on Christmas Day 1963, when the first group of relatives was about to arrive for Christmas dinner, his mother told him bluntly: 'I've made an appointment for the 28th. I'm taking you to a nerve specialist.'

Terrified by what that might mean – what in God's name was a nerve specialist? – he locked himself in his room and scribbled a harsh, almost cruel account of his relationship with his family:

I'm going to see a nerve specialist. My hands have gone cold with fear. But the anxiety this has brought on has allowed me to examine my home and those in it more closely.

Mama doesn't punish me in order to teach me, but just to show how strong she is. She doesn't understand that I'm a nervous sort and that occasionally I get upset, and so she always punishes me for it. The things that are intended to be for my own good she always turns into a threat, a final warning, an example of my selfishness. She herself is deeply selfish. This year, she has never, or hardly ever, held my hand.

Papa is incredibly narrow-minded. He is really nothing more than the house financier. Like Mama, he never talks to me, because his mind is always on the house and his work. It's dreadful.

Sônia lacks character. She always does what Mama does. But she's not selfish or bad. The coldness I feel towards her is gradually disappearing.

Mama is a fool. Her main aim in life is to give me as many complexes as possible. She's a fool, a real fool. Papa's the same.

The diary also reveals that the fear induced by the proposed visit to the specialist was unjustified. A day after the appointment he simply mentions the visit along with other unimportant issues:

Yesterday I went to the psychiatrist. It was just to meet him. No important comment to make.

I went to see the play *Pobre Menina Rica*, by Carlos Lyra and Vinicius de Moraes and then I had a pizza.

I decided to put off my whole literary programme until 1965. I'm going to wait until I'm a bit more mature.

He managed to achieve the required grades to pass the year and, according to the rules of the house, he therefore had the right to a holiday, which, this time, was to be in Belém. His holidays with his paternal grandparents, Cencita and Cazuza, had one enormous advantage over those spent in Araruama. At a time when a letter could take weeks to arrive and a long-distance phone call sometimes took hours if not days to put through, the distance – more than 3,000 kilometres – between Rio and Belém meant that the young man was beyond the control of his parents or from any surprise visits. Adventures that were unthinkable in Rio were routine in Belém: drinking beer, playing snooker and sleeping out of doors with his three cousins, whose mother had died and who were being brought up by their grandparents. Such was the excitement and bustle of life there that within the first few days of his holiday, he had lost his penknife, his watch, his torch and the beloved Sheaffer fountain pen he had bought with his prize money. One habit remained: no matter what time he went to bed, he devoted the last thirty minutes before going to sleep to writing letters to his friends and reading the eclectic selection of books he had taken with him – books ranging from Erle Stanley Gardner's detective story *The Case of the Calendar Girl*, to the encyclical *Pacem in Terris*, published in March 1963 by Pope John XXIII ('Reading this book is increasing my understanding of society,' he wrote).

He filled his letters to friends with news of his adventures in Belém, but in his letters to his father there was only one subject: money.

> You've never put your money to such good use as when you paid for this trip for me. I've never had such fun. But if all the money you've spent on the trip is to produce real benefits, I need more cash. There's no point in you spending 140,000 on a trip if I'm not going to have fun. If you haven't got any spare money, then no problem. But it isn't right to spend all your money on the house while my short life passes me by.

Belém appears to have been a city destined to provoke strong feelings in him. Three years before, on another trip there, he had at last had the chance to clarify a question that was troubling him: how were babies made? Earlier, he had plucked up the courage to ask Rui, a slightly older friend, but the reply, which was disconcertingly stark, appalled him: 'Simple: the man puts his dick in the woman's hole and when he comes, he leaves a seed in her stomach. That seed grows and becomes a person.'

He didn't believe it. He couldn't imagine his father being capable of doing something so perverted with his mother. As this was not something that could be written about in a letter, he waited for the holidays in Belém so that he could find out from an appropriate person – his cousin, Fred, who as well as being older, was a member of the family, someone whose version he could trust. The first chance he had to speak to his cousin alone, he found a way of bringing the subject up and repeated the disgusting story his friend in Rio had told him. He almost had an asthma attack when he heard what Fred had to say: 'Your friend in Rio is right. That's how it is. The man enters the woman and deposits a drop of sperm in her vagina. That's how everyone is made.'

Paulo reacted angrily. 'You're only telling me that because you haven't got a mother and so you don't have a problem with it. Can you really imagine your father penetrating your mother, Fred? You're out of your mind!'

That loss of innocence was not the only shock Belém had in store for him. The city also brought him his first contact with death. Early on the evening of Carnival Saturday, when he arrived at his grandparents' house after a dance at the Clube Tuna Luso, he was concerned to hear one of his aunts asking someone, 'Does Paulo know?' His grandfather Cazuza had just died unexpectedly of a heart attack. Paulo was extremely upset and shocked by the news, but he felt very important when he learned that Lygia and Pedro – since they were unable to get there in time – had named him the family's representative at his grandfather's funeral. As usual, he preferred to keep his feelings to himself, in the notes he made before going to sleep:

Carnival Saturday, 8th February
This night won't turn into day for old Cazuza. I'm confused and overwhelmed by the tragedy. Yesterday, he was laughing out loud at jokes and today he's silent. His smile will never again spread happiness. His welcoming arms, his stories about how Rio used to be, his advice, his encouraging words – all over. There are samba groups and carnival floats going down the street, but it's all over.

That same night he wrote 'Memories', a poem in three long stanzas dedicated to his grandfather. The pain the adolescent spoke of in prose and verse appeared sincere, but it was interwoven with other feelings. The following day, with his grandfather's corpse still lying in the drawing room, Paulo caught himself sinning in thought against chastity several times, when he looked at the legs of his female cousins, who were there at the wake. On the Sunday evening, Cazuza's funeral took place – 'a very fine occasion', his grandson wrote in his diary – but on Shrove Tuesday, during the week of mourning, the cousins were already out having fun in the city's clubs.

That holiday in Belém was not only the last he would spend there: it also proved to be a watershed in his life. He knew he was going to have a very difficult year at school. He felt even more negative about his studies than he had in previous years; and it was clear that his days at St Ignatius were numbered and equally clear that this would have consequences at home. There were not only dark clouds hanging over his school life either. At the end of the month, the day before returning to Rio, he flipped back in his diary to the day when he had written of his grandfather's death and wrote in tiny but still legible writing: 'I've been thinking today and I've begun to see the terrible truth: I'm losing my faith.'

This was not a new feeling. He had experienced his first religious doubts – gnawing away at him implacably and silently – during the retreat at St Ignatius when, troubled by sexual desire and tortured by guilt, he had been gripped by panic at the thought of suffering for all eternity in the apocalyptic flames described by Father Ruffier. He had turned to his diary to talk to God in a defiant tone ill suited to a true Christian: 'It was You who created sin! It's Your fault for not making me strong enough to resist! The fact that I couldn't keep my word is Your fault!' The following morning, he read this blasphemy and felt afraid. In desperation, he took his fellow pupil Eduardo Jardim to a place where they would not be seen or heard and broke his vow of silence to open up his heart to him.

His choice of confidant was a deliberate one. He looked up to Jardim, who was intelligent, read a lot and was a good poet without being a show-off. A small group of boys from St Ignatius to which Paulo belonged would

meet in the garage at Jardim's house to discuss what each had been reading. But it was mostly the strength of Jardim's religious convictions that
made him not only a good example but also the perfect confidant for a
friend with a troubled soul. Paulo told him that everything had started with
one doubt: if God existed and if this God had created him in His own
image and likeness, then why did He delight in his suffering? As he asked
these questions Paulo had arrived at the really big one – the unconfessable
doubt: did God really exist? Fearing that others might hear him, Jardim
whispered, as though in the confessional, words that were like salt being
rubbed into his friend's wounds: 'When I was younger and was scared that
my faith in God would disappear, I did everything I could to keep it. I
prayed desperately, took cold baths in winter, but my faith was very slowly
disappearing, until, finally, it disappeared completely. My faith had gone.'

This meant that even Jardim had succumbed. The more Paulo tried
to drive away this thought, the less he was able to rid his mind of that
image of a small boy taking cold baths in the middle of winter just so that
God would not disappear – and God simply ignoring him. That day Paulo
Coelho hated God. And so that there would be no doubt regarding his
feelings he wrote: 'I know how dangerous it is to hate God.'

A perfectly banal incident when he was returning from the retreat had
soured his relations with God and His shepherds still more. On the way
from the retreat house to the school, Paulo judged that the driver of the
bus was driving too fast and putting everyone's life at risk. What started
out merely as a concern became a horror movie: if the bus had an accident and he were to die, his soul would be burning in hell before midday.
That fear won out over any embarrassment.

He went to the front of the bus, where his spiritual guide was sitting,
and said: 'Father Ruffier, the driver is driving too fast. And I'm terrified of
dying.'

Furious, the priest snarled at the boy: 'You're terrified of dying and I'm
outraged that you're such a coward.'

As time passed, Paulo's doubts became certainties. He began to hate
the priests ('a band of retrogrades') and all the duties, whether religious
or scholastic, that they imposed on the boys. He felt the Jesuits had
deceived him. Seen from a distance, sermons he had once believed to

contain solid truths were now remembered as 'slowly administered doses of poison to make us hate living', as he wrote in his diary. And he deeply regretted ever having taken those empty words seriously. 'Idiot that I was, I even began to believe that life was worthless,' he wrote, 'and that with death always watching, I was obliged to go to confession on a regular basis so as to avoid going to hell.' After much torment and many sleepless nights, at almost seventeen years of age, Paulo knew that he no longer wanted to hear about church, sermons or sin. And he hadn't the slightest intention of becoming a good student during his second year on the science course. He was equally convinced that he would invest all his beliefs and energy in what he saw not as a vocation but as a profession – that of being a writer.

One term was more than enough for everyone to realize that the college had lost all meaning for him. 'I have gone from being a bad pupil to being a dreadful pupil.' His school report shows that this was no exaggeration. He was always near the bottom of the class, and he managed to do worse in each exam he sat. In the first monthly tests he got an average of just over 5, thanks to a highly suspect 9 in chemistry. In May, his average fell to 4.4, but alarm bells only started to ring in June, when his average fell to 3.7.

That month, Pedro and Lygia were called to a meeting at the school and asked to bring his report book. The news they received could not have been worse. A priest read out the fifth article of the school rules, which all parents had to sign when their son was admitted to the school and in which it was stated that those who did not achieve the minimum mark required would be expelled. If Paulo continued along the same path, he would undoubtedly fail and his subsequent expulsion from one of the most traditional schools in the country would thereafter blot his scholastic record. There was only one way to avoid expulsion and to save both student and parents from such ignominy. The priest suggested that they take the initiative and move their son at once to another school. He went on to say that St Ignatius had never done this before. This exception was being made in deference to the fact that the pupil in question was the grandson of one of the first pupils at the college, Arthur Araripe Júnior, 'Mestre Tuca', who had gone there in 1903.

Pedro and Lygia returned home, devastated. They knew that their son smoked in secret and they had often smelled alcohol on his breath, and some relatives had complained that he was becoming a bad example for the other children. 'That boy's trouble,' his aunts would whisper, 'he's going to end up leading all his younger cousins astray.' What, up until then, had been termed Paulo's 'strange behaviour' was restricted to the family circle. However, if he were to leave St Ignatius, even without being expelled, this would bring shame upon his parents and reveal them as having failed to bring him up properly. And if, as his father was always saying, a son was a reflection of his family, then the Coelhos had more than enough reason to feel that their image had been tarnished. At a time when corporal punishment was commonplace among Brazilian parents, Pedro and Lygia had never lifted a hand against Paulo, but they were rigorous in the punishments they meted out. So when Pedro announced that he had enrolled Paulo at Andrews College, where he would continue in the science stream, he also told his son that any future holidays were cancelled and that his allowance was temporarily suspended – if he wanted money for cigarettes and beer he would have to work.

If this was meant as a form of punishment, then it backfired, because Paulo loved the change. Andrews was not only a lay college and infinitely more liberal than St Ignatius but co-educational, which added a delightful novelty to the schoolday: girls. Besides this, there were political discussions, film study groups and even an amateur drama group, which he joined before he even met any of his teachers. He had ventured into the world of the theatre a year earlier, when, during the long end-of-year holiday, he had locked himself in his room, determined to write a play. He would only come out for lunch and dinner, telling his parents that he was studying. After four days, he finished *The Ugly Boy*, which he pretentiously referred to as 'a *petit guignol* à la Aluísio Azevedo', a synopsis of which he recorded in his diary:

In this play, I present the ugly person in society. It's the story of a young man rejected by society who ends up committing suicide. The scenes are played out by silhouettes, while four narrators describe the feelings and actions of the characters. During the interval between the first and second acts, someone at the back of the stalls sings a really slow bossa nova [a style of Brazilian music that has its roots in samba and cool jazz] whose words relate to the first act. I think it will work really well. This year it's going to be put on at home in the conservatory.

Fortunately, his critical sense won out over his vanity, and a week later, he tore up this first incursion into play-writing and gave it a six-word epitaph: 'Rubbish. I'll write another one soon.' And it was as a playwright (as yet unpublished) that he approached the amateur theatre group at Andrews College, known as Taca.

As for schoolwork, teachers and exams, none of these seemed to have concerned him. On the rare occasions when these topics merited a mention in his diary, he would dismiss them with a short, usually negative sentence: 'I'm doing badly at school, I'm going to fail in geometry, physics and chemistry'; 'I can't even get myself to pick up my schoolbooks: anything serves as a distraction, however stupid'; 'Classes seem to get longer and longer'; 'I swear I don't know what's wrong with me, it's beyond description.' Admitting that he was doing badly at school was a way of hiding the truth: he was on the slippery slope.

Up until October, two months before the end of the year, all his marks in every subject had been below 5. His father thought that it was time to rein him in once and for all and carry out his earlier threat: his cousin, Hildebrando Góes Filho, found Paulo work in a dredging company that operated at the entrance to the port of Rio de Janeiro. The pay wasn't even enough to cover Paulo's travel and cigarettes. Every day after morning classes, he would rush home, have lunch and take a bus to Santo Cristo, an area by the docks. A tugboat would take him over to the dredger, where he would spend the rest of the day with a slate in his hand, making a cross each time the machine picked up the rubbish from the seabed and deposited it in a barge. It seemed to him utterly pointless and reminded him of the Greek myth of Sisyphus, who is forced to push a stone up to the top of a mountain only to have the stone roll back down to the bottom, so that he has to begin his task all over again. 'It's never-ending,' Paulo wrote in his diary. 'Just when I think it's finished, it starts again.'

The punishment had no positive result. He continued to do badly at school and when he knew he ran the risk of failing the whole year, he recorded the fact quite shamelessly: 'A friend has told me I'm going to be kept down in maths,' he wrote. 'And meanwhile the morning is so beautiful, so musical, that I'm even rather happy. Oh, God, what a life. What a life, what a life.' At the end of the year, his report confirmed the expected results: his final average of 4.2 meant that he had failed in every subject.

Paulo seemed to be growing ever more indifferent to the world in which he found himself. He accepted uncomplainingly the work on the dredger and didn't even care when all he received from his parents at Christmas was a penknife. The only thing that interested him was writing, whether in the form of novels, plays or poetry. He had recently returned to poetry and was writing furiously. After some thought, he had concluded that it was no disgrace to write verses if he was not yet ready to start writing his novel. 'I have so many things to write about! The problem is that I can't get started and I haven't got the patience to carry on with it,' he moaned, and went on: 'All the same, that is my chosen profession.'

As he settled into the house in Gávea, he discovered that there were others among the young who were interested in books and literature. Since there were fifteen boys and girls, they created a literary club, which they called Rota 15, the name Rota being derived from Rua Rodrigo Otávio, which crossed Rua Padre Leonel Franca, where Paulo's house was, and at the corner of which they would all meet. Paulo's poetic output was such that when Rota 15 decided to produce a mimeographed booklet of poetry he contributed an anthology of thirteen poems (among them the award-winning 'Thirteen-year-old-Woman'), and he added at the end his biography: 'Paulo Coelho began his literary career in 1962, writing short articles, then moved on to poetry. He entered a poem in the Academia Literária Santo Inácio in 1963 and in the same year won the top prize.' Rota 15 collapsed amid scandal when Paulo accused the treasurer of stealing the petty cash in order to go and see the French singer Françoise Hardy in concert in Rio.

He already believed himself to be a poet of sufficient standing not to have to depend any more on insignificant little magazines produced locally or by small groups. With the self-confidence of an old hand he felt that the time had come for him to fly higher. His dream was to be praised for his work – a laudatory quote would work wonders – in the respected weekly literary column 'Escritores e Livros', produced by José Condé, from Pernambuco, in the newspaper *Correio da Manhã*. The waspish Condé, who was able to make or break reputations in one paragraph, was the joint author of *Os Sete Pecados Capitais* [*The Seven Cardinal Sins*], a collection published by Civilização Brasileira, the other authors being Guimarães Rosa, Otto Lara Resende, Carlos Heitor Cony and Lygia Fagundes Telles, among other equally important writers. Paulo admired Condé's dry style and hoped that the critic's sharp eye would perceive the talent hidden in his work.

He added new poems to the anthology published by Rota 15, typed it up and sent off the carefully bound volume to the editors of *Correio da Manhã*. The following Wednesday, when 'Escritores e Livros' appeared, he rushed to the newspaper stand, desperate to read Condé's opinion of his work. His surprise was such that he cut out the column and stuck it in his diary, writing above it: 'A week ago, I wrote to J. Condé sending him my poetry and asking for his opinion. This is what appeared in the newspaper today.' The reason for his fury was a ten-line postscript at the foot of the writer's column: 'To all young show-offs who are desperate to get themselves a name and publish books, it would be worthwhile recalling the example of Carlos Drummond de Andrade, who only published three volumes totalling 144 poems in 15 years … And only the other day, a critic said that Ernest Hemingway rewrote that small masterpiece *The Old Man and the Sea* no fewer than twenty times.'

Paulo took this personally and felt crushed by such an aggressive response. While only a short while before he had been thanking God for the joy of having discovered his vocation, his self-confidence gave way to a sea of doubt. 'Maybe I'm not cut out to be a writer,' he wrote. But he soon recovered his self-belief. Like the friend who used to take cold baths in order not to lose faith in God, he had to fight to realize his dream. Condé had dealt him a blow, but he was not prepared to lie down. He spent the whole day thinking of nothing but that literary column. In order to take his mind off it he tried watching an episode of *Dr Kildare*, about a young doctor, played by Richard Chamberlain, working in a large hospital. He switched off before the end and wrote in his notebook: 'In today's episode of *Dr Kildare*, the director of the hospital says to the doctor: "I shouldn't have tried to change your life, Jim. We were all born with an ideal." I've applied these words to being a writer and have decided that's what I'll be.' Thrilled by his own determination, he wrote a parody of Kipling's 'If ...':

> If you can ask your friends and enemies for a chance.
> If you can hear a 'no' and take it as a 'maybe'.
> If you can start from the bottom and yet still value the little that
>   you have.
> If you can improve yourself each moment and reach the heights
>   without succumbing to vanity.
> Then you'll be a writer.

Immersed in these lofty ideas, he viewed with horror the prospect of going back to Andrews College. Tormented by the mere thought of it, he dreamed up a plan which, if it succeeded, would free him from school for a good two years: to get a study grant and leave the country, as several of his schoolfriends had done. His parents found renewed hope when he applied to join the American Field Service, a cultural exchange programme that was much in vogue at the time. Judging by his marks, he wasn't entirely useless at English (a subject in which, by his standards, he always did fairly well), and that would certainly help in obtaining the grant. For two weeks, he dedicated his free time to getting together all the necessary documents: school certificates, passport-size photos, references. When the exams came around, the seven other applicants in his group for the one place were whittled down until there remained only Paulo and two others who were to take the decisive test – the interview in English with someone from the United States.

On the day, he was so nervous that as he sat down in front of the examiner – a girl his own age – he felt a jolt, as though he had been punched in the chest. He set aside his atheism and silently begged God to let this be a false alarm. It was not: he was having an asthma attack. A dry whistle rose from his lungs while, eyes bulging, he patted his pockets, searching for his inhaler. He tried to talk, but all that came out was a whisper. The American girl didn't know what to do. After a few minutes, the attack subsided. Pulling himself together, he managed to complete the interview, but he left with misgivings: 'I think that asthma attack has ruined my chances.' Indeed, a month before he would have been due to leave for the United States, a telegram arrived informing him that he had not been selected. Instead of feeling downhearted at this failure, Paulo attributed it not to his poor performance but to the fact that his mother had visited the States earlier. 'I think they'd prefer people whose relatives have never been to the United States,' he wrote, finishing with a statement worthy of the fox in the fable when faced with the bunch of grapes he cannot reach: 'They believe, at least this is how I interpret it, that I'm too much of an intellectual for America.'

It was at this time that a new, overwhelming passion entered his life: a flesh-and-blood passion with brown eyes and long legs and answering to the name of Márcia. At seventeen, Paulo was still skinny and rather short, even by Brazilian standards. He weighed 50 kilos, which was at least 10 kilos below the ideal for his height of 1.69 metres (he remains this height to this day). Added to this, he was not an attractive adolescent. 'I was ugly, skinny, lacking in charm and incapable of getting a girl-friend,' he has said in various interviews throughout his life. 'I had an inferiority complex about the way I looked.' While the majority of boys wore short-sleeved, close-fitting shirts, to show off their muscles, he would always wear a long-sleeved shirt that concealed his narrow shoulders and thin arms. A disproportionately wide leather belt held up his faded jeans which, as fashion decreed, were tight on the legs. He wore the same metal-framed spectacles with tinted lenses that, years later, would become the trademark of the Beatle John Lennon. His hair was almost shoulder-length, and he had started to cultivate a thin moustache and a tuft of hair under his lower lip.

Márcia was a year younger than Paulo and lived almost next door. She was also a pupil at Andrews College and a member of Rota 15. In spite of vigilance on the part of her parents and older brother, she was seen by her colleagues as a fun-loving girl and was, therefore, in great demand. With his self-confidence at rock bottom, Paulo didn't even notice her looking at him when he was arguing with the other 'intellectuals' in the group about films, books and plays. Although the majority of the group didn't even know the meaning of the word, they almost all felt that they were 'existentialists'. Paulo never wore smart clothes, he didn't have a car and he wasn't strong, but Márcia melted whenever she heard him talking about books or reciting famous poems. He, however, was oblivious to this until she took the initiative.

On New Year's Eve 1964, Paulo closed yet another notebook with the melancholy words: 'Today is the last day of 1964, a year that's coming to an end with a sob hidden in the dark night. A year crowned with bitterness.' And it was in this same downbeat mood that he met up with his friends two days later, on a Saturday, to go to the show *Opinião*, featuring the singer Nara Leão, at the Arena Theatre in Copacabana. The group took their seats and Márcia happened to sit next to him. When the lights dimmed and Nara began to sing, Márcia felt something brush her hand. She glanced sideways and saw Paulo's hand lying close to hers. She immediately entwined her fingers in his and squeezed lightly. He was so astonished that his first reaction was one of panic: what if he had an asthma attack right there? However, he calmed down. 'I was certain that God had guided Márcia's hand towards mine,' he recalled later. 'In that case, why would He give me an asthma attack?' So he began to breathe like any mortal and the two fell desperately in love.

When the show came to an end, Nara Leão gave several encores, but, still holding hands, the young couple took advantage of the dark, and escaped from the crowded theatre. They took off their shoes and walked barefoot, hand-in-hand, along Copacabana beach. Paulo put his arms around her and tried to kiss her, but Márcia pulled back gently, saying: 'I've never been kissed on the mouth before.'

He reacted like a veritable Don Juan: 'Don't worry. I've kissed lots of girls. You'll like it.'

In the suffocating heat and under the starry Rio night, the two liars shared a long kiss, which both would remember warmly more than forty years later. The year 1965 could not have got off to a more encouraging start.

Paulo's relationship with Márcia brought him a peace of mind he had never known before, not even during the best times in Araruama and

Belém. He wasn't even upset when he learned that he hadn't been placed in a poetry competition held by the Instituto Nacional do Mate. 'Who cares about prizes,' he wrote magnanimously, 'when they're loved by a woman like Márcia?' He now filled whole pages of his diary with drawings of hearts pierced by love's arrow and with their two names written on them.

This happiness was short-lived. Before the summer was over, Márcia's parents found out the name of her boyfriend, and they were adamant that he was not the one for her. And when she wanted to know the reason for this ban, her mother was disconcertingly frank: 'In the first place he's really ugly. I can't understand what a pretty girl like you could see in such an ugly, awkward boy. You're someone who likes parties, and he doesn't even know how to dance and would be embarrassed to ask a girl to dance. The only thing he's interested in is books. Added to that, he looks rather sickly ...'

Márcia retorted that he was perfectly healthy. He had asthma, like millions of others, but it could be cured and certainly wasn't a blot on his character. Her mother feared that he might have other, contagious illnesses: 'I've even been told that he's an existentialist and a communist. So we're not going to discuss it any further.'

For her daughter, the matter was far from being closed. She recounted the entire episode to her boyfriend and the two decided to deal with the situation as best they could. They began to meet secretly in the homes of mutual friends, but because there were very few safe places, their intimate moments together were exceedingly rare and usually occurred in a pedalo on Lake Rodrigo de Freitas. Not that they ever went beyond the preliminaries. Paulo pretended to be experienced, but in fact up until then he had had only one sexual relationship, some months earlier, when, taking advantage of his parents' absence, he had managed to convince Madalena, a pretty maid whom his mother had recently employed, to go up to his room with him. Although she was only eighteen, Madá – as she was known – was experienced enough for the boy to retain a happy memory of that first night.

When they learned that their daughter was still meeting 'that creature' behind their backs, Márcia's parents increased their vigilance and refused to allow her to speak to Paulo on the phone. However, it was soon discovered that they had each put an alarm clock under their pillow to wake them at four in the morning when, in the silence of the night, they could whisper words of love, their mouths pressed to the receiver. The punishment for this disobedience was still harsher: she was to remain in the house for a month. Márcia refused to give up. With the help of the maid she would send notes to her boyfriend in which she would say when he should go and stand beneath the window of her room, where she was shut away. One morning, she woke to find a declaration of love scrawled in the tarmac in enormous letters: 'M: I love you. P.'

Márcia's mother returned to the charge: Paulo wasn't right for her, it wouldn't work out, he had no future and no prospects. The girl responded, undaunted, that she would certainly not break up with her boyfriend. She planned to marry Paulo one day. On hearing this, one of her aunts suggested that a sickly boy like him might not have the physical strength to fulfil his conjugal obligations. 'You know what I'm talking about, don't you, my dear,' she went on. 'Marriage, sex, children … Do you think that, weak as he is, he'll be able to lead a normal life?' Márcia appeared unconcerned by such threats. As soon as she had served her term of punishment, she went back to meeting Paulo. They had discovered an ideal spot: the church of Our Lady of the Conception, which was close to both their houses. They never sat next to each other, but one would sit in front of the other so that they wouldn't arouse suspicion, and there they would talk in whispers. Despite all their precautions, they were caught by Márcia's father, who dragged her home screaming and punished her by beating her with a belt.

She, however, seemed firmly determined to love, become engaged to and marry her Prince Charming. His parents weren't over-enthusiastic about their son's choice either. Since it was usual for his friends to hold small parties in their homes, Paulo managed to persuade his parents to allow him to hold one in theirs. It was a disaster. When they saw their son dancing cheek-to-cheek with his girlfriend, his father stood, arms crossed, beside them, staring angrily until Márcia, embarrassed, moved away and joined a group of girlfriends. And he did the same with Paulo's other guests. If he saw a boy and girl dancing too close or with the boy's hand below the girl's waist, he would stand right next to them until they 'showed some manners'. In addition, the master of the house had forbidden all alcohol, even an innocent beer.

This was the first and last party held in the Coelhos' large pink house. But nothing could shake Paulo's happiness. Márcia's birthday was approaching, and their love was not yet two months old, when her mother suggested they have a talk. Not being a believer in corporal punishment, she tried another tack: 'If you break up with him, you can go to the best boutique in Rio and buy all the clothes you want.' Her mother knew her daughter's weak spot: vanity. Márcia's initial reaction was that the suggestion was unacceptable – 'downright blackmail'. However, after some reflection, she decided that she had more than proved her love and that they both knew that they couldn't pursue their love against their parents' wishes. They were both under age and dependent – there was no future in it. If she had to give in, then at least it was at a good price. She accepted. When he read Márcia's letter telling him that their romance was over, Paulo burst into tears and wrote of his frustration: 'For someone like me, who dreamed of transforming Gávea into a Brazilian Verona, there could be no sadder end than being thrown over for a couple of dresses.'

Abandoned by his Great Love – as he described Márcia in his diary – he once again fell into depression. His parents were concerned about his state of mind and, taking pity on him, they decided to make an exception. Although holidays in Araruama had been forbidden because of his failure at Andrews College, he would be allowed to spend Carnival there with his cousins. Paulo arrived by bus on the Friday night and spent the weekend feeling miserable, not even wanting to go and see the girls at the dances in the city. On the following Monday evening, he accepted an invitation from three friends to have a beer in a bar near his Uncle José's house.

When the table was covered in beer mats, showing how many drinks had been consumed, one of the boys, Carlinhos, had an idea: 'My parents are away and the car is in the garage just waiting to be taken out. If any of you knows how to drive we can go for a spin round the town.'

Although he had never driven a car, Paulo announced: 'I can drive.'

They paid the bill, went to Carlinhos's house and took the car. While the four of them were driving up the main street, where there were crowds of people and carnival parades, there was a general power failure. Although it was pitch dark, Paulo drove on through the mêlée of pedestrians and carnival-goers. Suddenly he saw a group of revellers in carnival costumes making their way towards the car.

Not knowing how to react, he swerved and accelerated. Then one of his friends yelled: 'Watch out for the boy!'

It was too late. They all felt something hit the car's front bumper, but Paulo went on accelerating while his friends looked back, terrified, shouting: 'Put your foot down, Paulo! Put your foot down! Get out of here! You've killed the boy!'

CHAPTER 5

First encounter with Dr Benjamim

THE BOY WAS LUÍS CLÁUDIO, or Claudinho, the son of a tailor, Lauro
Vieira de Azevedo. He was seven years old and lived in Rua Oscar
Clark, near the house where Paulo was staying. The violence of the collision was such that the boy was thrown some distance, with his stomach
ripped open and his intestines exposed. He was taken unconscious to the
Casa de Caridade, the only hospital in Araruama, where it was found that
the blow had ruptured his spleen. To control the haemorrhaging the
doctor in A&E gave him a blood transfusion, but Claudinho experienced
a sudden drop in blood pressure and nearly died.

After the collision, Paulo and his friends had not only failed to go to
Claudinho's aid but also fled the scene of the accident. They took the car
back to Carlinhos's house and, with the city still in darkness, went to the
home of another of the boys who had been in the car, Maurício. On their
way there, they realized that news of the accident was spreading. Terrified
by rumours that the boy had died, they made a pact of silence: no one
would ever utter a word about the incident. They all went their separate
ways. In order not to arouse suspicion, when Paulo arrived at his uncle's
home, he 'cynically' (his own word) acted as though nothing had
happened. However, half an hour later came the moment of truth:
Maurício and Aurélio, the fourth member of the group, had been named

by a witness and arrested, and while in police custody they revealed the identity of the driver.

Paulo's uncle took him to a room and told him of the gravity of the situation: 'The boy's life is hanging by a thread. We must just hope that he survives, because if he dies, things will get very ugly for you. Your parents have been told everything and they're on their way from Rio to talk to the police and the magistrate. Meanwhile, you're not leaving the house. You're safe here.'

His uncle knew what the tailor was like and was concerned that he might do something crazy. His fears were confirmed that night. After visiting his dying son in hospital, Lauro appeared at the gates of the house where Paulo was hiding, along with two unpleasant-looking men. A revolver stuck in his belt, Lauro wagged a finger at José and said: 'Dr Araripe, we don't know yet whether Claudinho will live or die. As long as that's the case, your nephew is not to leave Araruama. And if my son dies, Paulo will die too, because I'll come here personally and kill him.'

Late that night, Lygia and Pedro arrived in Araruama and, even before going to see their son, they went to the magistrate's house, who told them that the 'perpetrator' could only leave the city with his permission. His parents' arrival did nothing to alleviate Paulo's despair and he spent a sleepless night. Lying in bed, he wrote in a tremulous hand:

> This is the longest day of my life. I feel terrible, not knowing how the child is. But the worst thing was when we arrived at Maurício's house, after the accident, and everyone was saying that the boy was dead. I wanted to run away, to disappear. I can't think of anything but you, Márcia. I'm going to be charged with driving without a licence. And if the child's condition worsens, I'll be tried and might be sent to prison.

This was hell on earth. On Shrove Tuesday news of the two incidents – the accident and the tailor's threat – had spread rapidly, drawing inquisitive crowds to Rua Oscar Clark, eager to witness the climax to the drama. Early on, Lygia and Pedro decided to visit Claudinho's parents to offer their apologies and to get news of the boy's condition, for Claudinho was still unconscious. Lygia put together a large basket of fruit for the boy's mother to take to him. As she and her husband were approaching the house, which was on the same side of the road as José's, Lauro ordered them to turn back, because he was not prepared to talk. He repeated his threat – 'Your son will only leave this town if my son survives' – and he said that Lygia could take the fruit back: 'No one here is dying of hunger. I don't want charity, I want my son back.'

Paulo left his room only to ask for news of the boy. He recorded each piece of information in his notebook:

They went to the hospital this morning. The boy's temperature is going down, let's hope that his father withdraws his complaint to the police.

[...] The whole town knows everything and I can't leave the house because they're out looking for me. I heard that yesterday, at the dance, there was a detective waiting for me at the door.

[...] The boy's temperature has gone up again.

[...] It looks as though I might be arrested at any moment, because someone told the police I'm over eighteen. Everything depends on the boy.

Claudinho's temperature rose and fell several times. He regained consciousness on the Wednesday morning, two days after the accident, but it wasn't until late that night that the agony ended, when the doctors reported that he was out of danger and would be discharged in a few days.

Early on the Thursday, Pedro Coelho took his son to make a statement to the magistrate, who had him sign an agreement to pay all the medical and hospital expenses. The boy survived and suffered no long-term consequences, apart from an enormous scar on his abdomen that would remain with him for life. Destiny, however, appears to have decided that his meeting with death was to be on Carnival Monday, for thirty-four years later, on 15 February 1999 – another Carnival Monday – Luís Cláudio, by this time a businessman, and married with two daughters, was dragged from his house in Araruama by two masked men with guns, who were apparently in the pay of a group of hijackers of transport lorries. He was viciously tortured, then tied up, soaked in petrol, set alight and burned to death.

Claudinho's survival in 1965 did nothing to improve Pedro Coelho's mood. When Paulo returned to Rio, he heard that, as a punishment for having caused the accident and for having lied, he would not be allowed out at night for a month. Added to this, his allowance, which he had regained after leaving his job on the dredger in December, was once again to be stopped until he had repaid his father the 100,000 cruzeiros (some US$1,750 in today's terms) for the hospital fees.

Two months after the beginning of term, the first report from Andrews College revived the hopes of the Coelho family: although he had done badly in some subjects, their son had received such good marks in Portuguese, philosophy and chemistry that his average had risen to 6.1, which may have been only so-so, but was certainly an improvement for someone who hadn't even been able to manage a 5. Everyone was hopeful: but in his second report, his average dropped to 4.6 and in the third he managed only 2.5. The days when the reports arrived became days of retribution for Paulo. Pedro Coelho would rant and rave, take away more of Paulo's privileges and threaten even worse punishments. Paulo, however, appeared indifferent to all of this. 'I'm fed up with school,' he would tell his friends. 'I'll leave as soon as I can.'

He channelled all the energy and enthusiasm he failed to put into his schoolwork into the idea of becoming a writer. Unwilling to accept the fact that he was not yet a famous author, and convinced of his own talent, he had decided that his problem could be summed up in four words: a lack of publicity. At the beginning of 1965, he would take long walks with his friend Eduardo Jardim along Copacabana beach, during which he would ponder what he called 'the problem of establishing myself as a recognized writer'.

His argument was a simple one: with the world becoming more and more materialistic (whether through communism or capitalism, it made no difference), the natural tendency was for the arts to disappear and, with them, literature. Only publicity could save them from a cultural Armageddon. His main preoccupation was with the written word, as he frequently explained to Jardim. Since it wasn't as widely disseminated as music, literature was failing to find fertile ground among the young. 'If someone doesn't enthuse this generation with a love of literature,' he would tell his friend, 'it won't be around much longer.' To conclude, he revealed the secret of success: 'That's why publicity is going to be the main element in my literary programme. And I'm going to control it. I'm going to use publicity to force the public to read and judge what I write. That way my books will sell more, but, more importantly, I'll arouse people's curiosity about my ideas and theories.' In spite of Jardim's look of astonishment when he heard this, Paulo continued with his plans for the final phase of his conquest of the reading public: 'Then, like Balzac, I shall write articles under a pseudonym both attacking and defending my work, but that's a different matter.'

Jardim did not appear to agree with anything he was hearing: 'You're thinking like a businessman, Paulo. Remember, publicity is an artificial thing that forces people to do what they don't want.'

Paulo was so convinced of the effectiveness of his ideas, though, that he had stuck to his desk at home a summary of the tasks he would have to carry out during that year in order to achieve fame:

Literary programme for the Year 1965
Buy all the Rio newspapers each day of the week.
Check the book reviews, who writes them and the names of the
    editors of the papers.
Send articles to the relevant people and a covering note to the
    editors. Telephone them, asking when the article will appear.
    Tell the editors what my ambitions are.
Find contacts for publication.
Repeat this process for magazines.
Find out whether anyone who has received my texts would like to
    receive them on a regular basis.
Repeat the same process with radio stations. Send my own
    proposal for a programme or send contributions to current
    programmes. Contact the relevant people by phone, asking
    when my contribution will be transmitted, if it is.

Find out the addresses of famous writers and write to them
    sending my poetry and asking for their comments and for help
    in placing them in the papers they write for. Write again if
    there's no reply.
Go to all book signings, lectures, first nights of plays, and try to get
    talking with the big names and get myself noticed.
Organize productions of plays I've written and invite people
    belonging to the literary circle of the older generation, and get
    their 'patronage'.
Try to get in touch with the new generation of writers, hold drinks
    parties, go to places where they go. Continue with my internal
    publicity campaign, keeping my colleagues informed of my
    triumphs.

The plan seemed infallible, but the truth is that Paulo continued to be humiliatingly, painfully unknown. He didn't manage to get anything published; he didn't get to know any critics, journalists or anyone who could open a door for him or reach out a hand to help him up the ladder of success. To make matters worse, he continued to do badly in his studies and was clearly miserable at having to go to college every day – what was the point when his marks went from bad to worse? He spent the days in a state of abstraction, as if his mind were in another world.

It was during this state of lethargy that he got to know another boy at school, Joel Macedo, who was studying classics. They were the same age, but Joel was the opposite of Paulo: he was extroverted and politically articulate, and one of the youngest members of the so-called Paissandu generation – film-lovers and intellectuals who would meet at the old-fashioned Paissandu cinema in the Flamengo district. He was a cultural activist, led the Taca drama group and was responsible for *Agora*, a small newspaper published by the pupils of the college, whose editorial team he invited Paulo to join. The newspaper was at loggerheads with the conservative directors of the college because it criticized the arrests and other arbitrary measures taken by the military government.

A new world opened up to Paulo. Joining the Paissandu set meant rubbing shoulders with Rio's intellectual elite and seeing close to the leading lights of the left-wing opposition. The cinema and the two nearby bars – the Oklahoma and the Cinerama – attracted film directors, musicians, playwrights and influential journalists. The latest European films were shown at midnight sessions on a Friday, when the 700 available tickets sold out in minutes. Paulo wasn't much interested in political or social problems, but his deep existential anxieties fitted the profile of the typical denizen of Paissandu and he quickly made himself at home.

One day, he was forced to confess to Joel why he never went to the midnight film sessions, which were, after all, the most popular ones. 'Firstly because I'm not yet eighteen and the films shown there are usually banned for minors,' he explained, adding: 'And if I get home after eleven o'clock my father won't open the door to me.' Joel couldn't accept that someone of seventeen had a set time for getting home. 'The time has come for you to demand your freedom. The problem of your age is easy enough to solve: all you have to do is change your date of birth on your student card, as I did.' He also offered to solve the problem of the curfew: 'After the midnight sessions you can sleep in my parents' house in Ipanema.' From then on, with his card duly falsified and a guaranteed roof over his head, Paulo was free to enter the enchanted world of Jean-Luc Godard, Glauber Rocha, Michelangelo Antonioni, Ingmar Bergman and Roberto Rossellini.

However, one problem remained: tickets, beer, cigarettes and travel all cost money. Not a fortune, obviously, but with his allowance suspended he didn't have a penny to his name, nor any idea as to how to get some money. To his surprise, a partial solution came from his father. Pedro was a friend of Luís Eduardo Guimarães, the editor of the *Diário de Notícias*, which, at the time, was an influential newspaper in Rio. Guimarães was also the son-in-law of its owner, Ondina Dantas. Pedro fixed up a meeting between his son and the journalist, and a few days later Paulo began to work as a cub reporter. The work, alas, would be unpaid until he was given a proper contract. The problem of money remained, therefore, but there was one compensation: the job was a step towards liberating himself from parental control. He was almost never at home. He would go out in the morning to college, return home briefly for lunch, then spend the afternoon at the newspaper office and the evening at the Paissandu. He spent so many nights at Joel's parents' apartment that it became his second home.

As is the case with all publications, the least exciting tasks fell to the juniors, such as reporting on any potholes that were holding up the flow of traffic or any domestic arguments that ended up at the police station, or compiling lists of the dead in the public hospitals for the deaths section in the next day's edition. It was not unusual for the new boy to arrive at the office and be told by Silvio Ferraz, the chief reporter at the *Diário de Notícias*: 'Go and talk to shopkeepers to see whether business is suffering from the downturn.' He may have been earning nothing and dealing only with unimportant matters, but Paulo felt he was an intellectual, someone who wrote every day, no matter about what. There was also another great advantage. When his colleagues at college or someone from the Paissandu set asked what he was doing, he would say: 'I'm a journalist. I write for the *Diário de Notícias*.'

He was so busy with the newspaper, the cinema and amateur dramatics that he had less and less time left for Andrews College. His father was in despair when he discovered that, at the end of April, his son had an average of 2.5 (contributed to by a zero in Portuguese, English and chemistry), but Paulo seemed to be living in another world. He did exactly what he wanted to and came home at night when he wanted. If he found the door unlocked, he would go in. If his father had, as he usually did, carefully locked everything up at eleven, he would simply take the Leblon–Lapa bus and, minutes later, be sleeping in Joel's house. His parents didn't know what else they could do.

In May, a friend asked him for a favour: he wanted a job in the Crédito Real de Minas Gerais bank and needed two references. As this was the bank where Paulo's father had an account, perhaps he could be persuaded to write one of the necessary letters? Paulo promised to see to it, but when he brought up the subject with his father he received a blunt refusal: 'Absolutely not! Only you could possibly think that I would support your vagrant friends.'

Upset and too ashamed to tell his friend the truth, Paulo made a decision: he locked himself in his room and typed up a letter full of praise for the applicant, adding at the bottom 'Engenheiro Pedro Queima Coelho de Souza'. He signed it and put the letter in an envelope – problem solved. Everything went so well that the subject of the letter felt obliged to thank its writer for his kindness with a telephone call. Dr Pedro couldn't understand what the boy was talking about: 'Letter? What letter?' On hearing the words 'bank manager', he said: 'I wrote no letter! Bring that letter here. Bring it here immediately! This is Paulo's doing! Paulo must have forged my signature!' He rang off and rushed to the bank, looking for evidence of the crime – the letter, the proof that his son had become a forger, a fraudster. Paulo arrived home that evening, unaware of what had happened. He found his father in a fury, but that was nothing new. Before going to sleep, he wrote a short note in his diary: 'In a month and a half I've written nine articles for *Diário de Notícias*. I've got a trip to Furnas set up for 12th June, when I'm going to meet the most important people in the political world, such as the president, the most important governors and ministers of state.'

The following morning, he woke in a particularly good mood, since a rumour had been going round at the newspaper that he was going to be taken on officially, which would mean he would be a real journalist, with a press card and a guaranteed salary. When he went downstairs, he was surprised to find his parents already up and waiting for him. Pedro was beside himself with rage, but he said nothing.

It was Lygia who spoke: 'Paulo, we're worried about your asthma and so we've made an appointment with the doctor for a check-up. Eat your breakfast because we've got to leave soon.'

A few minutes later, his father took the Vanguard out of the garage – a rare occurrence – and the three drove along the coast road towards the city centre. Seated in the back, absorbed in thought, Paulo gazed out at the fog over the sea, which made Guanabara bay look simultaneously melancholy and poetic. When they were halfway along Botafogo beach the car took a left turn into Rua Marquês de Olinda, drove another three blocks and drew up alongside a wall more than 3 metres high. The three got out and went over to a wrought-iron gate. Paulo heard his father say something to the gatekeeper and, moments later, saw a nun arrive to take them to a consulting room. They were in the Casa de Saúde Dr Eiras, a large hospital occupying various buildings and large mansions in the woods at the bottom of a hill.

The nun went ahead, showing his parents the way, with Paulo behind, not understanding what was going on. The four of them took a lift to the ninth floor and, as they walked down a long corridor towards the consulting room, the nun opened a door and showed Pedro and Lygia a bedroom with two beds and a window with an iron grille. She smiled, saying: 'This is where the boy will sleep. As you can see, it's a nice bright, spacious room.'

Paulo couldn't understand what he was hearing and had no time to ask, since, by then, they were all in the doctor's consulting room. Seated behind a desk was the psychiatrist Dr Benjamim Gaspar Gomes, a fifty-two-year-old man, bald, with small eyes and a pleasant face.

Astonished, Paulo turned to his parents: 'If I've just come here for asthma tests, why have you booked a room for me?'

Pedro said nothing and Lygia gently tried to explain to her son that he was being admitted to an asylum. 'You're not going to school any more, and you're not going to sleep at home. You left St Ignatius so that you wouldn't be expelled and you've ended up failing at Andrews. On top of that you ran over the boy in Araruama ...'

Then his father spoke for the first time: 'This time, you've really overstepped the mark. Forging a signature, as you did mine, isn't just a prank – it's a crime.'

Things moved rapidly from then on. His mother said that she and his father had had a long talk with Dr Benjamim – a colleague of Pedro's and a person whom the family trusted implicitly – and that they were all agreed that he was too excitable and needed medication, so it would be a good idea for him to spend a few days in this 'rest home'. Before he could recover from the shock, his parents stood up, said goodbye and disappeared down the tiled corridor.

Suddenly he found himself alone, locked up in an asylum with his school file under his arm and a jacket over his shoulders, not knowing what to do. As though he thought it might still be possible to escape from this nightmare, he said to the doctor: 'You mean you're going to lock me up like a madman without examining me – no interview, nothing?'

Dr Benjamim smiled: 'You're not being admitted as a madman. This is a rest home. You're just going to take some medicine and rest. Besides, I don't need to interview you, I have all the information I need.'

No one with any common sense would think that the information given by Paulo's father could justify this treatment: his parents' complaints – that he was irritable, hostile, a bad student and 'even politically opposed to his father' – were not very different from the complaints that nine out of ten parents make about their adolescent children. His mother had more precise concerns and thought that her son 'had problems of a sexual nature'. The three reasons for this suspicion are surprising, coming as they do from an intelligent and sophisticated woman like Lygia: her son had no girlfriends, he had refused circumcision to correct an overtight foreskin – phimosis – and, finally, it seemed, lately, that his breasts were developing like those of a girl. There was, in fact, an explanation for all of these 'symptoms', including the change in his breasts, which was nothing more than the side effect of a growth hormone prescribed by a doctor to whom she herself had taken him.

The only problem of a psychiatric nature that might have concerned his parents was one of which they were in fact unaware. Some months earlier, during one of his many sleepless, anxiety-filled nights, he had decided to kill himself. He went into the kitchen and began to block all the air vents with sticky tape and dusters. However, when it came to turning on the gas inlet from the street to the oven, his courage failed him. He saw with sudden clarity that he didn't want to die: he only wanted his parents to notice his despair. He describes how, as he removed the last strip of tape from behind the door and started to go back to his room, he realized, terrified, that he had company: it was the Angel of Death. There was good reason for his panic, since he had read somewhere that, once summoned to Earth, the Angel never left empty-handed. He recorded the conclusion to this macabre encounter in his diary:

I could sense the smell of the Angel all around me, the Angel's breath, the Angel's desire to take someone away. I remained silent and silently asked what he wanted. He told me that he had been summoned and that he needed to take someone, to give an account of his work. Then I picked up a kitchen knife, jumped over the wall and landed in an empty plot of land where the people in the shanty towns kept their goats running free. I grabbed hold of one of them and slit its throat. The blood spurted up and went right over the wall, splattering the walls of my house. But the Angel left satisfied. From then on, I knew that I would never try to kill myself again.

Unless his parents had been so indiscreet as to read his diary – as he suspected some time later – the sacrifice of the goat, which at the time was attributed to some perverse evil-doer, could not have been one of their reasons for having him admitted to the asylum.

Still absorbing the shock of this new situation, Paulo was led to his room by a male nurse. As he leaned against the iron bars at the window, he was surprised by the beauty to be found in such a wretched place. From the ninth floor he had an unbroken view of the white sands of Botafogo beach, the Flamengo gardens and, in the background, the spectacular outline of Morro da Urca and Pão de Açucar. The bed beside his was empty, which meant that he would have to suffer his torment alone. In the afternoon, someone arrived from his house and handed over at the gate a suitcase with clothes, books and personal possessions. The day passed without incident.

Lying on his bed, Paulo thought of the options open to him: the first, of course, was to continue with his plan to be a writer. If this didn't work out, the best thing would be to go mad as a convenient means to an end. He would be supported by the state, he wouldn't have to work any more nor take on any responsibilities. This would mean spending a lot of time in psychiatric institutions, but, after a day wandering the corridors, he realized that the patients at the clinic didn't behave 'like the mad people you see in Hollywood films': 'Except for some pathological cases of a catatonic or schizophrenic nature, all the other patients are perfectly capable of talking about life and having their own ideas on the subject. Sometimes they have panic attacks, crises of depression or aggression, but they don't last for long.'

Paulo spent the following days trying to get to know the place to which he had been confined. Talking to the nurses and employees, he discovered that 800 mentally ill people were interned at the clinic, and divided up according to the degree of their insanity and social class. The floor he was on was for the so-called 'docile mad' and those referred by private doctors, while the remainder, the 'dangerously mad' and those dependent on public health services, were in another building. The former slept in rooms with a maximum of two beds and a private bathroom and during the day they could move freely around the entire floor. However, you could only take the lift, the doors of which were locked, when accompanied by a nurse and a guide nominated by a doctor. All the windows, balconies and verandahs were protected by iron grilles or walls made of decorative air bricks through which one could still see. Those being paid for by social services slept in dormitories of ten, twenty and even thirty beds, while those considered to be violent were kept in solitary confinement.

The Dr Eiras clinic was not only an asylum, as Paulo had originally thought, but a group of neurological, cardiological and detox clinics for alcoholics and drug addicts. Two of its directors, the doctors Abraão Ackerman and Paulo Niemeyer, were among the most respected neuro-surgeons in Brazil. While hundreds of workers dependent on social security lined up at their doors waiting for a consultation, famous people with health problems also went there. During his time in the clinic as a patient, Paulo received weekly visits from his mother. On one of these visits, Lygia arrived accompanied by Sônia Maria, who was fifteen at the time and had insisted on going to see her brother in hospital. She left in a state of shock. 'The atmosphere was horrendous, people talking to themselves in the corridors,' she was to recall angrily some years later. 'And lost in that hell was Paulo, a mere boy, someone who should never have been there.' She left determined to speak to her parents, to beg them to open their hearts and remove her brother from the asylum, but she lacked the courage to do so. If she was unable to argue in defence of her own rights, what could she do for him? Unlike Paulo, Sônia spent her life in submission to her parents – to such a point that, even when married and a mother, she would never smoke in front of her father and concealed from him the fact that she wore a bikini.

As for Paulo's suffering, this, according to Dr Benjamim, who visited him each morning, was not as bad as it might have been, thanks to 'a special way he had of getting himself out of difficult situations, even when he was protesting against being interned!' According to the psychiatrist, 'the fact that Paulo did not suffer more is because he had a way with words'. And it was thanks to that 'way with words' that he avoided being subjected to a brutal treatment frequently inflicted on the mentally ill at the clinic: electroshock treatment. Although he was well informed about mental illnesses and had translated books on psychiatry, Dr Benjamim was a staunch defender of electroconvulsive therapy, which had already been condemned in a large part of the world. 'In certain cases, such as incurable depression, there is no alternative,' he would say confidently. 'Any other therapy is a cheat, an illusion, a palliative and a dangerous procrastination.' However, while he was a patient, Paulo was subjected to such heavy doses of psychotropic substances that he would spend the whole day in a daze, slouching along the corridor in his slippers. Although he had never experimented with drugs, not even cannabis, he spent four weeks consuming packs and packs of medication that was supposedly detoxifying, but only left him more confused.

Since almost no one knew he was in the asylum, he had little news of his friends. One day, he had an unexpected visit from the friend who was indirectly responsible for his presence there by asking for a reference, and who left the clinic with a mad idea – never carried out: that of rallying the members of the defunct Rota 15 group to kidnap him. However, Paulo's tortured soul only found true peace when his latest love appeared: Renata Sochaczewski, a pretty girl whom he had met at an amateur theatrical group, who was to become a great actress under the name Renata Sorrah, and whom Paulo affectionately called 'Rennie' or 'Pato'. When she failed to get in to visit him, Renata would furtively send him little love notes. These contained such messages as 'Stand at the window because I'm waiting to wave goodbye to you', or 'Write a list of what you want and give it to me on Friday. Yesterday I phoned but they didn't tell you.'

When he was allowed out, four weeks after being admitted, Paulo was in a very fragile state, but he nevertheless tried to take a positive lesson from his journey into hell. It was only when he got home that he found the mental energy to make notes in his diary:

In the meantime, I've been in Casa de Saúde Dr Eiras, where I was admitted for being maladjusted. I spent twenty-eight days there, missed classes, lost my job and was released as if I had been cured, even though there was no reason for my ever having been admitted in the first place. My parents have really done it this time! They ruin my chances at the newspaper, ruin my academic year and spend loads of money only to find that there was nothing wrong with me. What I have to do now is start all over again, accepting what's happened as a joke and a well-intentioned mistake. (The worst of it is that the day I was admitted, I was going to be given a job on the permanent staff at the newspaper.)

All the same, it was OK. As a patient on my floor said, 'All experiences are good experiences, even the bad ones.' Yes, I've learned a lot. It gave me a chance to mature and gain in self-confidence, to make a more careful study of my friends and notice things I'd never really thought about before. Now I'm a man.

While Paulo may have left the clinic convinced that there was nothing wrong with him, this was not the opinion of the psychiatrist Dr Benjamim Gomes. The hospital file in the archives of the clinic held a dark prognosis that read more like a condemnation: 'A patient with schizoid tendencies, averse to social and loving contact. He prefers solitary activities. He is incapable of expressing his feelings or of experiencing pleasure.' Judging from this piece of paper, Paulo's suffering was only just beginning.

CHAPTER 6

Batatinha's début

THE FEW FRIENDS WHO HAD WITNESSED Paulo's twenty-eight days of suffering in the clinic were surprised when he was let out. Although physically exhausted and looking more fragile, he made no attempt to hide the fact that he had been admitted to an asylum. On the contrary, when he reappeared in Rua Rodrigo Otávio, he boasted to a circle of friends that he had lived through an experience unknown to any of them: being treated as a madman. His descriptions of the people and events at the clinic, many of them invented, were so extraordinary that some of his friends even expressed envy at not having been in such an interesting place.

Lygia and Pedro were concerned about their son's behaviour. Fearing that his confinement might stigmatize him at school and at work, they treated the matter with total discretion. His father had decided to tell Andrews College and the *Diário de Notícias* that Paulo's absence was due to his having to go away unexpectedly. When they learned that their son was telling everyone the truth, Pedro warned him: 'Don't do that. If people get to know that you've had mental problems, you'll never be able to stand as a candidate for President of the Republic.'

Not having the least desire to be president of anything at all, Paulo appeared to have returned from the clinic with a renewed appetite for what he called 'the intellectual life'. Now he had a new place where he could hang out, besides the amateur theatre at the college and the Cine Paissandu. The director of the Serviço Nacional de Teatro (SNT), Bárbara Heliodora, had got permission from the government to transform the old headquarters of the Students' Union (which had been ransacked and burned by extreme right-wing groups on the day of the military coup) into the new National Drama Conservatory. Without restoring the building or painting over the marks left by the damage caused by the vandals, the Centro Popular de Cultura, as it had been known, was turned into the Teatro Palcão, a 150-seat theatre which, although it didn't enjoy the freedom it had previously enjoyed, would once again become a centre of cultural debate permanently filled by workshops, rehearsals and drama group productions. What would later become the Teatro Universitário Nacional (National University Theatre), an occasional drama group comprising only students, was also born there. Paulo's sole experience in this area was his play *The Ugly Boy*, which he had torn up soon after writing it, plus two or three other plays that had also gone no further than his own house. However, he was sure that he had some ability in the field and plunged into the newly formed Conservatory.

When he returned to the *Diário de Notícias*, it became clear to Paulo that his absence of almost a month had put paid to or at least delayed his chances of being taken on as a reporter, but he stayed on, unpaid and uncomplaining. Working in a place that allowed him to write every day, even if only on the trivial topics that usually fell to him, was a good thing. At the end of July 1965, he was sent off to report on the history of the Marian Congregation in Brazil. He was beginning to gain experience as a reporter and had no difficulty in carrying out the task; at the organization's headquarters, he interviewed members of the community, noted down numbers and wrote a short article describing the history of the Marians from the time they had arrived in Brazil with the first Portuguese Jesuit missionaries. The following morning on his way to school, he bought a copy of the *Diário de Notícias* at the newspaper stand and smiled proudly when he saw his article. The sub-editors had made some small changes, but they were still essentially his words being read by thousands of readers at that very moment.

When he arrived at the newspaper office after lunch, he learned that his head was on the block. The Marians were furious about the article and had gone straight to the owner of the newspaper to complain. They accused him of having invented facts and attributing them to the organization's leaders. The cub reporter was indignant when he heard this, and although his colleagues told him to lie low until the whole thing had blown over, he decided that it would be best to clear up the matter straight away. He sat outside the owner's glass-walled office, the so-called fishbowl, and waited two hours for her to arrive.

On entering the fishbowl, he remained standing in front of her desk. 'Dona Ondina, I'm the person who wrote the article on the Marians and I've come to explain —'

She didn't even let him finish the sentence: 'You're sacked,' she said.

Surprised, he countered with: 'But Dona Ondina, I'm about to be taken on by the newspaper.'

Without even looking up, she said again: 'You're sacked. Please leave.'

Paulo left, regretting his naivety. If he had waited a few days, as he had been advised, she would probably have forgotten about the matter. Now there was no way of saving the situation. He returned home with his tail between his legs. Although shaken by the incident, his ability to fantasize seemed limitless. Recording in his diary his regret at having taken the initiative, he described his dismissal as if it were a case of political persecution:

> I could have done all kinds of things to avoid being fired! I could have given in and gone over to the right simply in order to keep my job on the newspaper. But no. I wanted to be a martyr, crucified for his ideas, and they put me on the cross before I could give any kind of message to humanity. I couldn't even say that I was innocent, that I was fighting for the good of all. But no! Die now, you filthy dog. I'm a worm. A C-O-W-A-R-D! I was sacked from the 'DN' for being a subversive. Now I've got nothing but night school and lots of time doing nothing.

The *Diário de Notícias* was not a right-wing newspaper; nor had he been dismissed for political reasons.

Paulo appeared prepared to take advantage of his time in the clinic. He had been labelled 'a madman', and he intended to enjoy the impunity that protects the mentally ill and do whatever he wanted. To hell with school and his parents: he wanted to follow his dream. In his own words, he had become a 'delinquent' who went around with gangs, but since he lacked the physical strength of other boys, he thought that he could become an 'intellectual delinquent' – someone who read things that none of his friends had read and knew things that no one else knew. He belonged to three different groups – Paissandu, the Conservatory and what remained of Rota 15 – but whenever there was any sign of violence, he felt ashamed that he didn't have the courage even to break up a fist-fight.

He knew, however, that displays of physical strength were not the way forward. Whereas before he had felt himself to be 'an existentialist on the road to communism', now he saw himself as 'a street communist'. He had read Henry Miller's famous trilogy *Sexus, Plexus* and *Nexus*, and glanced over the works of Marx and Engels, and he felt confident enough to talk on such topics as 'true socialism', 'the Cold War' and 'the exploitation of the worker'. In a text entitled 'Art in Brazil', he quotes Lenin as having spoken of the need to take two steps back when it was clear that this was the only way of taking one step forward. 'Art cannot flee from this premise. It must first adapt to man and then, having gained his confidence, respect and love, it can lead him along the road to reality.' His basis for taking a route he had earlier rejected was simple: 'I am an intellectual, and since all intellectuals are communists, I am a communist.' The mother of a girl he was friendly with accused him of 'putting ideas' in the heads of the poor people in the street. 'From Henry Miller to communism is only a step,' he wrote; 'therefore, I'm a communist.' What he would only confess to his diary was that he loathed Bergman and considered Godard 'a bore' and Antonioni 'annoying'. In fact what he really liked was to listen to The Beatles, but it wasn't quite right for a communist to say this in public.

As he had predicted, his studies were relegated firmly to the background. In August, fearing that he would fail the year, the school summoned Lygia and Pedro to deal with three issues: low grades, too many absences and 'the student's personal problems'. Since the start of classes after the July holidays he had not achieved marks above 2.5 in any subject and during that time he had not been to a single maths lesson, which explained why he had never got more than 3 in the subject since moving to the college. He would leave home every morning and go to school, but once there, involved as he was with the drama group, he would spend whole days without entering the classroom. The verdict presented to his parents was worrying: either their son paid more attention to his studies or he would be expelled. Although the college did not adopt the same strategy as that used at St Ignatius, the director of studies subtly suggested to his parents that 'to avoid the worst', it might be best to move him before the end of the year to a 'less demanding' educational establishment. Put bluntly: if they didn't want to have the shame of seeing their son fail again, the best thing would be to enrol him in a college where the pupil only had to pay his monthly fees promptly in order to guarantee success. Lygia and Pedro were indignant at this suggestion. Neither of them had lost hope of Paulo returning to the straight and narrow, and to accept such an idea meant a humiliating surrender. There was no way they would let him end up in a fifth-rate school.

Paulo, meanwhile, seemed to be living on another planet. His life within the world of theatre, which was a hotbed of opposition to the military regime, brought him close to young people who were becoming politically militant. Now all the films and plays he watched were political, and he had incorporated into his vocabulary left-wing slogans such as 'More bread, fewer guns' and 'United, the people will never be defeated'.

One night, when he went with a group of his friends to see *Liberdade, Liberdade* [*Freedom, Freedom*], which was being put on by Oduvaldo Viana Filho and Paulo Autran at the Teatro Opinião, the play was interrupted halfway through. A dishevelled young man got up on the stage and spoke out against the military dictatorship. He was Vladimir Palmeira, the student leader who went on to become a Member of Parliament and who was urging the audience to join yet another student march against the regime. On the few occasions when Paulo decided to take part in such marches, his real objective was to be seen by his father, whose office was in the centre of the city, where all the protest marches ended up. In fact, the world of politics that he was being drawn into had never much mattered to him. Apart from one or two notes, such as the results of the presidential elections in 1960 won by Jânio Quadros, his diary reflects his indifference to both politics and politicians. When the army had taken power in the April of the previous year, Paulo was speculating loftily in his diary on the existence of heaven and hell. Two weeks before the coup, when the whole country was in uproar, he filled several pages in his diary describing the misfortunes of a 'sixteen-year-old girl' he had met in the street: 'To think that this girl ran away from home and that in order to survive, she has been subjected to the most humiliating of things, although she has still managed to keep her virginity. But now she'll have to lose that just so she can eat.' And he ended: 'It's at times like this that I doubt the existence of God.'

However, that was the past. Now he felt himself to be a member of the resistance, although his criticisms of the dictatorship never went beyond the limits of his diary and even then were very timid. It was in his diary that he recorded his dissatisfaction with the existing situation, for example, in a satirical article entitled 'J'accuse', in which he placed The Beatles, Franco, Salazar and Lyndon Johnson on one side and on the other de Gaulle, Glauber Rocha and Luís Carlos Prestes:

I accuse the rich, who have bought the consciences of the politicians. I accuse the military, who use guns to control the feelings of the people. I accuse the Beatles, Carnival and football of diverting the minds of a generation that had enough blood to drown the tyrants. I accuse Franco and Salazar, who live by oppressing their compatriots. I accuse Lyndon Johnson, who oppresses countries too poor to resist the flow of dollars. I accuse Pope Paul VI, who has defiled the words of Christ.

But is there anything good in the world around me? Yes, it's not all disappointment. There's de Gaulle, who revived France and wants to spread freedom throughout the world. There's Yevtushenko, who raised his voice against a regime, knowing that he could be crushed without anyone knowing, but who saw that humanity was prepared to accept his thoughts, free as doves. There's Khrushchev, who

allowed the poet to express himself as he wished. There's Francisco
Julião and Miguel Arraes, two true leaders who knew how to fight to
the end. There's Ruy Guerra and Glauber Rocha, who brought to
popular art a message of revolt. There's Luís Carlos Prestes, who
sacrificed everything for an ideal. There's the life beating inside me
so that one day I can speak out too. There's the world in the hands of
the young. Perhaps, before it's too late, they will realize what this
means. And fight to the death.

The first job opportunity to arise, meanwhile, was light-years away from
the battle against the military dictatorship and the exploitation of under-
developed countries by American imperialism. An actors' cooperative
called Grupo Destaque was rehearsing a dramatized version of the children's classic *Pinocchio*, which was to be performed at the end of 1965,
and the directors had a problem. The show required seven scene-changes,
and the directors were worried that each time the curtain fell, the audience, mostly children, would start wandering around the theatre and delay
the start of the next scene. The producer, the Frenchman Jean Arlin,
came up with a simple solution: they would get another actor to appear
on the stage during each interval and distract the children until the
curtain rose again. He recalled an ugly, awkward, but witty young man,
Paulo Coelho, who had been introduced to him by Joel Macedo. He would
be perfect for the role. This was hardly resistance theatre, and the role
didn't even have a script, which meant he would simply have to improvise,
and it was unlikely he would get paid very much. As a cooperative
venture, after each show, the takings would be shared out, most of them
going to pay first for the hire of the theatre, and then the technicians,
lighting assistants and scene-shifters. If anything was left over, then it
would be divided equally among the actors, each of whom would get only
enough to pay for a snack. All the same, Paulo accepted the invitation on
the spot.

During his first rehearsal, he chose to wear a ragged pair of dungarees
and an old hat and waited in the wings to make his entrance. The only
instruction he had received from the director, the Argentine Luís Maria
Olmedo, who was known as Cachorro, was to improvise. When the

curtain fell for the first scene-change, he went on stage, pulling funny faces, and said whatever came into his head: 'When Little Potato starts to grow, he spreads across the ground. When Little Mama falls to sleep she puts her hand upon her heart.'

From then on, to his friends in the theatre he was known as Batatinha, or Little Potato. Although he considered himself to be a useless actor, during the following weeks he worked so hard at his role that when *Pinocchio* was about to open, his appearances had become so much part of the show that his name appeared in the programme and on the posters. At each rehearsal, he elaborated a little more on his performance – although always sticking to the time allowed for the scene-change – inventing strange names, making faces, jumping around and shouting. Deep down, he thought the whole thing ridiculous, but if that was the door that would allow him to enter the world of the theatre, he would go through it. In Grupo Destaque he worked with professionals who made their living from the theatre. After the rehearsals, the cheerful, lively group would leave the Miguel Lemos theatre, walk along the beach to Rua Sá Ferreira, four blocks away, and make an obligatory stop at the Gôndola bar, where the actors, technicians and directors who packed the stages of Copacabana's twenty theatres would meet every night.

Paulo felt he was in heaven. He was eighteen now, which meant he could drink when he wanted, go to any film or play and stay out all night without having to answer to anyone. Except, of course, to his father, Pedro Coelho, who took a dim view of his son's burgeoning theatrical vocation. This was not only because he hardly ever went to school and was on the verge of being expelled again. For his parents, the world of the theatre was a 'den of homosexuals, communists, drug addicts and idlers' with whom they would prefer their son not to mix. At the end of December, though, they gave in and accepted his invitation to the preview of *Pinocchio*. After all, this was a children's classic, not the indecent, subversive theatre that was enjoying such success in the country.

Paulo had reserved seats for his parents, his sister and his grandparents and, to his surprise, they all turned up. On the first night, the cultural section of the *Jornal do Brasil* published an article and his name appeared in print for the first time. He was last on the list, but for someone who was just beginning it was the right place. He recorded the feeling of being on stage in a short but emotional note in his diary: 'Yesterday was my début. Excitement. Real excitement. It was just unbelievable when I found myself there in front of the audience, with the spotlights blinding me, and with me making the audience laugh. Sublime, truly sublime. It was my first performance this year.' The family's attendance at the first night did not mean an armistice, however. When they learned that Paulo had failed at Andrews, his parents forced him to attend group therapy three times a week, still convinced that he had mental problems.

Indifferent to the hostility on the domestic front, he was having a wonderful time. In a matter of weeks, he had practically created a new character in the play. When the curtain fell on one scene, he would sit on the edge of the stage, unwrap a delicious toffee or sweet and start to eat it.

The children would watch greedily and when he asked one of the children in the front row: 'Would you like one?' the whole audience would yell: 'I want one! I want one!'

To which he would reply heartlessly: 'Well, too bad. I'm not going to give you one!'

Batatinha would take another bite or lick and turn to the audience again: 'Would you like one?'

More shouting, and again he would refuse. This would be repeated until the curtain rose for the next act.

A month and a half after the first night, *Pinocchio* moved to the Teatro Carioca, which was on the ground floor of an apartment block in Flamengo, a few metres from the Paissandu cinema. One afternoon when he was rehearsing, Paulo noticed that a very beautiful girl with blue eyes and very long hair had sat down in one of the rear stalls seats and seemed to be watching him closely. It was Fabíola Fracarolli, who lived on the eighth floor of the building, had noticed the open door and, out of curiosity, gone in to take a look. The following day, Fabíola returned and, on the third day, Paulo decided to approach her. She was sixteen and she lived in a small rented apartment with her widowed mother, who was a dressmaker, and her maternal grandmother, a nutty old woman who sat all day clutching a bag full of old papers, which she said were 'her fortune'.

Up to the age of fifteen, Fabíola had been afflicted with an enormous, grotesque nose à la Cyrano de Bergerac. When she learned that the only boy she had managed to attract had been paid to take her out by her cousins, she didn't think twice. She climbed on to the window ledge and said to her mother: 'Either you pay for plastic surgery or I'll jump!' Weeks later, when she had recovered from the surgery, she was parading a neat, sculptured nose. It was this new Fabíola who fell madly in love with Paulo.

Things were going well for Paulo when it came to women. While continuing his relationship with Renata Sorrah, he had decided to forgive Márcia and take her back as a girlfriend. This didn't stop him beginning a steady relationship with Fabíola. Her mother seemed to take pity on the puny young man with breathing problems and welcomed him into the family. He would have lunch and dinner with them almost every day, which made his life as Batatinha all the more comfortable. As if such kindness were not enough, soon Fabíola's mother, Beth, moved her bed into her sick mother's bedroom, thus freeing up a small room, which Paulo began to use as a studio, office and meeting room. To make the place seem less domestic, he covered the walls, ceiling and even the floor with pages from newspapers. When Beth was not around, his workspace became the bedroom where Fabíola had her first sexual experience. However, Paulo still could not understand why such a beautiful girl like her would be attracted to the rather sickly person he thought himself to be.

Riddled with insecurity and driven by what was certainly a mad streak, he gave her an ultimatum: 'I can't believe that a woman as beautiful as you, with your charm, your beautiful clothes, can be in love with me. I need to know that you really love me.'

When Fabíola replied confidently 'I'll do whatever you want me to do', he said: 'If you really love me, let me stub this cigarette out on your thigh. And you're not to cry.'

The girl lifted the edge of her long Indian wrapover skirt, like someone waiting to have an injection. Then she smiled at him without saying a word. Paulo took a long drag on his cigarette and stubbed it out on her smooth, tanned leg. With her eyes closed, Fabíola heard the hiss and smelled the repellent stench of the hot ash burning her skin – she would bear the scar for the rest of her life – but she didn't utter a sound or shed a tear. Paulo said nothing, but thought: She really does love me.

Although he made constant declarations of love, his feelings for Fabíola were ambiguous. While, on the one hand, he was proud to be seen in the fashionable places of Rio hand-in-hand with such a beautiful girl, on the other, he was embarrassed by her silliness and her extraordinary ignorance about almost everything. Fabíola was what, in those days, was known as a *cocota* or bimbo. When she announced over a few beers that Mao Tse Tung was 'the French couturier who created the Mao suits', Paulo wished the ground would open up and swallow him. But it was such a comfortable relationship, which made no demands on him, and she was so pretty that it was worth putting up with her stupid remarks with good grace.

The day she was invited to his house, she was astonished. Judging by her boyfriend's ragged appearance and his lack of money (she often gave him some of her allowance so that he could buy cigarettes and take the bus), Fabíola had always imagined that he was poor and homeless. Imagine her surprise, then, when she was received by a butler wearing white gloves and a jacket with gold buttons. For a moment, she assumed Paulo must be the son of one of the employees, but no, he was the son of the master of the house – 'an enormous pink house with a grand piano and vast courtyard gardens', she said later, recalling that day. 'Just think – in the middle of the drawing room there was a staircase that was identical to the one in *Gone With the Wind* ...'

Although he was eighteen and enjoying relative independence, Paulo still sometimes behaved like a child. One night, he stayed late at Márcia's house, listening to recordings of poetry (her family had given in and decided to accept him), and on returning home, which was only a few metres away, he came across what he called 'a group of nasty-looking individuals'. In fact, they were simply some boys with whom he'd had words a few days earlier when he complained about the noise they were making playing football. However, when he saw them armed with sticks and bottles, he was terrified, went back to Márcia's apartment and called home, waking his irascible father. Dramatic and theatrical as ever, he begged: 'Papa, come and collect me from Márcia's house. But come with a revolver because twelve criminals are threatening to kill me.' He would not leave until he looked out of the apartment window and saw his father in pyjamas, with a catapult in his hand, thus guaranteeing him a safe return home.

This paternal zeal did not mean that the situation at home had improved. Things were still as tense as ever, but his parents' control over his life had slackened. His performance during the second term at Andrews had been so dreadful that he wasn't actually allowed to take the end-of-year exams and was thrown out. The only solution was to take the route Pedro had sworn never to accept: to look for a college that was 'less demanding'. The choice was Guanabara, in Flamengo, where Paulo hoped to finish his schooling and then apply for a university course, although not in engineering, as his father so wanted. By opting to take the evening course at the college, he forced his parents to relax their vigilance on his timekeeping and give him a key to the house, but this freedom was won at a price: if he wanted independence and to choose a college for himself, to do drama and get home whenever he wanted, then he would have to find work. Pedro found his son a job where he could earn money selling advertising space in the programmes for the Jockey Club races, but after weeks and weeks of trying, the new entrant into the world of work hadn't managed to sell a single square centimetre of advertising space.

His lack of success did not dismay his father, who suggested another option, this time with Souza Alves Acessórios, a company specializing in the sale of industrial equipment. Although he hated doing anything he was forced to do, Paulo decided to agree for the sake of financial independence, because this was a job with a fixed salary and he wouldn't have to sell anything to anyone. On the first day, he turned up in a suit and tie with his unruly hair slicked down. He wanted to know where his desk would be and was surprised when the manager led him to an enormous shed, pointed to a broom and told him: 'You can start here. First you can sweep out this storeroom. When you've finished, let me know.'

Sweep out a storeroom? But he was an actor, a writer. Had his father fixed him up with a job as a cleaner? No, this must be some kind of joke, a prank they played on all the new employees on their first day at work. He decided to play the game, rolled up his sleeves and swept the floor until lunchtime, by which time his arms were beginning to ache. When the job was finished, he put on his jacket and, smiling, told his boss that he was ready. Without even looking at the new employee, the man handed him a sales slip and pointed to the door: 'Get twenty boxes of hydrometers from that room and take them to dispatch, on the ground floor, with this sales slip.'

This could only have been done deliberately to humiliate him: his father had found him work as a mere factory hand. Despondently, he did what he had been ordered to do and, after a few days, discovered that the routine was always the same: carrying boxes, packing water and electricity meters, sweeping the floor of the storeroom and the warehouse. Just as when he had worked on the dredger, he again felt like Sisyphus. As soon as he finished one thing, he was given something else to do. Weeks later, he wrote in his diary: 'This is like a slow suicide. I'm just not going to cope with waking up at six every morning, starting work at seven thirty to sweep the floor and cart stuff around all day without even stopping for lunch, and then having to go to rehearsals until midnight.'

He survived only a month and a half in the job and had no need to ask if he could leave. The manager decided to call Pedro and tell him that the boy was no good 'for this type of work'. When he left the building for the last time, Paulo had 30 cruzeiros in his pocket – the wages to which he was entitled. It was understandable that he couldn't do the work. Apart from performing in *Pinocchio*, which was on six days a week, he had begun rehearsing another children's play, *A Guerra dos Lanches* [*The War of the Snacks*], which was also directed by Luís Olmedo. 'I've got a role in this new play,' he wrote proudly, 'thanks to my spectacular performance as Batatinha in *Pinocchio*.' Now he was going to work as a real actor, sharing the stage with his friend Joel Macedo and a pretty brunette called Nancy, the sister of Roberto Mangabeira Unger, the perfect student who had come first in almost every subject at St Ignatius. After the tiring routine of rehearsals, the play had its first night in the middle of April 1966. Seeing how nervous Paulo was, Luís Olmedo kissed him on the forehead and said: 'You can do it, Batatinha!'

Paulo got off to a good start. Dressed as a cowboy, all he had to do was to step on to the stage to provoke roars of laughter from the audience, and so it continued. When the show ended, he was fêted as the best actor of the night. As the compliments came flooding in, Luís Olmedo hugged and kissed him (much to the embarrassment of Paulo's parents, who had attended the first night), saying: 'Batatinha, there are no words to describe your performance tonight. You were the hit of the evening, you had the audience eating out of your hand. It was wonderful.'

On the final night of *Pinocchio*, he repeated his success. Batatinha was the only actor – even though he wasn't really an actor – who merited an extra round of applause. If it weren't for the total absence of money, he would have been leading the kind of life he had always dreamed of. He had several girlfriends, he was reasonably successful as an actor, and he had also learned to play the classical guitar and now went everywhere with the instrument on his shoulder, just like his bossa nova idols. However, as had been happening for some time now, his waves of happiness were always cut short by bouts of deep depression. For example, this diary entry, written after reading a biography of Toulouse-Lautrec, dates from that apparently happy and exciting period of his life:

I've just this minute finished one of the most moving real-life stories I've ever read. It's the biography of a wealthy, talented artist, from an aristocratic family, who had achieved fame in his youth, but who, despite this, was the unhappiest man in the world, because his grotesque body and his incredible ugliness meant that he was never loved. He died of drink in the prime of life, his body worn down by his excesses. He was a man who, in the dark, noisy cafés of Montmartre, spent time with Van Gogh, Zola, Oscar Wilde, Degas, Debussy, and from the age of eighteen lived the kind of life all intellectuals aspire to. A man who never used his wealth and social position to humiliate others, but, on the other hand, his wealth and social position never brought a crumb of sincere love to a heart hungry for affection. In some ways, this man is very like me. Henri de Toulouse-Lautrec, whose life is brilliantly described by Pierre La Mure, in the 450 pages of *Moulin Rouge*. I'll never forget this book.

He continued reading a lot, but now, as well as making a note in his diary of each book he read, as he had always done, he would give each book a classification, like that given by professional critics. One star, bad; two, good; three, very good; four, brilliant. On one page in June, he wrote of his surprise at his own voracious literary appetite: 'I've beaten my record: I'm reading five books at the same time. This really can't go on.' And he wasn't reading lightweight stuff either. That day, he had on his bedside table *Crime and Punishment* by Dostoevsky; *Fear and Trembling* by Kierkegaard; *For People Under Pressure: A Medical Guide* by David Harold Fink; *Masterpieces of World Poetry*, edited by Sérgio Milliet; and *A Panorama of Brazilian Theatre* by Sábato Magaldi.

In that same month in 1966, Paulo finally got up the courage to show Jean Arlin the first play he had written as an adult: a three-act play, *Juventude sem Tempo* [*Ageless Youth*]. This was, in fact, a miscellany of poetry, speeches and texts by various authors: Bertolt Brecht, Carlos Lacerda, Morris West, Manuel Bandeira, Vinicius de Moraes, Carlos Drummond de Andrade, Jean-Paul Sartre and, of course, Paulo Coelho. Arlin found it interesting, fiddled with it here and there and decided to try it out. And there was more – since it was a simple play with hardly any scenery or props, he decided to put it on at the first Festival de Juventude, which was going to be held during the holidays in Teresópolis, 100 kilometres from Rio.

Since, besides being an author, he was also an actor, in the second week of July, Paulo went to Teresópolis with Grupo Destaque, against his parents' orders, naturally. He was excited by the festival and even entered a poem in the festival competition, which was to be judged by the poet Lêdo Ivo and the critic Walmir Ayala. The play was a disaster and the result of the poetry competition wouldn't be announced until a month later, but what mattered was that he'd had the courage to try.

The atmosphere at home hadn't changed at all. Besides continuing to nag him about getting home early – he rarely returned before one in the morning – his parents were now insisting that he have his hair cut, something he hadn't done for six months. When he arrived back late at night, he could rely on having to listen to a half-hour lecture before he could go to bed.

On one such night, Pedro was waiting for him at his bedroom door, looking very threatening: 'Once again you've overstepped the mark. As from tomorrow, we're going back to the old regime: the doors of this house will be locked at eleven at night; anyone left outside then can sleep in the street.'

Paulo spent the following day going from his 'studio' in Fabíola's home to rehearsals of *A Guerra dos Lanches*, for which the audiences were becoming smaller and smaller. In the evening, he went to the Paissandu to see Godard's latest film, *La Chinoise*; although he didn't much like the director, he was interested in attending the debate on the film that was to be held afterwards. There he met Renata and at the end of the evening the two went out to supper together. There was hardly anyone else in the restaurant when they finally asked for the bill and set off towards Leblon. Hand in hand, they walked almost 3 kilometres along the beach to Rua Rita Ludolf, where Renata lived. Exhausted, Paulo hoped desperately that a bus on the Lapa–Leblon route would come by, and it must have been almost four in the morning when he put his key in the front door, except that the key wouldn't go in. It was only then that he realized that his father must have had the lock changed.

At that hour in the morning, he couldn't possibly go to Joel's or Fabíola's. Furious, he grabbed a handful of stones and began to break all the glass in windows and doors at the front of the house. Woken by the noise, his parents at first decided to ignore him, but fearing that the neighbours would call the police, Pedro went downstairs and opened the door to his son. Making no secret of the fact that he had drunk too much, Paulo stalked across the glass-strewn drawing room and went upstairs without listening to a word his father was saying.

That night he went straight to sleep, but he had a dreadful nightmare. He dreamed that there was a doctor sitting on the edge of his bed taking his blood pressure and two male nurses standing at the door of the room holding a straitjacket. It was only then that he realized with horror that this was no dream. His father had called the emergency services of the mental asylum to admit him again. This time by force.

CHAPTER 7

Ballad of the Clinic Gaol

Wednesday, 20 July

08:00 I was woken up to have my blood pressure taken. Still groggy with sleep, I thought it was a dream, but gradually, the reality of the situation began to sink in. It was the end. They told me to get dressed quickly. Outside the house stood a car from the Emergency Psychiatric Service. I had never imagined how depressing it would be to get into such a car.

A few neighbours watched from a distance as the thin youth with long hair bowed his head to get into the car. Yes, bowed his head. He was defeated.

09:30 All the necessary bureaucratic documents have been filled out. And here I am again on the ninth floor. How fast things happened! Yesterday, I was happily walking with my girlfriend, a little worried, but certainly not expecting this. And here I am again. If I'd stayed out all night rather than gone home, I wouldn't have had that scene with my parents. I think of my girlfriend sometimes. I miss her.

Here everyone is sad. There are no smiles. Eyes stare into emptiness, seeking something, perhaps an encounter with the self. My room-mate is obsessed with death. To tease him, I play the Funeral

March on the guitar. It's good to have my guitar here. It brings a little joy into this atmosphere laden with sadness – the profound sadness of those who aspire to nothing in life and want nothing. The only thing that consoles me is that they still know how to sing.

15:00 I was talking to a young man who has been in here for two years now. I told him I couldn't bear it and wanted to get out. And he said in all sincerity: 'Why? It's great here. You don't have to worry about anything. Why struggle? Deep down, nobody cares about anything anyway.' I felt afraid, afraid that I might start thinking like him. I now feel real anguish, the anguish of not knowing when I will stop seeing the world through bars. It's indescribable. The anguish of the man sentenced to life imprisonment, knowing that one day he'll be given parole. But when will that day come? In a month? Three months? A year? Never?

17:00 Never?

19:20 I can't leave this floor, I can't phone anyone or write letters. A little while ago, I tried (in secret) to phone my girlfriend. She couldn't come to the phone, she was having supper. But what if she hadn't been having supper? What would I have said to her? Would I have complained about my lot, got angry? What would I have said? Who would I have been saying it to? Can I still speak?

I'm shocked at how calmly people accept being shut up in here. I'm afraid I might come to accept it too. If every man is an incendiary at 20 and a fireman at 40, then I reckon I must be 39 years and eleven months old. I'm on the brink of defeat. I felt this when my mother was here this afternoon. She looks down on me. This is only the first day, and yet I already feel half-beaten. But I must not let myself be beaten.

Thursday, 21 July

08:00 Yesterday they gave me a really powerful drug to make me sleep and I'm only just coming to. During the night, for no apparent reason, my room-mate woke me to ask if I was in favour of masturbation. I said I was and turned over. I really don't understand why he would ask me that. Or perhaps I dreamed it, but it was certainly strange. Flávio, my room-mate, normally spends long periods in complete silence. When he does speak, he always asks the same question: How are things outside? He still wants to maintain contact with the outside world. Poor thing. He's proud of his bohemian lifestyle, but now he's in here and admits that he's ill.

I will never do that. I'm fine.

11:30 I've just realized that they've emptied my wallet. I can't buy anything. Rennie, my girlfriend, promised to visit me today. I know it's forbidden, but I need to talk to her. I spoke to her on the phone, but I kept the tone light, to disguise my depression.

The people here like to show me new things. I'm fond of them really. Roberto is always showing me things – a way of calculating someone's age, a voltmeter, etc. Flávio is obsessed with knowing important people. There are endless interesting cases here. One man is always sniffing his food, another doesn't eat anything for fear of getting fat, a third talks only about sex and sexual aberrations. My room-mate is lying down, staring into space, looking fed up. They're playing a love song on the radio. I wonder what he's thinking about. Is he desperately searching for himself or is he just drifting aimlessly, lost and defeated?

I talk to some of the other patients. Some have been here for three months, others nine; still others have been here for years. I won't be able to bear this.

'Now from the sixth hour there was darkness over all the land unto the ninth hour. And about the ninth hour Jesus cried with a loud voice, saying: My God, my God, why hast thou forsaken me?'

Music, the sun beyond the barred windows, dreams, all of this brings with it a terrible melancholy. I remember the theatre at Teresópolis, where we put on my play *Timeless Youth*. It flopped, but it was still a great experience. Those were happy days, when I was free to see the sun come up, go horseback riding, to kiss my girlfriend and to smile.

Not any more. Not any more. Sleep dulls the ability to reason, and I'll end up like everyone else in here.

14:10 I'm waiting for Rennie. My doctor came to my room to bring me an anthology of French poets. That's good, because I'm starting to learn French. He remarked on the fact that I seemed calm, that I appeared to be enjoying myself. And sometimes I do enjoy it here. It's a world apart, where one just eats and sleeps. That's all. But there always comes a moment when I remember the world outside and then I feel like leaving. Not so much now. I'm getting used to it. All I need is a typewriter.

I know that my girlfriend will come (or try to come) today. She must be curious to find out what's happening to me. She'll visit another two or three times and then she'll forget about me. *C'est la vie.* And I can do nothing about it. I'd like her to come every day to cheer me up as only she can, but that won't happen. I don't even know if they'll let her visit me today. Still, it's a pleasant prospect – the enjoyable suspense of waiting.

14:45 It's a quarter to three and she hasn't arrived. She won't come now. Or perhaps they wouldn't let her in.

Friday, 22 July
11.50 Rennie came yesterday. She brought me a load of photos of her in the States and promised to write a dedication on one of them for me. I like Rennie. I feel sad to think that I haven't treated her as well as I should. I was cold and distant. And she was so affectionate.

So far, the rest of my things from home haven't arrived. As soon as my typewriter gets here, I'm going to have to type out an essay on psychiatry that Dr Benjamim set me. I've finished the anthology of French poets he lent me. Now I'm going to read *The Leopard* by Lampedusa.

It's odd, I'm starting to get used to the idea of staying here.

12:00 I'm beginning to allow sleep to overwhelm me. A heavy, dreamless sleep, sleep-as-escape, the sleep that makes me forget that I'm here.

14:00 I've stopped reading *The Leopard*. It's one of the most boring books I've ever read. Monotonous, stupid and pointless. I abandoned it on page 122. It's a shame. I hate leaving anything half-finished, but I couldn't stand it. It makes me sleepy. And I must avoid sleep at all costs.

14:30 It's not good to leave something half-done.

14:45 Conversation with my room-mate:

'I don't want to live here, in Flamengo, in Copacabana, or in any of those places.'

'So where do you want to live, Flávio?'

'In the cemetery. Life has lost all meaning for me since Carnival in 1964.'

'Why?'

'The person I loved most in the world didn't want to go with me to the Carnival ball at the Teatro Municipal.'

'Oh, come on Flávio, don't be so silly. There are plenty more fish in the sea. [Pause.] Do you still love her?'

'Him. He was a boy. Now he's doing his entrance exams to study medicine and I'm stuck in here, waiting for death.'

'Don't talk nonsense, Flávio.'

'He phoned me yesterday. He's a bit effeminate. It would make me so happy if he came to see me. I attempted suicide because of him. I drank ether spray mixed with whisky on the night of the ball. I ended up in the Emergency Department. Now he's out there and I'm in here, waiting for death.'

He's a strange guy, Flávio. He seems totally schizoid, but sometimes he talks perfectly normally, like now. I feel sad and powerless. He's made several suicide attempts in here. He's often spoken to me about the bohemian life he used to lead, and I've noticed a certain pride in his voice when he did so. I know from my own experience that all bohemians feel proud of being bohemian.

Flávio is crying.

15:00 The patients here can sometimes be very funny. Ápio, for example, who's fifty-six, told me yesterday that the Bolshevik Revolution was financed by the Americans. And there's a young man, the only other patient who's about the same age as me, who makes everybody laugh.

I can't write any more. Flávio is crying.

Saturday, 23 July

10:00 Last night, I managed to phone Rennie, who told me that she was still my girlfriend and still loved me very much. That made me so happy, and I probably said a load of silly things. I'm a sentimental fool. When I stopped talking, the telephonist butted in and I couldn't say anything else. Rennie's coming here on Monday. I hope I don't spend all the time complaining. It's awful, I feel inferior.

Luís said he'd come at midday.

Beside me is a boring guy called Marcos. He's been here since I got out, that's a year ago now. He keeps taking my radio so that he can listen to the football.

I diplomatically expelled him from my room.

20:30 It's half past eight at night, but it feels much later here. Luís came. He raised my spirits a little. I phoned Rennie and spouted more nonsense.

Sunday, 24 July

It's Sunday morning. I'm listening to the radio and I'm filled by a terrible sense of solitude, which is slowly killing me. It's Sunday morning, a sad, dull Sunday. I'm here behind bars, not talking to anyone, immersed in my solitude. I like that phrase: immersed in my solitude.

It's Sunday morning. No one is singing; the radio is playing a sad song about love and weeping. A day with few prospects.

Rennie is far away. My friends are far away. Probably sleeping off a night of partying and fun. I'm all alone here. The radio is playing an old-fashioned waltz. I think about my father. I feel sorry for him. It must be sad for someone to have a son like me.

On this Sunday morning, I feel my love for Rennie die a little. I'm sure her love for me must be dying too. My hands are empty, I have nothing to offer, nothing to give. I feel powerless and defenceless, like a swallow without wings. I feel bad, wicked, alone. Alone in the world.

Everything here is at once monotonous and unpredictable. I cling fearfully to my photos of Rennie, my money and my cigarettes. They are the only things that can distract me a little.

Monday, 25 July

I long for you and the nearer the time gets to your visit, the more I long to see you. Yesterday, on the phone, you said that you were still my girlfriend, and I'm very glad to have a girlfriend. It makes me feel less alone in here, the world seems a nicer place, even from behind bars. And it will be even nicer when you arrive. And so this morning, I open myself entirely to you, my love, and give you my heart. I feel a bit sad because you're far away and can't be with me all the time, but I'm a man now and have to survive this ordeal alone.

It's funny, I feel possessive. Yesterday, I talked to Luís and Ricardo on the phone. They'll come and see me on Tuesday. I know it's an effort for them. Luís's father is in hospital and Ricardo has to study. But they'll come. And that makes me glad. I've learned that people can get happiness and joy out of the saddest things. I've learned that I'm not as alone as I thought. There are people who need me and care about me. I feel a bit nostalgic, but happy.

Tuesday, 26 July

Yesterday, I read the whole of *Our Man in Havana* by Graham Greene. I haven't yet had time (ha, ha, ha) to write anything about the book. But it distracted me. I enjoyed it.

Sunday, 31 July

13:00 At this hour on this day, in this hospital, I have just received the news that in the poetry competition run by the newspaper *Diário de Notícias*, I came ninth out of 2,500 entries in the general category and second in the honourable mention category. My poem will probably appear in the anthology they're going to publish.

I'm happy. I wish I was outside, telling everyone, talking to everyone. I am very, very happy.

Here, behind bars, I wonder if Tatá still remembers me, her first boyfriend. I don't know if she's grown a lot, if she's thin or fat, if she's an intellectual or a member of high society. She might have been crippled or lost her mother, she might have moved into a mansion. I haven't seen her for eight years, but I'd like to be with her today. I haven't heard from her once since then. The other day, I phoned and asked if she used to go out with a guy called Coelho. She just said 'Yes' and hung up.

Saturday, 6 August

Rennie, my love, I feel a terrible need to speak to you. Now that Dr Benjamim has threatened me with insulin and electroconvulsive therapy, now that I've been accused of being a drug addict, now that I feel like a cornered animal, utterly defenceless, I want so much to talk to you. If this was the moment when my personality was about to be completely transformed, if in a few moments' time the systematic destruction of my being was about to begin, I would want you by my side, Rennie.

We'd talk about the most ordinary things in the world. You'd leave smiling, hoping to see me again in a few days' time. You would know nothing and I would pretend that everything was fine. As we stood at the door to the lift, you'd see my eyes fill with foolish tears, and I'd say it was because our conversation had been so boring it had made me yawn. And downstairs, you'd look up and see my hand through the bars waving goodbye. Then I'd come up to my room and cry my heart out thinking about what was and what should have been and what can never be. Then the doctors would come in with the black bag, and the electric shocks would enter me and fill my whole body.

And in the solitude of the night, I would pick up a razor blade and look at your photo next to the bed, and the blood would flow; and I would say to you softly, as I looked at your smiling face: 'This is my blood.' And I would die without a smile on my face, without shedding a tear. I would simply die, leaving many things undone.

Sunday, 7 August

Conversation with Dr Benjamim:

'You've no self-respect. After your first admission, I thought you'd never be back, that you'd do all you could to become independent. But, no, here you are again. What did you achieve in that time? Nothing. What did you get from that trip to Teresópolis? What did you get out of it? Why are you incapable of achieving anything on your own?'

'No one can achieve anything on their own.'

'Maybe, but tell me, what did you gain by going to Teresópolis?'

'Experience.'

'You're the sort who'll spend the rest of his life experimenting.'

'Doctor, anything that is done with love is worthwhile. That's my philosophy: if we love what we do, that's enough to justify our actions.'

'If I went and fetched four schizophrenics from the fourth floor, I mean real schizoids, even they would come up with a better argument than that.'

'What did I say wrong?'

'What did you say wrong?! You spend your whole time creating an image of yourself, a false image, not even noticing that you're failing to make the most of what's inside you. You're a nothing.'

'I know. Anything I say is pure self-defence. In my own eyes, I'm worthless.'

'Then do something! But you can't. You're perfectly happy with the way things are. You've got used to the situation. Look, if things go on like this, I'm going to forget my responsibilities as a doctor and call

in a medical team to give you electroconvulsive therapy, insulin,
glucose, anything to make you forget and make you more biddable.
But I'm going to give you a bit more time. Come on, be a man. Pull
yourself together!'

Sunday, 14 August – Father's Day
Good morning, Dad. Today is your day.
For many years, this was the day you'd wake up with a smile on
    your face
and, still smiling, accept the present I brought to your room,
and, still smiling, kiss me on the forehead and bless me.
Good morning, Dad, today is your day,
and I can neither give you anything nor say anything
because your embittered heart is now deaf to words.
You're not the same man. Your heart is old,
your ears are stuffed with despair,
your heart aches. But you still know how to cry. And I think you're
    crying
the timid tears of a strict, despotic father:
you're weeping for me, because I'm here behind bars,
you're weeping because today is Father's Day and I'm far away,
filling your heart with bitterness and sadness.

Good morning, Dad. A beautiful sun is coming up,
today is a day of celebration and joy for many,
but you're sad. And I know that I am your sadness,
that somehow I became a heavy cross
for you to carry on your back, lacerating your skin,
wounding your heart.
At this very moment, my sister will be coming into your room
with a lovely present wrapped in crêpe paper,
and you'll smile, so as not to make her sad too. But inside you,
your heart is crying,
and I can say nothing except dark words of revolt,
and I can do nothing but increase your suffering,

and I can give you nothing but tears and the regret
that you brought me into the world.

Perhaps if I didn't exist, you'd be happy now,
perhaps you'd have the happiness of a man who only ever wanted
     one thing:
a quiet life,
and now, on Father's Day,
you receive the reward for your struggle, in the form of kisses,
trinkets bought with the small monthly allowance
that has remained untouched for weeks in a drawer
so that it could be transformed into a present,
which, however small, assumes vast proportions in the heart of
     every father.

Today is Father's Day. But my Dad had me admitted
to a hospital for the insane. I'm too far away
to embrace you; I'm far from the family,
far from everything, and I know that
when you see other fathers surrounded by their children,
showering them with affection, you'll feel a pang
in your poor embittered heart. But I'm in here
and haven't seen the sun for twenty days now,
and if I could give you something it would be the darkness
of someone who no longer aspires to anything or yearns for
     anything in life.
That's why I do nothing. That's why I can't even say:
'Good morning, dear father, may you be happy;
you were a man and one night you engendered me;
my mother gave birth to me in great pain,
but now I can give you a little of the treasure
placed in my heart
by your hard-working hands.'
I can't even say that. I have to stay very still
so as not to make you even sadder,

so that you don't know that I'm suffering, that I'm unhappy in here,
in the midst of this quietness, normally only to be found in heaven,
if, of course, heaven exists.
It must be sad to have a son like me, Dad.

Good morning, Dad. My hands are empty,
but I give you this rising sun, red and omnipotent,
to help you feel less sad and more content,
thinking that you're right and I'm happy.

Tuesday, 23 August

It's dawn, the eve of my birthday. I'd like to write a message full of
optimism and understanding in this notebook: that's why I tore out
the previous pages, so devoid of compassion and so sad. It's hard,
especially for someone of my temperament, to withstand thirty-two
days without going out into the courtyard and seeing the sun. It's
really hard, believe me. But, deep down, I know I'm not the most
unfortunate of men. I have youth flowing in my veins, and I can start
all over again thousands of times.

It's the eve of my birthday. With these lines written at dawn, I
would like to regain a little self-confidence.

'Look, Paulo, you can always do your university entrance exams
next year: you've still got many years ahead of you. Make the most
of these days to think a little and to write a lot. Rosetta, your typewriter, your loyal companion-at-arms, is with you, ready to serve
you whenever you wish. Do you remember what Salinger wrote:
"Store away your experiences. Perhaps, later, they'll be useful to
someone else, just as the experiences of those who came before
were useful to you." Think about that. Don't think of yourself as
being alone. After all, to begin with, your friends were a great
support. Being forgotten is a law of life. You'd probably forget about
one of your friends if they left. Don't be angry with your friends
because of that. They did what they could. They lost heart, as you
would in their place.'

Thursday, 1 September

I've been here since July. Now I'm becoming more and more afraid. I'm to blame for everything. Yesterday, for example, I was the only one to agree to having an injection to help me sleep, and I was the only one to obey the nurse and lie down; the others, meanwhile, continued kicking up a ruckus. One of the nuns who help out here took a dislike to my girlfriend and so she's not allowed to visit me any more. They found out I was going to sell my shirts to the other patients and they wouldn't let me: I lost an opportunity to earn some money. But I managed to persuade my friends to bring me a gun, a Beretta. If I need to, I'll use it.

Interruption for a hair cut.

Right, my hair's all gone. Now I'm left with a baby face, feeling vulnerable and mad as hell. Now I feel what I feared I might feel: the desire to stay here. I don't want to leave now. I'm finished. I hadn't cut my hair since February, until the people in this hospital gave me an option: cut your hair or stay here for good. I preferred to cut my hair. But then came the feeling that I'd destroyed the last thing remaining to me. This page was going to be a kind of manifesto of rebellion. But now I've lost all will. I'm well and truly screwed. I'm finished. I won't rebel again. I'm almost resigned.

Here ends this ballad and here ends me.
With no messages to send, nothing, no desire to win,
a desire that had its guts ripped out by human hatred.
It was good to feel this. Total defeat.
Now let's start all over again.

CHAPTER 8

Shock treatment

ONE SUNDAY IN SEPTEMBER 1966, Paulo was wandering along the corridors of the clinic after lunch. He had just been re-reading 'The Ballad of the Clinic Gaol', which he had finished writing the day before, and he felt proud of the thirty-five typewritten pages that he had managed to produce in a month and a half at the mental asylum. In fact, it was not so very different from the work that had inspired him, Oscar Wilde's 'The Ballad of Reading Gaol', written in 1898, after his release from prison, where he had served two years for homosexual offences. Paulo's final sentence on the last page – 'Now let's start all over again' – might seem like mere empty words, a rather glib ending. Starting all over again meant only one thing: to get out of the hell that was the clinic as quickly as possible and restart his life. However, a terrifying idea was daily becoming more of a reality: if it was up to the doctors or his parents, he would continue to rot on the ninth floor for a long time.

Absorbed in these thoughts, he hardly noticed the two male nurses who came over to him and asked him to go with them to another part of the building. They led him to a cubicle with tiled floor and walls, where Dr Benjamim was waiting. In the centre of the room was a bed covered with a thick rubber sheet and, to one side, a small machine that looked like an ordinary electric transformer with wires and a handle, much like the equipment used clandestinely by the police to torture prisoners and extract confessions.

Paulo was terrified: 'Do you mean I'm going to have shock treatment?'

Kindly and smiling as ever, the psychiatrist tried to calm him: 'Don't worry, Paulo. It doesn't hurt at all. It's more upsetting seeing someone else being treated than receiving the treatment yourself. Really, it doesn't hurt at all.'

Lying on the bed, he watched a nurse putting a plastic tube in his mouth so that his tongue wouldn't roll back and choke him. The other nurse stood behind him and stuck an electrode that looked like a small cardiac defibrillator to each of his temples. While he stared up at the peeling paint on the ceiling, the machine was connected. A session of electroconvulsive therapy was about to begin. As the handle was turned, a curtain seemed to fall over his eyes. His vision was narrowing until it was fixed on one point; then everything went dark.

At each subsequent turn of the handle his body shook uncontrollably and saliva spurted from his mouth like white foam. Paulo never knew how long each session lasted – Minutes? An hour? A day? Nor did he feel any sickness afterwards. When he recovered consciousness he felt as though he were coming round after a general anaesthetic: his memory seemed to disappear and he would sometimes lie for hours on his bed, eyes open, before he could recognize and identify where he was and what he was doing there. Apart from the pillowcase and his pyjama collar, which were wet with dribble, there was no sign in the room of the brutality to which he had been subjected. The 'therapy' was powerful enough to destroy his neurones, but the doctor was right: it didn't hurt at all.

Electroconvulsive therapy was based on the idea that mental disturbance resulted from 'electrical disturbances in the brain'. After ten to twenty sessions of electric shocks applied every other day, the convulsions caused by the succession of electric charges would, it was believed, 'reorganize' the patient's brain, allowing him to return to normal. This treatment was seen as a great improvement on other treatments used at the time such as Metazol and insulin shock: it caused retrograde amnesia, blocking any memory of events immediately prior to the charges, including their application. The patient would therefore have no negative feelings towards the doctors or his own family.

After that first session, Paulo woke late in the afternoon with a sour taste in his mouth. During the torpor that dulled both mind and body after the treatment, he got up very slowly, as if he were an old man, and went over to the grille at the window. He saw that it was drizzling, but he still did not recognize his room, where he had been taken following the treatment. He tried to remember what lay beyond the door, but couldn't. When he went towards it, he realized that his legs were trembling and his body had been weakened by the shocks. With some difficulty, he managed to leave his room. There he saw an enormous, empty corridor and felt like walking a little through that cemetery of the living. The silence was such that he could hear the sound of his slippers dragging along the white, disinfected corridor. As he took his first steps, he had the clear impression that the walls were closing in around him as he walked, until he began to feel them pressing on his ribs. The walls were enclosing him so tightly that he could walk no farther. Terrified, he tried to reason with himself: 'If I stay still, nothing will happen to me. But if I walk, I'll either destroy the walls or I'll be crushed.'

What should he do? Nothing. He stayed still, not moving a muscle. And he stayed there, for how long, he doesn't know, until a female nurse led him gently by the arm, back to his room, and helped him to lie down. When he woke, he saw someone standing beside him, someone who had apparently been talking to him while he slept. It was Luís Carlos, the patient from the room next door, a thin mulatto who was so ashamed of his stammer that he would pretend to be dumb when meeting strangers. Like everyone else there, he also swore that he wasn't mad. 'I'm here because I decided to retire,' he would whisper, as though revealing a state secret. 'I asked a doctor to register me as insane, and if I manage to stay here as a madman for two years, I'll be allowed to retire.'

Paulo could not stand hearing such stories. When his parents visited, he would kneel down, weep and beg them to take him away, but the answer was always the same: 'Wait a few more days. You're almost better. Dr Benjamim is going to let you out in a few days.'

His only contacts with the outside world were the ever-more infrequent visits from the friends who managed to get through the security.

By taking advantage of the comings and goings at the gate, anyone with a little patience could get through, taking in whatever he or she wanted. So it was that Paulo managed to get a friend to smuggle in a loaded 7.65 automatic revolver, hidden in his underpants. However, once rumours began to spread among the other patients that Paulo was walking around armed, he quickly stuffed the Beretta into Renata's bag, and she left with the gun. She was his most frequent visitor. When she couldn't get through security, she would leave notes at the gate to be given to him.

The fool in the lift knows me now and today he wouldn't let me come up. Tell the people there that you had a row with me, and maybe that band of tossers will stop messing you around.

I feel miserable, not because you've made me miserable, but because I don't know what to do to help you.

[…] The pistol is safe in my wardrobe. I didn't show it to anyone. Well, I did show it to António Cláudio, my brother. But he's great; he didn't even ask whose it was. But I told him.

[…] I'll deliver this letter tomorrow. It's going to be a miserable day. One of those days that leave people hurting inside. Then I'm going to wait for fifteen minutes down below looking up at your window to see if you've received it. If you don't appear, it will be because they haven't given you the letter.

[…] Batata, I'm so afraid that sometimes I want to go and talk to your mother or Dr Benjamim. But it wouldn't help. So if you can, see if you can sit it out. I mean it. I had a brilliant idea: when you get out, we'll take a cargo ship and go to Portugal and live in Oporto – good idea?

[…] You know, I bought a pack of your favourite cigarettes because that way I'll have a little bit of the taste of you in my mouth.

On his birthday, it was Renata who turned up with a bundle of notes and letters she had collected from his friends with optimistic, cheerful messages, all of them hoping that Batatinha would soon return to the stage. Among this pile of letters full of kisses and promises to visit there was one message that particularly excited him. It was a three-line note from Jean Arlin: 'Batatinha my friend, our play *Timeless Youth* is having its first night on 12 September here in Rio. We're counting on the presence of the author.'

The idea of running away surfaced more strongly when Paulo realized that with his newly cropped hair he was unrecognizable, even to his room-mate. He spent two days sitting on a chair in the corridor pretending to read a book but in fact watching out of the corner of his eye the movements of the lift – the only possible escape route, since the stairs were closed off with iron grilles. One thing was sure: the busiest time was Sunday, between midday and one in the afternoon, when the doctors, nurses and employees changed shift and mingled with the hundreds of visitors who were getting in and out of the packed lift.

In pyjamas and slippers the risk of being caught was enormous. But if he were dressed in 'outdoor clothes' and wearing shoes, it would be possible to merge unnoticed with the other people crowding together so that they wouldn't miss the lift; then he could leave the building complex. Concealed behind his open book, Paulo mentally rehearsed his escape route dozens, hundreds of times. He considered all the possible obstacles and unexpected incidents that might occur and concluded that the chances of escaping were fairly high. It would have to be soon, though, before everyone got used to his new appearance without his usual shoulder-length curly mane.

He spoke of his plan to only two people: Renata and Luís Carlos, his 'dumb' neighbour in the clinic. His girlfriend not only urged him on but contributed 30 cruzeiros – about US$495 today – from her savings in case he should have to bribe someone. Luís Carlos was so excited by the idea that he decided to go too, as he was fed up with being stuck in the clinic. Paulo asked whether this meant he was giving up his idea of using mental illness as a way of retiring, but his fellow inmate replied: 'Running away is part of the illness. Every mad person runs away at least once. I've run away before, and then I came back of my own accord.'

Finally the long-awaited day arrived: Sunday, 4 September 1966. Duly dressed in 'normal people's clothes', the two friends thought the lift ride down, stopping at every floor, would never end. They kept their heads lowered, fearing that a doctor or nurse they knew might get in at any moment. It was a relief when they reached the ground floor and went up to the gate, not so fast as to arouse suspicion, but not so slowly as to be easily identified. Everything went exactly to plan. Since there had been no need to bribe anyone, the money Renata had given Paulo was enough to keep them going for a few days.

Still with Luís Carlos, Paulo went to the bus station and bought two tickets to Mangaratiba, a small town on the coast, a little more than 100 kilometres south of Rio. The sun was starting to set when the two of them hired a boat to take them to an island half an hour from the mainland. The tiny island of Guaíba was a paradise as yet unspoiled by people. Heloísa Araripe, 'Aunt Helói', Paulo's mother's sister, had a house on Tapera beach, and it was only when he arrived there, still with the 'dumb' man in tow, that he felt himself safe from the wretched clinic, the doctors and nurses.

The place seemed ideal as a refuge, but hours after getting there, the two realized that they wouldn't be able to stay there for long, at least not the way things were. The house was rarely used by Aunt Helói, and had only a clay filter half full with water – and this of a highly suspicious green colour. The caretaker, a man from Cananéia who lived in a cabin a few metres from the house, showed no interest in sharing his dinner. They were by now extremely hungry, but the only relief for their rumbling stomachs was a banana tree. When they woke the following day, their arms and legs covered in mosquito bites, they had to go to the same banana tree for breakfast, lunch and, finally, dinner. On the second day, Luís Carlos suggested that they should try fishing, but this idea failed when they discovered that the stove in the house had no gas and that there was no cutlery, oil or salt in the kitchen – nothing. On the Tuesday, three days after their arrival, they spent hours in the depot waiting for the first boat to take them back to the mainland. When the bus from Mangaratiba left them at the bus station in Rio, Paulo told his fellow fugitive that he was going to spend a few days in hiding until he had decided what to do with his life. Luís Carlos had also concluded that their adventure was coming to an end and had decided to go back to the clinic.

The two said goodbye, roaring with laughter and promising that they would meet again some day. Paulo took a bus and knocked on the door of Joel Macedo's house, where he hoped to remain until he had worked out what to do next. His friend was delighted to receive him, but he was worried that his house might not be a good hiding-place, as Lygia and Pedro knew that Paulo used to sleep there when he stayed out late. If he were to leave Rio, the ideal hiding-place would be the house that Joel's father had just finished building in a condominium at Cabo Frio, a town 40 kilometres from Araruama. Before setting out, Joel asked Paulo to have a bath and change his clothes, as he didn't fancy travelling with a friend who hadn't washed or had clean clothes for four days. A few hours later, they set off in Joel's estate car, driven by Joel (after the trauma of the accident, Paulo hadn't even touched a steering wheel).

The friends spent the days drinking beer, walking along the beach and reading Joel's latest passion, the plays of Maxim Gorki and Nikolai Gogol. When the last of Renata's money had gone, Paulo thought it was time to return. It was a week since he had run away and he was tired of just wandering about with nowhere to go. He went to a telephone box and made a reverse-charge call home. On hearing his voice, his father didn't sound angry, but was genuinely concerned for his physical and mental state. When he learned that his son was in Cabo Frio, Pedro offered to come and fetch him in the car, but Paulo preferred to return with Joel.

Lygia and Pedro had spent a week searching desperately for their son in mortuaries and police stations, and this experience had changed them profoundly. They agreed that he should not return to the clinic and even said that they were interested in his work in the theatre; and they appeared to have permanently lifted the curfew of eleven o'clock at night. Paulo distrusted this offer. 'After a week of panic, with no news of me,' he was to say later, 'they would have accepted any conditions, and so I took advantage of that.' He grew his hair again, as well as a ridiculous beard, and no one told him off. In his very limited free time, he devoted himself to girls. Besides Renata and Fabíola (Márcia was not around much), he had also taken up with Genivalda, a rather plain, but very intelligent girl from the northeast of Brazil. Geni, as she preferred to be called, didn't dress well, she didn't live in a smart part of town and she didn't study at the Catholic university in Rio or at one of the smart colleges. However, she seemed to know everything and that ensured her a place in the Paissandu circle.

Paulo's growing success with women was due not – as with Fabíola – to any surgical intervention but to a change in fashion. The 'counterculture' revolution that was spreading across the world was transforming not only political patterns and behaviour but also people's idea of what was attractive. This meant that men who had always been considered ugly up until then, such as the rock star Frank Zappa or, in Brazil, the musician Caetano Veloso, had overnight become ideals of modern beauty. The new criterion for beauty demanded that the virile, healthy and carefully shaven man be replaced by the dishevelled, ill-dressed and physically frail variety.

As a beneficiary of this new trend, Paulo had only one problem: finding a place where he could make love. He was eager to make up for lost time, and as well as his long-standing girlfriends, there were various others whom he chanced to meet. At a time when motels did not exist and morality demanded a marriage certificate when registering in a hotel, there were few alternatives for the young who, like him, did not have a bachelor pad. Not that he could complain, though, since as well as the lenient attitude of Fabíola's mother and grandmother, who shut their eyes and ears to what was going on in the newspaper-plastered 'studio', he could count on the assistance of Uncle José, in Araruama, whose door was always open to whomever Paulo might bring back at the weekends or on holidays.

Even so, when he made an unexpected conquest, he always managed to find a solution to suit the situation. On one occasion, he spent hours indulging in amorous preliminaries with a young aspiring actress in a pedalo on Lake Rodrigo de Freitas. After visiting numerous dives and by then feeling pretty high – on alcohol, since neither took any drugs – Paulo and the girl ended up having sex in the apartment where she lived with a great-aunt. As it was a one-room apartment, they enjoyed themselves before the astonished eyes of the old woman, who was deaf, dumb and senile – an experience he was to repeat several times. On another occasion, he confessed to his diary that he had had sex in still more unusual circumstances:

I invited Maria Lúcia for a walk on the beach with me; then we went to the cemetery to talk some more. That's why I'm writing today: so that, later, I'll remember that I had a lover for one day. A young girl

completely devoid of preconceptions, in favour of free love, a young
girl who's a woman too. She said that she could tell from my physical type that I would be hot stuff in bed. And the two of us, with a few
interruptions due to exhaustion or a burial taking place, made love
the whole afternoon.

Weeks after he ran away from the clinic, however, the problem of having
to find somewhere to make love was resolved. Thanks to the mediation
of his maternal grandfather, Tuca, Paulo's parents gave him permission
to try an experiment: living alone for a while. His new home was one
offered by his grandfather: a small apartment that he owned in the
Marquês de Herval building on Avenida Rio Branco, right in the commercial centre of Rio.

The apartment, which was a few blocks from the red light district,
could not have been worse. During the day, the area was a noisy tumult
of street vendors, traders, beggars and sellers of lottery tickets, with
buses and cars travelling in every direction. From seven in the evening,
there was a complete change of scene. As the brightness of day gave
way to darkness, the day workers were replaced by prostitutes,
layabouts, transvestites, pimps and drug traffickers. It was entirely
unlike the world Paulo came from, but it didn't matter: it was his home,
and he, and no one else, was in charge. As soon as he contacted his
friends in the Grupo Destaque, Paulo learned that the promised production of *Timeless Youth* in Rio had been cancelled for lack of funds. Some
of the group who had been in *Pinocchio* and *A Guerra dos Lanches* were
now engaged on another venture, in which Paulo immediately became
involved: a play for adults. For some weeks, under the auspices of the
Teatro Universitário Nacional, the group had been rehearsing an adaptation of *Capitães da Areia* [*Captains of the Sands*], a novel written thirty
years before by the Brazilian writer Jorge Amado. Blond, blue-eyed and
tanned, the director and adapter, Francis Palmeira, looked more like one
of the surfers who spent their time looking for waves in Arpoador; but,
as a precocious fifteen-year-old, he had already had one play, *Ato
Institucional*, banned by the censors. Jorge Amado was so thrilled to see
this group of young people putting on drama by established writers that

he not only authorized the adaptation but also wrote a foreword for the
programme:

> I have entrusted the students with the adaptation of my novel *Capitães
> da Areia* and have done so confidently and gladly: students nowadays
> are in the vanguard of everything that is good in Brazil. They are the
> untiring fighters for democracy, for the rights of man, for progress, for
> the advance of the Brazilian people, against dictatorship and oppres-
> sion. In the novel on which they have based their play, I also conveyed
> my faith in the Brazilian people and registered my protest against all
> forms of injustice and oppression. The first edition of *Capitães da
> Areia* was published a week before the proclamation of the 'Estado
> Novo', a cruel and ignorant dictatorship – which seized and banned
> the book. The novel was a weapon in the struggle. Today it has taken
> on a new dimension: the stage, which makes contact with the public
> all the more immediate. I can only wish the students of the Teatro
> Universitário Nacional the greatest success, certain that they are, once
> again, working for the good of democracy and of Brazil.

It was obvious that there would be problems. The first was with the
Juizado de Menores (the Juvenile Court), which acted in the interests of
minors and threatened to ban the rehearsals unless those under eighteen
were able to show that they had permission from their parents. This
meant all the young people in the group, starting with the show's director. Then, just a few days before the first night, the rehearsals were interrupted by the arrival of Edgar Façanha, Member of Parliament and the
head of censorship in Rio, together with a member of the Serviço
Nacional de Informações, or SNI, who wanted to see a certificate from the
censor's office, without which the play could not be performed. When it
became clear that no such certificate existed, during the ensuing argument the police arrested one of the actors, Fernando Resky, and left a
warning that if they wanted to open on 15 October 1966, as planned, they
should submit a copy of the script to the censor as soon as possible. Days
later, the script was returned with certain words deleted – 'comrade',
'dialogue', 'revolution' and 'freedom' – and one entire sentence cut: 'All

homes would be open to him, because revolution is a homeland and a family for all.' As they had already had such difficulty putting on the play, the group thought it best to accept the cuts without protest or appeal.

Although there were thirty actors in the play, Paulo had a reasonably prominent part. He was Almiro, the homosexual lover of Barandão, who dies of smallpox at the end of the play. Jorge Amado had promised to be at the preview, but as he was in Lisbon for the launch of his most recent novel, he asked no less a figure than 'Volta Seca', one of the street boys from Salvador who had been the inspiration for the main characters in the book, to represent him. The news in the Rio papers that *Capitães da Areia* had been censored proved a magnet to audiences. On the first night, all 400 seats in the Teatro Serrador in the centre of Rio were filled. Only two of the people Paulo had invited were missing: Renata and Dr Benjamim.

After his second period at the clinic, Paulo had formed a strange relationship with the psychiatrist. It wasn't just affection, despite all that Paulo had been through there: it was more that being close to the doctor and being able to talk to him about his doubts gave him a sense of security he hadn't felt before. At the time, such a relationship between doctor and patient was considered one of the side effects of retrograde amnesia. Many years later, however, Paulo himself diagnosed it as what came to be called Stockholm Syndrome, the sudden and inexplicable feelings of emotional dependence some hostages feel towards their hostage-takers. 'I established the same relationship of hostage and hostage-taker with Dr Benjamim,' he said in an interview. 'Even after leaving the clinic, during the great crises of my youth and problems with my love life, I would go and talk to him.'

Capitães da Areia ran for two months. Apart from that first night, it wasn't a wild success, but the takings were large enough to pay the expenses and there was even some money left over to be shared out among the actors and technicians. There was also praise from respected critics.

After the euphoria of the production, Paulo once again became depressed. He felt empty and lost, and frequently kicked to pieces anything that got in his way in his grandfather's apartment. Alone in that

hostile, unfamiliar neighbourhood, with no one to turn to during his periods of melancholy and no one to share his rare moments of joy, he would
often fall into despair. When these crises arose, he poured out his heart
to his diary. Once, he sat up all night filling page after page with something
he called 'Secrets of a Writer': 'Suddenly my life has changed. I've been
left high and dry in the most depressing place in Brazil: the city, the
commercial centre of Rio. At night, no one. During the day, thousands of
distant people. And the loneliness is becoming such that I've begun to
feel it's like something alive and real, which fills every corner and every
street. I, Paulo Coelho, aged nineteen, am empty-handed.'

His proximity to the red light district meant that he became a regular
client in the brothels that lined the streets from the bottom of the Lapa to
Mangue. It didn't matter that these women weren't very elegant and bore
no physical resemblance to the rich girls he fancied. He could talk about
anything to a prostitute and realize all his secret fantasies without scan-
dalizing anyone – even when these fantasies meant doing absolutely nothing, as he recorded in his diary:

> Yesterday I went with the oldest woman in the area – and the oldest
> woman I've slept with in my whole life (I didn't screw her, I just paid
> to look). Her breasts looked like a sack with nothing in it and she
> stood there in front of me, naked, stroking her cunt with her hand. I
> watched her, unable to understand why she made me feel both pity
> and respect. She was pure, extremely kind and professional, but she
> was a really old woman, you can't imagine just how old. Perhaps
> seventy. She was French and had left a copy of *France Soir* lying on
> the floor. She treated me with such care. She works from six in the
> evening to eleven o'clock at night; then she catches a bus home and
> there she's a respectable old lady. No one says, Oh my God! I can't
> think of her naked because it makes me shudder and fills me with
> such a mixture of feelings. I'll never forget this old woman. Very
> strange.

While sometimes he would pay and not have sex, on other occasions he
would have sex and pay nothing, or almost nothing ('Yesterday I was on

inspired form and I managed to get a prostitute without paying anything – in the end she took a sweater that I'd pinched from a friend'). Then, for weeks on end, he devoted every page in his diary to his crazed love for a young prostitute. One day, the woman disappeared with another client, without telling him, and once again he went crazy. He may have been an adult, but only the innocence of a boy in matters of love could explain his jealousy at having been betrayed by a prostitute. 'I wanted to cry as I've never cried before, because my whole being resided in that woman,' he moaned. 'With her flesh I could keep loneliness at bay for a while.' On hearing that his loved one had returned and that she was revealing inti-mate facts about him to all and sundry, he wrote: 'I've heard that she's slandering me … I've realized that as far as she's concerned, I'm a nobody, a nothing. I'm going to give away the name of the woman to whom I gave everything that was pure in my putrefied being: Tereza Cristina de Melo.'

During the day, Paulo continued to live the life of his dreams: girl-friends, rehearsals, study groups, debates about cinema and existential-ism. Although he had hardly set foot in his new college, he had managed to move up a year, which allowed him to think of taking the entrance exam for a degree. On the few occasions when he appeared at the family home – usually in order to scrounge a meal or ask for money – he made up stories in order to shock his parents, saying that he had been in the most outlandish places in Rio. 'I read in the newspapers about the places frequented by free-living young people and lied, saying that I had been there, just to shock my father and mother.' Although he almost never played his guitar, he took it with him everywhere, 'just to impress the girls!'

When night fell, though, the bouts of melancholy and loneliness returned. There came a time when he could take them no more. For three months, night after night, he had done battle with a constant nightmare, and he felt he had to take a step back. He packed up all his belongings in a box and, sad and humiliated, he asked his parents to have him back in the house to which he had never imagined he would return.

CHAPTER 9

The great escape

THE EASE WITH WHICH HE MIXED with women of all classes, from prostitutes in Mangue to elegant young bimbos at the Paissandu, gave everyone the impression that Paulo had no doubts about his sexual proclivities. This, however, was merely an impression. His life in the world of the theatre, where homosexuality was practised freely, had aroused a doubt so secret that he didn't even reveal it to his diary: did he have 'sexual problems', as his mother had suspected when she had first had him admitted to the clinic? Or, in plain language, was he homosexual? Although he was almost twenty, this was still a dark, mysterious area for Paulo. Unlike most Brazilian boys of the time, he had had his first sexual encounter with a woman, the sexually precocious and experienced Madá, rather than with a male friend. He had never felt the desire to have physical relations with a man, and had never even fantasized about such an encounter. Several times, though, when he saw groups of homosexual friends talking during intervals in rehearsals, he tormented himself with troubling questions: 'What if they're right? What if their sexual choice is better than mine?'

Life had taught him that it was better to be the first to jump into the icy river than to suffer in line until it was his turn. Instead of continuing to torment himself with endless doubts, he knew that there was only one way to resolve the problem: try it out. When he read a text from Marx saying something like 'practice is the deciding factor', he interpreted it as a prompt to take action. One evening, when he was still living in his grand-father's apartment in the city centre, he summoned up his courage and went round the various gay bars until, fortified by a few whiskies, he decided to take the plunge. He went up to a boy of his age, a professional, who was waiting for customers, and got straight to the point.

'Hi. How do you fancy going to bed with me?'

Paulo was ready for anything, but certainly not the reply he got: 'No. I don't want to.'

Paulo felt as surprised as if he had been punched. How come? He was going to pay, after all! The boy turned his back on him and left him standing, glass in hand. When he tried again in another nightclub and received a second 'No', he brought his brief homosexual experiment to an end. Weeks later, frantically engaged in work, he appeared to have forgotten the matter.

While the career of Paulo Coelho the writer continued to be an evident failure, the same could not be said about Coelho the playwright and producer. His first solo foray into the world of the arts, in children's theatre, was a production of a cinema classic, *The Wizard of Oz*. He not only adapted the script but also directed the play and cast himself as the Lion. Lacking funds for costly props and costumes, he simply painted whiskers on his face and stuck two cloth ears on his head; the tail was a rope sewn on to his trousers, the end of which he would twist round his forefinger during the show. Almost the only thing he took from the film was the song 'Somewhere Over the Rainbow'. The remainder of the score was composed by Antônio Carlos Dias, or Kakiko, a musician and actor with whom Paulo had shared a dressing room during the production of *Capitães da Areia*. To everyone's surprise, *The Wizard of Oz* took in enough to cover the costs of the production and the salaries of actors and tech-nicians *and* made a profit – money that Paulo squirreled away for their next production. Having his name appear on the entertainment pages of the newspapers was also something akin to success: on one day in 1967, his name appeared in three different places in the cultural sections of the Rio press. At the Teatro de Arena he was the author and director of

O Tesouro do Capitão Berengundo [*The Treasure of Captain Berengundo*]; at the Santa Terezinha his name was on the posters for an adaptation of his *Aladdin and His Magic Lamp*; and at the Teatro Carioca he was appearing as an actor in Walmir Ayala's *A Onça de Asas* [*The Winged Jaguar*].

Children's plays brought in a little money, but it was only in adult theatre that he could achieve the fame and prestige he craved. The production of *Capitães da Areia* had made this clear. In March, he was asked to act in a big production of Brecht and Weil's *The Threepenny Opera*. The show had been a great success in São Paulo with a cast of famous actors, and the Rio cast did not lag far behind, and was also full of well-known stars. The play was to be the first production at the theatre in the Sala Cecília Meirelles. Paulo played a blind beggar, a role that needed little acting ability, but his name would be printed in the programme alongside all the big names.

After several weeks of rehearsal, they were ready for the first night. A few days before, the company was invited to give a live performance of the play in the studios of TV Rio, the most important of the city's television stations. When it was due to go out, someone realized that the actor Oswaldo Loureiro, who was to sing the theme song, was missing. Since Paulo was the only one of the group who knew the words of 'Mack the Knife' by heart, he received the most exposure on the programme. The reasonable success of the production established him further in his new profession.

He was back in his parents' house and the play was still showing when the Devil of homosexuality decided to tempt him again. This time the initiative was not his but that of an actor of about thirty who was also working on the play. In fact the two had only exchanged a few words and looks, but one night, after the show, the older man approached him.

He came straight to the point: 'Would you like to come back to my place and have sex?'

Nervous and rather taken aback, Paulo said the first thing that came into his head: 'Yes, I would.'

They spent the night together. Although much later, Paulo recalled feeling rather disgusted to find himself exchanging caresses with a man, he nevertheless had sex with him, penetrating and being penetrated. Paulo returned home the following day even more confused than before. He had felt no pleasure and yet he still remained unsure as to whether or not he was homosexual. Some months later, he decided to try again and chose someone from among his stage friends. In the man's studio flat in Copacabana, he felt horribly embarrassed when his partner suggested they take a bath together. His feelings of unease continued throughout the night, and they only managed to have full sex when the sun was already coming up. Paulo Coelho was now convinced, once and for all, that he was not homosexual.

Despite his doubts about his sexuality, he continued to find success with women. He had left Márcia and finished his friendship with Renata, but he continued his relationship with Fabíola, who seemed to be growing more beautiful by the day. He had become a gifted bigamist, though, having fallen for Genivalda, from Sergipe, the ugly, brilliant Geni whose witty comments delighted the intelligentsia who hung out at the Paissandu. After besieging her unsuccessfully for weeks, he finally took her away for a weekend at Uncle José's house in Araruama. On their first night together, he was surprised to hear Geni, who seemed such a woman of the world, asking him in a whisper to be gentle because this was her first sexual experience. Since there was no suitable place for them to meet, the first months of their 'honeymoon' were awkward, but they were fruitful: at the beginning of June, Geni telephoned him to say that she was pregnant with his child. Paulo immediately decided that he wanted the child, but had no time to say so, as she immediately announced that she was going to have an abortion. He suggested a meeting so that they could talk, but Geni was determined: she had made her decision and, besides, she wanted to put an end to their relationship. She rang off and disappeared from his life as if she had never existed.

Paulo entered another downward spiral. Upset by the news of the pregnancy and Geni's sudden disappearance, he set about looking for her everywhere until he learned that she had returned to her hometown of Aracaju, where she was intending to have the abortion. Keen to dissuade her, but with no means of finding her when she was almost 2,000 kilometres away, he once again succumbed to fits of depression, interrupted by short periods of euphoria. Pages and pages of his diary, written during sleepless nights, reflect this:

> I breathe solitude, I wear solitude, I crap solitude. It's awful. I've never felt so alone. Not even during the long bitter days of my adolescence. Not that solitude is anything new. It's just that I'm getting tired of it. Soon I'll do something mad that will terrify the world.
>
> I want to write. But what for? Why? Alone, my brain fills with existential problems, and I can only make out one thing in all that noise and confusion: a desire to die.

This rather melodramatic vein also appears in his moments of happiness. He recorded these rare and short-lived moments of optimism with a total lack of modesty: 'My hour to give birth has arrived, as foreseen in a poem I wrote in the clinic. This morning I was born, along with the morning light. The time has come for me to show the world who I am.'

In 1967, the world still did not know who Paulo Coelho was; indeed, it ran the risk of losing him, judging by his frequent bouts of depression and the insistence with which he spoke of death and suicide. At the end of June, after enduring another sleepless night, he had a sudden attack of rage. He put his diary away in the drawer, locked his bedroom door and began to break everything. He started with his guitar, which he smashed over his desk with a crash that sounded like a bomb exploding. The neighbours, who at that time, around six in the morning, had not yet got up, were astonished to hear the racket coming from the Coelho household. He broke his portable red plastic tape recorder and his short-wave radio and anything else he came across.

There was nothing left to destroy, but his fury was not yet spent. He went over to his bookcase and set to work on the ten volumes of his Sherlock Holmes collection. He ripped them up one by one and then went to the shelf containing books by Brazilian authors and continued his destruction until the bedroom floor was covered in the tattered remains of books. He went into the small bathroom next door and, using the fingerboard of his guitar as a cudgel, smashed the mirror. When the noise stopped for a moment, he heard his father pounding on the door, demanding that he open up, but he would not stop. He ripped down and tore into tiny pieces the two texts he had stuck on his door – a prayer by St Francis of Assisi and the words of 'Barbara' by the French poet Jacques Prévert, and then he did the same thing with the posters decorating his room: Goya's *La Maja Desnuda*, Bosch's *Garden of Delights* and *The Crucifixion* by Rubens. Panting, he saw that only one thing had remained intact: the white armchair where, as he once wrote, he would sit and cry or look up at the starry sky. Having nothing he could use to smash it, he opened the window and hurled it out into the garden at the side of the house. It was only then, when there was nothing left standing or intact, that he decided to open the door. He hardly had time to notice that it was no longer his father who was knocking. Two male nurses held him down and one injected him with what seemed to be a powerful sedative.

When he opened his eyes, he recognized the peeling paint on the ceiling. He was back lying on a bed on the ninth floor of the clinic. The first precaution the nurses had taken as soon as he came round from sedation was to take him to the liftmen and tell them: 'This is the patient who ran away from here last year. Take a good look at his face and this time be more careful.'

Nothing in the clinic had changed since his previous stays there. Except for Flávio, who had tried to kill himself with whisky and ether spray, they were all there, including Luís Carlos, his companion in flight. The faces were the same as before, as was the suffering. On the first day, Paulo was submitted to a session of electroshock therapy so strong that when Fabíola came to visit him some hours later, he was still unconscious, drooling and with his face contorted by the violence of the electrical charges to his brain. In spite of the love and care shown him by his girlfriend – this time, Fabíola was the only person, apart from his parents, to visit him – he could not get the absent Geni and the baby out of his mind.

A week after being admitted to the clinic, during which time he was subjected to three electroshock sessions, Paulo was once again thinking of running away. And once again his chosen companion was Luís Carlos, who was unable to bear the routine of the hospital any longer. The opportunity arose on a day when a member of Dr Benjamim's team was checking his mouth and noticed that a wisdom tooth was coming through. He thought that he had found the cause of Paulo's problems: 'Now I know what's wrong. It's a tooth coming through and causing pressure in your head. That's what's making you agitated and causing your crises. I'm going to ask the dentist to take out the tooth and then you'll be all right.'

While they were looking for a nurse to take him to the dental clinic, he found Luís Carlos and told him: 'It's now or never! They're going to take me to the dentist and I'm going to try to escape. See if you can too. If all goes well, we'll meet in an hour at the café opposite the clinic.'

He walked down the paths separating the different clinic buildings, constantly watched by the male nurse, who, when they reached the door of the consulting room, looked at his watch and agreed with the dentist that since the extraction would take about half an hour, he would go to the toilet and then return straight away to take the patient back to the unit housing the mentally ill. However, the consultation lasted less than five minutes. After a quick examination, the dentist told him he could go: 'I don't know who invented such a stupid story! Since when has a wisdom tooth made anyone mad? You can sit outside and wait for the nurse to take you back to your floor.'

This was the moment. Paulo hurried along the corridors and, keeping his head down, crossed the woods on the edge of the complex and joined the crowd of visitors and doctors at the gate. Minutes later, he was free.

He ran to the café on the corner of Rua Assunção and Rua Marquês de Olinda and, to his surprise, saw Luís Carlos waiting for him with a glass of beer in his hand – it was all he could afford with the few coins he had in his pocket. They celebrated their success and decided to get out of the café before anyone on the ninth floor noticed they were missing and came looking for them (security seems to have been somewhat lax that day, since it was only two days later, on 9 July, that the doctors realized the two had disappeared). As they were leaving, Paulo managed to sell his wrist-watch at the bar, although since there was no time for haggling, he received only 300 new cruzeiros (US$380), less than half its true value. The fugitives walked three blocks along Rua Marquês de Olinda, sat on the grass and spent hours in silence, enjoying the delicious pleasure of seeing the shimmering Urca beach with Sugar Loaf Mountain in the background. It was exactly the same view that they had from the windows of the asylum, only now there was no grille in front of them.

Paulo told Luís Carlos what he was planning: 'I'm going to the bus station to buy a ticket to Aracaju. I need to find a girlfriend of mine who is or was expecting my baby. If you want to come with me, the money from the watch is enough to pay for you, too.'

Luís Carlos was surprised at the thought of such a long journey, but having no better plan and having nowhere to go, he accepted the invitation. As the bus did not leave until eight the following morning, the pair spent the night on the benches at the bus station. The tickets had cost them 80 cruzeiros, leaving more than enough money to buy food on the long bus ride. Luís Carlos wanted to know how they were going to survive when they reached their destination, but Paulo reassured him, saying: 'There are people there who will take care of that.' After crossing the states of Rio de Janeiro, Minas Gerais and Bahia, with stops at fifteen towns along the way, two days later, on the morning of 9 July 1967, they arrived in Aracaju. It was only then that Luís Carlos learned that Paulo had no address, telephone number or any other way of finding his beloved Genivalda in a town of 170,000 inhabitants. His sole local reference was the name of Mário Jorge Vieira, a young poet and militant member of the banned Brazilian Communist Party (PCB).

Thanks to the lies he invented, a day later, Paulo and his friend, whom he introduced as 'my dumb secretary', were installed in journalist Marcos Mutti's comfortable home, and he appeared in the social columns of the local press, described either as 'university student and actor' or as 'young playwright from Rio'. These references were always accompanied by extravagant stories: 'Mingling with the artistic community of Aracaju is the theatre actor Paulo Coelho, who recently appeared in Rio in the play *Oedipus Rex* alongside Paulo Autran. It seems that Coelho has come to admire our green landscape and to plant new seeds in the region's almost non-existent theatrical history.'

After a week of searching, he lost all hope of finding Geni. He heard nothing of her until many years later, when he learned that she had indeed had an abortion and that, some time later, when still young, she had been run over and killed. Frustrated in the one objective that had taken him to Aracaju, he planned to return to Rio, but the hospitality he was receiving was such that he stayed on. Treated with the respect granted to a star, he gave a long interview to the *Gazeta de Sergipe*, in which he was presented to the newspaper's readers: 'A strange individual arrived here on the 9th. Long-haired, unshaven, thin, and rather odd-looking, but with lots of ideas in his head, lots of hope and an enormous desire to propagate art throughout Brazil. He is, in short, an artist. A young man of twenty who has left his home (he is the son of one of the best-known families in Rio de Janeiro) for the love of art. His is a mind turned towards Humanity.'

Feeling himself to be at a safe distance (or protected perhaps by the impunity granted to the mad, to children and to native Indians), Paulo suddenly grew courageous and made use of the piece in the newspaper in order, for the first time, to criticize the military dictatorship – or rather, even more dangerous, the then President of the Republic, Marshal Artur da Costa e Silva. 'I'm not going to keep quiet just because some super-annuated marshal picks up a rifle and claims to be defending the morals and freedom of a people who don't even know what freedom is.' This was starting to look less like an interview and more like a manifesto, a call to arms. 'I haven't travelled thousands of kilometres to Aracaju in order to keep quiet. I won't lie to myself or to those around me.' The result of this vehemence was that he was offered a space in the newspaper to write a signed political article for the following Saturday's edition.

On the Friday, however, he discovered that there were two people in the city who were looking for 'the guy from Rio', wanting to kill him. He was convinced that these must be Geni's relatives, intent on defending their daughter's honour by spilling the blood of her abuser, and his courage disappeared in a flash. He decided to make a run for it and was just about to leave when Luís Carlos reminded him about the article he had promised for the newspaper. Paulo opened up the leather bag he was wearing slung over his shoulder and took out a cutting from a Rio newspaper he had picked up on a bench at the bus station in Vitória da Conquista, in Bahia, one of the fifteen stops on the way to Aracaju. He asked his hosts whether he could use their typewriter and copied, word for word, an article casti-gating the military dictatorship for having disenfranchised Brazilians. He kept the title and simply changed the author's name to his. Still with Luís Carlos, he spent the remainder of his money on two bus tickets to Salvador – the furthest his money would take him.

Years later, furious to learn that they had been duped and the article plagiarized, the people in Sergipe who had met Paulo at the time gave a rather different account of his sudden departure from Aracaju. 'He and his so-called dumb secretary didn't take a shower for two weeks and smoked cannabis all day,' recalls Ilma Fontes. 'That's why Paulo Coelho was thrown out of Marcos Mutti's house: for spending the day smoking cannabis in a strictly residential street.' Two weeks without washing was not perhaps anything new in his life, but smoking cannabis was certainly not one of Paulo's habits in July 1967.

When they got off the bus in the Salvador capital of Bahia without a penny in their pockets, the two men walked 10 kilometres to the Obras Sociais Irmã Dulce, a charitable institution known throughout Brazil. After joining a long line of beggars holding aluminum bowls for their daily soup ration, they went up to a small table, where the poor were received individually by the nun, to whom Paulo referred in his diary as 'Irma la Douce'. He explained to the sad-eyed little nun that he needed money to buy two bus tickets to Rio. The ragged appearance of these two mendicants spoke volumes, and so she asked no questions and wrote in tiny writing on a piece of paper bearing the name of the institution:

These young men are requesting free transport to Rio.
Irmã Dulce – 21/7/67

All they needed to do was to exchange the slip of paper at the bus station for two tickets. In Bahia, any piece of paper signed by the nun had the value of a voucher for a plate of food, having a relative taken into hospital or, as in their case, a bus ticket.

Paulo spent the forty-hour journey from Salvador to Rio drawing up the synopsis of a book about their escape and their journey to the northeast of the country. No – not just one book: in keeping with his megalomaniac temperament, he planned to write no fewer than nine books, each with twelve chapters. By the end of the journey, he had filled fifteen pages of his diary with details of each volume and their chapter titles ('Preparing the Escape'; 'My Travelling Companions'; 'The General's Son'; 'My Long Hair and Other People's Short Ideas'; 'Pedro's Pistol, or When the Bahians Shit Themselves'; 'Sleeping in Kerosene Cans at 7° Centigrade' …), but the project never got any further than that.

At the Rio bus station, he and Luís Carlos sadly parted company. Once again, Paulo was going home and the 'dumb' man was on his way back to the clinic, where he was to remain, playing the part of madman, for as long as it took to gain his dreamed-of pension.

Less than a year later, Paulo was plunged into misery and despair again, and he again smashed up his room. This time, when he opened his door, he found not the male nurses bearing syringes or straitjackets but a pleasant young doctor, who asked politely: 'May I come in?'

It was the psychiatrist Dr Antônio Ovídio Clement Fajardo, who often used to send patients for treatment at the Dr Eiras clinic. When Lygia and Pedro had heard the first sounds of things being broken in their son's room, they had called Dr Benjamim, but when he couldn't be found and since it was an urgent matter, they had contacted Dr Fajardo. When he spoke on the telephone to Pedro, the doctor had asked for basic information about Paulo.

'Is he armed?'

'No.'

'Is he an alcoholic?'

'No.'

'Is he a drug addict?'

'No.'

This made matters simpler.

Fajardo asked again: 'May I come in?'

Hearing this unusual question repeated, Paulo didn't know how to respond. 'Come in? But haven't you come to take me to the clinic?'

The doctor replied: 'Only if you want me to. But you haven't answered my question: may I come in?'

Seated on the bed, the doctor looked around the room, as though assessing the extent of the damage, and continued quite naturally: 'You've broken everything, haven't you? Excellent.'

Paulo couldn't understand what was going on. The doctor went on, explaining in professorial tones: 'What you've destroyed is your past. That's good. Now that it's no longer here, let's begin to think about the future, all right? My suggestion is that you start coming to see me twice a week so that we can talk about your future.'

Paulo was astonished. 'But doctor, I've just smashed up my room again. Aren't you going to send me to the clinic?'

The doctor replied dispassionately: 'Everyone has their mad side. I probably do, but you don't put people away just like that. You're not mentally ill.'

Only after this episode did peace return to the Coelho household. Much later, he wrote: 'I think my parents were convinced I was a hopeless case and preferred to keep an eye on me and to support me for the rest of my life. They knew I would get into "bad company" again, but it didn't enter their heads to have me re-admitted to the clinic.' The problem was that their son was not prepared to continue living under parental control. He was ready to accept anything but a return to his grandfather's depressing studio flat in the city centre. The short-term solution, which would last for a few months, came once again from his grandparents. Some years earlier, Tuca and Lilisa had moved into a house near by, which had over the garage a small apartment with a bedroom, bathroom and independent entrance. If Paulo wished – and if his father was in agreement – their grandson could move in there.

Their grandson wanted this so much that, before his father had time to say no, he had moved everything that remained from the wreck of his room into his new home – his bed, his desk, his few clothes and his typewriter, which he had carefully protected from his frenzy. He soon realized that the apartment was like a gateway to paradise: given his grandparents' extreme liberality, he could come and go as he pleased and, within the broad limits of decency, he could entertain whomever he wanted, day or night. His grandparents' tolerance was such that, years later, Paulo vaguely recalled that it was probably there that he tried cannabis for the first time.

With no control over their son and with his grandparents making no attempt to control his behaviour either, some months later, Paulo's father suggested he should move somewhere more comfortable. If interested, he could go back to living alone, not in Tuca's studio but in a comfortable apartment Pedro had been given in payment for a building he had constructed in Rua Raimundo Correa in Copacabana. Paulo was suspicious of this generosity, and discovered that the offer concealed another reason: his father wanted to get rid of a tenant who was frequently late in paying his rent. Since the law said that a contract could only be broken by the landlord if the dwelling was to be used by a close relative of the owner, this was the solution to two problems, both Paulo's and his father's. Like almost any offer coming from Pedro, it had its drawbacks: Paulo could use only one of the three bedrooms, since the other two were permanently locked and empty. Also, access was always to be by the door in the basement, since the main entrance was to be kept locked and the key to remain with his father. Paulo had only to go to a local second-hand shop to buy some lamps and a bookcase and the place was ready to live in.

Paulo retained happy memories of the days he spent in Rua Raimundo Correa. Other affairs with other girls began and ended, but Fabíola remained faithful to him. She swallowed her jealousy and, as she later recalled, put up with the 'Renatas, Genis and Márcias ... but in the difficult times, I was there for him, it was pure love – pure love.' Many years later, when he was famous, Paulo recalled that time with nostalgia: 'I experienced a period of enormous happiness, enjoying the freedom I needed in order, finally, to live the "artist's life". I stopped studying and devoted myself exclusively to the theatre and to going to bars frequented by intellectuals. For a whole year, I did exactly what I wanted. That was when Fabíola really came into my life.'

Now a full-time playwright – he had managed to complete his course at Guanabara, but had no plans as yet to take the university entrance exam – he turned the dining room of his new apartment into a workshop for scenery, costumes, compositions and rehearsals. He annoyed his neighbours by painting in Italian over the front door – which he never used – the words written above the gates of Dante's Inferno: 'Lasciate ogni speranza, voi che entrate' ['Abandon hope all ye who enter here']. He translated plays, directed and worked as an actor. The more successful productions made up for the failures, and so he was able to live without depending exclusively on support from his parents. When he needed more funds, he tried to make money at poker and snooker tables and by betting on horses at the Jockey Club.

At the end of 1968, he resolved to try the only aspect of theatre he had not yet worked on: production. He adapted the classic *Peter Pan*, which he wanted to direct and in which he also wanted to perform, but he was shocked to find that his savings were not nearly enough to cover the production's costs. He was still pondering how to resolve the problem when Fabíola came to his apartment one night, opened her bag and took out bundles of notes in rubber bands – more than 5,000 cruzeiros (US$11,600), which she scattered over the bed, explaining: 'This is my present for your production of *Peter Pan*.'

Fabíola told him that as she was about to turn eighteen, she had decided to tell her mother, grandmother and all her other relatives and friends that instead of clothes and presents she would prefer money. She had contacted people everywhere – her mother's rich clients and godparents whom she hadn't seen for years – and here was the result: the bundles on the bed were not a fortune, but the money was more than enough to make putting on the play a viable proposition. Paulo was overwhelmed by the gift: 'One girlfriend swapped me for two dresses and now you've exchanged all the dresses and presents for me. Your action has entirely changed my view of women.'

Fabíola not only got the money for the production but also sold advertising space in the programme and came to an agreement with the restaurants around the Teatro Santa Terezinha in the Botanical Gardens: in exchange for their names being printed on any advertising material, they would allow the actors and technicians to have dinner for free. Paulo repaid all he owed her by inviting her to take the title role. He was to be Captain Hook. With a score by Kakiko, *Peter Pan* played to packed houses throughout its run, which meant that every cent invested was recovered. And contrary to the notion that says that public success means critical failure, the play went on to win a prize at the first Children's Theatre Festival in the state of Guanabara. Paulo's dream remained the same – to be a great writer – but meanwhile, he had no alternative but to live by the theatre. These cheering results made him decide to turn professional, and soon he was a proud member of the Brazilian Society of Theatre Writers (SBAT).

In 1969, he was invited to work as an actor in the play *Viúva porém Honesta* [*A Widow but Honest*], by Nelson Rodrigues. In a break in rehearsals, he was drinking a beer in the bar beside the Teatro Sérgio Porto when he noticed that he was being watched by an attractive blonde woman seated at the counter. He pretended to look away, but when he turned round again, there she was, with her eyes fixed on him and with a discreet smile on her lips. This flirtation cannot have lasted more than ten minutes, but she made such an impression on Paulo that he wrote in his diary: 'I can't say how it all started. She appeared suddenly. I went in and immediately felt her looking at me. Despite the crowd, I knew that she had her eyes fixed on me and I didn't have the courage to look straight back at her. I had never seen her before. But when I felt her gaze something happened. It was the beginning of a love story.'

The beautiful mysterious blonde was Vera Prnjatovic Richter, eleven years Paulo's senior, who at the time was trying to end her fifteen-year marriage to a rich industrialist. She was always well dressed, she had a car – which was still fairly rare among women at the time – and she lived in a huge apartment in one of the most expensive areas of Brazil, Avenida Delfim Moreira, in Leblon. From Paulo's point of view she had only one obvious defect – she was going out with the actor Paulo Elísio, a bearded Apollo known for his bad temper and for being a karate black belt. However, the feelings recorded in his diary were to prove stronger than any martial arts.

CHAPTER 10

Vera

B RAZIL BEGAN 1969 immersed in the most brutal dictatorship of its entire history. On 13 December 1968, the President of the Republic, Artur da Costa e Silva – the 'superannuated marshal' to whom Paulo had referred in his interview – had passed Institutional Act number 5, the AI-5, which put paid to the last remaining vestiges of freedom following the military coup of 1964. Signed by the President and countersigned by all his ministers, including the Minister of Health, Leonel Miranda, the owner of the Dr Eiras clinic, the AI-5 suspended, among other things, the right to *habeas corpus* and gave the government powers to censor the press, the theatre and books, as well as closing down the National Congress.

It was not only Brazil that was about to erupt. In its sixth year of war in Vietnam, where more than half a million soldiers had been sent, the United States had elected the hawkish Richard Nixon as president. In April 1968, the black civil right's leader Martin Luther King, Jr, had been assassinated, and sixty-three days later it was the turn of Robert Kennedy. One of the symbols of counterculture was the musical *Hair*, in which, at one point, the actors appeared naked on stage. In May, French students had occupied the Sorbonne and turned Paris into a battlefield, forcing General Charles de Gaulle to hold talks with the French military chiefs in Baden-Baden, Germany. This worldwide fever had crossed the Iron

Curtain and reached Czechoslovakia in the form of the Prague Spring, a liberalizing plan proposed by the Secretary General of the Czech Communist Party, Alexander Dubček, which was crushed in August by the tanks of the Warsaw Pact, the Soviet Union's military alliance with its political satellites.

In Brazil, opposition to the dictatorship was beginning to grow. Initially, this took the form of peaceful student marches, in which Paulo rarely participated and, when he did so, it was more for fun and for the adventure of 'confronting the police' than as an act of political commitment. The political temperature rose with a rash of strikes called by workers in São Paulo and Minas Gerais, and reached alarming levels when the military intelligence services detected a growth in the number of guerrilla groups, which the regime loosely termed 'terrorists'. By the end of the year, there were, in fact, at least four armed urban guerrilla organizations: the Vanguarda Armada Revolucionária (VAR-Palmares), Ação Libertadora Nacional (ALN), Vanguarda Popular Revolucionária (VPR) and the Comando de Libertação Nacional (Colina). The Brazilian Communist Party, which took its inspiration from the Chinese Communist Party, had sent its first militants to Xambioá, in the north of Goiás (now on the frontier with the state of Tocantins), to mount a rural guerrilla assault in the region of the Araguaia River, on the edge of the Amazon rain forest. The extreme left attacked banks and set off bombs in barracks, while the extreme right organized attacks on one of the most visible centres of opposition to the regime: the theatre. Theatres in São Paulo and Rio were attacked or destroyed and there were an increasing number of arrests at street demonstrations as well as arrests of prominent people such as the ex-governor of Guanabara and civil leader of the 1964 coup, Carlos Lacerda, the composers Caetano Veloso and Gilberto Gil, and the journalist Carlos Heitor Cony, whose article Paulo had plagiarized in Aracaju.

Although he boasted of being 'the communist in the group', and although he was a witness to the violence being perpetrated on his profession – he was, after all, a playwright now and a member of the theatre union – Paulo seemed quietly indifferent to the political storm ravaging

Brazil. As with the military coup, the new law and its consequences didn't merit a mention in his diaries. The first words he wrote in 1969 are revealing as to the focus of his energies: 'It's New Year's Day. I spent the evening with adulterers, homosexuals, lesbians and cuckolds.'

In 1964, he could have attributed his lack of interest in politics to his youth, but now he was nearly twenty-two, the average age of most of those leading the political and cultural movements rocking the country. If any important change was occurring in his life, it was due not to the political maelstrom Brazil found itself in but to his new passion, Vera Richter.

Petite, blonde and elegant, she had been born in 1936 in Belgrade, the capital of the then kingdom of Yugoslavia (now the capital of Serbia), the daughter of a wealthy landowning family. Until the age of twenty, she had lived a normal upper-class life; then, when she was in her first year at the theatre studies department of the university, she began to sense political changes occurring across Central Europe. That, and the collectivization program begun in Yugoslavia by Tito, seemed to indicate that it was time for the rich to leave the country.

Since they had friends living in Rio de Janeiro, the Prnjatovic family – widowed mother, elder sister and Vera – decided this was to be their destination. Her mother and sister went first, and it was only some months later, when they were settled in Copacabana, that they sent a ticket for Vera. Speaking only English and the Italianate dialect of the area in which she had lived, she felt uncomfortable in Brazil. She ended up agreeing to a marriage arranged by her family – to a Yugoslav millionaire twelve years her senior. She recalled years later that even those who didn't know her well noticed how incompatible the two were. Like most twenty-year-old girls, she liked dancing, sports and singing, whereas her husband was shy and quiet and, when he wasn't running his import/export business, loved reading and listening to classical music.

When her eyes met Paulo's that night in the theatre bar, Vera's marriage was merely a formality. She and her husband lived under the same roof, but were no longer a couple. She had been attracted to the Teatro Carioca by an announcement in the newspaper saying that a

young director from Bahia, Álvaro Guimarães, was selecting students for
a drama course. Almost four decades later, she recalls that her first
impression of Paulo was not exactly flattering. 'He looked like Professor
Abronsius, the scientist with a big head in Roman Polanski's film *Dance of
the Vampires* – an enormous head on a tiny body. Ugly, bony, big lips and
protruding eyes, Paulo was no beauty.' But he had other charms: 'Paulo
was a Don Quixote! He was crazy. Everything seemed easy for him,
everything was simple. He lived in the clouds, he never touched the
ground. But his one obsession was to be someone. He would do anything
to be someone. That was Paulo.'

At the time of Vera's arrival on the scene, Paulo's relationship with
Fabíola was doomed anyway, but it finally ended when she caught him
with Vera. Fabíola suspected that Paulo was secretly meeting a young
Dutch actress who had appeared during rehearsals and she decided to
find out if her suspicions were true. One night, she sat on the doorstep of
the apartment in Rua Raimundo Correa and did not move until late in
the morning when he finally left with Vera. Deeply hurt, she ended the
affair. Some months later, she scandalized Lygia and Pedro, to whom she
had become quite close, by appearing nude on the cover of the satirical
weekly *Pasquim*.

As Paulo was to recall some years later, it was the experienced Vera
who really taught him how to make love, to speak a little English and to
dress a little better. But she could not help him overcome the trauma of
Araruama: he still shook at the mere thought of driving a car. Their
convergence of tastes and interests extended to their professional lives,
and Vera's money was the one thing that had been lacking in Paulo's
attempts to become immersed in the theatre. He divided his time between
his Copacabana apartment and Vera's luxurious apartment in Leblon,
where he would sleep almost every night, and where he bashed away for
weeks on end at his typewriter until he was able to announce proudly to
his partner that he had completed his first play for adults, *O Apocalipse*
[*The Apocalypse*]. The couple seemed made for each other. Vera not only
understood the entire play (a feat achieved by very few) but liked it so
much that she offered to put it on professionally, acting as its producer –
the person investing the money – while Paulo would be the director.

Everything went so well that, at the end of April 1969, the critics and editors of the arts sections of newspapers received an invitation to the preview and a copy of the programme listing the cast, in which Vera had the star part. Paulo's friend Kakiko, who had recently qualified as an odontologist and divided his time between his dental practice and his music, was to write the score.

Along with their invitation and the programme, journalists and critics received a press release written in pretentious, obscure language but which gave some idea of what *The Apocalypse* would be about. 'The play is a snapshot of the present moment, of the crisis in human existence, which is losing all its individual characteristics in favour of a more convenient stereotype, since it dogmatizes thought,' the blurb began, and it continued in the same incomprehensible vein. It then promised a great revolution in modern drama: the total abolition of characters. The play began with scenes from a documentary on the *Apollo 8* mission to the moon, after which the cast performed dance that was described as 'tribal with oriental influences'. Actors followed one another on to the stage, spouting excerpts from Aeschylus' *Prometheus Bound*, Shakespeare's *Julius Caesar* and the Gospels. At the end, before hurling provocative remarks at the audience, each actor acted himself, revealing traumatic events in his childhood.

The Apocalypse meant that Paulo would, for the first time, experience the thing that would persecute him for the rest of his life: negative criticism. On the days that followed the preview, the play was slated in every Rio newspaper. *The Apocalypse* was as big a disaster with the public as it was with the critics. It played for only a few weeks and left a large hole in the accounts of Paulo's first joint initiative with Vera – a hole that she quickly decided to fill.

The production coincided with an important change in their life as a couple. Vera's marriage had rapidly deteriorated, but since her husband continued to live in their shared apartment, she decided to put an end to that rather awkward situation and move with her lover to a place that had become a symbolic address in the counterculture movement in Rio at the end of the 1960s: Solar Santa Terezinha. Originally created as a night shelter for beggars, the Solar was a vast rectangular building with a central courtyard around which people had their bedrooms. It had the look of a large, decadent refuge, but it was considered 'hip' to live there. In the majority of cases each tenant had to share a bathroom with half a dozen other residents, but Paulo and Vera occupied a suite – a room with a bathroom – for which the monthly rent was about 200 cruzeiros (US$210).

At the end of July 1969, they decided to do something different. In the middle of August, the Brazilian football team was going to play Paraguay in Asunción in a World Cup qualifier, the finals of which were to be held in Mexico in 1970. Although he wasn't that interested in football, one Sunday, Paulo thrilled his foreign girlfriend by taking her to a match between Flamengo and Fluminense at the packed Maracanã stadium. Vera was mesmerized and began to take an interest in the sport, and it was she who suggested that they drive to Paraguay to watch the match. Paulo didn't even know that Brazil was going to play, but he loved the idea and started making plans.

He immediately discounted the idea of just the two of them driving the almost 2,000 kilometres to Asunción, a marathon journey on which Vera would be the only driver, since he had still not summoned up the courage to learn to drive. The solution was to call on two other friends for the adventure: the musician-dentist Kakiko and Arnold Bruver, Jr, a new friend from the theatre. They thought of Kakiko for another reason too: as well as being able to drive, he could guarantee hospitality for all in Asunción, in the home of a Paraguayan girlfriend of his father's. Bruver, like almost all those in Paulo's circle, was an unusual fellow. The son of a Latvian father and a Galician mother, he was thirty-three, a dancer, musician, actor and opera singer, and had been ejected from the navy, in which he had reached the rank of captain, for alleged subversion. It was only after accepting the invitation that Arnold revealed that he couldn't drive either. The next precaution was to ask Mestre Tuca, who had travelled with Lilisa by car to Foz do Iguaçu, on the frontier with Paraguay, to give them a route with suggestions of places to fill up the car with petrol, have meals and sleep.

On the cold, sunny morning of Thursday, 14 August, the four got into Vera's white Volkswagen. The journey passed without incident, with Vera and Kakiko taking turns at the wheel every 150 kilometres. It was evening when the car stopped at the door of the small hotel in Registro in the state of São Paulo. After twelve hours on the road they had covered 600 kilometres, about a third of the total distance. The locals eyed any strangers with understandable suspicion. Since the Department of Political and Social Order (the political police of the time, known as Dops) had disbanded the Student Union Congress some months earlier in Ibiúna, 100 kilometres from there, the small towns in the region were often visited by strangers and the locals had no way of telling if they were police or something else entirely. However, the four travellers were so tired that there was no time for their presence to arouse anyone's curiosity, for, on arriving, they went straight to bed.

On the Friday, they woke early, because the next stretch of the journey was the longest and they hoped to cover it in just a day. If all went well, by suppertime they would be in Cascavel, in the western region of Paraná, a 750-kilometre drive from there, and the last stop before reaching Asunción. But all did not go well: they were slowed down by the number of trucks on the road. The result was that, by ten o'clock that night, they were all starving and still had 200 kilometres to go.

It was at this point that Vera stopped the car in a lay-by and asked Kakiko to get out to see whether there was a problem with one of the tyres, because the car seemed to be skidding. As there was no sign of anything wrong, they decided that it must be the thick mist covering the area that was making the road slippery. Kakiko suggested that Vera should sit in the back and rest while he drove the rest of the way to Cascavel. After travelling for a further hour, he stopped at a petrol station to fill up. All their expenses were to be shared among the four, but when Vera looked for her purse, she realized that she had lost her bag with her money and all her documents, including her driving licence and car registration papers. She concluded that she must have dropped it when she had handed over the driving to Kakiko. They had no alternative but to go back to the place where they had stopped, 100 kilometres back, to try to find the bag. It took three hours to get there and back, without success. They looked everywhere, with the help of the car headlights, but there was no sign of the bag and no one in the local bars and petrol stations had seen it either. Convinced that this was a bad omen, a sign, Paulo suggested that they turn back, but the other three disagreed. They continued the journey and didn't reach Cascavel until early on the Saturday morning, by which time the car had a problem – the clutch wasn't working, and so it was impossible to carry on.

Because of the Brazil game, on the following day, almost everything in Cascavel was closed, including all the garages. They decided that they would continue on to Asunción by bus. They bought tickets to Foz do Iguaçu and, as Vera had no documents, they had to mingle with the crowds of tourists and supporters in order to cross the bridge separating Brazil from Paraguay. Once in Paraguay, they took another bus to the capital.

Immediately after settling into the home of Kakiko's father's girlfriend, they discovered that all tickets for the match had been sold, but they didn't mind. They spent the weekend visiting tribes of Guarani Indians on the outskirts of the city and taking tedious boat trips on the river Paraguay. On the Monday morning they began to think about getting the car repaired in Cascavel. With the disappearance of Vera's bag, they would have to take special care on the return journey: without the car documents they mustn't get caught breaking any laws and, without Vera's money, their expenses would have to be divided by three, which meant eating less and spending the night in cheaper places. They rejigged Tuca's route map and decided to go to Curitiba, where they would sleep and try to get a duplicate copy of the car documents and of Vera's driving licence.

At about ten at night – none of them remembers quite what time it was – hunger forced them to stop before reaching Curitiba. They parked the car by a steak house, just outside Ponta Grossa, having driven about 400 kilometres. To save money they used a ruse they had been practising since Vera had lost her bag: she and Paulo would sit alone at the table and ask for a meal for two. When the food arrived, Kakiko and Arnold would appear and share the meal with them.

Duly fed and watered, they were just about to resume their journey when a group of soldiers belonging to the Military Police entered the restaurant, armed with machine guns.

The man who appeared to be the head of the group went over to their table and asked: 'Is the white VW with Guanabara number plates parked outside yours?'

Kakiko, who was the only one officially allowed to drive, replied: 'Yes, it's ours.'

When the soldier asked to see the certificate of ownership, Kakiko explained in detail, watched by his terrified friends, how Vera had left her bag next to the car door and lost her purse and everything in it, and how the plan was to stay in Curitiba and see whether they could get a duplicate of the lost documents.

The man listened, incredulous, then said: 'You're going to have to explain all this to the police chief. Come with us.'

They were taken to a police station, where they spent the night in the freezing cold, sitting on a wooden bench until six in the morning, when the police chief arrived to give them the news himself: 'You are accused of terrorist activities and carrying out a bank raid. It's nothing to do with me now – it's up to the army.'

Although none of them had been taking much interest in the matter, the political situation had been getting worse in Brazil in the previous few months. Since the publication of the new law, AI-5, in December 1968, more than two hundred university professors and researchers had been compulsorily suspended, arrested or exiled. In the National Congress, 110 Members of Parliament and four senators had been stripped of their mandate and, elsewhere, about five hundred people had been removed from public office, either directly or indirectly accused of subversion. With the removal of three ministers from the Supreme Federal Tribunal, violence in the country had reached its height. In January, Captain Carlos Lamarca had deserted an army barracks in Quitaúna, a district of Osasco, taking with him a vehicle containing sixty-three automatic guns, three sub-machine guns and other munitions for the urban guerrilla movement. In São Paulo, the recently nominated governor Abreu Sodré had created Operação Bandeirantes (Oban), a unit that combined police and members of the armed forces, which was intended to crush any opposition. It immediately became a centre for the torture of enemies of the regime.

Two days before Paulo and his friends had been arrested, four guerrillas armed with machine guns – three men and a blonde woman – and driving a white Volkswagen with Guanabara number plates had attacked a bank and a supermarket in Jandaia do Sul, a town 100 kilometres north of Ponta Grossa. The police were now assuming that Paulo and his friends must be those people. Shivering with cold and fear, the four were taken in a prison van guarded by heavily armed soldiers to the headquarters of the 13th Battalion of the Armed Infantry (BIB), in the district of Uvaranas, on the other side of the city. Scruffy, dirty and cold, they climbed out of the van and found themselves in an enormous courtyard where hundreds of recruits were doing military exercises.

Half an hour after being placed in separate cells, made to undress and then dress again, interrogation began. The first to be called was Kakiko, who was taken to a cell furnished only with a table and two chairs, one of which was occupied by a tall, dark, well-built man in boots and combat gear with his name embroidered on his chest: 'Maj. Índio'. Major Índio ordered Kakiko to take a chair and then sat down in front of him. Then he spoke the words that Kakiko would remember for the rest of his life: 'So far no one has laid a finger on you, but pay very close attention to what I'm going to say. If you give just one bit of false information – just one – I'm going to stick these two fingers in your left eye, and rip out your eyeball and eat it. Your right eye will be preserved so that you can witness the scene. Understood?'

The first of the crimes of which Paulo and his friends were accused – an armed raid on a supermarket in Jandaia do Sul – had left no victims. But during the attempted raid on a bank in the same city, the guerrillas had shot the manager. The similarities between the four travellers and the guerrillas appeared to justify the suspicions of the military in Ponta Grossa. Although the raiders used nylon stockings to cover their faces, there was no doubt that they were three white men, one of them with long hair, like Paulo, and a blonde woman, like Vera, and that, like Paulo and his friends, they were driving a white Volkswagen with Guanabara number plates. Paulo's map also seemed to the authorities to be too careful and professional to have been produced by a grandfather eager to help his hippie grandson. Besides this, the chosen route could not have been more compromising: information from military intelligence had reported that the group led by Captain Carlos Lamarca might be preparing to establish a guerrilla nucleus in Vale do Ribeira – which was on the very route the friends had taken on their journey to Asunción. A dossier containing files on all four plus information on the car had been sent to the security agencies in Brasilia, Rio and São Paulo.

Besides their illegal arrest and the ever more terrifying threats, none of the four had as yet experienced physical violence. Major Índio had repeated his promise to eat one of their eyeballs to each of the others, insisting that this was not a mere empty threat: 'Up to now no one has laid a finger on you. We're giving you food and blankets on the assumption that you are innocent. But don't forget: if there's a word of a lie in your statements, I'll carry out my promise. I've done it before to other terrorists and I'll have no problems doing the same to you.'

The situation worsened on the Tuesday morning, when some of the supermarket employees were taken to the barracks to identify the suspects. With Paulo and Vera, the identification was made through a small opening in the cell doors, without their knowing that they were being observed. In the case of Arnold and Kakiko, the doors were simply opened, allowing the people – who were as terrified as the prisoners – a quick look inside. Although the assailants had had their faces covered when committing the crimes, and despite the very cursory identification procedure, in unlit cells, the witnesses were unanimous: those were the four who had committed the crime. The interrogations became more intense and more intimidating, and the same questions were repeated four, five, six, ten times. Vera and Arnold had to explain over and over to the succession of civil and military authorities who entered the cells to ask questions just what a Yugoslav woman and a naval officer suspended for subversion were doing in the area. Coelho cannot recall how often he had to answer the same questions: after such a long journey, how come they hadn't even bothered to see the match? How had Vera managed to cross the frontier with Paraguay in both directions without documents? Why did the map suggest so many alternative places to stay and fill up the car with petrol? Paulo commented to Arnold, in one of the rare moments they were alone in the same cell, that this was a Kafkaesque nightmare:

even the presence of his nebulizer to relieve his asthma attacks had to be explained in detail several times.

The nightmare continued for five days. On the Saturday morning, armed soldiers entered the cells and gave orders for the prisoners to collect their things because they were being 'moved'. Squashed in the back of the same olive-green van, the four were sure that they were going to be executed. When the vehicle stopped minutes later, much to their surprise, they got out in front of a bungalow surrounded by a garden of carefully tended roses. At the top of the stairs, a smiling soldier with grey hair and a bouquet of flowers in his hands was waiting for them. This was Colonel Lobo Mazza, who explained to the dazed travellers that everything had been cleared up and that they were indeed innocent. The flowers, which the officer had picked himself, were given to Vera by way of an apology. The colonel explained the reasons for their imprisonment – the growth of the armed struggle, their similarity to the assailants in Jandaia do Sul, the drive through Vale do Ribeira – and he made a point of asking each whether they had suffered any physical violence. Seeing their dirty, ragged appearance, he suggested they use the bathroom in the house and then offered them canapés accompanied by some good Scotch whisky. So that they would have no problems getting back to Rio, they were given a safe-conduct pass signed by Colonel Mazza himself. The journey was over.

CHAPTER 11

The marijuana years

ONCE HE WAS BACK IN RIO, Paulo entered the 1970s propelled by a new fuel: cannabis. This would be followed by other drugs, but initially he only used cannabis. Once they had tried the drug together for the first time, he and Vera became regular consumers. Being new to the experience, they had little knowledge of its effects, and before starting to smoke they would lock away any knives or other sharp household objects in a drawer 'to prevent any accidents', as she said. They smoked every day and on any pretext: in the afternoon so that they could better enjoy the sunsets, at night to get over the fact that they felt as if they were sleeping on the runway of Santos Dumont airport, with the deafening noise of aeroplanes taking off and landing only a few metres away. And, if there was no other reason, they smoked to allay boredom. Paulo recalled later having spent days in a row under the effect of cannabis, without so much as half an hour's interval.

Completely free of parental control, he had become a true hippie: someone who not only dressed and behaved like a hippie but thought like one too. He had stopped being a communist – before he had ever become one – when he was lectured in public by a militant member of the Brazilian Communist Party for saying that he had really loved the film *Les Parapluies de Cherbourg* – a French musical starring Catherine Deneuve.

With the same ease with which he had crossed from the Christianity of the Jesuits to Marxism, he was now a devout follower of the hippie insurrection that was spreading throughout the world. 'This will be humanity's final revolution,' he wrote in his diary. 'Communism is over, a new brotherhood is born, mysticism is invading art, drugs are an essential food. When Christ consecrated the wine, he was consecrating drugs. Drugs are a wine of the most superior vintage.'

After spending a few months at the Solar Santa Terezinha, he and Vera rented, together with a friend, a two-bedroom apartment in Santa Teresa, a bohemian district at the top of a hill near the Lapa, in the centre of the city, which had a romantic little tramway running through it that clanked as it went up the hill. In between moves, they had to live for some weeks in the Leblon apartment, along with Vera's husband, who had not yet moved out.

Cannabis usually causes prolonged periods of lethargy and exhaustion in heavy users, but the drug seemed to have the opposite effect on Paulo. He became positively hyperactive and in the first months of 1970, he adapted for the stage and produced *The War of the Worlds* by H.G. Wells, took part in theatre workshops with the playwright Amir Haddad and entered both the Paraná Short Story Competition and the Esso Prize for Literature. He even found time to write three plays: *Os Caminhos do Misticismo* [*The Paths of Mysticism*], about Father Cícero Romão Batista, a miracle worker from the northeast of Brazil; *A Revolta da Chibata: História à Beira de um Caís* [*The Chibata Revolt: History on the Dockside*], about the sailors' revolt in Rio de Janeiro in 1910; and *Os Limites da Resistência* [*The Limits of Resistance*], which was a dramatized compilation of various texts. He sent the latter off to the National Book Institute, an organ of the federal government, but it failed to get beyond the first obstacle, the Reading Commission. His book fell into the hands of the critic and novelist Octavio de Faria who, while emphasizing its good points, sent the originals straight to the archives with the words:

> I won't deny that this strange book, *The Limits of Resistance*, left me completely perplexed. Even after reading it, I cannot decide which literary genre it belongs to. It claims to comprise 'Eleven Fundamental

Differences', bears an epigraph by Henry Miller, and sets out to 'explain' life. It contains digressions, surrealist constructions, descriptions of psychedelic experiences, and all kinds of games and jokes. It is a hotchpotch of 'fundamental differences', which, while undeniably well written and intelligent, does not seem to me the kind of book that fits our criteria. Whatever Sr. Paulo Coelho de Souza's literary future may be, it's the kind of work that 'avant-garde' publishers like, in the hope of stumbling across a 'genius', but not the publishers of the National Book Institute.

At least he had the consolation of being in good company. The same Reading Commission also rejected at least two books that would become classics of Brazilian literature: *Sargento Getúlio*, which was to launch the writer João Ubaldo Ribeiro in Brazil and the United States, and *Objeto Gritante*, by Clarice Lispector, which was later to be published as *Água Viva*.

As if some force were trying to deflect him from his *idée fixe* of becoming a writer, drama continued to offer Paulo more recognition than prose. Although he had high hopes for his play about Father Cícero, foreseeing a brilliant future for it, only *A Revolta da Chibata* went on to achieve any success. He entered it in the prestigious Concurso Teatro Opinião, more because he felt that he should than with any hope of winning. The prize offered was better than any amount of money: the winning play would be performed by the members of the Teatro Opinião, which was the most famous of the avant-garde theatre groups in Brazil. When Vera called to tell him that *A Revolta* had come second, Paulo reacted angrily: 'Second? Shit! I always come second.' First prize had gone to *Os Dentes do Tigre* [*Tiger's Teeth*] by Maria Helena Kühner, who was also starting out on her career.

However, if his objective was fame, he had nothing to complain about. Besides being quoted in all the newspapers and praised by such critics as João das Neves and José Arrabal, that despised second prize brought *A Revolta* a place in the Teatro Opinião's much-prized series of readings, which were open to the public and took place every week. Paulo may have been upset about not winning first prize, but he was very anxious during the days that preceded the reading. He could think of nothing else all week and was immensely proud when he watched the actress Maria Pompeu reading his play before a packed house.

Months later, his acquaintance with Teatro Opinião meant that he met – very briefly – one of the international giants of counterculture, the revolutionary American drama group the Living Theatre, which was touring Brazil at the time. When Paulo learned that he had managed to get tickets to see a production by the group, he was so excited that he felt 'quite intimidated, as though I had just taken a big decision'. Fearing that he might be asked to give his opinion on something during the interval or after the play, he read a little Nietzsche before going to the theatre 'so as to have something to say'. In the end, he and Vera were so affected by what they saw that they wangled an invitation to the house where the group – headed by Julian Beck and Judith Malina – were staying, and from there went on to visit the shantytown in Vidigal. Judging by the notes in his diary, however, the meeting did not go well: 'Close contact with the Living Theatre. We went to the house where Julian Beck and Judith Malina are staying and no one talked to us. A bitter feeling of humiliation. We went with them to the *favela*. It was the first time in my life that I'd been to a *favela*. It's a world apart.'

The following day, although they had had lunch with the group and been present at rehearsals, the Americans' attitude towards them remained unchanged. 'Julian Beck and Judith Malina continue to treat us with icy indifference,' he wrote. 'But I don't blame them. I know it must have been very difficult to get where they are.' The next Paulo heard of the group and its leaders was some months later, when he heard that they had been arrested in Ouro Preto, in Minas Gerais, accused of possession and use of cannabis. The couple had rented a large house in the city and turned it into a permanent drama workshop for actors from all over Brazil. A few weeks later, the police surrounded the house and arrested all eighteen members of the group and took them straight to the Dops prison in Belo Horizonte.

In spite of protests from the famous across the world – Jean-Paul Sartre, Michel Foucault, Pier Paolo Pasolini, Jean-Luc Godard and Umberto Eco among others – the military government kept the whole group in prison for sixty days, after which they expelled all the foreign members, accusing them of 'drug trafficking and subversion'.

As for Paulo, some months after he and Vera had first been introduced to cannabis, the artist Jorge Mourão gave them a tiny block the size of a packet of chewing gum that looked as though it were made of very dark, almost black, wax. It was hashish. Although it comes from the same plant as cannabis, hashish is stronger and was always a drug that was consumed more in Europe and North Africa than in South America, which meant that it was seen as a novelty among Brazilian users. Obsessive as ever about planning and organizing everything he did, Paulo decided to convert a mere 'puff' into a solemn scientific experiment. From the moment he inhaled the drug for the first time he began to record all his sensations on tape, keeping a note of the time as well. He typed up the final result and stuck it in his diary:

Brief notes on our Experiment with Hashish
To Edgar Allan Poe

We began to smoke in my bedroom at ten forty at night. Those present: myself, Vera and Mourão. The hashish is mixed with ordinary tobacco in a ratio of approximately one to seven and put into a special silver pipe. This pipe makes the smoke pass through iced water, which allows for perfect filtration. Three drags each are enough. Vera isn't going to take part in the experiment, as she's going to do the recording and take photos. Mourão, who's an old hand at drugs, will tell us what we must do.

3 minutes – A feeling of lightness and euphoria. Boundless happiness. Strong inner feelings of agitation. I walk backwards and forwards feeling totally drunk.

6 minutes – My eyelids are heavy. A feeling of dizziness and sleepiness. My head is starting to take on terrifying proportions, with images slightly distorted into a circular shape. At this phase of the experiment, certain mental blocks (of a moral order) surfaced in my mind. Note: the effects may have been affected by over-excitement.

10 minutes – An enormous desire to sleep. My nerves are completely relaxed and I lie down on the floor. I start to sweat, more

out of anxiety than heat. No initiative whatsoever: if the house caught fire, I'd rather die than get up from here.

20 minutes – I'm conscious, but have lost all sense of where sounds come from. It's a pleasant phase that leads to total lack of anxiety.

28 minutes – The sense of the relativity of time is really amazing. This must be how Einstein discovered it.

30 minutes – Suddenly, I lose consciousness entirely. I try to write, but I fail to realize that this is just an attempt, a test. I begin to dance, to dance like a madman; the music is coming from another planet and I exist in an unknown dimension.

33 minutes – Time is passing terribly slowly. I wouldn't have the courage to try LSD ...

45 minutes – The fear of flying out of the window is so great that I get off my bed and lie on the floor, at the back of the room, well away from the street outside. My body doesn't require comfort. I can stay lying on the floor without moving.

1 hour – I look at my watch, unable to understand why I'm trying to record everything. For me this is nothing more than an eternity from which I will never manage to escape.

1 hour 15 minutes – A sudden immense desire to come out of the trance. In the depths of winter, I'm suddenly filled by courage and I decide to take a cold bath. I don't feel the water on my body. I'm naked. But I can't come out of the trance. I'm terrified that I might stay like this for ever. Books I've read about schizophrenia start parading through the bathroom. I want to get out. I want to get out!

1 hour and a half – I'm rigid, lying down, sweating with fear.

2 hours – The passage from the trance to a normal state takes place imperceptibly. There's no feeling of sickness, sleepiness or tiredness, but an unusual hunger. I look for a restaurant on the corner. I move, I walk. One foot in front of the other.

Not satisfied with smoking hashish and recording its effects, Paulo was brave enough to try something which, in the days when he was under his father's authority, would have ended in a session of electroshock therapy in the asylum: he made a copy of these notes and his parents almost died of shock when he gave it to them to read. From his point of view, this was perhaps not simply an act of provocation towards Lygia and Pedro. Although he confessed to his diary that he had 'discovered another world' and that 'drugs are the best thing in the world', Paulo considered himself to be no ordinary cannabis user but, rather, 'an activist ideologue of the hippie movement' who never tired of repeating to his friends the same extravagant claim: 'Drugs are to me what the machine gun is to communists and guerrillas.' As well as cannabis and hashish, the couple had become frequent users of synthetic drugs. Since the time when he had first been admitted to the clinic, he had been prescribed regular doses of Valium. Unconcerned about the damage these drug cocktails might cause to their nervous systems, the lovers became enthusiastic users of Mandrix, Artane, Dexamil and Pervitin. Amphetamines were present in some of these drugs and acted on the central nervous system, increasing the heartbeat and raising blood pressure, producing a pleasant sensation of muscular relaxation, which was followed by feelings of euphoria that would last up to fourteen hours. When they became tired, they would take some kind of sleeping drug such as Mandrix, and crash out. Drugs used in the control of epileptic fits or the treatment of Parkinson's disease guaranteed neverending 'trips' that lasted days and nights without interruption.

One weekend at Kakiko's place in Friburgo, 100 kilometres from Rio, Paulo carried out an experiment to find out how long he could remain drugged without stopping even to sleep, and was overjoyed when he managed to complete more than twenty-four hours, not sleeping and completely 'out of it'. Only drugs seemed to have any importance on this dangerous path that he was following. 'Our meals have become somewhat subjective,' he wrote in his diary. 'We don't know when we last ate and anyway we don't seem to miss food at all.'

Just one thing seemed to be keeping him connected to the world of the normal, of those who did not take drugs: the stubborn desire to be a writer. He was determined to lock himself up in Uncle José's house in Araruama and just write. 'To write, to write a lot, to write everything' was his immediate plan. Vera agreed and urged him on, but she suggested that before he did this, they should relax and take a holiday. In April 1970, the couple decided to go to one of the Meccas of the hippie movement, Machu Picchu, the sacred city of the Incas in the Peruvian Andes, at an altitude of 2,400 metres. Still traumatized by his journey to Paraguay, Paulo feared that something evil would happen to him if he left Brazil. It was only after much careful planning that the couple finally departed. Inspired by the 1969 film *Easy Rider*, they had no clear destination or fixed date of return.

On 1 May they took a Lloyd Aéro Boliviano aeroplane to La Paz for a trip that involved many novelties, the first of which Paulo experienced as soon as he got out at El Alto airport, in the Bolivian capital: snow. He was so excited when he saw everything covered by such a pure white blanket that he could not resist throwing himself on the ground and eating the snow. It was the start of a month of absolute idleness. Vera spent the day in bed in the hotel, unable to cope with the rarefied air of La Paz at 4,000 metres. Paulo went out to get to know the city and, accustomed to the political apathy of a Brazil under a dictatorship, he was shocked to see workers' demonstrations on Labour Day. Four months later, Alfredo Ovando Candia, who had just named himself President of the Republic for the third time, was ousted.

Taking advantage of the low cost of living in Bolivia, they rented a car, stayed in good hotels and went to the best restaurants. Every other day, the elegant Vera made time to go to the hairdresser's, while Paulo climbed the steep hills of La Paz. It was there that they encountered a new type of drug, which was almost non-existent in Brazil: mescalito, also known as peyote, peyotl or mescal – a hallucinogenic tea distilled from cut, dried cactus. Amazed by the calmness and tranquillity induced by the drink, they wallowed in endless visual hallucinations and experienced intense moments of synaesthesia, a confusion of the senses that gives the user the sense of being able to smell a colour or hear a taste.

They spent five days in La Paz drinking the tea, visiting clubs to listen to local music and attending *diabladas*, places where plays in which the Inca equivalent of the Devil predominated. They then caught a train to Lake Titicaca, the highest navigable lake in the world, where they took a boat across and then the train to Cuzco and Machu Picchu, after which they went by plane to Lima.

In Lima, they rented a car and headed for Santiago de Chile, passing through Arequipa, Antofagasta and Arica. The plan was to spend more time on this stretch, but the hotels were so unprepossessing that they decided to carry on. Neither Paulo nor Vera enjoyed the Chilean capital – 'a city like any other', he wrote – but they did have the chance to see Costa-Gavras's film *Z*, which denounced the military dictatorship in Greece and was banned in Brazil. At the end of their three-week trip, still almost constantly under the influence of mescalito, they found themselves in Mendoza, in Argentina, on the way to Buenos Aires. Paulo was eaten up with jealousy when he saw the attractive Vera being followed by men, particularly when she began to speak in English, which he still could not understand that well. In La Paz it had been the sight of snow that had taken him by surprise; in Buenos Aires it was going on the metro for the first time. Accustomed to low prices in the other places they had visited, they decided to dine at the Michelangelo, a restaurant known as 'the cathedral of the tango', where they were lucky enough to hear a classic of the genre, the singer Roberto 'Polaco' Goyeneche. When they were handed a bill for $20 – the equivalent of about US$120 today – Paulo almost fell off his chair to discover that they were in one of the most expensive restaurants in the city.

Although his asthma had coped well with the Andean heights, in Buenos Aires, at sea level, it reappeared in force. With a temperature of 39°C and suffering from intense breathing difficulties, he had to remain in bed for three days and began to recover only in Montevideo, on 1 June, the day before they were to leave for Brazil. At his insistence, they would not be making the return journey on a Lloyd Aéro Boliviano flight. This change had nothing to do with superstition or with the fact that they would have to travel via La Paz. Paulo had seen the bronze statue of a civilian pilot at La Paz airport in homage 'to the heroic pilots of LAB who have died in action': 'I'd be mad to travel with a company that treats the pilots of crashed planes as heroes! What if our pilot has ambitions to become a statue?' In the end, they flew Air France to Rio de Janeiro, where they arrived on 3 June in time to watch the first round of the 1970 World Cup, when the Brazilian team beat Czechoslovakia 4–1.

The dream of becoming a writer would not go away. Paulo placed nowhere in the short story competions he entered. He wrote in his diary: 'It was with a broken heart that I heard the news ... that I had failed to win yet another literary competition. I didn't even get an honourable mention.' However, he did not allow himself to be crushed by these defeats and continued to note down possible subjects for future literary works, such as 'flying saucers', 'Jesus', 'the abominable snowman', 'spirits becoming embodied in corpses' and 'telepathy'. All the same, the prizes continued to elude him, as he recorded in his notes: 'Dear São José, my protector. You are witness to the fact that I've tried really hard this year. I've lost in every competition. Yesterday, when I heard I'd lost in the competition for children's plays, Vera said that when my luck finally does arrive, it will do so all in one go. Do you agree?'

On his twenty-third birthday, Vera gave him a sophisticated microscope and was pleased to see what a success it was: hours after opening the gift, Paulo was still hunched over it, carefully examining the glass plates and making notes. Curious to know what he was doing, she began to read what he was writing: 'It's twenty-three years today since I was born. I was already this thing that I can see under the microscope. Excited, moving in the direction of life, infinitesimally small but with all my hereditary characteristics in place. My two arms, my legs and my brain were already programmed. I would reproduce myself from that sperm cell, the cells would multiply. And here I am, aged twenty-three.' It was only then that she realized that Paulo had put his own semen under the microscope. The notes continue: 'There goes a possible engineer. Another one that ought to have become a doctor is dying. A scientist capable of saving the Earth has also died, and I'm impassively watching all this through my microscope. My own sperm are furiously flailing around, desperate to find an egg, desperate to perpetuate themselves.'

Vera was good company, but she could be tough too. When she realized that, if he had anything to do with it, Paulo would never achieve anything beyond the school diploma he had got at Guanabara, she almost forced him to prepare for his university entrance exams. Her vigilance produced surprising results. By the end of the year, he had managed to be accepted by no fewer than three faculties: law at Cândido Mendes, theatre direction at the Escola Nacional de Teatro and media studies at the Pontifícia Universidade Católica (PUC) in Rio.

This success, needless to say, could not be attributed entirely to Vera: it had as much to do with Paulo's literary appetite. Since he had begun making systematic notes of his reading four years earlier, he had read more than three hundred books, or seventy-five a year – a vast number when one realizes that most Brazilians read, on average, one book a year. He read a great deal and he read everything. From Cervantes to Kafka, from Jorge Amado to Scott Fitzgerald, from Aeschylus to Aldous Huxley. He read Soviet dissidents such as Alexander Solzhenitsyn and Brazilians who were on police files such as the humourist Stanislaw Ponte Preta. He would read, make a short commentary on each work and rate them accordingly. The highest accolade, four stars, was the privilege of only a few writers, such as Henry Miller, Borges and Hemingway. And he blithely awarded 'zero stars' to books as varied as Norman Mailer's *American Dream*, Régis Debray's *Revolution in Revolution* and two Brazilian classics, *Os Sertões* [*Rebellion in the Backlands*] by Euclides da Cunha and *História Econômica do Brasil* [*An Economic History of Brazil*] by Caio Prado, Jr.

In this mélange of subjects, periods and authors, there was one genre that appeared to arouse Paulo's interest more than others: books dealing with the occult, witchcraft and satanism. Ever since he had read a short book written by the Spanish sorcerer José Ramón Molinero, *The Secret Alchemy of Mankind*, he had devoured everything relating to the invisible world beyond the human senses. When he finished reading *The Dawn of Magic* by the Belgian Louis Pauwels and the French-Ukrainian Jacques Bergier, he began to feel he was a member of this new tribe. 'I'm a magician preparing for his dawn,' he wrote in his diary. At the end of 1970, he had collected fifty works on the subject. During this time he had read, commented on and given star ratings to all six of the Hermann Hesse books published in Brazil, as well as to Erich von Däniken's best-sellers *The Chariots of the Gods* and *Return to the Stars*, Goethe's *Faust*, to which he gave only three stars, and to absurd books such as *Black Magic and White Magic* by a certain V.S. Foldej, which didn't even merit a rating.

One of the most celebrated authors of this new wave was Carlos Castaneda. Not only did he write on the occult: his own story was shrouded in mystery. He was said to have been born in 1925 in Peru (or in 1935 in Brazil, according to other sources) and had graduated in anthropology at the University of California, in Los Angeles. When he was preparing his doctoral thesis he decided to write autobiographical accounts of his experiences in Mexico on the use of drugs such as peyote, mushrooms and stramonium (known as devil's weed) in native rituals. The worldwide success of Castaneda, who even featured on the cover of *Time* magazine, attracted hordes of hippies, in search of the new promised land, from the four corners of the earth to the Sonora desert on the border where California and Arizona meet Mexico, where the books were set.

For those who, like Paulo, did not believe in coincidences, the fact that it was at precisely this moment that his mother made him the gift of a trip to the United States seemed like a sign. His grandmother Lilisa was going to Washington to visit her daughter Lúcia, who was married to the diplomat Sérgio Weguelin, and he would go with her and, if he wanted, extend the trip and go travelling alone or with his cousin Serginho, who was a few years younger. Besides giving him the opportunity to get to know first-hand the area about which Castaneda had written, the trip was useful in another way. His relationship with Vera appeared to be coming to an end. 'Life with her is getting complicated,' he complained at the beginning of 1971 in his diary. 'We don't have sex any more, she's driving me mad, and I'm driving her mad. I don't love her any more. It's just habit.' Things had reached such a low ebb that the two had stopped living together. Vera had returned to her apartment in Leblon and he had moved from Santa Teresa back to his grandparents' house before moving to Copacabana. Besides this, he announced in his diary that he was 'half-married' to a new woman, the young actress Christina Scardini, whom he had met at drama school and with whom he swore he was passionately in love. This was a lie, but during the month and a half he was away in America, she was the recipient of no fewer than forty-four letters.

At the beginning of May, after a celebratory farewell dinner given by his parents, he took a Varig flight with his grandparents to New York, where they were to catch an internal flight to Washington. When they arrived at Kennedy airport, Paulo and his grandmother couldn't understand why Tuca was in such a hurry to get the eleven o'clock plane to

Washington, for which the check-in was just closing. Lilisa and her grandson argued that there was no reason to rush, because if they missed that plane they could take the following flight, half an hour later. Out of breath from running, the three boarded the plane just as the doors were about to be closed. Tuca only calmed down once they were all sitting with their seatbelts buckled. That night, when they were watching the news at his uncle's house, Paulo realized that the hand of destiny had clearly been behind Tuca's insistence that they catch the 11.00 flight. The 11.30 flight, a twin-engined Convair belonging to Allegheny (later US Airways), had experienced mechanical problems and when the pilot tried to make an emergency landing near New Haven, 70 kilometres from New York, the plane had crashed, killing the crew and all thirty passengers on board.

While staying at his diplomat uncle's house in Bethesda, Maryland, half an hour from Washington, instead of writing a travel diary Paulo decided to use his copious correspondence with Christina to record his impressions. He seemed to be astounded by everything he saw. He could stand for ages, gazing at the automatic vending machines for stamps, newspapers and soft drinks, or spend hours on end in department stores without buying anything, amazed by the sheer variety of products. In his very first letter he regretted not having taken with him 'a sack of change' from Brazil, since he had discovered that all the machines accepted the Brazilian 20 centavo coin as if it were a 25 cent piece, even though it was worth only one fifth of the value. 'I'd have made great savings if I'd brought more coins,' he confessed, 'because it costs me 25 cents to buy a stamp for Brazil from the vending machines and to get in to see the blue movies they show in the porn shops here.'

Everything was new and everything excited him, from the supermarket shelves stacked with unnecessary items to the works of art at the National Gallery, where he wept as he actually touched with his own hands the canvas of *Death and the Miser* by Hieronymus Bosch. He knew perfectly well that touching a painting is a cardinal sin in any serious museum, but he placed his fingers not only on Bosch's 1485 work but on several other masterpieces too. He would stand in front of each work for some minutes, look around and, when he was certain he wasn't being watched by the security guards, commit the heresy of spreading all ten fingers out on the canvas. 'I touched a Van Gogh, a Gauguin, and a Degas, and I felt something growing in me, you know,' he told his girlfriend. 'I'm really growing here. I'm learning a lot.'

Nothing, however, seems to have struck him more, while in Washington, than the visits he made to the military museum and the FBI museum. The first, with its many exhibits relating to the participation of the United States in the two world wars, appeared to him to be a place 'where children are sent to learn to hate the enemies of the United States'. Not only children, to judge by his reaction. After visiting every bit of the museum and seeing planes, rockets and films about American military power, he left 'hating the Russians, wanting to kill, kill, kill, spitting hatred'. On his tour of the FBI museum, with a federal agent as his guide, he saw the Gangster Museum, with the original clothes and weapons used by famous gangsters, such as Dillinger, 'Baby Face', 'Machine Gun Kelly' and others, as well as the actual notes written by kidnapped hostages. In the corner of one room he was surprised to find a blinking light, under which was a plaque bearing the following words: 'Each time this light blinks, a type A crime (murder, kidnap or rape) is committed in the United States.' The problem was that the light blinked every three seconds. On the gun stand, the agent was proud of the fact that in the FBI, they shoot to kill. That night, on a card peppered with exclamation marks, he recorded his feelings:

These guys don't miss! They shot with revolvers and machine-guns, and always at the target's head! They never missed! And there were children, my love, watching all this! There were whole school parties at the FBI gun stand to find out how they defend the country! ... The agent told me that to join the FBI you have to be taller than 1.80m, have a good aim and be prepared for them to examine the whole of your past life. Nothing else. There's no intelligence test, only a shooting test. I'm in the most advanced country in the world, in a country enjoying every comfort and the highest social perfection. So why do such things happen here?

Concerned with his public image, Paulo usually appended a footnote, asking Christina not to show the letters to anyone. 'They're very private and written with no thought for style,' he explained. 'You can say what I've written, but don't let anyone else read them.' At the end of a marathon week of visits, he bought a train ticket to New York, where he was going to decide on his next move. In a comfortable red-and-blue second-class carriage on an Amtrak train, minutes after leaving the American capital, he felt a shiver run through him when he realized the purpose of the concrete constructions beside the railway line: they were fall-out shelters built in case of nuclear war. These dark thoughts were interrupted by a tap on his shoulder when the train was about to make its first stop in Elizabeth, New Jersey.

It was the conductor, wearing a blue uniform and with a leather bag round his waist, who said to him: 'Morning, sir, may I see your ticket?'

Surprised, and not understanding what he meant, Paulo responded in Portuguese: '*Desculpe.*'

The man seemed to be in a hurry and in a bad mood: 'Don't you understand? I asked for your ticket! Without a ticket nobody travels on my train.'

It was only at this point that Paulo understood, with deep dismay, that all Vera's efforts to make him into a model English speaker had been in vain. Without her to turn to, he realized that it was one thing to read books in English, and even then with the help of his lover or of dictionaries. It was quite another to speak it and, most of all, to understand what people were saying in the language. The disappointing truth was that there he was alone in the United States and he couldn't say a single, solitary word in English.

CHAPTER 12

Discovering America

PAULO'S FIRST IMPRESSION OF NEW YORK could not have been worse. In marked contrast to the cleanliness and colour he was accustomed to seeing on cinema screens and in books, the city that opened up to him through the train windows as soon as he passed through the Brooklyn tunnel and entered Manhattan Island appeared to be infested with beggars and ugly, poorly dressed, threatening-looking people. But this sight did not dishearten him. He wanted to stay only a few days in the city and then set off to find the original objective of his journey: the Grand Canyon in Arizona and the magical deserts of Mexico. He had US$300 and wanted to spend two months 'wandering from one side of the United States to the other'. The first thing he should do was to stop travelling by train and switch to Greyhound buses. He remembered having seen these buses in films, an elegant greyhound painted on the side. A pass costing US$99 gave you the right to travel for forty-five days to anywhere on the Greyhound network, more than two thousand towns across the United States, Mexico and Canada. Since his plan was to spend two months travelling, this meant that, with the money that remained, he could only afford to stay in YMCA hostels, which charged 6 dollars a night, including breakfast and dinner.

Two days was enough for New York to dispel the disappointment he had felt on arrival. Firstly, because, although the YMCA rooms were small – half the size of his room at his grandmother's house – and they had no bathroom, television or air conditioning, they were single and very clean, with bed linen changed daily. The staff were polite and while the food was not exactly haute cuisine, it was well cooked and tasty. Were it not for the discomfort of having to share a bathroom with all the other guests on the corridor, Paulo could happily have stayed there longer. The continuing problem was the language. Every day, in the dining room, he would annoy everyone else in the hungry, impatient queue with his inability to communicate to the cook what it was he wanted to eat. It was a relief to learn that the delicious beans served at the YMCA were called 'poroto'. Since this was a word he had no difficulty in pronouncing, the problem was solved: he would eat nothing but 'poroto' until his English improved.

New York's tolerant, liberal atmosphere also helped to reconcile him to the city. Paulo discovered that sex, cannabis and hashish were all available in the streets, especially in the areas around Washington Square, where groups of hippies spent their days playing guitars and enjoying the first rays of spring sunshine. One night, he arrived at the hostel restaurant only five minutes before the doors were to be closed. Even though almost all the tables were empty, he picked up his tray and sat down opposite a slim girl of about twenty, wearing what seemed to be the official uniform of hippie women the world over – an ankle-length Indian dress in multi-coloured cotton. A smile appeared on her freckled face and Paulo, sure that he had enough English to be polite, said: 'Excuse me?'

The girl didn't understand: 'What?'

Realizing that he was incapable of pronouncing even a banal 'excuse me', he relaxed and started to laugh at himself. Feeling more relaxed made communication easier, and, later that night, he and the girl, Janet, walked together through the city streets. However hard he tried to find out what it was she was studying, Paulo could not understand what the word '*belei*' meant. *Belei?* But what did studying '*belei*' mean? Janet drew back and jumped up, her arms wide, performed a pirouette, and then curtseyed deeply. So that was what it was! She was studying ballet!

At the end of the evening, on the way back to the hostel, where men and women slept on different floors, the young couple stopped on the steps of a building in Madison Square Garden to say goodbye. Between kisses and hugs, Janet slipped her hand below Paulo's waist, over his jeans, and then started back and said, almost spelling out the words so that he could understand: 'I've been with other boys before, but you ... Wow! You're the first one I've known who's had a square one.' Laughing, he had to explain that no, he did not have a square dick. Rather than leaving his documents in the wardrobe in the YMCA, he had put all his money and his return ticket to Brazil in his passport and put the whole lot in a supposedly safe place – his underpants.

It was under the guidance of Janet, with whom he would often have sex in quiet corners of parks and gardens, that he came to know a new world: the New York of the 1970s. He joined demonstrations against the war in Vietnam, went to concerts of baroque music in Central Park and was thrilled to go down some steps and find Pennsylvania station magically lit up. 'It's bigger than Central station in Rio,' he wrote to his girlfriend, 'only it's constructed entirely underground.' He was excited when he went to Madison Square Garden, 'where three months ago Cassius Clay was beaten by Joe Frazier'. His passion for the boxer who would later take the name Muhammad Ali was such that he not only watched all his fights but also compared his tiny physical measurements with those of the American giant. Although he had no specific date to return home, time seemed too short to enjoy everything that New York had to offer a young man from a poor country under a military dictatorship.

When he could, he tried to record in his letters the excitement he was experiencing:

> There are areas where everything – books, newspapers, posters – is written in Chinese, or Spanish or Italian. My hotel is full of men in turbans, Black Panther militants, Indians in long clothes, everything. Last night, when I left my room, I broke up a fight between two old guys of sixty! They were bashing the hell out of each other! I haven't even told you anything about Harlem yet, the black district, it's amazing, fantastic. What is NY? I think NY is the prostitutes walking the streets at midday in Central Park, it's the building where *Rosemary's Baby* was filmed, it's the place where *West Side Story* was filmed.

Before sealing the envelopes he would cover the margins of his letters with sentimental declarations of love ('adored, loved, wonderful woman', or 'I'll telephone you even if I've got to go without food for a day just to hear your voice for a minute') and a few lies, such as 'Don't worry, I won't cheat on you'.

At the end of a torrid, two-week affair with New York, Paulo realized that he was limited by two things: neither his hesitant English nor his savings would be enough for him to travel alone across the United States for two months. The question of money could be resolved with a clever piece of belt-tightening suggested by Janet: if he used his Greyhound ticket for night journeys lasting more than six hours, the bus would become his hotel bedroom. The language problem, though, seemed insoluble. His schoolboy vocabulary might be enough to cope with basic needs, such as sleeping and eating, but Paulo knew that the journey would lose its charm if he couldn't properly understand what other people were saying. Faced with a choice between returning to Brazil and asking for help, he opted for the latter: he made a reverse-charge call to his aunt's house in Washington and invited his cousin Sérgio, who spoke English fluently, to go with him. A few days later, the two young men, rucksacks on their backs and using the Greyhound buses as a hotel, headed off to Chicago, the first stop on the long haul to the Grand Canyon, in the heart of Arizona, more than 4,000 kilometres from Manhattan and so far away that the time there was three hours earlier than in New York.

The only records of this period are the letters he sent to Christina, and one notes the absence of any reference to his companion who was, after all, his saviour on the journey. This is not just a lapse, because, besides overlooking Sérgio's presence, Paulo told his girlfriend that he was travelling alone. 'Perhaps I'll leave my camera with Granny during the journey,' he wrote, 'because I'm alone and can't take photos of myself, and it's better to buy postcards than to waste film on landscapes.' He wanted to make this marathon trip sound like a bold adventure.

With no money to spare, he recorded all his expenses on a piece of paper with the amounts in dollars and Brazilian cruzeiros: a packet of cigarettes 60 cents, a hamburger 80 cents, a subway ticket 30 cents, a cinema ticket 2 dollars. Each time they missed the night Greyhound bus, his savings would shrink by 7 dollars, the price of a room in one of the more modest roadside hotels. New York, with its mixture of civilization and barbarism, had left him 'shaken up', and it was hard for him to adjust to the more rural states in the Midwest. 'After NYC I've got little to say,' he complained to Christina in a near unintelligible scrawl written as the bus was moving. 'I'm only writing because I'm really missing my woman.' The majority of the cities he visited merited only superficial mention in his correspondence. His impression of Chicago was that it was the 'coldest' city he had so far encountered. 'The people are absolutely neurotic, and totally and uncontrollably aggressive. It's a city where they take work very seriously.'

After spending five days on the road, Paulo's eyes lit up at the sight through the dusty bus window of a road sign saying 'Cheyenne – 100 miles'. In the state of Wyoming, on the border with Colorado, in the heart of the American West, this was a city he felt he had known since childhood. He had read so many books and magazines and seen so many Westerns set in Cheyenne that he thought himself capable of reconstructing from memory the names of the streets, hotels and saloons where the cowboy and Indian adventures had taken place. His astonishment at seeing the road sign stemmed from the fact that he hadn't realized the city actually existed. In his mind, Cheyenne was a fantasy appropriated by the authors of books, films and cartoons in stories of the Wild West that he had read and seen during his childhood and adolescence.

He was disappointed to discover that while there were still cowboys in the city, in boots, Stetsons and belts with bull's buckles, and revolvers in holsters, they now travelled in convertible Cadillacs. The only traces of the Cheyenne he had seen in John Ford's *Cheyenne Autumn* were the carriages used by the local Amish community, which forbids the use of such modern inventions as lifts, telephones and cars. But his greatest disappointment was when he discovered that Pioneer Street, the favourite place for cowboys to hold duels in the evening in the mythical Cheyenne, had been transformed into a busy four-lane highway lined with shops selling electronic gadgets.

The obvious route to the Grand Canyon was to travel some 1,000 kilometres southwest, then cross Colorado and part of New Mexico into Arizona. However, because they both wanted to go to Yellowstone Park and make the most of their Greyhound ticket, they travelled in the opposite direction, northwards. When they realized that the closest stopping-off place to the park was Idaho Falls, 300 kilometres from Yellowstone, Paulo decided to take two risks. First, he spent US$30 on hiring a car. Second, since he had not taken his driving test he lied to the car-hire firm and presented his membership card of the Actors' Union in Rio as a Brazilian driving licence.

Although he was aware that he risked being arrested if stopped by a traffic policeman, he drove for the whole day past the glaciers in the park and the geysers spewing out hot water and sulphur on to the snow, and saw bears and deer crossing the road. In the evening, they went to return the car and decided to catch a Greyhound bus where they could shelter from the cold. Although it was the middle of summer and the two had experienced temperatures of up to 38°C, two hours from the Canadian border, the cold was so unbearable that the heating in the car wasn't enough to keep them warm. As neither had suitable clothes for such low temperatures, when they arrived at the bus station in Boise, the capital of Idaho, they rushed to the Greyhound ticket office to ask what time the next night bus left. Going where? Anywhere that wasn't so cold. If the only destination with available seats at that time of night was San Francisco, then that was where they would go.

In the middle of the night, as the bus was crossing the Nevada desert, he wrote a letter to Christina boasting of how he had tricked the man at the car-hire firm with his false licence, but regretting the fact that the extra expense of hiring the car had 'messed up my budget'. He also said that he had discovered the reason for the strong smell of whisky pervading the Greyhound bus: 'Everyone here has a small bottle in his pocket. They drink a lot in the United States.' The letter is interrupted halfway through and starts again some hours later:

I was going to go straight to San Francisco, but I discovered that gambling in Nevada is legal, so I spent the night here. I wanted to play and see how other people play. I didn't make any friends at the casino; they were all too busy gambling. I ended up losing 5 dollars in a one-armed bandit – you know, those betting machines where you pull a handle. There was a cowboy sitting next to me wearing boots, hat and neckerchief, just like in the films. In fact the whole bus is full of cowboys. I'm in the Far West on the way to San Francisco, where I'm due to arrive at eleven at night. In seven hours' time, I'll have crossed the American continent, which not many other people have.

When they reached San Francisco, exhausted after travelling for twenty-two days, the cousins signed in at a YMCA hostel and spent the day sleeping, in an attempt to catch up on more than a hundred hours spent sitting in cramped buses.

The cradle of the hippie movement, San Francisco had as great an impact on Paulo as New York. 'This city is much freer than NYC. I went to a really smart cabaret and saw naked women making love with men on the stage in front of rich Americans with their wives,' he told her, excited but regretting the fact that he'd been unable to see more. 'I went in quickly and saw just a bit of the show, but as I didn't have enough money to buy a seat, I got thrown out.' He was astonished to see adolescents buying and consuming LSD pills quite openly; he bought some hashish in the hippie district, smoked it on the street and no one stopped him. He also took part in demonstrations against the war in Vietnam and saw a pacifist march by Buddhist monks being broken up by a gang of young blacks with truncheons. 'You breathe an air of complete madness in the streets of this city,' he said in a letter to Christina.

After five 'mind-blowing' days, the cousins caught another bus in the direction of the Grand Canyon. They got off halfway there, in Los Angeles, but as it was 4 July, Independence Day, the city was dead, and they stayed only a few hours. 'Nothing was open, and it was almost impossible to find somewhere to have a coffee,' he complained. 'The famous Hollywood Boulevard was a complete desert, with no one on the streets, but we did see how luxurious everything here is, even the most ordinary bar.' And since the cost of living in Los Angeles was incompatible with the backpackers' funds, they didn't stay the night. They took another bus and, twenty-four hours after leaving San Francisco, reached Flagstaff, the entrance to the Grand Canyon.

The extortionate prices of the hotels and restaurants were almost as impressive as the beauty of the canyon. Since there were no YMCA hostels in the area, they bought a nylon tent, which meant a 19-dollar hole in their tiny stash of savings, and spent the first night in a hippie camp, where at least free hashish was guaranteed. As soon as the sun began to rise, they took down their tent, filled their rucksacks with bottles of water and tinned food, and left on foot for the Grand Canyon. They walked all day beneath the blazing sun and when they decided to stop, exhausted and hungry, they discovered that they were at the widest point of the Canyon, which measures 20 kilometres from side to side. It is also the deepest; between them and the river was a drop of 1,800 metres. They pitched their tent, lit a small bonfire to heat up their tins of soup and fell asleep, exhausted, not waking until dawn the next day.

When Sérgio suggested they go down to the river, Paulo was terrified. As there was absolutely no one around, apart from them, and they were on a path little used by tourists, he was worried that should they get into difficulties, there would be no one to come to their aid. However, Sérgio was determined: if Paulo didn't want to, he would go alone. He put all his stuff in his rucksack and began the descent, oblivious to his cousin's protests: 'Serginho, the problem isn't going down, but coming back! It's going to get really hot and we've got to climb the equivalent of the stairs in a 500-storey building! In the blazing sun!'

Impervious, his cousin didn't even turn round. There was nothing for Paulo to do but pick up his rucksack and follow him down. The beauty of the area dispelled some of his fears. The Grand Canyon looked like a 450-kilometre gash in the desert of red sand, at the bottom of which was what appeared to be a tiny trickle of water. This was, in fact, the torrential Colorado River, which rises in the Rocky Mountains in the state of Colorado and flows more than 2,300 kilometres until it runs into the Sea of Cortez in Mexico, crossing six more American states (Arizona, California, Nevada, Utah, New Mexico and Wyoming). To be down there was indescribable.

After walking for some five hours, Paulo stopped and suggested to his cousin that they end their adventure there and begin the climb back up, saying: 'We didn't eat much last night, we haven't had a proper breakfast and up to now we haven't had any lunch. Take a look and see how far we've got to climb.'

His cousin remained determined. 'You can wait for me here, because I'm going down to the river bank.'

He continued walking. Paulo found some shade where he could sit, smoked a cigarette and enjoyed the splendour of the landscape as he sat in total silence. When he looked at his watch, he realized it was midday. He walked on a few metres, trying to see Sérgio, but there was no sign of him. Indeed, as far as the eye could see, there was no one, no tourist, no Indians, not a soul for kilometres and kilometres. He realized that if he were to go down a little farther, he would come to a rocky ledge from where he would have a wider view of the area. However, even from there, he couldn't see his cousin. He began to shout out his name, waiting a few seconds after each shout, before shouting again. His voice echoed between the walls of red stone, but there was neither sign nor sound of his cousin. He was beginning to think that they had taken the wrong path. From fear to panic was but a step. Feeling entirely defenceless and alone, he became terrified. 'I'm going to die here,' he kept saying: 'I'm going to die. I can't take any more. I'm not going to get out of here. I'm going to die here, in this wonderful place.'

He was aware that, in midsummer, the temperatures around the Grand Canyon could be over 50°C. His water had run out and it was unlikely that there would be a tap in the middle of that desert. Added to which, he had no idea where he was, since there were so many intersecting paths. He started to shout for help, but no one appeared, and he heard nothing but the echo of his own voice. It was past four in the afternoon. Desperate to find his cousin, he began to run, stumbling, in the direction of the river, knowing that every step he took meant another he would have to climb up on his return.

The sun was burning his face when he finally reached a sign of civilization. Fixed to a rock was a metal plate with a red button and sign saying: 'If you are lost, press the red button and you will be rescued by helicopters or mules. You will be fined US$500.' He had only 80 dollars left and his cousin must have about the same in his pocket, but the discovery of the sign made him certain of two things: they were not the first to be so foolish as to take that route; and the risk of dying began to fade, even though it might mean a few days in jail until their parents could send the money for the fine. However, first of all, Paulo had to find Sérgio. He went another 200 metres farther down, never taking his eyes off the red button, which was his one visible reference mark, and after a bend in the path, he came across a natural belvedere where there was a metal telescope with a coin slot. He inserted 25 cents, the lens opened and he began to scan the river banks, looking for his travel companion. There he was, in the shadow of a rock and apparently as exhausted as Paulo. He was sound asleep.

Rejecting the idea of summoning a helicopter, they climbed up to the top again, and it was midnight by the time they got there. They were exhausted, their skin was puffy with sunburn, but they were alive. After the long day, the idea of spending another night in the hippie camp was so appalling that Paulo made a suggestion: 'I think we deserve two things tonight: dinner in a restaurant and a night in a hotel.'

They found a comfortable, cheap motel, left their rucksacks in their room and went into the first restaurant they came to, where each ordered a T-bone steak so big it barely fitted on the plate. It cost 10 dollars – the amount they usually spent each day. They barely had the strength to pick up knife and fork. They were both starving, though, and ate as quickly as they could. Five minutes later, however, they were in the toilet, throwing up. They returned to the motel and collapsed on to their beds for the last night they would spend together on their journey: the following day Sérgio would be returning home to Washington and Paulo was to go on to Mexico.

The original reason he had accepted his mother's gift of a plane ticket had been that it would give him the chance to make a pilgrimage to the mysterious deserts that had inspired Carlos Castaneda, but he had been so thrilled by the novelty of the country as a whole that he had almost forgotten this. Now, with his entire body aching after his adventure in the Grand Canyon, and with money fast running out, he felt a great temptation to return to Brazil. His Greyhound pass was still valid for a few more days, though, and so he carried on as planned. Grown accustomed to the wealth of America, he was appalled by the poverty he found in Mexico, which was much like Brazil. He tried all the mushroom syrups and hallucinogenic cactus teas that he could, and then caught the bus back to New York, where he spent three more days, after which he flew home to Brazil.

CHAPTER 13

Gisa

A WEEK AFTER RETURNING TO BRAZIL, having recovered from his trip, Paulo had still not decided what to do with his life. One thing was certain: he was not going back to the law faculty, so he left the course in the middle of the academic year. He continued to attend classes in theatre direction at the Guanabara State Faculty of Philosophy – which would later become the University of Rio de Janeiro – and he did everything he could to get his articles published in Rio newspapers. He wrote an article about the liberal attitude towards drugs in the United States and sent it to the most popular humorous weekly of the period, *Pasquim*, which went on to become an influential opponent of the dictatorship. He promised St Joseph that he would light fifteen candles to him if the text was published and, every Wednesday, he was the first to arrive at the newspaper stand on the corner near his home. He would avidly leaf through the magazine only to return it to the pile, disheartened. It was not until three weeks later that he realized the article had been rejected. Although this rejection tormented him for days, it was not enough to put paid to his dream of becoming a writer. When he realized that *Pasquim*'s silence was a resounding 'No', he made a strange note in his diary: 'I've been thinking about the problem of fame and have concluded that my good fortune hasn't yet turned up. When it does, it's going to be quite something.'

The problem was that while he waited for it to turn up, he needed to earn a living. He still enjoyed working in the theatre, but the returns weren't usually enough even to cover the costs of putting on the production. This led him to accept an invitation to teach on a private course preparing students for the entrance exam for theatre courses given by the Federation of Isolated State Schools in the State of Guanabara. It wouldn't contribute anything to his future plans, but, on the other hand, it wouldn't take up much time and it guaranteed him a monthly salary of 1,600 cruzeiros, some US$350.

On 13 August 1971, a little more than a month after his return from the United States, Paulo received a phone call from Washington. His grandfather, Arthur Araripe or Tuca, had just died. He had suffered severe cranial trauma when he fell down the stairs at his daughter's house in Bethesda, where he was staying, and had died instantly. Appalled by the news, Paulo sat in silence for a few minutes, trying to collect his thoughts. One of the last images he had of Tuca, smiling and sporting a beret as they arrived at the airport in Washington, seemed so fresh that he could not accept that the old man had died. Paulo felt that if he went out on to the verandah he would find Tuca dozing there, mouth open, over a copy of the *Reader's Digest*. Or, as he loved to do, provoking his hippie grandson with his reactionary ideas, saying for instance that Pelé was 'an ignorant black man' and that Roberto Carlos was 'an hysterical screamer'. Then he would defend right-wing dictators, starting with Salazar in Portugal and Franco in Spain (on these occasions, Paulo's father would join in and insist that 'any idiot' could paint like Picasso or play the guitar like Jimi Hendrix). Instead of getting annoyed, Paulo would roar with laughter at his obstinate grandfather's over-the-top remarks, because, for all his conservatism, and perhaps because he himself had been a bit of a bohemian during his youth, he was the only member of the family who respected and understood the strange friends Paulo went around with. Having known him for so many years, and having built a closer relationship with him during the time he spent in his grandparents' small house, Paulo had come to consider Tuca to be almost a second father to him. A generous, tolerant father, the very opposite of his real father, the harsh and irascible Pedro. For these reasons, his grandfather's unexpected death was all the more painful, and the wound opened up by that loss would take time to heal.

Paulo continued to teach and to go to his theatre course, with which he was beginning to find fault. 'In the first year, the student learns to be a bit of a chiseller and to use personal charm to achieve whatever he or she wants,' he wrote in his diary. 'In the second year, the student loses any sense of organization he had before and in the third, he becomes a queer.' His proverbial paranoia reached unbearable levels when he learned that the detective Nelson Duarte, who was accused of belonging to the Death Squad, was going around the Escola Nacional de Teatro looking for 'cannabis users and communists'. On one such visit, the policeman was confronted by a brave woman, the teacher and speech and hearing therapist Glória Beutenmüller, who wagged her finger at him and said: 'My students can wear their hair as long as they like – and if you arrest one of them, they'll have to be dragged out of here.'

Protected by the secrecy of his diary, Paulo made a solitary protest against these arbitrary arrests:

> Nelson Duarte again issued a threat against students and teachers with long hair, and the school issued a decree, banning long hair. I didn't go to the class today because I haven't decided whether I'm going to cut mine or not. It's affected me deeply. Cutting my hair, not wearing necklaces, not dressing like a hippie … It's unbelievable. With this diary I'm writing a real secret archive of my age. One day, I'll publish the whole thing. Or else I'll put it all in a radiation-proof box with a code that's easy to work out, so that one day someone will read what I've written. Thinking about it, I'm a bit worried about even keeping this notebook.

In fact, he had already made plenty of notes showing that he didn't share the ideas of many of his left-wing friends who opposed the dictatorship. His diary was peppered with statements such as: 'There's no point getting rid of this and replacing it with communism, which would just be the same shit' and 'Taking up arms never solved anything'. But the repression of any armed conflict was at its height and mere sympathizers as well as their friends were being rounded up. Censorship meant that the press could not publish anything about the government's use of violence against its opponents, but news of this nevertheless reached Paulo's ears, and the shadow cast by the security forces seemed to get closer by the day. One of his friends was imprisoned by the political police merely because he had renewed his passport in order to go to Chile during the period of Salvador Allende's rule. A year earlier, Paulo had learned that a former girlfriend of his, Nancy Unger, had been shot and apprehended in Copacabana while resisting arrest. He found out that Nancy, along with sixty-nine other political prisoners, had been exiled from Brazil, in exchange for the Swiss ambassador Enrico Giovanni Bucher, who had been kidnapped by command of the Popular Revolutionary Front. In the end, the repression became too much even for those who weren't part of the armed resistance. Persecuted by the censors, the composer Chico Buarque went into self-imposed exile in Italy. Gilberto Gil and Caetano Veloso moved to London after having their heads shaved in an army barracks in Rio. Gradually, Paulo was starting to hate the military, but nothing would make him overcome his fear and open his mouth, and say in public what he felt. Appalled that he could do nothing against a regime that was torturing and killing people, he fell into depression.

In September 1971, the army surrounded and killed Captain Carlos Lamarca in the interior of Bahia. When Paulo read excerpts from the dead guerrilla's diary that were published by the press, he wrote a long and bitter outburst that gives a faithful picture of his inner conflicts. Once again, he confessed that he avoided talking about the police in his diary for one reason only: fear. But how could he continue not protesting against what was going on around him? It was when he was alone, locked in his room that he gave expression to his pain:

> I'm living in a terrible climate, TERRIBLE! I can't take any more talk about imprisonment and torture. There is no freedom in Brazil. The area in which I work is subject to vile and stupid censorship.
>
> I read Lamarca's diary. I admired him only because he fought for his ideas, nothing more. Today, though, when I see the demeaning

comments in the press, I felt like shouting, like screaming. I was really angry. And I discovered in his diary a great love for someone, a poetic love that was full of life, and the newspaper called it 'the terrorist's dependence on his lover'. I discovered a man who was full of self-doubt and hyper-honest with himself, even though he fought for an idea that I consider wrong.

The government is torturing people and I'm frightened of torture, I'm frightened of pain. My heart is beating far too fast now, simply because these words could compromise me. But I have to write. The whole thing is fucked. Everyone I know has either been imprisoned or beaten up. And none of them had anything to do with anything.

I still think that one day they're going to knock on the door of this room and take this diary. But St Joseph will protect me. Now that I've written these lines, I know that I'm going to live in fear, but I couldn't continue to keep quiet, I needed to let it out. I'm going to type because it's faster. It needs to be fast. The sooner this notebook is out of my room the better. I'm really frightened of physical pain. I'm frightened of being arrested like I was before. And I don't want that to happen ever again: that's why I try not to think about politics at all. I wouldn't be able to resist. But I will resist. Up until now, 21st September 1971, I was scared. But today is an historic day – or perhaps just a few historic hours. I'm liberating myself from the prison that I built, thanks to all Their practices.

It was very difficult for me to write these words. I'm repeating this so that I won't ever delude myself when I re-read this diary in a safe place, thirty years from now, about the times I'm living through now. But now I've done it. The die is cast.

Sometimes he would spend all day locked in his room at the back of his grandmother's house, smoking cannabis and trying to make a start on that dreamed-of book, or at least a play, or an essay. He had notebooks full of ideas for books, plays and essays, but something was missing – inclination? inspiration? – and when evening came, he still hadn't written a line. Otherwise, he taught for three hours a day and then went to the university. He would go in, talk to various people and, when he got fed up with doing that, end up alone in a bar near by, drinking coffee, chain-smoking and filling pages of notebooks with ideas.

It was on one such evening that a girl appeared, wearing a miniskirt and high boots. She had very long, thick dark hair. She sat down beside Paulo at the bar, ordered a coffee and struck up a conversation with him. She had just qualified as an architect and her name was Adalgisa Eliana Rios de Magalhães, or Gisa, from Alfenas in Minas Gerais; she was two years older than Paulo. She had left Minas for Rio in order to study at the Federal University and was now working for the Banco Nacional da Habitação, although what she liked best was drawing comic strips. She was as slender as a catwalk model, and had an unusual face in which her dark melancholy eyes contrasted with a sensual mouth. They talked for some time, exchanged telephone numbers and parted. Once again, Paulo dismissed any possibility of a relationship developing, writing: 'She's ugly and has no sex appeal.'

Unlike Paulo – and this was something he never knew – Gisa had been an active militant in opposition to the military regime. She had never taken part in armed action or anything that might involve risking her life – and this, in the jargon of repression, meant that she was a 'subversive', rather than a 'terrorist' – but following her first year in architecture, she had been a member of several clandestine left-wing cells that had infiltrated the student movement. It was through the students' union at the university that she joined the Brazilian Communist Party, or PCB, where she handed out pamphlets at student assemblies with copies of *Voz Operária* [*The Worker's Voice*]. She left the party and joined the Dissidência da Guanabara, which changed its name in 1969 to Movimento Revolucionário 8 de Outubro, or MR-8, and was one of the groups responsible for the kidnapping of the United States ambassador Charles Elbrick. Although she herself was never anything more than a low-ranking militant, Gisa was nevertheless an activist, and, when she met Paulo, she was having an affair with a young architect from Pernambuco, Marcos Paraguassu de Arruda Câmara. He was the son of Diógenes de Arruda Câmara, a member of the elite in the Partido Comunista do Brasil, who had been in prison in Rio since 1968, and was himself a militant.

In spite of Paulo's scornful remark after their first meeting, over the next few days, the two met up again every night in the small bar next to the theatre school. A week later, he walked her back to the apartment where she lived with her brother, José Reinaldo, at Flamengo beach. She invited him up, and they listened to music and smoked cannabis until late. When her brother arrived home at two in the morning, he found them lying naked on the sitting-room carpet. Less than a month later, Gisa broke up with Marcos Paraguassu: she and Paulo had decided to live together. Paulo moved in three weeks later, once she had managed to get rid of her brother, and immediately proposed that they get married in a month and a half, on Christmas Eve. Gisa accepted, despite feeling slightly uncomfortable about the speed with which he had moved into her home and his habit of walking around the apartment naked.

Hoping perhaps that marriage would help her son to settle down, Paulo's mother reacted as warmly as she had with his previous girl-friends. Then, on 22 November, three months after they had met, Paulo recorded in his diary: 'Gisa is pregnant. It looks as though we're going to have a son.' The fact that the baby would be a boy born under the sign of Leo appears to have made him still more excited at the thought of fatherhood. 'My powers will be re-born with this son,' he wrote delight-edly. 'In the next eight months I'll redouble my energy and climb higher and higher.'

The dream lasted less than a week. After his initial excitement, Paulo began to feel a sense of horror whenever he thought of it, which was all the time. When reality dawned, and he saw that it would be absolute madness to have a child when he had no permanent employment and no means of supporting a family, the first person to be told of his decision was not Gisa but his mother. To Paulo's surprise, Lygia turned out to be not quite the committed Catholic when he told her that he was going to suggest to his girlfriend that she have an abortion. She agreed that having the child was not a good idea. Gisa resisted at first, before agreeing that she, too, was convinced that it would be irresponsible to have the baby. With the help of friends they found a clinic that specialized in clandestine abortions – abortion being a crime – and arranged the operation for 9 December 1971.

Neither managed to sleep the night before. In the morning, they got up in silence, had a bath and went in search of a taxi. They arrived at the clinic at seven on the dot, the time of the appointment. It was a surprise for them both when they saw that there were about thirty women there, the majority very young, and many with their husbands or boyfriends – all looking miserable. On arrival, each woman gave her name to the nurse, left a small pile of notes on the table – cheques were not accepted – and waited to be called. Although there were plenty of chairs, the majority preferred to stand. Five minutes later, Gisa was taken by another nurse to a staircase going up to the second floor. She left with her head bowed, without saying goodbye. In a matter of minutes, all the women had been called, with only a few men remaining in the waiting room.

Paulo sat on one of the chairs, took a notebook out of his bag and began to write – in a very small hand so that his partners in misfortune would not be able to read what he was writing. Whether knowingly or not, each tried to conceal his concern with some gesture or other. Paulo was constantly blinking; the man on his right would empty half the tobacco from his cigarette into the ashtray before lighting up; another kept flipping through a magazine, meanwhile staring into space. Despite his tic, Paulo did not appear to be nervous. He was, it was true, feeling an unpleasant sense of physical smallness, as though he had suddenly become a shrunken dwarf. Background music was coming from two loud-speakers, and although no one was really listening to it, they all kept time by tapping their feet or rattling their key rings. As he watched these move-ments, Paulo noted in his diary: 'They are all trying to keep their bodies as busy as possible and in the most varied ways, because their subcon-scious is clearly telling them: "Don't think about what's going on in there".' They all kept looking at the clock, and each time footsteps were heard, heads would turn toward the staircase. Occasionally, one would complain about how slowly time seemed to be passing. A small group tried to put aside their thoughts by talking quietly about football. Paulo merely observed and wrote:

A young man next to me is complaining about the delay and says that he's going to be late collecting his car from the garage. But I know he's not really like that. He's not thinking about his car, but he wants me to believe that so that he can play the part of the strong man. I smile and gaze into his neurones: there's his wife with her legs open, the doctor is inserting forceps, cutting, scraping and filling everything up with cotton wool once it's over. He knows that I know, turns the other way and is still, without looking at anything, breathing only deeply enough to stay alive.

At 8.30 in the morning, half the women had left and there was no sign of Gisa. Paulo went to the bar around the corner, had a coffee, smoked a cigarette and went back to the waiting room and his notebook, impatient and concerned that perhaps things were not going well for his girlfriend. An hour later, there was still no news. At 9.30 he put his hand in his pocket, hurriedly took out his fountain pen and wrote: 'I felt that it was now. My son returned to the eternity he had never left.'

Suddenly, no one knew from where, or why, they heard a sound that no one had really expected to hear in such a place: a loud, healthy baby's cry, followed immediately by a shout of surprise from a young lad in the waiting room: 'It's alive!'

For a moment, the men appeared to have been freed from the pain, misery and fear that united them in that gloomy room and they broke into a wild, collective burst of laughter. Just as the laughter stopped, Paulo heard footsteps: it was Gisa, returning from the operation, almost three hours after their arrival. Paler than he had ever seen her and with dark rings around her eyes, she looked very groggy and was still suffering from the effects of the anaesthetic. In the taxi on the way home, Paulo asked the driver to go slowly, 'because my girlfriend has cut her foot and it's hurting a lot'.

Gisa slept the whole afternoon and when she woke she couldn't stop crying. Sobbing, she told him that just as she was about to be anaesthetized, she had wanted to run out: 'The doctor put a thin tube inside me and took out a baby that was going to be born perfect. But now our son is rotting somewhere, Paulo ...'

Neither could sleep. It was late at night when she went slowly over to the desk where he was sitting writing and said: 'I hate to ask you this, but I've got to change the dressing and I think I'll manage to do it alone. But if it's very painful, can you come into the bathroom with me to help?'

He smiled and replied with a supportive 'Of course', but once the bathroom door was shut, Paulo begged St Joseph a thousand times to save him from that unpleasant task. 'Forgive me my cowardice, St Joseph,' he murmured, looking up, 'but changing that dressing would be too much for me. Too much! Too much!' To his relief, minutes later, she released him from that obligation and lay down on the bed again. Since leaving the abortion clinic, Gisa had only stopped crying when she fell asleep.

On the Saturday, Paulo took advantage of the fact that she seemed a little better and went off to do his teaching. When he got back in the evening, he found her standing at the bus stop in front of their building. The two returned home and only after much questioning from him did she confess what she had been doing in the street: 'I left the house to die.'

Paulo's reaction was astonishing. He immediately said: 'I'm really sorry I interrupted such an important process. If you've decided to die, then go ahead and kill yourself.'

Her courage had failed her, though.

On the third night without sleep, Gisa only opened her mouth to cry, while he could not stop talking. He explained carefully that she had no way out: after being called to Earth, the Angel of Death would only go back if he could take a soul with him. He said that there was no point in turning back, because the Angel would follow her for ever, and even if she didn't want to die now, he could kill her later, for example by letting her be run over. He recalled how he had faced the Angel when he was an adolescent and had cut the throat of a goat so that he would not have to hand over his own life. The way out was to stand up to the Angel: 'You need to challenge him. Do what you decided to do: try to kill yourself but hope that you'll escape with your life.'

When Gisa closed her eyes, exhausted, he went back to his diary, where he pondered the mad course of action he was proposing to his girlfriend:

I know that Gisa isn't going to die, but she doesn't know it and she can't live with that doubt. We have to give a reply to the Angel in some way or other. Some days ago, a friend of ours, Lola, slashed her whole body with a razor blade, but she was saved at the last moment. Lots of people have been attempting suicide recently. But few succeeded and that's good, because they escaped with their lives and managed to kill the person inside them whom they didn't like.

This macabre theory was not just the fruit of Paulo's sick imagination but had been scientifically proven by a psychiatrist whom he frequently visited, and whom he identified in his diary merely as 'Dr Sombra', or 'Dr Shadow'. The theory was that one should reinforce the patient's traumas. The doctor had told him quite categorically that no one is cured by conventional methods: 'If you're lost and think that the world is much stronger than you are,' he would say to his patients, 'then all that's left for you is suicide.' According to Paulo, this was precisely where the brilliance of his thesis lay: 'The subject leaves the consulting room completely devastated. It's only then that he realizes that he has nothing more to lose and he begins to do things that he would never have had the courage to do in other circumstances. All in all, Dr Sombra's method is really the only thing in terms of the subconscious that I have any real confidence in. It's cure by despair.'

When they woke the following day – a brilliant, sunny summer Sunday – Paulo did not need to try to convince Gisa any further. He realized this when she put on a swimsuit, took a bottle of barbiturates from the bathroom cupboard – he thought it was Orap, or pimozide, which he had been taking since his first admission to the clinic – and emptied the contents into her mouth, swallowing it all down with a glass of water. They went out together into the street, she stumbling as she walked, and proceeded down to the beach. Paulo stayed on the pavement while Gisa waded into the water, where she began swimming out to sea. Although he knew that with that amount of medication in her she would never have the strength to swim back, he waited, watching until she was just a black dot among the glittering waves, a black dot that was moving farther and farther away. 'I was scared, I wanted to give in, to call her, to tell her not to do it,' he wrote later, 'but I knew that Gisa wasn't going to die.'

Two men doing yoga on the beach went up to him, concerned that the girl was nearly out of sight, and said: 'We should call the lifeguard. The water's very cold and if she gets cramp she'll never get back.'

Paulo calmed them with a smile and a lie: 'No need, she's a professional swimmer.'

Half an hour later, when a group of people had begun to collect on the pavement, foreseeing a tragedy, Gisa began to swim back. When she reached the beach, pale and ghostly looking, she threw up, which probably saved her life, because she vomited up all the tablets. The muscles in her face and arms were stiff from the cold water and from the overdose. Paulo held her as they went to the house and then wrote the results of that 'cure by despair' in his diary:

> I'm thinking: Who's the Angel going to content himself with this time, now that Gisa is in my arms? She cried and was very tired, and of course she did still have eight tablets inside her. We came home, and she fell asleep on the carpet, but woke up looking quite different, with a new light in her eyes. For a while, we didn't go out for fear of contagion. The suicide epidemic was spreading like anything.

If anyone had looked through his diaries during the months prior to Gisa's attempted suicide, they would not have been surprised by Paulo's bizarre behaviour. Since reading Molinero's book, *The Secret Alchemy of Mankind*, he had become deeply immersed in the occult and in witchcraft. It was no longer just a matter of consulting gypsies, witch doctors and tarot readers. At one point, he had concluded that 'The occult is my only hope, the only visible escape'. As if he had put aside his dream of becoming a writer, he now concentrated all his energies on trying to 'penetrate deep into Magic, the last recourse and last exit for my despair'. He avidly devoured everything relating to sorcerers, witches and occult powers. On the bookshelves in the apartment he shared with Gisa, works by Borges and Henry Miller had given way to things such as *The Lord of Prophecy*, *The Book of the Last Judgement*, *Levitation* and *The Secret Power of the Mind*.

He would frequently visit Ibiapas, 100 kilometres from Rio, where he would take purifying baths of black mud administered by a man known as 'Pajé Katunda'.

It was on one such trip that Paulo first attributed to himself the ability to interfere with the elements. 'I asked for a storm,' he wrote, 'and the most incredible storm immediately blew up.' However, his supernatural powers did not always work. 'I tried to make the wind blow, without success,' he wrote a little later, 'and I ended up going home frustrated.' Another trick that failed was his attempt to destroy something merely by the power of thought: 'Yesterday Gisa and I tried to break an ashtray by the power of thought, but it didn't work. And then, would you believe it, straight afterwards, while we were having lunch here, the maid came to say that she had broken the ashtray. It was bizarre.'

Sects had also become an obsession with Paulo. It might be Children of God or Hare Krishnas, followers of the Devil's Bible or even the faithful of the Church of Satan, whom he had met on his trip to the United States. All it took was a whiff of the supernatural – or of sulphur, depending on the case. Not to mention the myriad groups of worshippers of creatures from outer space or UFO freaks. He became so absorbed in the esoteric world that he eventually received an invitation to write in a publication devoted to the subject, the magazine *A Pomba*. Published by PosterGraph, a small publishing house dedicated to underground culture and printing political posters, this contained a miscellany of articles and interviews on subjects of interest to hippie groups: drugs, rock, hallucinations and paranormal experiences. Printed in black and white, every issue carried a photographic essay involving some naked woman or other, just like men's magazines, the difference being that the models for *A Pomba* appeared to be women recruited from among the employees in the building where the magazine was produced. Like dozens of other, similar publications, *A Pomba* had no influence, although it must have had a reasonable readership, since it managed to survive for seven months. For half the salary he received at the school, Paulo accepted the position of jack-of-all-trades on the magazine: he would choose the subjects, carry out the interviews, write articles. The visual aspect – design, illustrations and photographs – was Gisa's job. It appears to have been a good idea, because after only two issues under Paulo's editorship, the owner of PosterGraph, Eduardo Prado, agreed to his proposal to launch a second publication, entitled *2001*. With two publications to take care of, his salary doubled, and he had to give up teaching.

While he was doing research for an article on the Apocalypse, it was suggested to Paulo that he should go and see someone who called himself 'the heir of the Beast in Brazil', Marcelo Ramos Motta. He was surprised to find that the person he was to interview lived in a simple, austere apartment with good furniture and bookcases crammed with books. There was just one eccentric detail: all the books were covered with the same grey paper, without any indication as to the content apart from a small handwritten number at the foot of the spine. The other surprise was Motta's appearance. He wasn't wearing a black cloak and brandishing a trident, as Paulo had expected, but instead had on a smart navy-blue suit, white shirt, silk tie and black patent-leather shoes. He was sixteen years older than Paulo, tall and thin, with a thick black beard, and a very strange look in his eye. His voice sounded as if he were trying to imitate someone. He did not smile, but merely made a sign with his hand for the interviewer to sit down, and then sat down opposite him.

Paulo took his notepad out of his bag and, to break the ice, asked: 'Why are all the books covered in grey paper?'

The man did not appear in the mood for small talk and said: 'That's none of your business.'

Startled by his rudeness, Paulo began to laugh: 'I'm sorry, I didn't mean to offend you. I was just curious.'

Motta continued in the same vein: 'This is no matter for children.'

When the interview was over, Paulo wrote and published his article, but he couldn't stop thinking about that strange man and his library of books with blank spines. After several refusals, Motta agreed to meet him again and this time he opened the conversation by saying: 'I'm the world leader of a society called AA – Astrum Argentum.' He got to his feet, picked up a copy of The Beatles' record *Sgt. Pepper's Lonely Hearts Club Band* and pointed out one of the figures on the crowded collage on the cover. This was a bald, elderly man, the second along in the photo, next to an Indian guru: 'This man is called Aleister Crowley, and we are the proponents of his ideas in the world. Go and find out about him, and then we'll talk again.'

It was only after searching through libraries and second-hand book-shops that Paulo discovered that there were very few books available in Brazil about the old man on the cover of The Beatles' album, lost among the images of Mae West, Mahatma Gandhi, Hitler, Jesus Christ and Elvis Presley. While he was preparing to go back to speak to the mysterious Motta, he continued to produce the two magazines with Gisa. Since the budget was not enough to take on even one collaborator, he wrote almost everything. So that the readers would not realize what a tiny budget the magazines had to survive on, he used a variety of pseudonyms as well as his own name.

At the beginning of 1972, a stranger appeared in the office, which was a modest room on the tenth floor of a commercial building in the centre of Rio de Janeiro. He was wearing a shiny suit – one of those crease-resistant ones – and a thin tie, and carried an executive briefcase, and he announced that he wanted to talk to 'the writer Augusto Figueiredo'. At the time, Paulo did not connect the visitor with the person who had phoned him some days earlier, also asking for Augusto Figueiredo. It was enough to awaken his dormant paranoia. The man had the look of a policeman and must have come there after a tip-off, looking for drugs, perhaps. The problem was that Augusto Figueiredo did not exist; it was one of the names Paulo used to sign his articles.

Terrified, but trying to appear calm, he attempted to get rid of the visitor as quickly as possible, saying: 'Augusto isn't here. Do you want to leave a message?'

'No. I need to talk to him. Can I sit and wait for him?'

The man was definitely a policeman. He sat at a table, picked up an old copy of *A Pomba*, lit a cigarette and started to read, with the air of someone with all the time in the world. An hour later, he was still there. He had read every past copy of the magazine, but showed no sign of wanting to leave. Paulo recalled the lesson he had learned as a child, when jumping off the bridge into the river: the best way to curtail suffering was to face the problem head on. He decided to tell the truth – for he was absolutely certain this man was a policeman. First, though, he took the precaution of going through all the drawers in the office to make sure that there were no butts left over from cannabis joints.

He summoned up his courage and, blinking nervously, confessed that he had lied: 'You must forgive me, but there is no Augusto Figueiredo here. I'm the person who wrote the article, Paulo Coelho. What can I do for you?'

The visitor smiled broadly, held out his arms as if about to embrace him and said: 'Well, you're the person I want to talk to, man. How do you do? My name is Raul Seixas.'

CHAPTER 14

The Devil and Paulo

APART FROM THEIR INTEREST in flying saucers and having both been disastrous students during their adolescence, Raul Seixas and Paulo Coelho appeared to have little in common. Seixas was working as a music producer for a multinational recording company, CBS; his hair was always tidy and he was never seen without a jacket, tie and briefcase. He had never tried drugs, not even a drag on a cannabis joint. Coelho's hair, meanwhile, was long and unruly, and he wore hipsters, sandals, necklaces, and spectacles with octagonal purple lenses. He also spent much of his time under the influence of drugs. Seixas had a fixed address, and was a real family man, with a daughter, Simone, aged two, while Paulo lived in 'tribes' whose members came and went according to the seasons – in recent months his 'family' had been Gisa and Stella Paula, a pretty hippie from Ipanema who was as fascinated as he was by the occult and the beyond.

The differences between the two men were even more marked when it came to their cultural baggage. At twenty-five, Paulo had read and given stars to more than five hundred books, and he wrote articulately and fluently. As for Raul, despite having spent his childhood surrounded by his father's books – his father worked on the railways and was an occasional poet – he didn't seem particularly keen on reading. However, one date in their lives had different meanings but was equally important to each of them. On 28 June 1967, when Paulo was drugged and taken to the ninth floor of the Dr Eiras clinic for his third admission, Seixas was twenty-two and getting married to the American student Edith Wisner in Salvador, Bahia, where he was born. Both believed in astrology, and if they had studied their respective astrological charts they would have seen that the zodiac predicted one certain thing: the two were destined to make a lot of money, whatever they did.

When Raul Seixas entered his life, Paulo Coelho was immersed in the hermetic and dangerous universe of satanism. He had begun meeting Marcelo Ramos Motta more frequently and, after devouring weighty volumes on pentacles, mystical movements, magical systems and astrology, he could understand a little of the work of the bald man on The Beatles' LP cover. Born in Leamington Spa, England, on 12 October 1875, Aleister Crowley was twenty-three when he reported that he had encountered in Cairo a being who transmitted to him the *Liber AL vel Legis* [*The Book of the Law*], which was his first and most important work on mysticism, the central sacred text of Thelema.

The Law of Thelema proclaimed the beginning of an era in which man would be free to realize all his desires. This was the objective contained in the epigraph 'Do what thou wilt shall be the whole of the Law', which was considered the basic rule of conduct by Crowley's followers. Among the instruments recommended to achieve this state were sexual freedom, the use of drugs and the rediscovery of oriental wisdom. In 1912, Crowley entered the sect known as Ordo Templi Orientis (OTO), a Masonic, mystical, magical type of organization of which he soon became the head and the principal theorist. He called himself 'the Beast', and built a temple in Cefalu, in Sicily, but was expelled from Italy by the Mussolini government in 1923, accused of promoting orgies. During the Second World War, Crowley was summoned by the writer Ian Fleming, creator of James Bond and an officer in British Naval Intelligence, to help the British consider how superstitions and mysticism among the Nazi leaders could be put to good use by the Allies. It was also Aleister Crowley who, through Fleming, suggested to Winston Churchill that he should use the V for Victory sign, which was, in fact, a sign of

Apophis-Typhon, a god of destruction capable of overwhelming the energies of the Nazi swastika.

In the world of music it was not only The Beatles who became, in their case only briefly, Thelemites, which was the name given to Crowley's followers. His satanic theories attracted various rock artists and groups such as Black Sabbath, The Clash, Iron Maiden and Ozzy Osbourne (who wrote the classic 'Mr Crowley'). The famous Boleskine House, where Crowley lived for several years, later became the property of Jimmy Page, the Led Zeppelin guitarist. But the English Beast's ideas also inspired terrible tragedies: in August 1969, his American disciple Charles Manson headed the massacre of four people who were shot, stabbed and clubbed to death in a mansion in Malibu. Among the victims was the actress Sharon Tate, aged twenty-six, who was expecting a baby by her husband, the director Roman Polanski.

Paulo appeared to be so influenced by these readings and supernatural practices that not even the atrocities committed by Manson brought him back down to earth. The murderer of Sharon Tate was described as 'the most evil man on Earth' by the jury that condemned him to death, although this sentence was subsequently commuted to life imprisonment. When he read the news, Paulo wrote in his diary: 'The weapons of war nowadays are the strangest you can find. Drugs, religion, fashion ... It's something against which it's impossible to fight. When looked at like this, Charles Manson is a crucified martyr.'

Until he met Paulo Coelho, Raul Seixas had never heard of Crowley or of the nomenclature used by those people. He knew nothing about Astrum Argentum, OTO or *Liber Oz*. He liked reading about flying saucers, but the main object of his interest had always been music, and more precisely rock and roll, a musical genre with which Paulo had only a glancing relationship – he liked Elvis Presley, knew the most famous groups and that was it. Seixas's passion for rock music had meant he had to repeat his second year at São Bento College in Salvador three times, and at eighteen he had had some success in performances in Bahia as leader of the group Os Panteras – The Panthers. However, at the insistence of his future father-in-law, an American Protestant pastor, he abandoned his promising musical career and returned to his studies. He made up for lost time with a revision course, and when he took his entrance exams for the law faculty, he was among the top entrants. 'I just wanted to prove to people, to my family, how easy it was to study and pass exams,' he said many years later, 'when for me it wasn't important in the least.' During the first months of his marriage, he supported the family by giving guitar and English lessons. Before he was even three months into his marriage, though, Seixas succumbed to temptation.

In October 1967, the singer Jerry Adriani went to Salvador after being hired for a show at the smart Bahian Tennis Club, where the muse of bossa nova, Nara Leão, was also performing, along with the comedian Chico Anysio. Adriani was, by then, regarded as a national star among the youth music movement, Jovem Guarda, but dismissed by more sophisticated audiences as tacky. On the day of the show, a tennis club employee told the singer that his performance had been cancelled: 'The group you've hired has got several black musicians in it, and no blacks are allowed in the club.'

Although the Afonso Arinos law had been in place since 1951, making racial discrimination a crime, 'Blacks didn't enter the Club even through the kitchen door', in the words of the song 'Tradição', by another famous Bahian, Gilberto Gil. This prejudice was even harsher here, since this was a club in Bahia, a state where more than 70 per cent of the population were black and of mixed race. Instead of calling the police, the show's impresario chose to hire another group. The first he could think of were the defunct Os Panteras, who in the past few months had changed their name to The Panthers. Seixas was thrilled at the idea of reviving the group and went off into the city to look for his old accompanists: the bassist Mariano Lanat, the guitarist Perinho Albuquerque and the drummer Antônio Carlos Castro, or Carleba – all of them white. The show was a great success, and Os Panteras left the stage to loud applause. At the end of the show, Nara Leão whispered in Jerry Adriani's ear: 'That group are really good. Why don't you ask them to play with you?'

When, that evening, he received an invitation from the singer for the group to go with him on a tour of the north and the northeast, due to start the following week, Seixas was thrilled. An invitation to tour with a nationally famous artist such as Jerry Adriani wasn't one that was likely to come around twice. However, he also knew that accepting the proposal would be the end of his marriage, and that was too high a cost.

He said he was sorry, but he had to refuse: 'It would be an honour to go on tour with you, but if I leave home now, my marriage will be finished.'

Jerry Adriani doubled the stakes: 'If that's the problem, then problem solved: your wife is invited too. Bring her with you.'

As well as giving the couple a rather amusing, unusual honeymoon, the tour was so successful that when it ended, Jerry Adriani convinced Raul and his musicians to move to Rio and turn professional, and at the beginning of 1968 they were all in Copacabana. This adventure did not end happily. Although they managed to record one LP of their own, in the years that followed, the only work that came their way was playing as a backing group to Adriani. There were times when Seixas had to ask his father for a loan to pay the rent on the house where he, Edith and the other members of the group were living. Going back to Bahia because they had run out of money was a very hard thing to do, particularly for Raul, the leader of the group, but there was no other solution. Much against his will, he started giving English lessons again and was beginning to think that his musical career was over when a proposal came from Evandro Ribeiro, the director of CBS, to return to work in Rio, not as a band leader but as a music producer. His name had been suggested to the management of the record company by Jerry Adriani, who was interested in getting his friend back on the Rio–São Paulo circuit, which was the centre of Brazilian music production. Wanting to get even with the city that had defeated him, Seixas did not think twice. He asked Edith to organize the move and, a few days later, he was working, in jacket and tie, in the polluted city centre of Rio, where the CBS offices were. Within a few months, he had become music producer to various well-known artists, starting with Adriani.

At the end of May 1972, Raul had walked the seven blocks between the CBS building and the offices of *A Pomba* not merely to praise the non-existent Augusto Figueiredo's writings on extraterrestrials. He had in his briefcase an article that he himself had written on flying saucers and wanted to know if *A Pomba* might be interested in publishing it. Paulo politely accepted it, said that he would indeed be happy to publish the article, and drew him out on the subject of UFOs and life on other planets. He had an ulterior motive for this. The mention of CBS had sparked a rather more materialistic interest: since Raul enjoyed the magazine and was an executive in a multinational, he might well be persuaded to place advertisements for CBS in *A Pomba*. The short meeting ended with Raul inviting Paulo to dinner at his house the following night, a Thursday. At the time, Coelho never took any decision without consulting his 'family', Gisa and their flatmate, Stella Paula. Even something as banal as whether or not to go to someone's house was subjected to a vote: 'We had a truly ideological discussion in that tiny hippie group to decide whether or not we should go and have a drink at Raul's house.'

Even though he realized that, apart from an interest in UFOs, the two appeared to have nothing in common, Paulo, with one eye on the possibility of getting some advertising revenue from CBS, decided to accept the invitation. Gisa went with him, while Stella Paula, who was outvoted, felt no obligation to go along as well. On that Thursday evening, on his way to supper, Paulo stopped at a record shop and bought an LP of Bach's Organ Preludes. The bus taking them from Flamengo to Jardim de Alah – a small, elegant district between Ipanema and Leblon, in the south of Rio, where Raul lived – was stopped at a police checkpoint. Since the crackdown by the dictatorship in December 1968, such checks had become part of life for Brazilians in the large cities. However, when Gisa saw the police get on the bus and start asking the passengers to show their papers, she felt it was a bad sign, a warning, and threatened to call off the meeting. Paulo, however, would not be moved, and at eight that evening, as agreed, they rang the bell of Raul's apartment.

The meeting lasted three hours. When he left, the obsessive Paulo stopped at the first bar they came to and scribbled on the cover of his Bach LP every detail of their visit to the man he still referred to as 'the guy'. Every blank space on the record cover was taken up with tiny, almost illegible writing:

We were greeted by his wife, Edith, and a little girl who must have been three at most. It was all very respectable, very proper. They brought in little dishes with canapés … It's years since I've eaten in someone's house where they had little dishes with canapés. Canapés, how ridiculous!

So then the guy comes in: 'Would you like a whisky?'

Well, of course we wanted a whisky! A rich man's drink. Dinner was hardly over and Gisa and I were desperate to leave.

Then Raul said: 'Oh, I wanted to play you some of my music.'

Oh, shit, we were going to have to listen to music as well. All I wanted was to get some advertising out of him. We went into the maid's room and he picked up his guitar and played some marvellous music. When he finished, the guy said to me: 'You wrote that stuff on flying saucers, didn't you? Well, I'm planning on going back to being a singer. Would you like to write some lyrics for me?'

I thought: Write lyrics? Me write lyrics for this guy who's never touched drugs in his life! Never put a joint in his mouth. Not even an ordinary cigarette. Anyway, we were just leaving and I hadn't yet mentioned the advertisement. I plucked up courage and asked: 'Since we're going to publish your article, do you think you could manage to get an advertisement for CBS in the magazine?'

Imagine my astonishment when he said that he had resigned from CBS that very day: 'I'm moving to Philips because I'm going to follow my dream. I wasn't born to be a manager, I want to be a singer.'

At that moment I understood: I'm the conventional one, this guy deserves the greatest respect. A guy who leaves a job that gives him everything, his daughter, his wife, his maid, his family, his canapés! I left feeling really impressed with the guy.

Gisa's premonitions were not entirely unfounded. She had mistaken the year, but not the date. While it marked Paulo's first step in the direction of one of his dreams – fame – 25 May was, by coincidence, going to be a crucial date, a watershed in his life: the day chosen by destiny, some years later, for his first appointment with the Devil, a ceremony he was preparing for when he met Raul Seixas. Under Marcelo Ramos Motta's guidance he felt he was a disciple of the Beast's battalions. He was determined to immerse himself in the malignant forces that had seduced Lennon and Charles Manson, and began the process by being accepted into the OTO as a 'probationer', the lowest rank in the sect's hierarchy. He was fortunate that his guide was not Motta but another militant in the organization, a graduate employee of Petrobras, Euclydes Lacerda de Almeida, whose magical name was Frater Zaratustra, or Frater Z, and who lived in Paraíba do Sul, 150 kilometres from Rio. 'I received a letter, rude as ever, from Marcelo,' Paulo wrote to Frater Z when he heard the news. 'I'm forbidden from contacting him except through you.' It was a relief to have a well-educated man like Euclydes as his instructor rather than the uncouth Marcelo Motta, who treated all his subordinates appallingly. Extracts from letters sent to militants of the OTO by Parzival XI (as Motta self-importantly called himself) show that Paulo was being quite restrained when describing the leader of the followers of the Devil as 'rude':

I'd prefer you not to write to me any more. If you do, send a stamped, addressed envelope for the reply – or you won't get a reply.

[…] Be aware of just where you are on the vertebrate scale, monkey!

[…] If you're incapable of getting up on your own two legs and looking for the Way through your own efforts then stay on all fours and howl like the dog you are!

[…] You're no more than a drop of shit on the end of the monkey's cock.

[…] If suddenly your favourite son, or you, were to fall ill with a fatal disease that required an expensive operation and you could only use OTO money, then rather let your son die, or die yourself, than touch the money.

[…] You haven't seen anything yet. Wait until your name is known as a member of the OTO. The Army's secret service, the CIA, Shin-Beth [Israeli military intelligence], the Russians, the Chinese and innumerable Roman priests disguised as members of the sect will try to get in contact with you.

On at least two occasions Paulo's name appears in correspondence from Parzival XI to Euclydes. In the first, one gets the impression that Paulo will be working on the publication by Editora Três, in São Paulo, of the book *The Equinox of the Gods*, by Crowley and translated into Portuguese by Motta: 'I got in touch with Editora Três through their representative in Rio, and we shall soon see whether or not they're going to publish *Equinox of the Gods*. Paulo Coelho is young, enthusiastic and imaginative, but it's too early for us to assume that they really will publish the book.' In the second, Euclydes is castigated for having told Paulo too much and too soon about Parzival XI's power: 'Paulo Coelho said that you told him I destroyed the Masons in Brazil. You talk too much. Even if it were true, Paulo Coelho doesn't have the magical maturity to understand how these things are done, which is why he's confused.'

At the time, Paulo had had his own experiences of being in contact with the Devil. Some months before getting to know Motta and the OTO, during one of his regular anxiety crises, he was full of complaints. The reasons were many, but behind them lay the usual fact: he was nearly twenty-five and still just a nobody, without the remotest chance of becoming a famous writer. The situation seemed hopeless and the pain this time was such that, instead of asking for help from the Virgin Mary or St Joseph as he usually did, he decided to make a pact with the Prince of Darkness. If the Devil gave him the power to realize all his dreams, Paulo would give him his soul in exchange. 'As an educated man who knows the philosophical principles that govern the world, humanity and the Cosmos,' Paulo wrote in his diary, 'I know perfectly well that the Devil does not signify Evil, but just one of the poles in the equilibrium of humanity.' Using a fountain pen with red ink ('the colour of this supernatural being'), he began to write out his pact in the form of a letter to the Devil. In the first line he made it clear that he was setting out the conditions and was not willing to deal with intermediaries:

> You have wanted this for a long time. I felt that You were beginning to close the circle around me and I know that You are stronger than I am. You are more interested in buying my soul than I am in selling it. Whatever the case, I need to have an idea of the price that You are

going to pay me. For this reason, from today, 11 November 1971, until 18 November, I'm going to do an experiment. I will speak directly to You, the King of the Other Pole.

In order to confirm this agreement he took a flower out of a vase and crushed it, at the same time proposing to Satan a kind of spectral test: 'I'm going to crush this flower and eat it. From now on, for the next seven days, I'm going to do everything I want and I'm going to get what I want, because You will be helping me. If I'm satisfied with the results, I will give You my soul. If a ritual is necessary, I take it upon myself to carry it out.'

As a proof of good faith, Paulo promised the Devil that, during this experimental period, he would reciprocate by not praying to or saying the names of those considered sacred by the Catholic Church. But he did make it clear that this was a test, not a lifelong contract. 'I retain the right to go back,' he went on, still in red, 'and I want to add that I'm only doing this because I find myself in such a state of complete despair.'

The agreement lasted less than an hour. He closed his notebook, and went out to have a cigarette and walk along the beach. When he returned home, he was deathly pale, terrified at the mad thing he had done. He opened his notebook again and wrote in capital letters that took up the whole page:

PACT CANCELLED
I OVERCAME TEMPTATION!

Paulo felt sure that he had tricked the Devil, but this ruse did not work for long. Although he and the Devil did not meet this time, he continued to invoke the spirit of evil in his articles for *A Pomba* and in a new enterprise in which he had become involved, the storyboards for comic strips. Beings from the Beyond created by him were brought to life in Gisa's drawings and began to illustrate the pages of the magazine. The positive reaction to the series *Os Vampiristas*, which told of the troubles and adventures of a small, peaceful solitary vampire, convinced Gisa to send her work to King Features, an American agency that distributed comic strips, but she received no reply. The couple did, though, manage to get some of their work into two of the main daily Rio newspapers, *O Jornal* and *Jornal do Brasil*, creating a special cartoon about the little vampire for the latter's children's supplement, which came out on Sundays. They also created a highly popular character, Curingão, whose image was used on lottery tickets. From time to time, one of their comic strips even appeared in *Pasquim*, the magazine favoured by the Rio intelligentsia.

A Pomba was managing to survive with almost no advertising revenue and even achieved sales of 20,000, a real achievement in the tiny counterculture market; however, by the middle of 1972, it was heavily in debt, and looked set to take *2001* down with it. When the publisher, Eduardo Prado, announced that he was thinking of closing both publications, Paulo and Gisa moved to the newspaper *Tribuna da Imprensa*, where they produced a whole page that was published on Saturdays and given the name of the magazine that had died after only two issues – *2001*.

This change of medium was another step towards their work emerging from the subworld of flying saucers, elves and sorcerers to reach a wider public. Although in comparison with the other Rio dailies, *Tribuna* didn't publish many copies, it had earned respect as a fighter. It had been founded in 1949 by the journalist Carlos Lacerda in order to combat the ideas, the supporters and the future government of President Getúlio Vargas (1951–54) and now, under the editorship of Hélio Fernandes, it was the favourite target for the military dictatorship's censors. The arrival of Paulo and Gisa in the old building on Rua do Lavradio, near Lapa, coincided with the most repressive period in the entire history of the dictatorship, and this was reflected in the daily life of the paper. For three years, the offices of *Tribuna* had been visited every night by army officers, who would read everything and then decide what could and could not be published. According to Hélio Fernandes, a fifth of their daily output was thrown in the rubbish bin by the censors. He himself was an example of what happened to those targeted by the regime's violence, for he had been arrested no fewer than twenty-seven times since 1964 and imprisoned twice. However, since the military were not too concerned about alchemy and the supernatural, the page produced by Paulo and Gisa remained untouched.

The visibility they achieved in the paper encouraged Paulo to go to the advertising department of Petrobras and show them a comic strip he and Gisa had created to be handed out at their petrol stations.

The man they met had approved the idea, but then Paulo, eager to make the project a success, said: 'Just so that there's no risk to Petrobras, we can work for free for the first month.'

The man turned round and said: 'For free? Sorry, but you're clearly a real amateur. Here no one does anything for free. Go and do a bit more work and try again when you're a professional.'

In August, while he was still smarting from this rejection, Paulo received an invitation to go with his mother and maternal grandmother, Lilisa, for a three-week trip to Europe. He was heavily into his journalistic work, and hesitated before agreeing, but then it wasn't every day that one was invited on a trip to Europe with all expenses paid. Added to this, he could leave several cartoons ready, as well as the *Tribuna* page, for Gisa to illustrate and design while he was away, since his mother's invitation did not include his girlfriend. During the twenty-one day trip, which started in Nice and ended in Paris, with stops in Rome, Milan, Amsterdam and London, Paulo visited museums, ruins and cathedrals. Apart from two or three occasions in Amsterdam, when he escaped his mother's vigilance in order to smoke a joint, the trip meant that he went almost a month without his daily intake of drugs.

Having been brought up by a methodical, obsessive mother, Paulo was furious with what he found when he arrived home. He wrote: 'The house is a complete tip, which really annoyed me. It hasn't even been swept. The electricity bill hasn't been paid, nor has the rent. The page for *Tribuna* hasn't been handed in, which is utterly irresponsible. I'm so upset by all this that I have nothing else to say.'

However, not everything was bad. While he was away, a tempting invitation had arrived in the post. Professor Glória Albues, who worked for the education department in Mato Grosso, had finally organized a project that the two had thought up when they had met up in Rio. The idea was that Paulo would spend three weeks every two months in three cities in Mato Grosso – Campo Grande, Três Lagoas (now in Mato Grosso do Sul, a state that did not exist at the time) and Cuiabá – teaching a course in theatre and education for teachers and pupils in state schools. The salary was tempting – 1,500 cruzeiros a month, which was double what he earned on *A Pomba* and *2001*. There was another reason that led Paulo to exchange the delights of Rio for the inhospitable lands of Mato Grosso. When the idea for the course had first come up, he hadn't been involved with the OTO, but now, eager to spread Crowley's ideas, the thought came to him: Why not change the course into a black magic workshop?

CHAPTER 15

Paulo and Raul

EITHER ALONE OR WITH GISA, who was following him on his journey to satanism, Paulo began to try out some so-called magical exercises. One he frequently performed consisted in going to a park to pick a leaf of *Sansevieria trifasciata*, a plant with hard, pointed leaves, popularly known in English as mother-in-law's tongue and in Brazil as St George's sword. Performed in public, this exercise was likely to expose the novice to a certain amount of ridicule, since it was then necessary to walk ten steps holding the plant as though it were a real sword, turn towards the setting sun and then bow to the four points of the compass, pointing the 'sword' at each and shouting at the top of one's voice: 'Strength lies in the West!' Each step to the left was accompanied by a roar, with eyes raised heavenwards: 'Knowledge lies in the South! Protection lies in the East! Victory lies in the North!'

He would then take the leaf home, where he would cut it into eleven pieces (eleven being the Thelemites' magic number) with a penknife or an ordinary knife that he had previously thrust into the ground, and then heated over a fire and washed in sea water. After this he would arrange the eleven pieces on the kitchen table to form the symbol of Mars – a circle topped by a small arrow, which also represents the male sex – while boiling up some water in a saucepan. He would then mix the pieces up with the torn petals of two yellow roses and add them to the boiling water. The entire ceremony had to be performed so that the thick, viscous liquid thus produced would be ready at precisely eleven at night, which, according to the *Liber Oz*, is the hour of the Sun. He would then add it to his bath water, in which he would immerse himself until midnight, the hour of Venus. After performing one such ceremony, Paulo dried himself and wrote in his diary, with the house in almost total darkness and his notebook lit just by a single candle:

> I realize that this ritual might appear naive. It lasted in total almost two hours. But all I can say is that for the greater part of the time I was in touch with a different dimension, where things are interconnected in the Laws (Second Causes). I can feel the mechanism, but I am not yet able to understand it. Nor can I rationalize the mechanism. I feel only that intuition works in close conjunction with rationalization and that these two spheres almost touch each other. Something leads me to believe that the Devil really does exist.

Another ceremony he frequently performed was the so-called Ritual of the Lesser Pentagram, which involved spreading out on the floor a white sheet on which one had to paint a green five-pointed star. The star was surrounded by a length of twine dipped in sulphur, with which Paulo would draw the symbol of Mars. He would turn off all the lights, and then hang a lamp from the ceiling, immediately above the centre of the pentagram, so that it created a column of light. With sword in hand and completely naked, he would turn to the south, step into the middle of the sheet and adopt the 'Dragon pose' – a yoga position in which the person crouches on the floor with one leg forward and the other back – and then jump up and down like a toad while repeating invocations to the Devil. On one of these occasions, the ceremony ended very strangely, as he recorded in his diary:

> After half an hour, my personal problems began seriously to interfere with my concentration, thus wasting a great deal of energy. I

changed from the Dragon pose to the Ibis pose, finally crouching in the centre of the circle, shaking my body. This made me sexually excited and I ended up masturbating, even though I was only thinking about the column of light over the circle. I ejaculated into the column of light in several successive spasms. This brought me a feeling of total confirmation. Obviously I felt very guilty while I was masturbating, but this soon passed, so profound was my state of ecstasy.

It was during this time that Paulo was preparing for his first stay in Mato Grosso. He left various texts and storyboards ready for *Tribuna* and the other publications he was working for and typed out a programme for the course. Anyone not in the know would have had difficulty identifying any magical or satanic content. 'I used this trick on purpose, so that no one would realize,' he confessed years later, 'because I knew it was an act of supreme irresponsibility to use magical techniques and rituals in order to give classes to teachers and adolescents ... There I was performing black magic: I was using them without their knowledge, innocently, for my own magical experiments.' Before leaving, Paulo asked permission from Frater Zaratustra to use Hermes Trismegistus' *Emerald Tablet* on the course. This was a text containing such statements as: 'By this means wilt thou partake of the honours of the whole world. And Darkness will fly from thee', and 'With this thou wilt be able to overcome all things and transmute all that is fine and all that is coarse.'

Unaware that they were to be used as guinea pigs in the experiments of a satanic sect, the people of Mato Grosso received him with open arms. The local press heralded his arrival at each of the towns participating in the project with praise, hyperbole and even a pinch of fantasy. After comparing him with Plínio Marcos and Nelson Rodrigues, two of the greatest names in Brazilian drama, the Campo Grande *Diário da Serra* congratulated the government for having invited Paulo to bring to Mato Grosso a course 'that was crowned with success in Rio de Janeiro, Belém do Pará and Brasília'. The treatment conferred on him by the *Jornal do Povo*, in Três Lagoas, was even more lavish:

Now it's the turn of Três Lagoas. We have the opportunity to experience one of the great names in Brazilian theatre: Paulo Coelho. He
may not look it, but Paulo Coelho is a great man! The prototype of
concrete art, in which everything is strong, structured and growing ...
Such a figure could not help but be noticed, and that is what drives
him on and what makes of him a natural communicator. While not
wishing to exaggerate, we could compare him symbolically with
Christ, who also came to create.

He had not received such reverential attention since Aracaju, when he
had plagiarized an article by Carlos Heitor Cony. Cast in the role of full-
time missionary, Paulo took advantage of his few free hours to become
still more steeped in mysticism, and it didn't much matter to him how he
gained access to this mysterious world. In Três Lagoas, 'with the help of
a Tibetan who is there fulfilling a mission', he went to the headquarters
of the Brazilian Society of Eubiosis, a group that argued for living in
harmony with nature, and also the Masonic lodge of the Grand Order of
Brazil. When he learned that there was a village of acculturated Indians
on the edge of the city, he decided to visit them in order to find out about
native witchcraft. After his three weeks were up, he recorded the first
results of his time there:

At the beginning my work with the *Emerald Tablet* was a real disappointment. No one really understood how it worked (not even me,
despite all the workshops and improvisations I had done). All the
same the seed was sown in the minds of the students and some of
them really changed their way of thinking and began to think in
different ways. One female pupil went into a trance during a class.
The vast majority reacted negatively and the work only took on
some meaning on the last day of the classes when I managed one
way or another to break down their emotional barriers. Obviously,
I'm talking about a purely theatrical use of the *Tablet*. Perhaps if the
last day had been the first I could have done something interesting
with them.

Ah, before I forget: one day, I went for a walk in the city to collect
some plants (I had just finished reading Paracelsus and was going to
perform a ceremony) and I saw a cannabis plant growing outside a
branch of the Bank of Brazil. Imagine that!

On his return to Rio, Paulo learned from a colleague at *Tribuna* that the
editorial team at *O Globo* was looking for staff. The idea of writing for
what claimed to be 'the greatest newspaper in the country' was very
tempting, and he managed to arrange an interview with Iran Frejat, the
much-feared editor. If he got a job there, he would have at his disposal a
fantastic means of spreading the ideals of the OTO. Several times in his
correspondence with Frater Zaratustra he had suggested allowing the
weekly page in *Tribuna* to be used by the sect, but they had never asked
him to do so. When he told Raul Seixas of his interest in a position at *O
Globo*, his friend tried to dissuade him from the idea, again suggesting a
musical partnership: 'Forget it. Don't go and work for some newspaper,
let's write music. TV Globo are going to re-record *Beto Rockefeller* [an
innovative and very successful soap opera that was shown on the now
defunct TV Tupi from 1968 to 1969] and they've asked me to write the
soundtrack. Why don't we do it together? I'll write the music and you can
write the lyrics.'

While Paulo was still torn between the supernatural and the need to
earn a living, Raul was building his career as a singer, devoting himself
entirely to music. He had an LP on sale – *Sociedade da Grã Ordem
Kavernista*, which was recorded almost secretly at CBS a few weeks before
he resigned – and he was getting ready for the seventh International Song
Festival being put on by Rede Globo. For Paulo, accepting a partnership
would mean going back to poetry, which he had sworn never to do. For
the moment at least the position at *O Globo* seemed more achievable and
this was what he was going to try for.

He turned up at the appointed time for his interview with Frejat,
introduced himself to the chief reporter, who appeared to be in a very
bad mood, and sat down in a corner of the office waiting to be called.
Before leaving home, he had put a book of poems by St John of the
Cross in his bag to help take his mind off things while waiting. At two in

the afternoon, an hour after he had arrived, Frejat had still not even so much as glanced at him, although he had walked past him several times, giving orders and handing out papers to various desks. Paulo stood up, got himself a coffee, lit a cigarette and sat down again. When the clock showed three he lost patience. He ripped the pages out of the book he was reading, tore them into tiny pieces, gathered them up and deposited them on Frejat's desk.

This unexpected gesture caught the journalist by surprise, and he burst out laughing and said: 'What's up, boy? Have you gone mad?'

Paulo said quietly, but forcefully: 'I've been waiting for two hours – didn't you notice? Are you behaving like this just because I want a job? That's so disrespectful!'

Frejat's response was a surprising one: 'Oh, I'm sorry. I didn't realize you were here for the job. Well, let's give you a test. If you pass it, the job's yours. You can start now. Go to the Santa Casa and count the dead.'

The dead? Yes, one of his daily tasks would be to go to the Santa Casa de Misericórdia and to two other large hospitals in Rio to get lists of the names of the dead, which would then appear on the newspaper's obituary pages the following day. In spite of his previous experience on *Diário de Notícias* and *Tribuna*, he was going to start at *O Globo* as a cub reporter. As a trainee, on the lowest rung of the ladder, he would work seven hours a day, with one day off a week, for a salary of 1,200 cruzeiros a month – some US$408. His first weeks at the paper were spent on 'reports on still lives', or 'coverage of a pacifist demonstration' as he called his daily visits to the city's mortuaries. The famous, such as politicians and artists, were the domain of the more experienced reporters, who would write obituaries or 'memorials'. When this macabre daily round finished early he would go to the red light district of Mangue to chat to the prostitutes.

Although he didn't have a formal contract, which was the case with the majority of cub reporters on most Brazilian newspapers (meaning that they had no form of social security), he could have his meals at *O Globo*'s very cheap canteen. For a mere 6 cruzeiros – US$1.75 – he could have lunch or dinner in the canteen, along with the owner of *O Globo*, Roberto Marinho. A few days after meeting Marinho in the canteen queue, Paulo learned from Frejat that 'Dr Roberto', as he was known, had issued an ultimatum: either Paulo cut his hair, which at the time was down to his shoulders, or he need not return to the office. Working on *O Globo* was more important than having long hair, and so he gave in to the demand without protest and trimmed his black mane.

Paulo was, in fact, used to reporting on two or three emergency situations, which meant that his superiors could see that this cub reporter with dark circles under his eyes knew how to write and had the confidence to carry out an interview. While he was never singled out to report on matters of major importance, he went out on to the streets every day with the other more experienced reporters, and, unlike some of them, he almost never returned empty-handed. What his superiors didn't know was that when he failed to find the interviewees he needed, he simply made them up. On one such occasion, he was told to file a report on people whose work centred on Carnival. He spent the day out in the streets, returned to the office and, in the early evening, handed to his editor, the experienced Henrique Caban, five pages of interviews with, among others, 'Joaquim de Souza, nightwatchman', 'Alice Pereira, waitress' and 'Adilson Lopes de Barros, bar owner'. The article ended with an 'analysis of the behaviour of the inhabitants of Rio during Carnival', a statement made by a 'psychologist' going by the highly suspicious name of 'Adolfo Rabbit'. That night Paulo noted at the top of his carbon copy of the article, which he had taken home, something that neither Caban nor anyone else would ever know: 'This material was COMPLETELY invented.'

While he may occasionally have resorted to such low stratagems, he was, in fact, doing well at the newspaper. Less than two months after starting work, he saw one of his interviews – a real one this time – with Luis Seixas, the president of the National Institute of Social Security (INPS), on the front page of the next day's edition of *O Globo*: 'Free medicine from the INPS'. Following this he was given the news that if he moved to being *pauteiro de madrugada* (sub-editor on the early-morning shift), he would receive a 50-per-cent salary increase. Most applicants for the position were put off by having to work every day from two until nine in the morning; however, for an insomniac like him, this was no problem.

The *pauteiro* began by reading all the competing newspapers, the first editions of which had been bought at the newspaper stands in the centre of town, and comparing them with the early edition of *O Globo*, in order to decide which items might be worth including in later editions of *O Globo*. Once this was done, he would listen to the radio news to see what were going to be the major news items of the day and then draw up guidelines for the reporters when they arrived at nine o'clock as to what they should investigate and whom they should interview. He also had to decide which of the night's events, if any, merited the presence of a reporter or photographer. At first, he longed for something important to happen while he was working. 'One of these days, some really big news story will break while I'm on duty, and I'll have to cover it,' he noted in his diary. 'I'd prefer a different shift, but working this one isn't unpleasant, if it weren't for that bastard Frejat, who keeps me hanging on here in the morning.' During his six months in the post, only one thing required him to mobilize reporters and photographers: the murder of the footballer Almir Albuquerque, or 'Pernambuquinho', a forward in the Flamengo football team, who was shot by Portuguese tourists during a fight in the Rio Jerez restaurant in the South Zone of the city. Mostly, though, the nights passed without incident, which left time for him, as he sat alone in the office, to fill pages of notes that he later stuck into his diary.

I don't think Frejat likes me. He told someone that I'm a 'pseudo-intellectual'.

[…] As I said to Gisa, what I like about journalism is that no one lasts long … Frejat's fall is long overdue and it's going to happen, because the whole production team is pressing for it. There are no nice people in journalism. Anyone nice is basically fucked.

[…] I read in the newspaper that someone knifed his wife to death because she never did anything. I'm going to cut out the article and leave it for Gisa to read. I hope she gets the message.

[…] Adalgisa went to Minas leaving the house a complete tip. She didn't hand in our pages to *Tribuna*, she didn't pay the electricity bill and she didn't even wash any clothes. These things make me so angry. It seems that she hasn't got the slightest idea of what living together means. Now I've got no cash to pay the electricity bill and the house is going to be in darkness. When she spoke to me on the phone she said that she's had too much work, but it's nothing to do with that. She's just completely irresponsible.

Before joining *O Globo* Paulo had agreed to lead the drama course in Mato Grosso, and at the end of 1972, after much insistence, he managed to get the newspaper to give him three weeks' unpaid leave. However, at the beginning of the following year the problem arose again. 'I'm going to have to choose between the course in Mato Grosso and the work here on the biggest newspaper in the country,' he wrote in his diary. 'Caban says I can't go, and if I have to give up one of them, I'm going to have to leave the paper.' Besides, Raul Seixas was continuing to pursue him with the idea of working together, and to show that his interest in having him as a lyricist was genuine, Seixas had done a very seductive thing: he let it be known that the song 'Caroço de Manga', which he had written for the theme music of the new version of *Beto Rockefeller*, was in fact by him and Paulo Coelho. Although it was not uncommon in the recording world for a composer to 'share authorship' of a composition with a friend, this also meant an equal division of any royalties. Raul Seixas was slowly beginning to win a place in his life. Paulo wrote:

It's so peaceful working at night. I didn't take a bath today. I slept from nine in the morning until seven at night. I got up to find that Gisa hadn't done any work. We telephoned Raul telling him that we can't meet him today.

[…] I'm tired. I spent all day typing and now I can't remember the music I promised Raul.

[…] Raul is full of silly scruples about writing commercial music. He doesn't understand that the more you control the media, the more influence you have.

As he had foreseen, in April 1973, Paulo had to decide whether or not to continue at *O Globo*. As had become his normal practice whenever he had to make a decision, however unimportant, he left it to the I Ching or the Book of Changes, to choose. He was alone at home and, after a period of concentration, he threw the three coins of the Chinese oracle on the table and noted in his diary the hexagrams that were revealed. There was no doubt: the I Ching warned him against working on the newspaper and advised him that it would mean 'a slow and prolonged exercise leading to misfortune'. He needed nothing more. The following morning, his short-lived career on *O Globo* came to an end. The outcome had been good, even as regards his bank balance. The money he had earned by selling his and Gisa's cartoons, along with what he had been paid for the course at Mato Grosso, their page in *Tribuna* and his work at *O Globo*, not only covered his day-to-day expenses but meant that he, ever cautious, could start investing his modest savings in the stock market. 'I lost my money buying shares in the Bank of Brazil. I'm ruined ...' he recorded at one stage in his diary, only to cheer up a few days later. 'The shares in Petrobras that were only 25 when I bought them are at 300 today.'

Between the time when he resigned from *O Globo* and the start of his partnership with Raul Seixas, Paulo did a little of everything. Alongside the various other bits of work he had been doing, he did some teaching and some theatre directing, and worked as an actor in a soft-porn movie. No longer having to spend his nights working in the editorial office, which had meant he had to sleep during the day, he began to meet up with Raul either at his place or his own in order to begin their much-postponed partnership. The thought of working together had another attraction for Paulo: if 'Caroço de Manga' was already generating substantial royalties, what would he earn if he were the lyricist on a hit song?

As someone who, in a very short space of time, had composed more than eighty songs recorded by various artistes – although he claimed not to like any of them – Raul had enough experience to be able to rid Paulo of any negative feelings he might still have about writing poetry. 'You don't have to say things in a complicated way when you want to speak seriously to people,' Raul would say during their many conversations. 'In fact, the simpler you are the more serious you can be.' 'Writing music is like writing a story in twenty lines that someone can listen to ten times without getting bored. If you can do that, you'll have made a huge leap: you'll have written a work of art everyone can understand.'

And so they began. As the months went by, the two became not just musical partners but great friends or, as they liked to tell journalists, 'close enemies'. They and their partners went out together and visited each other often. It did not take much for Raul and Edith to be seduced by the disturbing allure of drugs and black magic. At the time, in fact, drugs had taken second place in Paulo's life, such was his fascination for the mysteries revealed to him by Frater Zaratustra and the OTO. The much proclaimed 'close enmity' between Paulo and Raul wasn't just an empty expression, and appears to have arisen along with their friendship. While Raul had opened the doors of fame and fortune to his new friend, it was Paulo who knew how to reach the world of secret things, a universe to which ordinary mortals had no access. Raul held the route to fame, but it was Paulo who knew the way to the Devil.

The first fruits of their joint labours appeared in 1973 as an LP, *Krig-Ha, Bandolo!*, the title being taken from one of Tarzan's war cries. Of the five songs with lyrics by Paulo, only one, 'Al Capone', became a hit that people would hum in the street. *Krig-Ha* also revealed Raul Seixas to be an excellent lyricist in his own right. At least three of the songs he composed and wrote – 'Mosca na Sopa', 'Metamorfose Ambulante' and 'Ouro de Tolo' – continued to be played on the radio years after his death in 1989. The LP may not have been a blockbuster, but it meant that Paulo finally saw money pouring into his bank account. When he asked for his balance at his branch of the Banco do Brasil in Copacabana a few weeks after the launch of *Krig-Ha*, he couldn't believe it when he saw that the record company, Philips, had deposited no less than 240 million cruzeiros – about US$200,000 – which, to him, was a real fortune.

The success of the disc meant that Paulo and Gisa, Raul and Edith could really push the boat out. They flew to the United States and, after spending a childish week at Disney World in Florida, visited Memphis, the birthplace of Elvis Presley, and then spent a glorious, hectic month in New York. On one of their many outings in the Big Apple, the two couples knocked at the door of the Dakota building, the grey, neo-Gothic, somewhat sinister apartment block opposite Central Park where John Lennon lived and which had also provided the setting for that classic of satanism, *Rosemary's Baby*, directed by Roman Polanski. With typical Brazilian immodesty, Paulo and Raul seemed to assume that the success of *Krig-Ha* was recommendation enough for these two puny rockers to fraternize with the unassailable writer of 'Imagine'. On their return to Brazil, Paulo and Raul gave several interviews, some for international publications, in which they gave details of their conversation with Lennon, who despite a heavy cold had, according to them, received them with his wife, Yoko Ono, to chat, swap compositions and even consider the possibility of working together. A press release described their meeting:

> We only got to meet John Lennon the day before our return. We went there with a journalist from a Brazilian TV channel. As soon as we sat down, the journalist asked about his separation from Yoko. John immediately told the journalist to leave, saying that he wasn't going to waste his time on gossip. Because of this, the meeting began rather tensely, with John warning us that he would take a very dim view of any attempt on our part to capitalize on our meeting for the purposes of promoting ourselves in Brazil. After a few minutes, the tension lifted and we talked non-stop for half an hour about the present and the future. The results of this meeting will be revealed bit by bit as the situation develops.

It was a complete lie. As time went by the truth behind the story emerged. Paulo and Raul never visited John Lennon's apartment; nor were they received by Yoko Ono. The nearest they got to John Lennon was the porter at the Dakota building, who merely informed them over the intercom that 'Mr Lennon is not at home'. The same press release included another invention: that Lennon had been most impressed by the project Paulo and Raul were preparing to launch in Brazil, the Sociedade Alternativa, the Alternative Society.

The plan was to create a community based on an experiment developed by Aleister Crowley at the beginning of the twentieth century in Cefalu, in Sicily. The place chosen as the site of the 'City of the Stars', as Raul called it, was Paraíba do Sul, where Euclydes Lacerda, or Frater Zaratustra, lived. Raul had absorbed the world of drugs and magic so quickly that a year after his first meeting with Paulo, there was no sign of the smart businessman who had come to the office of *Pomba* to discuss flying saucers. He now sported a thick beard and a magnificent mane of black hair, and had started dressing extravagantly as well, favouring flares that were very tight in the leg and very wide at the bottom, and lamé jackets which he wore without a shirt underneath, thus revealing his pale, sunken, bony chest.

When they returned from their American trip, Raul and Paulo began to create what was to be by far their greatest success – the LP *Gita*. Of the eleven songs chosen for the disc, seven had lyrics by Paulo and of these at least three became the duo's theme tunes – 'Medo da Chuva', 'Gita' and 'Sociedade Alternativa'. 'Medo da Chuva' revealed the lyricist's somewhat unorthodox views on marriage ('It's a pity that you think I'm your slave/Saying that I'm your husband and I can't leave/Like the stones on the beach I stay at your side/Knowing nothing of the loves life brought me, but that I never knew …'). The title song, 'Gita', was no more than a translation of the dialogue between Krishna and Arjuna found in Bhagavad Gita, the Hindu sacred text which they had just read. The most intriguing song on the album, though, was the sixth, 'Sociedade Alternativa' – or, rather, what was intriguing was what the words concealed. At first sight, the words appear to be an innocent surrealist game based on a single chorus, which is repeated throughout the song:

> If I want and you want
> To take a bath in a hat
> Or to wait for Father Christmas
> Or to talk about Carlos Gardel
> Then let's do it!

It was the refrain that opens and closes the piece that concealed the mystery.

> Do what you want is the whole of the law.
> Viva! Viva! Viva the Sociedade Alternativa!

As if wanting to leave no doubt as to their intentions, the authors transcribed word for word entire texts from the *Liber Oz*, finally showing their hand and making their allegiances crystal clear. While Raul sang the refrain, a backing track of his own voice sang:

> Number 666 is called Aleister Crowley!
> Viva! Viva!
> Viva the Sociedade Alternativa!
> The law of Thelema
> Viva! Viva!
> Viva the Sociedade Alternativa!
> The law of the strong
> That is our law and the joy of the world
> Viva! Viva!
> Viva the New Age!

Although only the few initiates to the world of Crowley would understand this, Paulo Coelho and Raul Seixas had decided to become the spokesmen of OTO and, therefore, of the Devil. For many of their audience this was a coded message written to confuse the censors and arguing for a new society as an alternative to the military dictatorship. This also seemed to be the government's view, because when 'Sociedade Alternativa' was released, the censors forbade Raul to sing it when he toured Brazil.

With or without censorship, the fact is that everything was going so well that Paulo concluded that his days of material and emotional penury were over. That evening, as he sometimes did, instead of writing, he recorded his diary on tape, talking as if he were on stage:

> On 15 April 1974, at the age of twenty-six, I, Paulo Coelho, finally finished paying for my crimes. Only at twenty-six did I become fully aware of this. Now give me my reward.
> I want what's due to me.
> And what's due to me will be whatever I want!
> And I want money!
> I want power!
> I want fame, immortality and love!

While he was waiting for his other wishes to come true, he enjoyed the money, fame and love that had already come his way. At the beginning of May, Raul invited him and Gisa to go to Brasília, where he was going to do three shows during the Festival of the Nations being held in the federal capital on 10, 11 and 12 May. At the same time, they were going to start promoting the LP *Gita*, which was to be launched a few weeks later. A slave to the I Ching, Paulo threw the three coins several times until it was confirmed that the trip would present no danger.

They were staying at the smart Hotel Nacional when, on the Friday afternoon, the day of the first show, the two were summoned by the Federal Police to be given the usual talk by the censors as to what could and could not be sung in public. The colonel and bureaucrat who received them explained that in their case the only banned song was 'Sociedade Alternativa'. The sports stadium where the show was to be held was packed, and the first two shows passed off without incident. On the Sunday, the night of the final show, Raul, after spending the afternoon and evening smoking cannabis, had what he called 'a turn'. He was unable to remember a single word of the songs on the programme. While the band kept the audience entertained, he squatted at the edge of the stage and whispered to his partner, who was sitting in the first row: 'Help me, will you? I'm in deep shit. Get up here and keep the public quiet for a while, while I go and splash my face with water.' With the microphone in his hand, Raul introduced Paulo to the crowd as 'my dear partner' and left him to deal with the problem. Since the audience were already clapping in time to the band, shouting out the banned refrain, Paulo simply did the same and began to sing along with them:

Viva! Viva! Viva the Sociedade Alternativa!
Viva! Viva! Viva the Sociedade Alternativa!

When he returned to Rio, he described the weekend in Brasília in just a few lines: 'It was a very quiet trip. On Friday we talked to the censor and a colonel from the Federal Police. On Sunday, I talked to the crowd for the first time, although I was completely unprepared. Any mention of the Alternative Society is restricted to interviews.'

During that week Paulo made an important decision: he formalized his acceptance into the OTO as a probationer or novice, when he swore 'eternal devotion to the Great Work'. From 19 May 'of the year 1974 of the Common Era' onwards, for followers of the Devil, Paulo Coelho de Souza's 'profane name' would disappear and be replaced by the 'magical name' that he himself had chosen: Eternal Light, or Staars, or, simply, 313. After sending his oath off in the post, he noted in his diary: 'Having been invoked so often, He must be breathing fire from his nostrils somewhere near by.' He was. On the morning of 25 May, six days after his entrance into the world of darkness, Paulo was finally to have his much-desired meeting with the Devil.

CHAPTER 16

A devil of a different sort

T HE LARGE AMOUNT OF MONEY that Philips had deposited in Paulo's
bank account the previous year was just a hint of what was to come.
Following the enormous success of *Krig-Ha, Bandolo!* the recording
company launched a single featuring 'Gita' and 'Não Pare na Pista', the
latter written on the Rio–Bahia highway when the two were returning
from a few days' rest in Dias d'Ávila, in the interior of Bahia, where Raul's
parents lived. The aim of the single was merely to give the public a taster
of the LP that would be released in June, but in less than a month it had
sold more than a hundred thousand copies, which won the creators an
unexpectedly early Gold Disc, the first of six prizes that the two songs
went on to win. Each time a radio station unwittingly made an invocation
to the Devil as they played the refrain 'Viva! Viva a Sociedade Alternativa!'
meant more money for Raul and Paulo. In April 1974, Paulo bought a
large apartment in Rua Voluntários da Pátria, in Botafogo, a few blocks
from the estate where he had been born and spent his childhood, and he
moved in there with Gisa.

On Friday, 24 May, two weeks after their short stay in Brasília, Raul
telephoned to say that he had been ordered to go to the political police –
known as the Dops – on the following Monday in order to 'provide some
information'. Being accustomed to frequent invitations to discuss which

songs could appear in shows or on records, he didn't appear to be worried, but just in case, he asked his partner to go with him. As soon as he rang off, Paulo consulted the I Ching as to whether there was any risk in going to the Dops. Since the answer seemed to be 'No' – or at least so it seemed, for according to its followers, the interpretation of the oracle is not always very precise – he thought no more about the matter.

When he woke on the Saturday morning, Paulo found a note on the bedside table from Gisa, saying that she had gone out early and would be back soon. As he scanned the front page of the *Jornal do Brasil*, the date on the masthead caught his eye: it was exactly two years since he had met Raul, a meeting that had totally changed his life. He drank a cup of coffee, lit a cigarette, glanced through the window from where he could see the sun beating down on the pavement below and then went into his bedroom to put on some shorts before going for his usual hour-long walk. He could detect a slight smell of burning and checked the sockets and domestic appliances, but found nothing wrong. And yet the smell was getting stronger. No, it wasn't the smell of a fuse blowing, it was something else, something very familiar. He felt a chill in his stomach as his memory took him back to the place where he had smelled the same smell now filling the apartment: the morgue in the Santa Casa de Misericórdia that he had visited daily for some months when collecting data for the obituary page of *O Globo*. It was the macabre smell of the candles that appeared to be permanently burning in the hospital morgue. The difference was that the odour permeating everything around him now was so strong that it seemed to be coming from 100, even 1,000, candles all burning at the same time.

As he bent down to do up his trainers, he had the impression that the parquet floor was rising up and coming dangerously close to his face. In fact, his legs had unexpectedly given way beneath him, as if he were about to faint, throwing his chest forwards. He almost crashed to the ground. When the dizziness intensified, he tried to remember whether he had eaten anything strange, but no, it was nothing like that: he wasn't feeling nauseous, he was simply caught up in a kind of maelstrom that seemed to be affecting everything around him. As well as the attacks of giddiness, which came and went, he realized that the apartment was full of a dark mist, as though the sun had suddenly disappeared and the place was being invaded by grey clouds. For a moment, he prayed that he was merely experiencing the moment most feared by drug addicts – a bad trip, provoked by the use of LSD. This, however, was impossible. He hadn't taken LSD in ages, and he'd never heard of cannabis causing such hellish feelings.

He tried to open the door and go outside, but fear paralysed him. It might be worse outside than in. By now, along with the dizziness and the smoke, he could hear terrifying noises, as though someone or some being were breaking everything around him, and yet everything remained in its place. Terrified and lacking the strength to do anything, he felt his hopes revive when the telephone rang. He prayed to God to let it be Euclydes Lacerda – Frater Zaratustra – who could put an end to his suffering. He picked up the phone, but almost immediately put it down again when he realized that he was invoking God's name in order to speak to a disciple of the Devil. It was not Euclydes: the person calling was his friend Stella Paula, whom he had also recruited into the OTO. She was sobbing, as terrified as he was, and was calling to ask for help because her apartment was filled with black smoke, a strong smell of decomposition and other vile smells. Paulo broke down into uncontrollable sobs. He rang off and, remembering what he usually did when he'd had too much cannabis, he went to the refrigerator and drank several glasses of milk, one after the other, and then put his head under the cold-water tap in the bathroom. Nothing happened. The smell of the dead, the smoke and the dizziness continued, as did the noise of things breaking, which was so loud that he had to cover his ears with his hands to deaden it.

It was only then that he began to understand what was happening. Having broken all ties with Christianity, he had spent the last few years working with negative energies in search of something that not even Aleister Crowley had achieved: a meeting with the Devil. What was happening that Saturday morning was what Frater Zaratustra called a 'reflux of magical energies'. All his prayers had been answered. Paulo was face-to-face with the Devil. He felt like throwing himself out the window, but jumping from the fourth floor might not necessarily kill him, and might do terrible damage and perhaps leave him crippled. Crying like an abandoned baby, his hands shielding his ears and his head buried between his knees, he recalled fragments of the threats that Father Ruffier had pronounced from the pulpit of the chapel at St Ignatius College.

We are in hell! Here you can see only tears and hear only the grinding of teeth caused by the hatred of some against others.

[...] While we cry in pain and remorse the Devil smiles a smile that makes us suffer still more. But the worst punishment, the worst pain, the worst suffering is that we have no hope. We are here for ever.

[...] And the Devil will say: my dear, your suffering hasn't even begun!

That was it: he was in hell – a hell far worse than Father Ruffier had promised and which he seemed to be condemned to suffer alone. Yes, how long had this been going on – two hours? three? He had lost all notion of time, and there was still no sign of Gisa. Had something happened to her? In order to stop thinking, he began to count the books in the apartment, and then the records, the pictures, the knives, spoons, forks, plates, pairs of socks, underpants ... When he reached the end, he started again. He was standing bent over the kitchen sink with his hands full of cutlery when Gisa returned. She was as confused as he was, shivering with cold, and with her teeth chattering. She asked him what was happening, but Paulo didn't know. She became angry, saying: 'What do you mean, you don't know? You know everything!'

They clung to each other, knelt down on the kitchen floor and began to cry. When he heard himself confessing to Gisa that he was afraid to die, the ghosts of St Ignatius College again rose up before him. 'You're afraid of dying?' Father Ruffier had bawled at him once in front of his classmates. 'Well, I'm shamed by your cowardice.' Gisa found his cowardice equally shameful, especially in a man who, until recently, had been the great macho know-it-all, and who had encouraged her to become involved with the crazy warlocks of the OTO. However, in the midst of that mayhem, Paulo really didn't care what that priest or his girlfriend or his parents might think of him. The only thing he knew was that he didn't want to die, far less deliver his soul to the Devil.

He finally plucked up the courage to whisper in Gisa's ear: 'Let's go and find a church! Let's get out of here and go straight to a church!'

Gisa, the left-wing militant, couldn't believe her ears. 'A church? Why do you need a church, Paulo?'

He needed God. He wanted a church so that he could ask God to forgive him for having doubted His existence and to put an end to his suffering. He dragged Gisa into the bathroom, turned on the cold-water tap of the shower and crouched beneath it with her. The evil smell, the grey clouds and the noise continued. Paulo began to recite out loud every prayer he knew – Hail Mary, Our Father, Salve Regina, the Creed – and eventually she joined in. They couldn't remember how long they stayed there, but the tips of their fingers were blue and wrinkled by the time Paulo got up, ran into the sitting room and grabbed a copy of the Bible. Back in the shower, he opened it at random and came upon verse 24, chapter 9, of St Mark's gospel, which he and Gisa began to repeat, like a mantra, under the showerhead:

Lord, I believe! Help thou my unbelief ...
Lord, I believe! Help thou my unbelief ...
Lord, I believe! Help thou my unbelief ...

They repeated these words out loud hundreds, possibly thousands of times. Paulo renounced and forswore, again out loud, any connection with OTO, with Crowley and with the demons who appeared to have been unleashed that Saturday. When peace returned, it was dark outside. Paulo felt physically and emotionally drained.

Terrified by what they had experienced, the couple did not dare to sleep in the apartment that night. The furniture, books and household objects were all in their usual places, as if that emotional earthquake had never taken place, but it seemed best not to take any chances and they went to spend the weekend with Lygia and Pedro in Gávea. Since she had been with Paulo, Gisa had become a regular visitor to the Coelho household and was always made welcome, particularly by Lygia. Gisa's one defect – in the eyes of Paulo's parents – was her political radicalism. During the long Sunday lunches in Gávea when Paulo's parents, aunts, uncles and grandparents would meet, Gisa would always defend her ideas, even though she knew she was among supporters of Salazar, Franco and the Brazilian military dictatorship. Although everything indicates that she had gradually distanced herself from the political militancy of her student days, her views had not changed. When the couple left on Monday morning, Lygia invited them to a small dinner she was going to hold that evening for her sister Heloísa, 'Aunt Helói'. The two took a taxi back to their apartment – for Paulo had still not learnt to drive. There were no smells, no mists, no shards of glass, nothing to indicate that two days earlier the place had been the scene of what both were sure had been a battle between Good and Evil. When he chose the clothes he was going to wear after his shower, Paulo decided that he would no longer be a slave to superstition. He took from his wardrobe a pale blue linen shirt with short sleeves and pockets trimmed with embroidery, which was a present his mother had given him three years earlier and which he had never worn. This was because the shirt had been bought on a trip his parents had made to Asunción, the capital of the neighbouring country whose name, since his imprisonment in Ponta Grossa, he had never again pronounced. In wearing that shirt from Paraguay he wanted, above all, to prove to himself that he was free of his esoteric tics. He had lunch with Gisa and, at two in the afternoon, went over to Raul's apartment to accompany him to the Dops.

It took more than half an hour to travel the traffic-ridden 15 kilometres that separated Jardim de Alah, where Raul lived, and the Dops building in the centre of the city, and the two men spent the time discussing plans for the launch of their LP *Gita*. A year earlier, when the *Krig-Ha, Bandolo!* album had been released, the two, at Paulo's suggestion, had led a 'musical march' through the streets of the commercial area in old Rio, and this had been a great success. This 'happening' had garnered them valuable minutes on the TV news as well as articles in newspapers and magazines. For *Gita* they wanted to do something even more extravagant.

Calmly going to an interview with the political police when Brazil still had a military dictatorship, without taking with them a lawyer or a representative of the recording company, was not an irresponsible act. Besides being reasonably well known – at least Raul was – neither had any skeletons in the cupboard. Despite Paulo's arrest in Ponta Grossa in 1969 and their skirmishes with the censors, they could not be accused of any act that might be deemed to show opposition to the dictatorship. Besides, the regime had eradicated all the armed combat groups operating in the country. Six months earlier, at the end of 1973, army troops had destroyed the last centres of guerrilla resistance in Araguaia in the south of Pará, leaving a total of sixty-nine dead. Having annihilated all armed opposition, the repressive machinery was slowly being wound down. The regime was still committing many crimes and atrocities – and would continue to do so – but on that May Monday morning in 1974, it would not have been considered utter madness to keep an appointment with the political police, especially since any allegations of torture and the killing of prisoners were mostly made against the intelligence agencies and other sectors of the army, navy and air force.

When the taxi left them at the door of the three-storey building in Rua da Relação, two blocks away from the Philips headquarters, it was three on the dot on 27 May. While Paulo sat on a bench, reading a newspaper, Raul showed the summons to the man at a window and then disappeared off down a corridor. Half an hour later, the musician returned. Instead of going over to Paulo, who was getting up ready to leave, he went over to a public telephone opposite, pretended to dial a number, and began to sing in English: 'My dear partner, the men want to talk to you, not to me ...'

When Paulo failed to understand that Raul was trying to alert him to the fact that he might be in danger, Raul continued tapping his fingers on the telephone and repeating, as though it were a refrain: 'They want to talk to you, not to me ... They want to talk to you, not to me ...'

Paulo still didn't understand. He stood up and asked, smiling: 'Stop messing around, Raul. What are you singing?'

When he made to leave, a policeman placed a hand on his shoulder and said: 'You're not going anywhere. You've got some explaining to do.'

Paulo only had time to murmur a rapid 'Tell my father' to Raul before being led away. He was taken through a labyrinth of poorly lit corridors and across a courtyard until they reached a corridor with cells on either side, most of which appeared to be empty and from which emanated a strong smell of urine combined with disinfectant. The man with him stopped in front of one of them, occupied by two young men, shoved him inside and then turned the key in the lock. Without saying a word to the others, Paulo sat down on the floor, lit a cigarette and, panic-stricken, tried to work out what could possibly lie behind this imprisonment.

He was still immersed in these thoughts when one of the men, who was younger than he, asked: 'Aren't you Paulo Coelho?'

Startled, he replied: 'Yes, I am. Why?'

'We're Children of God. I'm married to Talita. You met her in Amsterdam.'

This was true. He recalled that during his trip to Holland, a young Brazilian girl had come up to him on seeing the Brazilian flag sewn on to the shoulder of his denim jacket. Like Paulo, the two young men had no idea why they were there. The Children of God sect, which had been started in California some years earlier, had managed to attract hundreds of followers in Brazil and now faced serious allegations, among which was that they encouraged sex with children, even between parents and their own children. The presence of the three in the Dops cells was like a snapshot of the state of political repression in Brazil. The much-feared, violent machine created by the dictatorship to confront guerrillas was now concerned with hippies, cannabis users and followers of eccentric sects.

It wasn't until about six in the evening that a plainclothes policeman with a pistol in his belt and holding a cardboard folder in his hand opened the door of the cell and asked: 'Which one of you is Paulo Coelho de Souza?'

Paulo identified himself and was taken to a room on the second floor of the building, where there was only a table and two chairs.

The policeman sat on one of them and ordered Paulo to sit in the other. He took from the folder the four-page comic strip that accompanied *Krig-Ha, Bandolo!* and threw it down on the table. Then he began a surrealist dialogue with the prisoner.

'What kind of shit is this?'

'It's the insert that accompanies the album recorded by me and Raul Seixas.'

'What does *Krig-Ha, Bandolo!* mean?'

'It means "Watch out for the enemy!"'

'Enemy? What enemy? The government? What language is it written in?'

'No! No, it's not against the government. The enemy are African lions and it's written in the language spoken in the kingdom of Pal-U-Don.'

Convinced that this skinny, long-haired man was making a fool of him, the policeman looked as if he was about to turn nasty, thus obliging Paulo to explain carefully that it was all a work of fiction inspired by the places, people and language of the Tarzan cartoons which were set in an imaginary place in Africa called Pal-U-Don.

The man was still not satisfied. 'And who wrote this stuff?'

'I did, and my partner, who's an architect, illustrated it.'

'What's your partner's name? I want to interview her too. Where is she now?'

Paulo panicked at the thought of involving Gisa in this nightmare, but he knew that there was no point in lying; nor was there any reason to lie, since they were both innocent. He looked at his watch.

'Her name is Adalgisa Rios. We were invited to supper this evening at my parents' house. She should be there by now.'

The policeman gathered up the papers, cigarettes and lighter he had scattered on the table, got up and ordered the terrified prisoner to follow him, saying: 'Right, let's go. Let's go and find your old lady.'

As he was being bundled into a black-and-white van bearing the symbol of the Rio de Janeiro Security Police, Paulo felt momentary relief. This meant that he had been officially arrested and, in theory at least, was under state protection. Hell meant being picked up in unmarked cars with false number plates by plainclothes policemen, men with no orders and no official mandate, and who had been linked with many cases of torture and with the disappearance, so far, of 117 political prisoners.

His parents could hardly believe it when they saw their son get out of the car, surrounded by four armed men. They said that Gisa had not yet arrived and wanted to know what was going on. Paulo tried to calm them down, saying that it was just a minor problem with *Krig-Ha, Bandolo!* It would soon be resolved, and he and Gisa should even be back in time for dinner.

Lygia Araripe Coelho de Souza holding her baby Paulo, Rio de Janeiro, 1947.

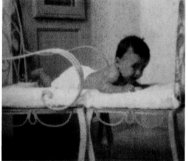

Paulo as a baby (*above*) and playing with his cousins (in sandals and shorts, *left*), Rio de Janeiro, 1950s.

Paulo, aged ten (second from left, first row), at Our Lady Victorious School, Rio de Janeiro, 1957.

Paulo, aged fifteen (fourth from left, second row from top), at St Ignatius College, a respected boys' schools in Rio de Janeiro, in 1962.

Left The forged school document Paulo used to get into the left-leaning 'Paissandu set' in 1965. Adding two years to his age gained him admittance to this group of intellectual film-lovers.

Below Paulo used to classify and rank the books he read. In this list, Martin Luther King wins his highest rating.

Left Fabíola Fracarolli in 1967, one of Paulo's many girlfriends during the late 1960s.

Right Paulo and Fabíola.

Paulo with fellow actors in an adaptation of Jorge Amado's *Capitães da Areia* at the Teatro Serrador in Rio de Janeiro, 1966.

Paulo (fifth from the left, front row) with cast and crew on the opening night of *Capitães da Areia*.

Paulo as Captain Hook (far right) and the other actors in his production of *Peter Pan*, 1969. Fabíola, who subsidised the production, played Peter Pan and Paulo's friend Kakiko (centre, front row) wrote the score.

Kakiko, Paulo, Vera
and Arnold (left to right)
make their first stop in
Registro on their ill-fated
trip to Asunción,
Paraguay, 1969.

Above Paulo during his
trip across the United States,
1971.

Left Paulo during his 24-hour
marijuana experiment at
Kakiko's house in Friburgo,
1971.

Paulo and his girlfriend Gisa (also *right*). Following the termination of her pregnancy, she took an overdose of barbiturates and nearly drowned.

Paulo used black magic techniques and rituals in the drama courses he ran in 1973 at schools in Mato Grosso, Brazil.

Right Paulo breaks his hour-long pact with the Devil, 11 November 1971.

Far right Paulo's registration card as prisoner no. 13720. He and Gisa were imprisoned on account of the *Krig-Ha, Bandolo!* comic strip, 1974.

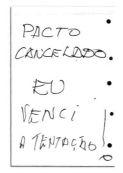

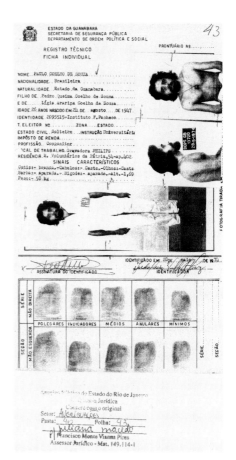

Right A leaflet advertising a presentation by the Crowleyites and the launch of Paulo's *Arquivos do Inferno.*

The psychedelic comic strip accompanying the *Krig-Ha, Bandolo!* LP, written by Paulo and Raul Seixas and illustrated by Gisa, that so intrigued the Brazilian police, 1974.

Paulo and Cissa leave the altar of St Joseph's Church, Rio de Janeiro, as man and wife, 2 July 1976.

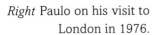

Right Paulo on his visit to London in 1976.

Left Paulo and Christina in January 1980.

Paulo and Christina bought this Mercedes-Benz from the Indian embassy in Budapest for their European trip in 1982 after having struggled in their previous car, a Citröen 2CV.

Left Paulo's visit to Dachau concentration camp in 1982 saw his birth as an author.

Below Nandor Glid's bronze memorial at the camp.

Left The cover of *Arquivos do Inferno* featured Paulo with Christina and his old Crowleyite colleague Stella, 1982. The preface was by 'Andy Wharol', who never read the book.

Left Béla Lugosi on the cover of *Manual Prático do Vampirismo*, 1985. Though credited as the main author, Paulo didn't write a single word and persuaded a friend to produce his chapters.

Left Paulo asked the I Ching in 1988 how to ensure 100,000 sales of *The Alchemist*. The oracle replied, 'The great man brings good luck.'

Below Paulo in Egypt in 1987. The trip would provide inspiration for *The Alchemist*.

Paulo and Christina in the Mojave desert in 1988, where they practised the spiritual exercises of St Ignatius Loyola.

Paulo cemented an image of Our Lady of Aparecida in a grotto in Glorieta Canyon, New Mexico, writing a message in the wet mortar beneath it. The image was subsequently stolen.

The cartoon that appeared in *Jornal do Brasil*, 1993. According to the accompanying article, putting books by Paulo on the school curriculum would make students more stupid.

Jacques Chirac congratulates Paulo at the Paris Expo convention centre in 1998, after he had been ignored by the official Brazilian delegation. Brazilian First Lady Ruth Cardoso looks on.

Paulo takes a photo of himself in the hotel bathroom, wearing the Légion d'Honneur with which he has just been decorated by the French president in 1999.

Below Paulo is received by Pope John Paul II in the Vatican, 1998.

Left Mônica Antunes, Paulo's literary agent, with Paulo and friends in Dubai.

Right Paulo and Christina in Prague in 2005 with their gift to the Infant Jesus of a gold-embroidered cloak, fulfilling a promise Paulo made three decades earlier.

Left Paulo signing books in Cairo, 2005. Egypt is the world's leading producer of pirate editions of his books.

In 2002 Paulo was chosen as one of the forty lifetime members of the Brazilian Academy of Letters. He is pictured here with four of his fellow 'immortals'.

Paulo, Marisa Letícia (First Lady of Brazil), Christina and President Lula (left to right) at a state banquet in the president's honour at Buckingham Palace, 2006.

Right Paulo meeting Vladimir Putin.

Left Fulfilling an old dream: Paulo pauses during his journey on the Trans-Siberian Railway, 2007.

Above The *Sunday Times* journalist Christina Lamb, the inspiration for the character of Esther in *The Zahir*.

Below The pamphlet commemorating 100 million books sold.

PAULO COELHO
100,000,000 COPIES

One of the policemen backed him up, assuring Lygia and Pedro: 'Yes, they'll be back before you know it.'

As on the outward journey, he sat in the back of the van with an armed policeman on either side and the other two in the front. Halfway there, Paulo asked if they could stop at a public telephone, saying that he needed to tell the recording company that there were some problems with the record. One of the policemen said 'No', but calmed him by saying that in a few hours he and Gisa would be free. His plan had not worked: in fact, Paulo had been hoping to call home to ask Gisa to get rid of a jar full of cannabis that was on the bookcase in the sitting room. He sat frozen and silent until they reached the door of the building where he lived. A policeman stayed with the van while the other three went upstairs with him, crowding into the small, slow lift which on that occasion seemed to take about an hour to arrive at the fourth floor. Inside, wearing an Indian sari, Gisa was just turning out the lights, ready to leave, when Paulo came in with the policemen.

'Sweetheart, these men are from the Dops and they need some information about the record I made with Raul and about the comic strip you and I did for Philips.'

Gisa was a bit frightened, but she seemed to take the matter calmly enough: 'Fine. Tell me what you want. What do you want to know?'

A policeman said that it didn't work that way: 'We can only take statements at the Dops headquarters, so we'll have to go back there.'

She didn't understand. 'Do you mean we're being arrested?'

The policeman answered politely: 'No. You're being detained so that you can provide us with some further information and then you'll be released. But before we leave, we'll just take a quick look around the apartment.'

Paulo's heart was beating so fast he thought he'd have a heart attack: they were sure to find the cannabis. Standing in the middle of the room with his arm around Gisa's shoulder, he followed the movements of the policemen with his eyes. One of them took a pile of about a hundred *Krig-Ha, Bandolo!* comic strips, while another rummaged through drawers and cupboards, and the third, who seemed to be the leader, scrutinized the books and records. When he saw a Chinese lacquered jar the size of a sweet tin, he picked it up, took off the lid and saw that it was full to the brim with cannabis. He sniffed the contents as though savouring a fine perfume, put the lid back on and restored it to its original place. It was only then that Paulo realized that the situation was infinitely worse than he had supposed: if the policeman was prepared to overlook a jar of cannabis, it was because he was suspected of far graver crimes. The Ponta Grossa incident came to mind: could it be that he was once again being confused with a terrorist or a bank robber?

It was only when they arrived at the Dops headquarters that he and Gisa realized that they would not be dining with his parents that evening. They were separated as soon as they arrived and ordered to exchange the clothes they were wearing for yellow overalls with the word 'PRISONER' written in capital letters on the top pocket. During the night of the twenty-eighth they were both photographed and identified and fingerprinted for the police files that had been created in their names; Paulo's number was 13720 and Gisa's 13721. They were then interrogated separately for several hours. Among the personal items confiscated along with their clothes were their watches, which meant that they lost all idea of time, particularly in the circumstances in which they found themselves – imprisoned in a place where there was no natural light.

The interrogation did not involve any physical torture and mainly had to do with the psychedelic comic strip that accompanied the *Krig-Ha, Bandolo!* LP and what exactly was meant by Sociedade Alternativa. This, of course, was after they had spent hours dictating to clerks what in the jargon of the Brazilian police is called the *capivara* – a careful, detailed history of a prisoner's activities up to that date. When Paulo said that he had been in Santiago in May 1970 with Vera Richter the police pressed him for information on Brazilians who lived there, but he had nothing to tell them, for the simple reason that he'd had no contact with any Brazilian exiled in Chile or anywhere else. Gisa, for her part, had a problem convincing her interrogators that the title of *Krig-Ha, Bandolo!* had come up during a brainstorming session at Philips when Paulo, standing on a table, had bellowed out Tarzan's war cry.

In Gávea, the Coelhos were frantic with worry. With the help of a friend, the secretary of the governor of what was then the state of

Guanabara, the journalist and businessman Antônio de Pádua Chagas Freitas, Lygia managed to find out, to everyone's relief, that her son had been arrested by the Dops and was being detained in their prison in Rua da Relação. This was some guarantee, however flimsy, that he would not join the list of the 'disappeared'. Since *habeas corpus* no longer existed, all they could do was to try to find people who might have some kind of link, either family or personal, with influential individuals in the security forces. Paulo's brother-in-law, Marcos, suggested seeking the help of a friend, Colonel Imbassahy, who had connections with the SNI (Brazil's National Intelligence Service), but Pedro decided to try legal routes first, however fragile these might be. It was Aunt Helói who suggested the name of the lawyer Antônio Cláudio Vieira, who had worked in the offices of 'Uncle Candinho', as the Coelho family called the ex-procurator general of the Republic, Cândido de Oliveira Neto, who had died a year earlier.

By five in the afternoon, they were all at the door of the prison. When he was told that only the lawyer, Vieira, could enter, Pedro mentioned that he knew one of the stars of the dictatorship. 'We're friends of Colonel Jarbas Passarinho.' He was speaking of the ex-governor of Pará, who had held ministerial positions in three military governments (he had been one of the signatories of the AI-5) and had been re-elected senator for Arena, a party that supported the regime. The policeman was unimpressed, saying that even someone in Jarbas's position had no influence in Dops.

While the lawyer was trying to get news about Paulo from the officer on duty, Pedro, Lygia, Sônia and her husband Marcos had to wait on the pavement in the drizzle.

After some minutes, Vieira came out with good news: 'Paulo is here and should be released today. The officer in charge is phoning his superior to see whether they will allow me to see him for a few minutes.'

The lawyer was summoned by the doorman and taken to a room where he would be allowed to speak to Paulo briefly. He was shocked by Paulo's appearance: while he hadn't been the victim of any physical violence, Paulo was very pale with dark rings under his eyes and had a strange zombie-like expression on his face. Vieira reassured him, saying he had been given a promise that he would be freed in the next few hours. And that was that. Lygia insisted that they remain on the pavement outside the Dops until her son was released, but the lawyer dissuaded her from this idea.

At about ten o'clock on the Tuesday night, one of the policemen, who had always seemed to Paulo to be the most sympathetic and least threatening, opened the cell door and gave him back the clothes and documents he'd had with him when he was arrested: he and Gisa were free to go. Paulo dressed quickly and met Gisa in the lobby, and the policeman accompanied the couple to the café next to the Dops, where they smoked a cigarette.

Anxious to get away from such a terrifying place, Paulo hailed a taxi and asked the driver to take them to his parents' house in Gávea. The driver set off; then, as the cab was travelling at speed past Hotel Glória, it was brought screeching to a halt by three or four civilian vehicles, among them two Chevrolet Veraneio estate cars, which at the time were the trademark vehicle used by the security police. Several men in plain clothes jumped out and opened the two rear doors of the taxi in which the couple were travelling and dragged Paulo and Gisa out by force. As Paulo was handcuffed and dragged along on his stomach across the grass, he caught sight of Gisa being thrown into an estate car, which drove off, tyres squealing. The last thing he saw before his head was covered in a black hood was the elegant white building of the Hotel Glória, lit up like fairyland.

Once in the back seat of the car, Paulo managed to murmur a question to one of the men with him: 'Are you going to kill me?'

The agent realized how terrified he was and said. 'Don't worry. No one's going to kill you. We're just going to interrogate you.'

His fear remained undiminished. His hands shaking, Paulo was able to overcome his fear and shame enough to ask his captor: 'Can I hold on to your leg?'

The man seemed to find this unusual request amusing. 'Of course you can. And don't worry, we're not going to kill you.'

CHAPTER 17

Paulo renounces the Devil

I T WAS NOT UNTIL THIRTY YEARS LATER, with the country's return to democracy, that Paulo learned he had been kidnapped by a commando group of the DOI-Codi (Department of Information Operations – Centre for Internal Defence Operations). Pedro Queima Coelho was concerned about the damage all this might inflict on his son's fragile emotional state and made a point of being at home so that he would be there to receive Paulo when he was freed. He spent a sleepless night beside a silent telephone and at eight in the morning took a taxi to the Dops. When he arrived, he was astonished to be told by the officer at the desk:

'Your son and his girlfriend were freed at ten o'clock last night.'

When Paulo's father stared at him in disbelief, the agent opened a file and showed him two stamped sheets of paper. 'This is the document for release and here are their signatures,' he said, trying to appear sympathetic. 'He was definitely released. If your son hasn't come home, it's probably because he's decided to go underground.'

The nightmare had begun. Paulo and Gisa had been added to the list of the regime's 'disappeared'. This meant that whatever might happen to them, it was no longer the responsibility of the state, since both had been released safe and sound after signing an official release document.

What happened after their kidnapping is still so swathed in mystery that in 2007, when he turned sixty, the author still had many unanswered questions. Records kept by the security police confirm that Raul was not detained and that on 27 May the Dops arrested the couple, having identified and questioned them during the night and throughout the day of the twenty-eighth. Documents from the army also show that following their kidnapping outside the Hotel Glória, Paulo and Gisa were taken separately to the 1st Battalion of the Military Police in Rua Barão de Mesquita, in the north of Rio, where the DOI-Codi had its offices, although there is no information about how long they were held at the barracks. Some family members state, albeit not with any certainty, that he could have spent 'up to ten days' in the DOI-Codi, but on Friday, 31 May, Paulo was in Gávea writing the first entry in his diary following his release: 'I'm staying at my parents' house. I'm even afraid of writing about what happened to me. It was one of the worst experiences of my life – imprisoned unjustly yet again. But my fears will be overcome by faith and my hatred will be conquered by love. From insecurity will come confidence in myself.'

However, among the documents taken from the archives of Abin, the Brazilian Intelligence Agency (the successor to the SNI, the National Intelligence Service), is a long interrogation with Paulo lasting from eleven o'clock on the night of 14 June until four in the morning of 15 June in the offices of the DOI-Codi. The mystery lies in the fact that he swears that he never returned to the DOI-Codi following his release. The lawyer Antônio Cláudio Vieira also states with equal certainty that he never accompanied him to Rua Barão de Mesquita; nor was he called a second time by the Coelho family to help their son. The same version is corroborated by Pedro, Paulo's sister Sônia Maria and her ex-husband, Marcos, who witnessed everything at close hand. Any suspicion that Paulo, in his terror, had betrayed his friends or put others in danger and now wanted to remove this stain from his record does not stand up to a reading of the seven pages typed on the headed notepaper of the then 1st Army. The first four pages are filled with a reiteration of the statement that Paulo had made in the Dops, a detailed history of his life up until then: schools, work in the theatre, trips within Brazil and abroad, prison in Paraná, *O Globo*, the course in Mato Grosso, *A Pomba*, his partnership with Raul ...

The part referring to his and Raul's membership of the OTO is so incomprehensible that the clerk had to write '*sic*' several times, just to make it clear that this really was what the prisoner had said:

> That in 1973 the deponent and Raul Seixas had concluded 'that the world is experiencing an intense period of tedium' [*sic*]; that on the other hand they realized that the career of a singer, when not accompanied by a strong movement, tends to end quickly. That the deponent and Raul Seixas then resolved 'to capitalize on the end of hippiedom and the sudden interest in magic around the world' [*sic*]; that the deponent began to study the books of an esoteric movement called 'OTO'. That the deponent and Raul Seixas then decided to found the 'Sociedade Alternativa', 'which was registered at the register office to avoid any false interpretations' [*sic*]; that the deponent and Raul Seixas were in Brasília and explained the precepts of the Sociedade Alternativa to the chiefs of the Federal Police and the Censors, stating 'that the intention was not to act against the government, but to interest youth in another form of activity' [*sic*].

When the police asked him to give the names of people he knew with left-wing tendencies, Paulo could recall only two: someone who used to go to the Paissandu, 'known by everyone as the Philosopher', and an ex-boyfriend of Gisa's in the student movement, whose name he also could not remember, but which he believed 'began with the letter H or A'. The certainty with which everyone states that he did not return to the DOI-Codi after being kidnapped is corroborated by his diary, in which there is absolutely no record of his making a further statement on the night of 14–15 June. The theory that the clerk had typed the wrong date doesn't hold up when one considers the fact that the statement is seven pages long, with the date – 14 June – typed on every page. The definitive proof that Paulo was indeed at the DOI-Codi on some date after 27 May, however, is to be found in one small detail: when he was photographed and identified in the Dops some hours after his arrest on 27 May, he had a moustache and goatee beard. On 14 June, he is described as having 'beard and moustache shaven off'.

As for Gisa, during the time in which she remained in the DOI-Codi she underwent two interrogations. The first started at eight on the morning of 29 May and only ended at four in the afternoon, and the second was held between eight and eleven on the morning of the following day, Thursday. On both occasions, she was treated as a militant member of the radical group Ação Popular (Popular Action) and of the Brazilian Communist Party, but, as in Paulo's case, she had little or nothing to tell them, apart from her work in the student movement when she was involved in several left-wing organizations.

During one of the nights when they were being held in the DOI, something happened that caused the final break between the two. With his head covered by a hood, Paulo was being taken to the toilet by a policeman when, as he walked past a cell, he heard someone sobbing and calling him: 'Paulo? Are you there? If it's you, talk to me!'

It was Gisa, probably also with a hood on her head: she had recognized his voice. Terrified at the thought that he might be placed naked in the 'refrigerator' – the closed cell where the temperature was kept deliberately low – he stayed silent.

His girlfriend begged for his help: 'Paulo, my love! Please, say yes. Just that, say that it's you!'

Nothing.

She went on: 'Please, Paulo, tell them I've got nothing to do with all this.'

In what he was to see as his greatest act of cowardice, he didn't even open his mouth.

One afternoon that week, probably Friday, 31 May, a guard appeared with his clothes, told him to get dressed and to cover his head with the hood. He was put on the rear seat of a car and, having been driven some way, thrown out in a small square in Tijuca, a middle-class district 10 kilometres from the barracks where he had been held.

The first days in his parents' house were terrifying. Every time someone knocked on the door, or the telephone rang, Paulo would lock himself in his room, afraid of being taken away again by the police, the military or whoever it was who had kidnapped him. In order to calm him a little, Pedro, touched by his son's paranoia, had to swear that he would not allow him to be imprisoned again, whatever the consequences. 'If anyone comes to take you without a legal summons,' he promised, 'he'll be greeted with a bullet.' Only after two weeks holed up in Gávea did Paulo have the courage to go out in the street again, and even then he chose a day when it would be easy to spot if someone was following him: Thursday, 13 June, when Brazil and Yugoslavia were playing the first match of the 1974 World Cup in Germany, and the whole country would be in front of the television supporting the national team. With Rio transformed into a ghost town he went by bus to Flamengo and then, after much hesitation, he plucked up the courage to go into the apartment where he and Gisa had lived until the Saturday on which they believed they had received a visit from the Devil. It was exactly as the police had left it on the Monday evening after searching it. Before the referee blew the final whistle of the match, Paulo was back in the shelter of his parents' home. One of the penances he imposed on himself, though, so that everything would return to normal as quickly as possible, was not to watch any of the World Cup matches.

The most difficult thing was finding Gisa. Since that dreadful encounter in the DOI-Codi prison he had had no more news of his girlfriend, but her voice crying 'Paulo! Talk to me, Paulo!' kept ringing in his head. When he eventually managed to call her old apartment, where she had gone back to live, it suddenly occurred to him that the phone might be tapped and so he didn't dare to ask whether she had been tortured or when she had been released. When he suggested a meeting in order to discuss their future, Gisa was adamant: 'I don't want to live with you again, I don't want you to say another word to me and I would prefer it if you never spoke my name again.'

Following this, Paulo fell into such a deep depression that his family again sought help from Dr Benjamim Gomes, the psychiatrist at the Dr Eiras clinic. Luckily for Paulo, this time the doctor decided to replace electric shocks with daily sessions of analysis, which, during the first weeks, were held at his home. Paulo's persecution mania had become so extreme that, on one outing, he became so frightened that he fainted in the street in front of a bookshop in Copacabana and was helped by passers-by. When Philips sent him the proofs for the record sleeve for *Gita*, which was about to be released, he couldn't believe his eyes: it was a photo of Raul with a Che Guevara beret bearing the red five-pointed star of the communists. Appalled, he immediately phoned Philips and demanded that they change the image; if they didn't, he would not allow any of his songs to appear on the record.

When they asked why, he replied so slowly that he seemed to be spelling out each word: 'Because I don't want to be arrested again and with that photo on the record sleeve, they'll arrest me again. Understood?'

After much discussion, he accepted that Raul could be shown wearing the Che beret, but he demanded a written statement from Philips stating that the choice was the entire responsibility of the company. In the end, a suggestion by a graphic artist won the day: the red star was simply removed from the photo, so that it looked as though the beret was merely an innocent beret with no sinister communist connotations.

Since Gisa refused to answer his calls, Paulo began to write her letters each day, asking forgiveness for what he had done in the prison and suggesting that they live together again. In one of these letters he wrote of his feelings of insecurity during the three years they had spent together:

> I didn't understand why, when you moved in with me, you brought just the bare minimum of clothes. I never understood why you insisted on continuing to pay the rent on the other empty apartment. I wanted to put pressure on you with money, saying I wouldn't pay any more, but you still kept on the other apartment. The fact that the other apartment existed made me really insecure. It meant that from one moment to the next you could escape my grasp and regain your freedom.

Gisa never replied, but he continued to write. One day, his father, clearly upset, took him to one side. 'Look, Gisa phoned me at the office,' he told him, his hand on his son's shoulder. 'She asked me to tell you not to write to her again.' Paulo ignored the request and went on writing: 'Today my father told me that you don't want to see me again. I also learned that you're working, which is good, and I felt both hurt and happy. I had just heard "Gita" on the radio. I was wondering whether you think of me when you hear that song. I think they were the most beautiful lyrics I've written so far. It contains all of me. Now I don't read, don't write and I've no friends.'

This was one of the symptoms of his paranoia, that all his friends had supposedly abandoned him for fear of being close to someone who had been seized and imprisoned by the security police. Whether this was real or imagined, what mattered was his belief that, apart from Raul, only two people held out a hand to him: the journalist Hildegard Angel and Roberto Menescal, one of the creators of the bossa nova and, at the time, a director of Polygram. Together with Phonogram, Polydor and Elenco, the company was one of the Brazilian arms of the Dutch multinational Philips, and one of its greatest rivals in Brazil was CBS, a subsidiary of the American company Columbia. Hilde, as she was and is known, continued to be a friend to Paulo even though she had painful reasons to avoid risking any more confrontations with the dictatorship: three years earlier, her youngest brother, Stuart Angel, who was a member of the guerrilla group MR-8, had been brutally asphyxiated at an air force barracks, with his mouth pressed to the exhaust pipe of a moving jeep. His wife, the economist Sônia Moraes Angel, a member of the ALN (National Liberationist Movement), had also died while being tortured by the DOI-Codi in São Paulo a few months earlier, at the end of 1973. As if these two tragedies were not enough for one family, Hilde and Stuart's mother, the designer Zuzu Angel, was to die two years later in a car accident that had all the hallmarks of an assassination attempt and became the subject of the film *Zuzu Angel*.

It was Hilde who, after much insistence, convinced Paulo to get back into circulation. She invited him to attend the debate 'Women and Communication' at which she was to participate with the feminist Rose Marie Muraro at the Museu Nacional de Belas-Artes. Paulo's justified paranoia would have reached unbearable levels had he known that among the audience was a spy, Deuteronômio Rocha dos Santos, who wrote a report on the meeting for the Section of Special Searches (part of the Dops) in which he said: 'among those present was the journalist and writer Paulo Coelho, a personal friend of Hildegard Angel'.

As soon as he felt strong enough to go around without fear of being kidnapped again, Paulo's first important step after what he referred to as the 'black week' was to search out the OTO. He had two reasons for going to see Frater Zaratustra: first, he wanted to understand what had happened in his apartment on that dreadful Saturday and, second, whatever the explanation, he was going to distance himself permanently from the sect. His fear of the Devil was such that he asked Euclydes-Zaratustra to meet him during the day at his parents' house, where he had gone back to live, and, for good measure, he invited Roberto Menescal to be there as a witness. This turned out to be a good idea: to his surprise, on the appointed day, who should appear at the house in Gávea but Parzival XI, the self-crowned world head of the sect – the sinister and uncouth Marcelo Ramos Motta. Paulo decided to come straight to the point. After summarizing what had happened at his home and in prison, he asked: 'I want to know what happened to me that Saturday and on the following days.'

Parzival XI eyed him scornfully. 'You always knew that with us what counts is the law of the strongest. I taught you that, remember? According to the law of the strongest, whoever holds out succeeds. Those who don't, fail. That's it. You were weak and failed.'

Menescal, who was listening to the conversation from a distance, threatened to attack the visitor – something that would have endangered the Coelhos' china and crystal, since Menescal practised aikido and the Crowleyite Ramos Motta was a black belt in ju-jitsu.

But Paulo restrained him and, for the first time, addressed the high priest by his real name: 'So is that what the OTO is, Marcelo? On Saturday, the Devil appears in my house, on Monday, I'm arrested and on Wednesday, I'm abducted? That's the OTO, is it? Well, in that case, my friend, I'm out of it.'

As soon as he found himself free from the sect, it was with great relief, as though he had sloughed off a great burden, that Paulo sat down at his typewriter and wrote an official document formalizing his rejection of the mysterious Ordo Templi Orientis. His brief and dramatic incursion into the kingdom of darkness had lasted less than two months:

Rio de Janeiro, 6 July 1974

I, Paulo Coelho de Souza, who signed my declaration as a Probationer in the year LXX, 19 May, with the sun in the sign of Taurus, 1974 e.v., ask and consider myself to be excluded from the Order because of my complete incompetence in realizing the tasks given me.

I declare that, in taking this decision, I am in a perfect state of physical and mental health.

93 93 / 93

As witness my hand,

Paulo Coelho

What Paulo believed to be a break with the Devil and his followers did not mean the end of his paranoia. In fact he felt safe only when at home with his parents and with the doors locked. It was during this period of despair that the idea of leaving Brazil for a while, at least until the fear subsided, first surfaced. With Gisa out of his life there was nothing to keep him in Brazil. The sales of *Gita* had outstripped even the most optimistic expectations and the money kept pouring into his bank account.

This coincided with another important moment in Paulo's progress: the launch of his first book. Although it was not the Great Work he dreamed of producing, it was nevertheless a book. It had been published at the end of 1973 by the highly regarded Editora Forense, which specialized in educational books, and was entitled *O Teatro na Educação* [*Theatre in Education*]. In it he explained the programme of courses he had given in state schools in Mato Grosso. Not even an admiring review by Gisa published on their weekly page in *Tribuna* had been able to get sales moving: a year after its launch, the book had sold only 500 copies out of an initial print run of 3,000. Although it was predictable that the work would pass almost unnoticed in the world of letters, this was still his first book and therefore deserved to be celebrated. When Gisa had arrived home on the day it came out, on the dining table stood two glasses and a miniature of Benedictine liqueur that Paulo had won at the age of fifteen and kept all that time, promising not to open it until he published his first book.

Not even this initial lack of success as an author or the wealth that came with fame, however, could shake the dream that he himself admitted had become an obsession: to be a writer known throughout the world. Even after he had become well known as a lyricist, that dream would return as strongly as ever when he was alone. A rapid flick through his diaries reveals, in sentences dotted here and there, that public recognition as a lyricist had not changed his plan one jot: he wanted to be not just another writer but 'world-famous'. He regretted that by the time they were his age, The Beatles 'had already conquered the world', but Paulo didn't lose hope that, one day, his dreams would be realized. 'I'm like a warrior waiting to make his entrance on the scene,' he wrote, 'and my destiny is success. My great talent is to fight for it.'

Raul had been very shaken by his friend's imprisonment, and Paulo had no difficulty in convincing him, too, to go abroad for a while. Less than ten days after their decision to leave Brazil, they were ready for departure. The fact that they had to go to the Dops to receive a visa to leave the country – a requirement imposed by the dictatorship on anyone wanting to travel abroad – so frightened Paulo that he had a serious asthma attack. But on 14 July 1974, a month and a half after his kidnapping, the two partners landed in New York with no fixed return date.

They each had on their arm a new girlfriend. Raul had separated from Edith, the mother of his daughter, Simone, and was living with another American, Gloria Vaquer, the sister of the drummer Jay Vaquer. Abandoned by Gisa, Paulo had started a relationship with the beautiful Maria do Rosário do Nascimento e Silva, a slim brunette of twenty-three. She was an actress, scriptwriter and film producer. She was also the daughter of a judge from Minas Gerais, Luiz Gonzaga do Nascimento e Silva, who, a week before the trip, had been named Minister for Social Services by General Ernesto Geisel, the President of the Republic. Despite her father's political activities, Rosário was a left-wing activist who hid those being persecuted by the regime and who had been arrested when filming statements by workers at the Central do Brasil railway station in Rio. When she met Paulo, through Hilde Angel, she was just emerging from a tempestuous three-year marriage to Walter Clark, the then director-general of the Globo television network.

The bank balance of any of those four travellers was more than enough for them to stay in comfort at the Hotel Plaza opposite Central Park or in the Algonquin, both natural staging posts for stars passing through New York. In the crazy 1970s, however, the in thing was to stay in 'exciting' places. So it was that Paulo, Rosário, Raul and Gloria knocked at the door of the Marlton Hotel, or, to be more precise, on the iron bars that protected the entrance of the hotel from the street gangs of Greenwich Village.

Built in 1900, the Marlton was famous for welcoming anyone, be they pimps, prostitutes, drug-dealers, film stars, jazz musicians or beatniks. Such people as the actors John Barrymore, Geraldine Page and Claire Bloom, the singers Harry Belafonte, Carmen McRae and Miriam Makeba and beat writer Jack Kerouac had stayed in some of its 114 rooms, most of which shared a bathroom on the landing. The fanatical feminist Valerie Solanas left one of those rooms in June 1968, armed with a revolver, to carry out an attack on the pop artist Andy Warhol that nearly killed him. Raul and Gloria's apartment, which had a sitting room, bedroom and bathroom, cost US$300 a month. Paulo and Rosário had only a bedroom and bathroom, which cost US$200, but there was no refrigerator, which meant they had to spend their days drinking warm Coke and neat whisky – this, of course, when they weren't smoking cannabis or sniffing cocaine, their main pastimes.

On 8 August 1974, the eyes of the whole world were turned on the United States. After two years and two months of involvement in the Watergate scandal, Richard Nixon's Republican government was suffering a very public death. The big decisions were taken in Washington, but the heart of America beat in New York. There seemed to be a more-than-usual electric atmosphere in the Big Apple. It was expected that at any moment either the President would be impeached or he would resign. After a night spent in a fashionable nightclub, Paulo and Rosário woke at three in the afternoon, went out for a big breakfast at Child, a rough bar a block away from the Marlton, and then returned to their room. They had a few lines of cocaine and when they came to, it was getting dark. On the radio on the bedside table, the reporter was announcing that in ten minutes there was to be a national radio and television transmission of an announcement by President Nixon.

Paulo jumped off the bed, saying: 'Come on, Maria! Let's go down and record the reactions of the people when he announces his resignation.' He put on a denim jacket but no shirt and his knee-high riding boots, grabbed his portable recorder – a heavy thing the size of a telephone directory – filled his pockets with cassette tapes and hung his cine camera round Rosário's neck, telling her to hurry: 'Come on, Maria! We can't miss this. It's going to be better than the final of the World Cup!'

He turned on the recorder when they got outside and began describing what he could see, as though making a live radio report:

> Paulo – Today is 8th August 1974. I am on 8th Street, heading for the Shakespeare restaurant. In five minutes' time the President of the United States is going to resign. Right, we've arrived. We're here in the Shakespeare, the TV is on but the broadcast hasn't started yet … What did you say?
>
> Rosário – I said I still think the American people aren't cold at all. Quite the contrary!
>
> Paulo – It's like a football match. The TV's on here in the bar of the Shakespeare restaurant. The broadcast hasn't started yet but there are already loads of people out in the street.
>
> Rosário – Everyone's shouting, can you hear?
>
> Paulo – I can!

In the crowded restaurant, the two managed to find a place in front of the television that was suspended from the ceiling, its volume on maximum. Wearing a navy-blue suit and red tie, Nixon appeared on the screen, looking very sombre. A church-like silence fell in the bar as he began to read the speech in which he resigned from the most important position in the world. For almost fifteen minutes, the people standing around made not a sound as Nixon explained the reasons that had led him to this dramatic decision. His speech ended on a sad note: 'To have served in this office is to have felt a very personal sense of kinship with each and every American. In leaving it, I do so with this prayer: may God's grace be with you in all the days ahead.'

As soon as the speech had ended Paulo was out in the street, closely followed by Maria do Rosário, with the microphone to his mouth like a radio announcer.

Paulo – Christ! I was really moved, Rosário, I really was! If one day I have to resign, I hope it's like that … But look! Nixon has just resigned and there's some guy dancing in the corner.

Rosário – Dancing and playing the banjo. This country's full of madmen!

Paulo – My feelings, at this moment, are completely indescribable. We're walking along 8th Street.

Rosário – The people are really so happy. Oh, it's just too much!

Paulo – They really are! They're sort of half-surprised, Maria. Really! The television crews are interviewing people in the streets! This is an historic day!

Rosário – There's a woman crying, a girl crying. She's genuinely upset.

Paulo – It's a truly fantastic moment, isn't it? Really, really fantastic!

The two returned to the Marlton, feeling very excited. Rosário got out at the third floor, where their apartment was, and Paulo took the lift up to the seventh, because he wanted Raul to listen to the tapes recording the madness that had taken hold of New York that evening. When he opened the door, without knocking, as was their habit, he found his partner lying flat out on the sofa, sleeping with his mouth open. On the small table next to him was a line of cocaine ready to be sniffed, a half-drunk bottle of whisky and a pile of money amounting to about US$5,000 in one hundred dollar bills. For someone coming from a public celebration as Paulo had, after having been witness to a spontaneous street festival, the shock of seeing his friend lying there, completely out of it, a victim of drugs and alcohol, was a real wake-up call. He was sad not only to see a friend in that state – a friend whom he had introduced to the world of drugs – but also because he realized that cocaine was leading him down the same path.

Paulo had never confessed this to anyone, not even to his diary, but he knew he was becoming drug-dependent. He returned to his room in a state of shock. He saw Rosário's slim body lying naked on the bed, lit only by the bluish light from the street.

He sat shamefaced beside his girlfriend and gently stroked her back as he announced in a whisper: 'Today is an historic day for me too. On 8 August 1974, I stopped sniffing cocaine.'

CHAPTER 18

Cissa

THEIR PLAN TO REMAIN IN NEW YORK for a few months was cut short by an unforeseen incident. One evening, Paulo was trying out an electric can-opener and accidently let the sharp blade slip, catching his right hand. Rosário tried to staunch the flow of blood with a bath towel, and it immediately became a ball of blood. He was taken by ambulance to a first-aid station in Greenwich Village, where he learned that the gadget had sliced the tendon in the third finger of his right hand. He had emergency surgery and ended up with nine stitches in his finger and had to wear a metal splint for several weeks, which immobilized his hand. A few days later, he and Rosário left for Brazil, while Raul and Gloria travelled on to Memphis.

On his return to Rio, Paulo found that he was strong enough to confront his ghosts and decided to live alone in the apartment where he had lived with Gisa. However, his courage was short-lived. On 10 September, after two weeks, he was once again berthed in the secure port of his parents' house in Gávea. Anxious to free himself of everything that might remind him of demons, prisons and abductions, before moving to their house, he sold all his books, records and pictures. When he saw his bare apartment, with nothing on the walls or shelves, he wrote in his diary: 'I have just freed myself from the past.' But it wasn't going to be that easy. His paranoia, fears and complexes continued to trouble him. He frequently confessed that he continued to feel guilty even about things that had happened during his childhood, such as having 'placed my hand on a girl's private parts', or even 'dreaming of doing sinful things with Mama'. But at least at home it was unlikely that anyone could simply abduct him, with no questions asked.

At a time when sexual promiscuity appeared to carry few risks, he recorded in his diary the women who came and went in his life without saying anything much about them, apart from some statement as to how well this woman or that had performed in bed. Sometimes he set up meetings with ex-girlfriends, but the truth is that he had still not got over the end of his affair with Gisa, to whom he continued to write and from whom he never received a reply. When he learned that Vera Richter was back with her ex-husband he noted: 'Today I went into town to resolve my psychological problem with a few shares in the Bank of Brazil. I was thinking of selling them and giving the money to Mário in exchange for having possessed Vera for more than a year. In fact it was Vera who possessed me, but in my muddled head I always thought it was the other way round.'

His partnership with Raul continued to produce impressive results, but the ship of the Sociedade Alternativa was beginning to let in water. Even before the 'dark night' and Paulo's imprisonment, disagreements between them and Philips as to the meaning of the Sociedade Alternativa had begun to arise. Everything indicates that Raul had been serious about creating a new community – a sect, religion or movement – that would practise and spread the commandments of Aleister Crowley, Parzival XI and Frater Zaratustra. For the executives of the recording company, however, the Sociedade Alternativa was nothing more than a brand name they could use to boost the sales of records. The president of Philips in Brazil, André Midani, a Syrian who had become a Brazilian national, had created an informal working group to help the company market its artists better. This dream team, which was coordinated by Midani and the composer Roberto Menescal, consisted of the market researcher Homero Icaza Sánchez, the writer Rubem Fonseca and the journalists Artur da Távola, Dorrit Harazim, Nelson Motta, Luis Carlos Maciel, João Luís de Albuquerque and Zuenir Ventura. The group would meet once a week in a suite in some luxury hotel in Rio and spend a whole day there discussing the profile and work of a particular Philips artist. At the first meeting, they would simply talk among themselves, and then the following week, they would repeat the exercise with the artist present. Those taking part were paid well – Zuenir Ventura describes how for each meeting he would receive 'four thousand or four million, I can't remember which, but I know that it was the equivalent of my monthly salary as a director of the Rio branch of the magazine *Visão*'.

When it was time for Paulo and Raul to face the group, it was Raul who was in the grip of paranoia. He was sure he was being followed by plainclothes policemen and had taken on a bodyguard, the investigator Millen Yunes, from the Leblon police department, who, in his spare time, was to accompany the musician wherever he went. When Paulo told him that Menescal had invited them to be questioned by the select group of intellectuals, Raul declared: 'It's a trick on the part of the police! I bet you the police have infiltrated the group in order to record what we say. Tell Menescal we're not going.'

Paulo assured his partner that there was no danger, that he knew most of the participants and that some were even people who were opposed to the dictatorship; finally he promised that neither Midani nor Menescal would play such a trick. Since Raul refused to budge, Paulo went alone to the meeting, but because of Raul's concerns, he placed a tape recorder on the table so that he could give the tapes to his partner afterwards. Before the discussion began, someone asked Paulo to explain, in his own words, what exactly the Sociedade Alternativa was. From what he can remember more than three decades later, he hadn't taken any drugs or been smoking cannabis; however, to judge by what he said, which was all captured on tape, you would think he must have taken something:

The Sociedade Alternativa reaches the political level, the social level, the social stratum of a people, you see? Shit, it also reaches the intellectuals in a country whose people are coming down from a trip, who are being more demanding ... So much so that there was a discussion in São Paulo about the magazine *Planeta*. I reckon *Planeta* is going to go bust in a year from now because everyone who reads *Planeta* is

bound to think that *Planeta* is a stupid magazine, well, it failed in
France, and so they invented *Le Nouveau Planète*, then *Le Nouveau
Nouveau Planète*, do you see what I mean? They ended up closing
down the magazine. That's what's going to happen with all these
people who are into macumba. No, no, no! I don't mean the prole-
tariat, but what people call the middle classes. The bourgeoisie who
suddenly decided to take an interest, you know. Intellectually, like.
Obviously there's another aspect to the question which is the aspect
of faith, of you going there and making a promise, and getting some
advantage, you know, things like that. Right, but in cultural terms
there's going to be a change, right? And the change is going to come
from abroad, just like it always does, do you see what I'm saying?
And it's never going to be filtered through a Brazilian product called
spiritualism. That's on the spiritual level, of course, because I think on
the political level I've been clear enough.

Clarity was obviously not his strong point, but the working group seemed
to be used to people like him. Paulo paused a second for breath, and then
went on:

So ... there's going to be this filtering. In my opinion, it's not filtering,
but no one's ever going to stop getting a buzz out of Satan, because
it's a really fascinating subject. It's a taboo like ... like virginity, do
you understand? So, when everyone starts talking about Satan, even
if you're afraid of the Devil and hate him, you really want to get into
it, do you understand? Because it's aggression, State agression turned
against itself, the aggression of repression, right? A series of things
turn up inside this scheme and you start to get into it ... It's not a trip
that's going to last very long, it hasn't even happened yet, the Satan
trip. But it's a phenomenon. It's the result of aggression, of the same
thing as free love, of the sexual taboo that the hippies opened up.
    [...] I haven't given, like, an overview of the Sociedade
Alternativa. I've just noted a few things, but I wanted to give an
overview of everything that we created, a general vision of the thing,
right? Anyway, where does Raul Seixas fit in with all this? The

Sociedade Alternativa serves Raul Seixas and he's not going to change his mind because we've spent two days talking about the Sociedade Alternativa and nothing but, right? The Sociedade Alternativa serves Raul Seixas in the sense that Raul Seixas is a catalyst for this type of movement, all right? It's been judged to be a myth. No one can explain what the Sociedade Alternativa is.

Do you see what I mean?

'More or less,' the journalist Artur da Távola replied. Since most of those present had understood none of this nonsense, the problem the group put to Paulo was a simple one: if this was the explanation he and Raul were going to give to the press, then they should prepare themselves to see the idea made mincemeat of by the media. Dorrit Harazim, who, at the time, was editor of the international section of the magazine *Veja*, thought that if they wanted to convince the public that the Sociedade Alternativa was not merely a marketing strategy but some kind of mystical or political movement, then they would need far more objective arguments: 'First of all, you need to decide whether the Sociedade Alternativa is political or metaphysical. With the arguments you put to us, it will be very hard for you to explain to anyone what the Sociedade Alternativa actually is.'

This was the first time the working group had reached a unanimous decision about anything, and it fell to Artur da Távola to remind them that they risked losing a gold mine: 'We need to be very careful because we're pointing out defects in a duo who sell hundreds of thousands of records. We mustn't forget that Raul and Paulo are already a runaway success.'

However, there was another matter bothering the group: Raul and Paulo's insistence on telling the press that they had seen flying saucers. They all believed that this was something that could affect the commercial standing of the duo, and they suggested that Paulo tell Raul to stop it. They had good reason to be concerned. Some months earlier, Raul had given a long interview to *Pasquim* and, inevitably, he was pressed by the journalists to explain the Sociedade Alternativa and his sightings of flying saucers, giving him the chance to ramble on at will. He explained that it was a society that wasn't governed by any truth or any leader, but had arisen 'like a realization of a new tactic, of a new method'. As his reply was somewhat unclear, he made another attempt to explain what he meant: 'The Sociedade Alternativa is the fruit of the actual mechanism of the thing,' he went on, adding that it had already crossed frontiers. 'We're in constant correspondence with John Lennon and Yoko Ono, who are also part of the Society.' With no one there to keep a check on him, Raul even made up facts about things that were public knowledge, such as his first meeting with Paulo. 'I met Paulo in Barra da Tijuca,' he told *Pasquim*. 'At five in the afternoon, I was there meditating and he was too, but I didn't know him then – it was then that we saw the flying saucer.' One of the interviewers asked whether he could describe the supposed UFO and he said: 'It was sort of … silver, but with an orange aura round it. It just stood there, enormous it was. Paulo came running over to me, I didn't know him, but he said, "Can you see what I see?" We just sat there and the saucer zigzagged off and vanished.' It was statements like these that made the Philips work group fear that the duo risked exposing themselves to public ridicule.

When the session ended, Paulo took the recorded tapes to his partner. Since the working group's comments had not been exactly flattering, instead of telling Raul to his face what had happened, Paulo preferred to record another tape on arriving home, in which he gave Raul his version of the meeting:

The working group's great fear is that the Sociedade Alternativa might work out and that you, Raul – listening to this tape – won't be up to the challenge. They're afraid that the Sociedade Alternativa will grow and that when you go to give an interview on what the Sociedade Alternativa is … as Artur da Távola said, you'll talk a lot but won't explain things. And the press will fall about laughing, will say it's a farce and your career will go up in smoke. What I mean is, Philips' main concern is that you're not up to it. The meeting was extremely tense. There's one point I really feel they won't budge on: your inability, Raul, to hold out. You'll hear that on the tape and I'm talking about it now because that's the impression I got.

Another thing that came up was the problem of the flying saucer, with everyone saying that it's stupid. They said, for example, that every time you repeat the story about the flying saucer, the press will just laugh at you. I decided to stay quiet and not say whether it was true or false. But the working group reckon that the flying saucer story should gradually be abandoned. I didn't say as much, but I left it open at least to the working group that we might deny the story about the flying saucer.

Although the idea of the Sociedade Alternativa proved alluring enough to attract hundreds of thousands of record buyers and an unknown number of Devil-worshippers from all over Brazil, time would prove the working group right. As time went on, the expression 'Sociedade Alternativa' would be remembered only as the chorus of a song from the 1970s.

Now, not long after his return from New York with his hand strapped up, and at the height of the success of *Gita* (which had been released in their absence), Paulo was invited by Menescal to join the working group as a consultant, with the same pay as the other members, which meant an additional US$11,600 per month. Money was flooding in from all sides. When he received the first set of accounts from the recording company for initial sales of *Gita*, he wondered whether to invest the money in shares or to buy a summer house in Araruama, but finally decided upon an apartment in the busy Rua Barata Ribeiro, in Copacabana. At this time, Paulo also wrote three sets of lyrics – 'Cartão Postal', 'Esse Tal de Roque Enrow' and 'O Toque' – for the LP *Fruto Proibido*, that the singer Rita Lee released at the beginning of 1975, and he also produced film scripts for Maria do Rosário. In between, he acted in the porn movie *Tangarela, a Tanga de Cristal*. In December 1974, the recording company abandoned the working group, but then, at Menescal's suggestion, André Midani contracted Paulo Coelho to work as a company executive, managing the creative department.

His new financial and professional security did not, however, have the effect of comforting his tortured soul. Until May 1974, he had just about managed to live with his feelings of persecution and rejection, but following his imprisonment, these appeared to reach an unbearable level.

Of the 600 pages of his diary written during the twelve months following his release, more than 400 deal with the fears resulting from that
black week. In one notebook of 60 pages chosen at random, the word
'fear' is repeated 142 times, 'problem' 118 times, and there are dozens of
instances of words such as 'solitude', 'despair', 'paranoia' and 'alien-
ation'. He wrote at the bottom of one page, quoting Guimarães Rosa: 'It
is not fear, no. It's just that I've lost the will to have courage.' In May
1975, on the first anniversary of his release from the DOI-Codi, he paid
for a mass of thanksgiving to be celebrated at the church of St Joseph,
his protector.

Since leaving prison, the person who gave him the greatest sense of
security – more even than Dr Benjamim and even perhaps his father –
was the lawyer Antônio Cláudio Vieira, whom Paulo considered responsible for his release. As soon as he returned from the United States, he
asked his father to make an appointment for him to thank Vieira for his
help. When he arrived at the lawyer's luxurious apartment with its spectacular view of Flamengo, Paulo was completely bowled over by the
lawyer's dark, pretty daughter, Eneida, who was a lawyer like her father
and worked in his office. During that first meeting, the two merely flirted,
but exactly forty-seven days later, Paulo proposed to Eneida, and she
immediately accepted. According to the social values of the time, not
only was he in a position to marry, but he was also a good prospect –
someone with enough money to maintain a wife and children. The new
album he had made with Raul, *Novo Aeon*, had been released at the end
of 1975. The two had written four of the thirteen tracks ('Rock do Diabo',
'Caminhos I', 'Tú És o MDC da Minha Vida' and 'A Verdade sobre a
Nostalgia'). The record also revealed Raul's continued involvement with
the satanists of the OTO: the ill-mannered Marcelo Motta had written
the lyrics of no fewer than five of the tracks ('Tente Outra Vez', 'A Maçã',
'Eu Sou Egoísta', 'Peixuxa – O Amiguinho dos Peixes' and 'Novo Aeon').
Although Raul and his followers considered the record a masterpiece,
Novo Aeon was not a patch on the previous albums, and sold only a little
over forty thousand copies.

Paulo clearly had enough money to start a family, but asking for the
girl's hand so quickly could only be explained by a burning passion, which,

however, was not the case. As far as Paulo was concerned, he had not only found a woman he could finally marry and 'settle down' with – as he had been promising himself he would do since leaving prison – but he would also have the guarantor of his emotional security, Antônio Cláudio Vieira, as his father-in-law. On the evening of 16 June 1975, after smoking a joint, Paulo decided that it was time to resolve the matter. He called Eneida, asking her to tell her parents that he was going to formalize his offer of marriage: 'I just need time to go home and pick up my parents. Then we'll come straight over.'

His parents were fast asleep, but were hauled out of their beds by their crazy son who had suddenly decided to become engaged. Whether it was the effects of the cannabis, or whether it was because he had never before played such a role, the fact is that when it came to speaking to his future father-in-law, Paulo's mouth went dry, and he choked and stammered and was unable to say a single word.

Vieira saved the situation by saying: 'We all know what you want to say. You're asking for Eneida's hand in marriage, aren't you? If so, the answer is "Yes".'

As they all toasted the engagement with champagne, Paulo produced a beautiful diamond ring that he had bought for his future wife. The following day, Eneida reciprocated Paulo's present by sending to his house an Olivetti electric typewriter, which the author continued to use until 1992, when he changed to working on a computer.

Not even three weeks had passed before his diary began to reveal that the engagement had perhaps been over-hasty: 'I have serious problems with my relationship with Eneida. I chose her for the security and emotional stability that she would give me. I chose her because I was looking for a counter-balance to my naturally unbalanced temperament. Now I understand the price I have to pay for this: castration. Castration in my behaviour, castration in my conversation, castration in my madness. I can't take it.'

To go back on his word and break off the engagement did not even enter his head, because it would mean not only losing the lawyer but gaining an enemy – the mere thought of which made his blood run cold. But Paulo realized that Eneida was also getting fed up with his strange habits.

She didn't mind if he continued to smoke cannabis, but she didn't want to use it herself, and Paulo was constantly at her to do just that. As for his 'sexual propositions', she made it quite clear: he could forget any ideas of having a *ménage à trois*. Eneida was not prepared to allow his girlfriends to share their bed. A split was, therefore, inevitable. When the engagement was only forty days old Paulo recorded in his diary that it had all come to an end:

> Eneida simply left me. It's been very difficult, really very difficult. I chose her as a wife and companion, but she couldn't hack it and suddenly disappeared from my life. I've tried desperately to get in touch with her mother, but both her parents have disappeared as well. I'm afraid that she has told her parents about my Castaneda-like ideas and my sexual propositions. I know that she told them about those. The break-up was really hard for me, much harder than I had imagined. My mother and father are going to be very shocked when they hear. And it's going to be difficult for them to accept another woman in the way they accepted my ex-fiancée. I know that, but what can I do? Go off again and immediately start looking for another companion.

The companion on whom he had his eye was a trainee, Cecília Mac Dowell, who was working on the press team at Philips. But before declaring himself to Cissa, as she was known, Paulo had a lightning romance with Elisabeth Romero, who was also a journalist and had interviewed him for a music magazine. They started going out together, and the affair took off. Beth rode a large Kawasaki 900 motorbike, and Paulo took to riding pillion. Although the affair was short-lived, it allowed Beth to witness an episode which Paulo was to describe dozens, if not hundreds of times in interviews published in the international press: the meeting he never had with his idol Jorge Luis Borges.

With the Christmas holidays approaching, Paulo invited Beth to go with him to Buenos Aires, where he intended to visit the great Argentinean writer. He had been putting off the trip for some time, reluctant to go to the police in order to ask for an exit visa to travel to the neighbouring country, fearing that he might be arrested again. They made no attempt to get in touch with Borges beforehand or to obtain some kind of letter of introduction, but the couple were nevertheless prepared to put up with the forty-eight-hour bus journey between Rio and Buenos Aires, armed only with Borges's address: Calle Maipu 900. As soon as they arrived, Paulo went straight there. The porter of the apartment block, in the centre of the city, told him that Don Jorge Luis was on the other side of the road having a coffee in the bar of an old hotel. Paulo crossed the road, went into the lobby and saw through the window the unmistakable silhouette of the great author of *El Aleph*, then seventy-six years old, seated alone at a table, drinking an espresso. Such was his excitement that Paulo didn't have the courage to go up to him. Creeping out as silently as he had entered, he left without saying a word to Borges – something he would always regret.

At the age of twenty-eight, he was to spend his first Christmas away from his family. On the path to Christian reconversion, on 24 December he invited Beth to go with him to midnight mass. Surprised by her refusal – she preferred to spend the night walking through the streets of Buenos Aires – he simply ended the relationship. He telephoned Cissa in Rio on the pretext of wishing her a happy Christmas and declared: 'I'm in love with you and I'll be home in three days' time. If you promise to meet me at the airport, I'll take a plane so we can be together as soon as possible.'

Small, like him, with brown eyes and a slightly aquiline nose, Cecília Mac Dowell was nineteen and doing media studies at university in Rio de Janeiro when she met Paulo. She was the daughter of Patrícia Fait, an American, and the wealthy and respected TB specialist Afonso Emílio de la Rocque Mac Dowell, the owner of a large clinic in Jacarepaguá. She had been educated at the traditional Colégio Brasileiro de Almeida in Copacabana, which had been set up and run by Nilza Jobim, the mother of the composer Tom Jobim. Although she came from a conservative background – her father came from the northeast and her mother had received a strict Protestant education – the Mac Dowells welcomed with open arms the hippie who had fallen in love with their youngest child. As the months went by, Patrícia and Afonso Emílio shut their eyes to the fact that Cissa spent every weekend with her boyfriend (who had rented out his apartment in Voluntários da Pâtria and moved to the two-roomed apartment in noisy Barata Ribeiro). Thirty years later, Cissa would look back and see some ulterior motives behind her parents' broad-mindedness: 'I think that because my two older sisters hadn't married, my parents lowered their expectations regarding future sons-in-law. They thought it best not to frighten off any potential candidates.'

Whatever her parents' reasoning, the fact is that at the end of the week, when the Mac Dowells went to their country house in Petrópolis, Cissa would put a few clothes and possessions into a cloth bag and set off to the apartment in Barata Ribeiro. The memory of his disastrous engagement to Eneida, however, continued to trouble Paulo whenever such a situation threatened to reappear: He wrote in his diary: 'This evening, we're having supper at Cissa's house and I hate that because it looks like we're engaged, and the last thing I want at the moment is to be someone's fiancé.' During one of his sessions with the psychiatrist, which he continued to attend frequently, Dr Benjamim Gomes suggested that his nervous tension arose from his problems with sexual relationships: 'He said that my lack of interest in sex is causing the tension I'm experiencing. In fact, Cissa is a bit like me: she doesn't insist that much on having sex. This suited me fine because I wasn't under any obligation, but now I'm going to use sex as a therapy to relieve tension. Dr Benjamim told me that the curve on the graph produced by electroshock treatment is the same as for an orgasm or for an epileptic fit. That's how I discovered sex as therapy.'

Although he still avoided any mention of an engagement, in March 1976, when his girlfriend returned from a three-week trip to Europe, Paulo proposed marriage. Cissa accepted with genuine happiness, but she laid down certain conditions: she wanted a real marriage, both in a register office and in church, with a priest, and with the bride in white and the groom in jacket and tie. He burst out laughing, telling her that he would accept all her demands in the name of love; 'besides I really needed to do something conventional and there was nothing better than marriage for that'.

Before the ceremony Paulo consulted the I Ching several times to discover whether he was doing the right thing, and he recorded in his diary his feelings of insecurity: 'Yesterday I was filled with a real dread of marriage and I was terrified. I reacted violently. We were both feeling a bit suspicious of each other and things turned ugly.' Two days later, his state of mind was quite different: 'I've been sleeping away from the apartment because I'm suffering from paranoia. I'm desperate for Cissa to come and live with me now. We really do love each other and understand each other and she's a very easy person to be with. But before she can do that, we have to go through the farce of the wedding.'

On 2 July, however, Paulo was even more dressed up than his fiancée had demanded. Punctually, at seven in the evening, as Chopin's Nocturne No. 2 was playing, he took his place to the right of the priest in St Joseph's Church. Compared with the Paulo Coelho who had allowed himself to be photographed drunk and dishevelled in New York two years earlier, the man at the altar looked like a prince. With short hair, and his moustache and goatee neatly trimmed, he was wearing a modern morning suit, with a double-breasted jacket, striped trousers, black shoes, a white shirt with cufflinks and a silver tie – identical clothes to those worn by his father and father-in-law, although not by his two best men, Roberto Menescal and Raul Seixas.

To the sound of Elgar's 'Pomp and Circumstance', five bridesmaids led the way for the bride, who arrived on her father's arm and wearing a long white dress. Among the dozens of guests filling the church, Raul Seixas was a most striking figure, in dark glasses, red bowtie and a jacket with matching red stitching. At the blessing of the rings, music filled the nave and the ceremony ended to the chords of Albinoni's Adagio. Afterwards, everyone went back to the bride's parents' apartment, where the civil ceremony was performed, followed by a magnificent dinner.

The honeymoon was nothing special. Since both had to get back to work, they spent a week in a summer house that belonged to Paulo's parents on the island of Jaguanum, off the Rio de Janeiro coast. Neither has particularly fond memories of that time. There is no reference to the trip in Paulo's diaries, and Cissa commented: 'Paulo wasn't very happy. I don't think he wanted all that formality … He agreed to it, but only, I think, because I insisted. But it wasn't the sort of honeymoon, where you'd say, oh, it was marvellous, we were so in love. No. No, I don't recall that. I know we spent a few days there, I can't say how many, and then went back to our little life in Rio.'

Their 'little life' was to start with a slight disagreement between husband and wife. Paulo insisted on living in his two-room apartment in Barata Ribeiro, not because it was cheap, but because it was near his parents, who had sold their house in Gávea and moved to a new apartment in Rua Raimundo Correia, in Copacabana, just a block away. The memories Cissa has of the first months of her marriage are not very encouraging:

> Living there was dreadful. The only bedroom looked directly out on to Rua Barata Ribeiro, which was incredibly noisy. But he was in his maternal phase and wanted it so that he could be close to his mother, who lived in the same district. Our apartment would hardly have fitted into a decent-sized living room. He had another apartment, but wanted to stay close to his mother. I had been brought up to be a good Protestant, and so I did everything I could for the sake of the marriage and learned to fall asleep to the noise from the street. We got married in July, and I think we stayed there for about six months.

This may not have been one of the most promising starts to a marriage, but the marriage survived. Sometimes, however, their fights were very noisy, as in the early hours of 24 August, Paulo's twenty-ninth birthday. Cissa was woken at two in the morning by a loud bang, as if a bomb had gone off in the building. She got up, terrified, and found her husband in the sitting room with a burnt-out firework in his hand. With the inevitable spliff in the other hand, he had decided to let off some rockets, to the despair of the neighbours. Everything was, of course, recorded on tape:

> Paulo – It's 1:59 on 24th August 1976. I'm twenty-nine. I'm going to let off a rocket commemorating who I am and I'm going to record the noise [sound of the rocket exploding]. Great! Everyone is coming to their windows.
> Cecília – Paulo!!
> Paulo – What? Everyone's awake, the dogs are barking …

Cecília – This is absurd!

Paulo – What?

Cecília – Are you mad?

Paulo – It made a fantastic noise! It echoed all over the city! I'm the champion! [laughing a lot] It's great that I bought these rockets the other day! It's great! God, it was fun! [laughing a lot] Fantastic! I think that I've really freed myself of a lot of things letting off that rocket!

Cecília – Come and sit here with me for a while. I'm frightened.

Paulo – Why are you frightened? Have you had a premonition or something?

Cecília – No Paulo, it's because I've had a difficult day.

Paulo – Ah, thank God for that! Jesus, this has been a real liberation, Cecília. Go on, you let off a rocket and you'll feel calm too, straight away. Stand here at the window and let off a rocket.

Cecília – No! Anyone hearing the noise will know where it came from. Forget about the rockets. Stay a bit with me, will you?

Paulo – [laughing a lot] Oh, this is so cool! Two o'clock in the morning, a rocket celebrating my birthday, the stars filling the sky. Oh, thank you, God! I'm going to let off my fireworks across the city! [sound of rockets exploding]

Cecília – Paulo! The porters in all the other buildings will see it's coming from here.

Cissa was in fact an easy person to live with, but she had a strong character and wouldn't be forced to do anything against her will. She accepted her husband's 'Castaneda-inspired ideas', as Eneida had, and would sometimes even join him in smoking a cannabis joint, but she wouldn't hear of any marital extravagances, which he called 'sexual propositions'. One day, Paulo woke late in the morning when, as usual, Cissa was at work. She had left a piece of paper on the bedside table with a handwritten note that seemed to burn his fingers as he read it. It said that if her husband had decided to 'settle down', then this certainly hadn't happened at home.

To whom it may concern:

I am quite relaxed about the 500 women Paulo has had in the past because none of them is a threat. But today I felt really worried about my marriage. When Paulo joked with a secretary that he was going to grab her arse, I thought that was really low-class, but it was much worse when I heard him suggest paying 'some guys' in Cinelândia to join in our sexual relationship. I knew he had done this before, but I never thought he would suggest something so disgusting to me, knowing me as Paulo knows me, and knowing what I think about it. So this morning I feel more alone than ever because I know I can't talk about it to anyone. The only thing I can see, and what I actually want at this moment, is to separate from Paulo as soon as possible, as soon as this stupid society allows it, but I know that it's going to be a real trauma for me and for my family.

They hadn't even been married for a year and already the marriage was floundering.

CHAPTER 19

London

H IS MARRIAGE MIGHT BE FALLING APART, but the same could not be
said of Paulo's professional life. In December 1976, Philips released
the fifth LP produced by Paulo and Raul, *Há Dez Mil Anos Atrás*, on which
ten of the eleven tracks had lyrics written by him. It immediately became
a phenomenal success. The album took its title from 'I Was Born Ten
Thousand Years Ago', a traditional American song of which there were
several versions, the most famous of which had been recorded by Elvis
Presley four years earlier. It was also only the second time that Paulo had
dedicated a song to anyone; in this case, the dedication was to his father,
Pedro Queima Coelho. It was an unusual way of paying him homage,
since the lyrics speak of the differences between himself and his father
and are slightly condescending. Although he only admitted it years later,
anyone who knew a little about his family history would realize that the
'Pedro' of 'Meu Amigo Pedro' ['My Friend Pedro'] was his father:

> Every time that I touch paradise
> Or else burn in hell,
> I think of you, my poor friend,
> Who always wears the same suit.

Pedro, I remember the old days
When we two used to think about the world.
Today, I call you square, Pedro
And you call me a bum.

Pedro, where you go I go too,
But everything ends where it started

And I've got nothing to say to you,
But don't criticize me for being the way I am,
Each one of us is a universe, Pedro,
Where you go I go too.

Success was synonymous with money and, as far as Paulo was concerned, money had to be transformed into bricks and mortar. By the end of 1976, he was the owner of a third property, a two-bedroom apartment in Rua Paulino Fernandes, in Flamengo, a few steps from the estate where he had been born and brought up. Despite the pleasure he took in being a property owner, there was a problem in being rich: the possible envy of other people, particularly communists. In this aspect, Paulo had become very conventional indeed. The long-haired hippie who, only a short time before, had challenged the consumer society and written ironical songs about materialism was now terrified of losing the money he had so eagerly accumulated. 'Today at the cinema I was gripped by this terrible fear of communism coming and taking away all my apartments,' Paulo confessed to his diary and added bluntly, 'I would never fight for the people. These words may come back to haunt me, but I would never do that. I fight for free thought and perhaps for an elite of privileged people who choose a society apart.'

The material stability that the world of music gave him, however, never seems to have diverted him from his old dream of becoming a great writer. In anxious moments he got to the point of feeling 'almost certain' that he would not achieve this. He was appalled each time he thought how close his thirtieth birthday was, the deadline he had given himself, and beyond which, he believed, he wouldn't have the slightest chance of being a literary success. But all it took to restore his enthusiasm was to read that Agatha Christie had accumulated a fortune of US$18 million simply from her book sales. On these occasions Paulo would plunge back into his daydreams: 'There's no way I want to publish my novels in Brazil. There's no market for them here. In Brazil, a book that sells 3,000 copies is deemed a success, while in the United States that would be considered a complete flop. There's no future here. If I want to be a writer I'm going to have to get out of here.'

Meanwhile, Paulo was obliged to submit to the routine of meetings and trips to São Paulo demanded by his position as a Philips executive. The company had decided to concentrate all its departments in one office, in the then remote Barra da Tijuca, a modern district that was just beginning to develop in Rio. He was against the move, not just because his work would then be 40 kilometres from his home – which meant he had to get over the trauma of that accident in Araruama, buy a car and take his driving test – but also because he was given a really tiny office. He complained to no one except his diary: 'I'm sitting in my new office, if that's what you can call the place I'm in now. Me and my team, comprising two secretaries, an assistant and an office boy, occupy an area of 30 square metres, i.e., 5 metres per person. This would be bad enough if it weren't for the fact that we also have to take into consideration the pile of obsolete furniture that has also been crammed into this small space.'

As well as the distance and discomfort, he realized that his job was all to do with vanity, prestige and squabbles over space in the media. This world of embattled egos and back-stabbings was hardly the ideal place for someone so tormented by fear and paranoia. If some big shot was less than effusive when he met him in the lift, Paulo would immediately see in this a threat to his job. Not being invited to a show or to some major launch in the music world was a guarantee of sleepless nights and page after despairing page in his diary. Being excluded from a company meeting could trigger an asthma attack. His insecurity reached extreme levels. A music producer who ignored him could provoke an internal crisis that almost prevented him from working. When a number of these symptoms coincided, Paulo would lose direction entirely.

I'm in a really bad way today, completely in the grip of paranoia. I think no one likes me, that they're going to play some dirty trick on me at any moment and that they don't pay me as much attention as they used to.

It all started when I was practically thrown out of a meeting this morning. It left me with a runny nose. Maybe the colds I get are psychosomatic. André Midani, the president of the company, came into the room and didn't even speak to me; my partner was in a foul mood, and I'm sure he's plotting against me. My name isn't mentioned in a newspaper column, when it should be.

To add to my persecution mania, I wasn't even invited to the launch of Nelson Motta's book. He's pretty much avoided me, and I've never been able to conceal my dislike of him.

I think people only tolerate me because I'm a friend of Menescal's. It really winds me up.

His dual role – as lyricist and Philips executive – also became a source of irrepressible fears. Paulo often had to produce lengthy reports for the Philips board containing critical appraisals of the most important artists contracted to the company, namely, his colleagues. Although only Midani, Menescal, Armando Pittigliani and one or two other directors read this information, it made him go cold just to think of that material falling into the hands or reaching the ears of the artists he had assessed. His fear was justifiable, as he was usually niggardly in his praise and harsh in his criticism. Paulo was nevertheless a more than dedicated worker whose enthusiasm for what he was doing often meant working late into the night. His work with Philips was one of the supports on which his fragile emotional stability was balanced. The second was his somewhat shaky marriage and the third, a new interest into which he threw himself body and soul, yoga. As well as this, and when things got too much, he asked for help from Dr Benjamim Gomes, who would get him back on track with an assortment of antidepressants.

In January 1977, Paulo had been convinced that Cissa was different from his previous partners. 'She is what she is, she's unlikely to change,' he wrote. 'I've stopped trying to change her because I can see how useless that is.' Gradually, however, he managed to interest his wife in at least one facet of his world – drugs. Cissa would never become a regular consumer, but it was because of him that she smoked cannabis for the first time and then experimented with LSD. Following a ritual similar to that adopted by Vera Richter when she smoked hashish for the first time, they had their first experiment with LSD on 19 March, St Joseph's feast day, after first kissing the saint's image. They turned on a tape recorder when Cissa placed the small tablet on her tongue and from then on she described her initial feelings of insecurity, how she felt, at first, sleepy and then experienced itching all over her body, finally reaching a state of ecstasy. At that moment, she began to hear 'indescribable' sounds. Sobbing, she tried unsuccessfully to describe what she felt: 'No one can stop what's going in my ears. I'll never forget what I'm hearing now. I need to try and describe it ... I know that you heard what I heard. I was looking at the ceiling of our little home. I don't know ... I think it's impossible to describe it, but I must ... Paulo, it's such an amazing thing.' Her husband monitored this 'research' and also provided the sound track. The opening was a headline from *Jornal Nacional*, on TV Globo, announcing high numbers of traffic accidents in Rio. Then came Bach's Toccata and Fugue, and Wagner's Wedding March. To calm his guinea pig he promised that should she have a bad trip, a simple glass of freshly squeezed orange juice would quickly reverse the effects of the lysergic acid.

While drugs may have masked his anxieties, they were not enough to drive them away. It was during one of his deep depressions that a super-hero appeared to him in his room, on a mission to save him. This was the heavyweight Rocky Balboa, the character played by Sylvester Stallone in the film *Rocky*. In the early hours, in March 1977, as he and Cissa sat in bed watching the Oscar awards on TV, Paulo was moved to see *Rocky* win no fewer than three statuettes, for best film, best director and best editing. Like Balboa, who had come back from nothing to become a champion, he, too, wanted to be a winner and was determined to win his prize. And still the only thing he was interested in becoming was a writer with a worldwide readership. It was already clear in his mind that the first step on the long road to literary glory was to leave Brazil and write his books abroad. The following day he went to Menescal and told him he was leaving. If it had been up to Paulo, the couple's destination would have been Madrid, but Cissa's preference won the day and in early May 1977, the two disembarked at Heathrow airport in London, the city chosen as the birthplace of his first book.

A few days later, they were settled in a studio flat in 7 Palace Street, halfway between Victoria station and Buckingham Palace, for which they paid £186 a month. It was a tiny apartment, but it was in a good location and there was a further attraction: a bath. When they arrived in London, they opened an account at the Bank of Brazil with US$5,000. Money was not exactly a problem for Paulo, but as well as being known for his parsimony, he had a legal problem, which was the limit of US$300 a month that could be transferred to Brazilians living abroad. In order to get round this, at the end of each month Paulo and Cissa mobilized grandparents, uncles, aunts and cousins to each send US$300 to Brazilian friends who were resident in London and they would then deposit the money in the couple's account in the Bank of Brazil. Thus they received about US$1,500 a month without paying any tax.

Paulo's incomings included payment for a music column he wrote in the weekly magazine *Amiga*. Cissa did some journalistic work for the Brazilian section of the BBC and published the occasional short, signed article in the *Jornal do Brasil*, as well, of course, as doing all housework, since her husband's contribution in this area was nil. Worse, he refused to allow any frozen food in the house and politely asked his wife to buy a cookery book. The problem was translating the recipes. The two spent hours trying to understand a recipe so that she could transform it into a meal. A weekly menu listing each day's meals was solemnly posted in a prominent place on one of the walls of the apartment. From these menus it can be seen that they only allowed themselves meat once a week, although they made up for this with frequent visits to Indian and Thai restaurants.

They never lacked for money and what they received was enough to cover their expenses, including the classes in yoga, photography and vampirism that Paulo attended, as well as outings, short trips and taking in London's many cultural highlights. Paulo and Cissa were always first in the queue when something was shown that would have been banned by the censors in Brazil, such as the film *State of Siege*, directed by Costa-Gavras, which was a denunciation of the dictatorship in Uruguay. Three months went by without any real work being done. Paulo wrote: 'I have worked a maximum two days a week. That means that, on average, in these three months in Europe I've worked less than a month. For someone who wanted to conquer the world, for someone who arrived full of dreams and desires, two days' work a week is very little.'

As there seemed no way to write the wretched, longed-for book, Paulo tried to fill his time with productive activity. The classes in vampirism inspired him to write a film script, *The Vampire of London*. He sent it by post to well-known producers, all of whom replied politely, making it clear that, as far as they were concerned, vampires did not make good box office. One of them very kindly offered 'to look at the film when it's finished and give you my opinion as to whether or not we are prepared to distribute it'.

By July, Paulo and Cissa realized that it would not be easy to find friends in London. To compensate for this lack in their lives they had a short visit from his parents. The exchange of correspondence with Brazil was growing, in the form of letters or, as Paulo preferred, tapes, whenever there was someone who could take them back to Brazil. Piles and piles of cassette tapes collected in the houses of his parents and friends, particularly in that of his dearest friend, Roberto Menescal, from whom he learned that Rita Lee had found a new writing partner – which, added to the rejections from producers and publishers, led to pages of lamentation:

> My partner has found another writing partner. I've been forgotten far more quickly than I imagined: in just three months. In just three months I've lost any importance I had to cultural life over there. No one's written to me for several days.
>
> What's been going on? What lies behind the mysteries that led me here? The dream I've dreamed all my life? Right now I'm close to realizing that dream and yet I feel as though I'm not ready for it.

At the end of 1977, when it was time to renew the six-month contract with their landlord, the couple decided to leave the apartment in Palace

Street for a cheaper one. They put a five-line advertisement in the classified column of a London newspaper saying: 'Young professional couple need flat from November 15th, London area with telephone.' Days later, they had settled in Bassett Road, in Notting Hill, near Portobello, where Paulo would later set his novel *The Witch of Portobello*. It was not such a smart address as Palace Street, but they were now living in a far larger apartment that was also better and cheaper than the other one.

While the course in vampirism didn't help Paulo become a screenplay writer, it nevertheless left a mark on his life. There he met and fell in love with a charming twenty-four-year-old Japanese masseuse, Keiko Saito, who was as interested as he was in that lugubrious subject. As well as being his colleague on the course, Keiko became his companion in handing out pamphlets in the street, one day protesting against the mass killings perpetrated by 'Marshal' Pol Pot in Cambodia, and another collecting signatures in favour of the legalization of cannabis in Great Britain. Paulo broached the subject with Cissa: 'I'm in love with Keiko and I want to know how you feel about me inviting her to come and live with us.' On the only occasion when he spoke publicly about this episode – an interview in 1992 with the journalist W.F. Padovani, who was working for *Playboy* at the time – Paulo revealed that his wife happily accepted his proposal:

Playboy – And what about your marriage to Cecília Mac Dowell?

Paulo – It took place in church.

Playboy – With the full regalia?

Paulo – Yes, and Raul Seixas was my best man. Cecília and I then went to live in London, where we enjoyed a *ménage à trois*.

Playboy – How did that happen?

Paulo – I did a course on vampires and fell in love with one of the students, a Japanese girl called Keiko. Since I loved Cecília too, I decided to live with them both.

Playboy – Did they meet?

Paulo – Oh, yes, we lived together for a year.

Playboy – And how was it in bed?

Paulo – I had sex with them both at the same time, but they didn't
    have sex with each other.

Playboy – Wasn't one jealous of the other?

Paulo – No, never.

Playboy – Wasn't there a time when you felt you wanted to make
    love just to one of them alone?

Paulo – As far as I can remember, no. It was a very intense love
    affair *à trois*.

Playboy – Cecília and Keiko didn't have sex, but what exactly did
    they feel for each other?

Paulo – They were very fond of each other. They knew how much I
    loved them and I knew how much they loved me.

Just as the Chinese and Soviet communist leaders used to do with political dissenters in official photos, Paulo airbrushed from the scene
described in *Playboy* an important character in this story, a young, long-
haired Brazilian music producer known as Peninha, who was also living
in London at the time. Paulo had always believed that Cissa was an easy
person to live with, but after living with her for a year he had learned that
he had married a woman who would not put up with any excesses. When
she realized that he was suggesting living with two women, like an
Arabian sheikh, in an apartment that had just one room and one bed, he
was astonished at her reaction:

'Keiko can come and live here, as long as you agree that Peninha can
move in too, because I'm in love with him as well.'

Paulo had no alternative but to agree to the involvement of this fourth
member of what he came to call 'the extended family', or the 'UN General
Assembly'. Whenever a relative of Cissa's or Paulo's arrived, Keiko and
Peninha had to vanish, as, for example, when Gail, Cissa's elder sister,
spent a week at the apartment.

To celebrate the New Year – the first and only one they spent in
England – the Coelhos travelled by train with the 'extended family' to
spend a few days in Edinburgh. The end of the year was always a time
for Paulo to weigh up triumphs and failures. He clearly wasn't going to
lay his hands on the imaginary Oscar that had been one of his reasons

for leaving Brazil in March. Months and months had passed without his producing a single line of the much dreamed-of book. Defeat followed defeat, as he confessed to his diary:

> It's been a time of rejections. Everything I've submitted to the various competitions I was eligible to enter has been rejected. The last remaining results arrived today. All the women I've wanted to go out with have rejected me. This isn't just my imagination. When I say 'all' I mean that there is not one exception.
>
> [...] Ever since I was a child I've dreamed of being a writer, of going abroad to write and becoming world-famous. Obviously London was the step I dreamed of taking when I was a child. The fact is that the results haven't been what I was hoping for. My first and greatest disappointment has been with myself. I've had six months here to feel inspired and I haven't had enough discipline to write a single line.

The image Paulo gave to other people was of a successful lyricist whose hobby was writing about London for Brazilian magazines. His old friend Menescal, however, with whom he corresponded frequently, began to suspect that his protégé was not very happy and thought that it was time for him to end his stay in London. Paulo agreed to return to Brazil, but he didn't want to return with his tail between his legs, as though defeated. If Philips invited him to go back to work there, he would return to Rio de Janeiro the next day. Menescal not only flew to London to make the offer but took with him Heleno Oliveira, a top executive of the multinational company. The job would not begin until March 1978, but it was the invitation Paulo needed, not the job. The day before leaving, he collected together the few pieces of writing he had managed to produce during those sterile months in London and put them in an envelope on which, after sealing it, he wrote his own name and address. Then, as he was drinking a whisky with Menescal in a modest pub in the Portobello Road, he 'accidentally' left the envelope on the bar. On his last night in the city, he explained to his diary the reason for this act: 'I've left everything I've written this year in that bar. It's the last chance for someone to discover

me and say: this guy's brilliant. So there's my name and address. If they
want to, they can find me.'

Either the package was lost or whoever found it did not consider its
contents particularly brilliant. The couple returned to Brazil in February
1978. During the flight, Cissa broke down in tears and Paulo summarized
the situation thus: 'In London all my hopes of becoming a world-famous
writer were dashed.'

As various of the characters he created later on would say: this was
just another defeat, not a failure. He and Cissa returned to the apartment
in Rua Barata Ribeiro, which had seemed unsuitable even before their trip
to England. As soon as they were back, Paulo began to predict dark times
for his marriage, if the 'emotional flexibility' that had prevailed in London
did not extend to Brazil:

> My relationship with Cissa could prove lasting if she showed the
> same emotional flexibility that existed in London. We have already
> advanced far enough for a small step back to be acceptable. On the
> other hand, there will be no opportunities. It is just going to be a ques-
> tion of time. Let's hope that everything turns out all right. Although
> I think that our return to Brazil means that we're more likely to split
> up than to stay together, because here we're less forgiving of each
> other's weaknesses.

Some months later, they moved to the fourth property that Paulo had
added to his small urban portfolio. Bought with the royalties that had accumulated during his absence, this was a comfortable three-bedroom apartment in Rua Senador Eusébio in Flamengo, two blocks from the Paissandu
cinema, three from the home of his ex-fiancée Eneida and a few metres
from where Raul Seixas lived. They decorated half the sitting-room wall
with photos and souvenirs of their trip to London, which began to take on
another meaning: while on the one hand, they reminded the couple of the
happy times they had spent there, on the other, they were, for Paulo, a
permanent reminder that he had not succeeded in writing 'the book'.

In March he took up his job as artistic producer with Philips and
during the months that followed, he resumed his routine as executive at

a recording company. Since he disliked getting up early, he was frequently woken at ten in the morning with a telephone call from his secretary, telling him that someone had been asking for him. He would drive from home to Barra da Tijuca in his own car and spend the rest of the day in endless meetings, many out of the office, with artists, directors of the company and journalists from the music world. In his office he ended up dealing with everything. In between fielding numerous telephone calls, he would sort out administrative matters, approve record sleeves and write letters to fans on behalf of famous artists.

The fact that Raul Seixas was near by didn't mean that the partners became close again. Indeed, at the end of the year, the two 'close enemies' were invited by WEA, Raul's new recording company, to try to recreate the partnership that had taken Brazil by storm, but the attempt failed. The LP *Mata Virgem*, for which Paulo wrote five lyrics ('Judas', 'As Profecias', 'Tá na Hora', 'Conserve seu Medo' and 'Magia de Amor'), was released at the beginning of 1979, but did not achieve even a tenth of the sales of such albums as *Gita* and *Há Dez Mil Anos Atrás*.

The fame that the two had experienced between 1973 and 1975 became a thing of the past, but Paulo had absorbed the lesson that Raul had taught him – 'Writing music is like writing a story in twenty lines that someone can listen to ten times without getting bored' – and was no longer dependent on his partner. Besides the five songs he wrote for *Mata Virgem*, in 1978 he wrote almost twenty songs in partnership with all the performers who were making a mark on the popular Brazilian music of the time. He had become a sort of jack-of-all-trades in show business, writing songs, directing and scripting shows, and when Pedro Rovai, a director of porn films, decided to make *Amante Latino*, he invited Paulo to write the script for that.

As was usually the case with his fragile emotional state, when his work was going well, his emotional life wasn't – and vice versa. This time was no different. The clear skies he was enjoying professionally clouded over when he returned home. The bitterness between him and Cissa gave way to ever more frequent arguments, and then came the endless silences that could last for days. In February 1979, he decided to go alone on a boat trip to Patagonia. When the liner anchored in Buenos Aires on the way back to Brazil, he phoned Cissa and suggested that they separate. Given how concerned he was with signs, it's surprising that he failed to realize that, three years earlier, he had proposed marriage to her by telephone and from Buenos Aires.

The separation took place on 24 March 1979, when Cissa left the apartment in Rua Senador Eusébio, and it was legally ratified on 11 June in a family court 50 metres from St Joseph's Church, where they had married. The hearing nearly didn't take place. Firstly, because Cissa had to go out at the last minute to buy a skirt, because the judge would not allow jeans in the court. Then, the lawyer had forgotten a document, which meant that they had to bribe an employee in the register office in order to get their certificate of legal separation.

Setting aside their disagreements, the two went out afterwards to have a civilized lunch in a restaurant. They each had a very different memory of the end of their marriage. Paulo wrote: 'I don't know how unhappy she is, but she certainly cried a lot. I didn't find the procedure in the least traumatic. I left and went back to work in other offices, other rooms, other worlds. I had a good dinner and enjoyed it more than I have for a long time, but that had nothing to do with the separation. It was all down to the cook, who made a really delicious meal.' Cissa, on the other hand, set down her feelings in a brief note written in English, which she posted to him. She found fault with him in the one area where he considered himself to be good – in bed: 'One of our main problems, in my view, was sex. I never understood why you didn't think about me in bed. I could have been much better if I had felt that you were thinking about my pleasure in bed. But you didn't. You never thought about it. So I began not to think about your pleasure either.'

For someone whose emotional stability was so dependent on a stable relationship with a woman who would help him through his psychological storms, the end of the marriage was sure to presage more depression and more melancholy. Not that he lacked for women – on the contrary. The problem now was that Paulo had got it into his head that they were sucking out the energy that he should be putting into his career as a writer. 'I've gone out a lot, had sex a lot, but with female vampires,' he wrote, 'and I don't want that any more.'

The person who appears to have been most seriously shaken by the separation was his mother. During Easter she wrote a long letter to her son, typewritten in single spacing. It does not appear to have been written by 'a fool', as Paulo called his mother more than once. The document reveals someone who had a knowledge of psychoanalytical jargon, which was unusual in a non-professional. She also insisted that it was he who was responsible for the separation, with his insecurities and his inability to recognize what he had lost:

My dearest son,

We have much in common, including the ease with which we express ourselves in letters. That's why, on this Easter Sunday, I'm sending you these lines in the hope that they will be of some help to you or at least let you know how much I love you, which is why I suffer when you suffer and am happy when you're happy.

As you can well imagine, you and Cissa are much on my mind. There's no need to tell me again that it's your problem and that I should simply keep out of it. That's why I don't really know whether I'll actually send you this letter.

When I say that I know you well I'm basing this simply on my mother's intuition, because much of you, unfortunately, was created far from us, and so there are lots of things I don't know. You were repressed during childhood and then suffocated by your own problems and ended up having to break off close relationships, break with convention and start from scratch. And although you were anxious, fearful, insecure, you succeeded. And how! But you also let go of a very repressed side to you, something you didn't know how to live with.

I only know Cecília a little, but she seems to me a practical woman. Strong. Fearless. Intuitive. Uncomplicated. It must have been a real shock to you when she paid you back in kind ... with her dependency, her hang-ups, her needs. She refused to carry your burden any more and that's what tipped the balance in your relationship. I don't know how it all ended, but you took it as a rejection, as lack of love, and couldn't accept it. There is only one way of resolving the problem: recognizing it. Identifying it. You told me that you don't know how to lose. We can only live life fully if we accept winning and we accept losing.

Lygia

Note: As you can see, I'm still a dreadful typist. But I've decided to beard the lion in his den, and I'm sending the letter.

My dear son: I prayed a lot for you today in my way. I prayed that God would encourage in you the certainty that it's in your hands to build your life, and that your life will always be the same as it has been up to now: full of conscious and honest decisions and full of moments of happiness and joy.

Much love,

L.

As he himself often wrote in his diary, there is nothing new under the sun. And as had been the case so often before in his life, the only way of compensating for an emotional defeat was to find new victories at work. So it seemed like a gift from God when he received an invitation in April 1979 – not even a month after his separation – to swap his job at Philips for that of product manager with their largest competitor, CBS. Included in the proposal was the prospect of prompt promotion to the post of artistic director. Following a succession of amorous and professional failures – the poor performance of the *Mata Virgem* album, the short-lived engagement to Eneida, the literary sterility in London, the end of his marriage – the invitation was a great relief, in large part because it would put him back in the media world of Rio and São Paulo, a world he hadn't frequented for some time. But it also awoke an unfamiliar and unpleasant side to his character: arrogance. Since one of his duties was to reorganize the artistic department, he started by rocking the boat. 'It's true, I did behave very arrogantly when I started work there,' he was to recall years later. 'I went round giving orders and giving the yes-men a really hard time; pure authoritarianism!' He suspected that money was being channelled out of the company and began to refuse to sign notes and invoices about which there might be any doubt.

Unaware that he was digging his own grave, he hired and fired, cut costs and closed departments, adding fuel to what was already a bonfire of egos and vanities. Meanwhile, those who had suffered most in his clean-up operation were plotting against him. One Monday, 13 August 1979, after two months and ten days in the job, he arrived at the company late in the morning and, having sent yet more heads rolling, was summoned to the office of Juan Truden, the president of CBS in Brazil. He was standing waiting for Paulo, smiling, his hand outstretched and with these words on his lips: 'My friend, you're fired.' Nothing more. No 'Good afternoon', no 'Hope it goes well'.

The impact was enormous, not simply because of the coldness of the dismissal but because he knew that this meant the end of his career as a recording executive. 'I was dismissed from the highest post, from the highest position in the profession, and I couldn't go back, I couldn't go back to being what I was at the beginning,' Paulo recalled years later in a statement at the Museum of Image and Sound in Rio de Janeiro. 'There were only six recording companies in Brazil and all the six positions I might really want were occupied.' Before packing his bags, he wrote a long, angry letter to Truden in which he said that, in view of the lack of structure in the company, 'CBS artists at the moment enjoy the dubious pleasure of being the most poorly served in the Brazilian market.' He finished dramatically, using an expression that had remained in the popular imagination since it had been used by the ex-president Jânio Quadros in his letter of resignation: 'And the same hidden forces that are responsible for my dismissal will one day have to face the truth. For you cannot hide the sun with a sieve, Sr Juan Truden.'

His dismissal ('for incompetence', as he learned later) was celebrated by the group of disaffected individuals he had created as manager, and would cause him still more humiliation. Some days later, at a social function, Paulo met Antônio Coelho Ribeiro, who had just been made president of Philips, the company Coelho had left in order to try his luck with CBS. When he saw him, Ribeiro said, in front of everyone: 'You always were a bluffer.'

Ten months later, Antônio Ribeiro, too, got the sack. When he heard the news, Paulo took from a drawer a present he had bought shortly after Ribeiro had publicly insulted him. He went to the Ribeiros' apartment and, when Ribeiro opened the door, Paulo hurriedly explained the reason for his presence there: 'Do you remember what you said to me when I was sacked? Right, now you can repeat those words every day as you look into your own eyes.' He unwrapped the object and handed it to Ribeiro. It was a wall mirror on which he had had the wretched words painted in capitals: 'YOU ALWAYS WERE A BLUFFER.' Once he had returned the insult, he turned, took the lift and left.

It was time for Paulo to heal his wounds. Now that he had been ejected from the world of show business, his name did not appear again in the press until the end of the year, when the magazine *Fatos&Fotos* published an article entitled 'Vampirology: a Science that Now Has its Own Brazilian Master'. He was the master, presenting himself as a specialist in the subject, and he announced that he was writing the script for a feature film on vampires, which was, in fact, never made. His unexpected dismissal from CBS had caught him unawares, and with the scars from the recent breakdown of his marriage still open he was unable to bear the setback alone. In his solitude, his mind oscillated between delusions of grandeur and feelings of persecution, which, at times, he managed to bring together in his diary in one sentence: 'Every day it seems harder to achieve my great ideal: to be famous and respected, to be the man who wrote the Book of the Century, the Thought of the Millennium, the History of Humanity.'

This seemed to be simply a repeat of what various doctors had diagnosed as paranoid schizophrenia or manic depression. The problem was that it was nearly time for his traditional end-of-year taking stock and, at thirty-two, he had still not succeeded in realizing his dream. There were moments when he seemed to accept being a writer like any other. 'Sometimes I think about writing an erotic story, and I know it would get published,' he noted in his diary. 'Besides which, I could devote myself to that one genre, which is gaining ground here now that pornographic magazines are being published again. I could think up some really good pseudonym.' These plans were followed by questions he could not answer. Why write erotic books? To earn money? He was already earning money and he still wasn't happy. In order not to have to accept that his problems were caused by no one but himself, he returned to the old story: he hadn't written before because he was married and Cissa didn't help. Now it was because he was alone and loneliness was preventing him from writing.

> I carry on with the same plans, which haven't yet died in me. I can resuscitate them whenever I want to; all I have to do is find the woman of my life. And I really do want to find her soon ...
>
> [...] I've been very, very lonely. I can't be happy without a woman at my side.
>
> [...] I'm tired of searching. I need someone. If I had a woman I could love, I'd be all right.

In his misery Paulo seemed to be confirming the popular belief that there's none so blind as those who will not see, because 'the woman of his life' had been right there before him for more than ten years without ever receiving from him a smile or even a handshake. It's surprising that such a pretty girl – petite, with dark hair, gentle eyes and porcelain skin – had gone unnoticed for such a long time by Paulo, the confirmed womanizer.

Paulo had met Christina Oiticica in 1968, when her uncle, Marcos, asked Sônia, Paulo's sister, to marry him. At Lygia's insistence, all the women invited to the formal engagement dinner were to wear long dresses. For the men, including Paulo, who was sporting a great dark mane of hair at the time and appeared to be completely out of it on drugs during the supper, she demanded dark suits. Christina and Paulo met several times in the years that followed at family gatherings and dinners without either really noticing the other. Naturally, one of these celebrations was for the marriage of Cissa and Paulo. When Paulo's sister took him to Christmas lunch in 1979 at Christina's parents' house, she was going out with Vicente, a young millionaire whose inheritance included, among other luxuries, a vast yacht. Destiny, however, had decided that she was to be the woman Paulo had so longed for. A week later, just as in a fairy tale, the two were together for ever.

CHAPTER 20

Christina

A FTER HER PRIMARY EDUCATION, Christina had been to Bennett College, a traditional Protestant establishment, where the Bible stories told during the Religious Knowledge lessons were the only thing that awoke in her a flicker of interest. She consistently failed in all other subjects, which meant that she had to leave the college and go from school to school until, like Paulo, she gave up completely. When she was seventeen, however, she was able to take a different educational route that would allow her to complete her secondary school studies in less than a year. It was only then that she returned to Bennett College, which had become a college of higher education, where she studied art and architecture. And at the end of 1979, when Paulo arrived at her parents' house for Christmas dinner, she was working as an architect.

Although they were practising Christians, Christina's parents were exceptionally liberal. If she wanted to go to lessons, she went. If she preferred to go to the cinema, no problem. And as soon as she was old enough, she was allowed to have her boyfriends sleep over at her parents' house without any objections on their part. Not, however, that she had that many boyfriends. Although she was very pretty, Chris was no flirt. She was a thoughtful girl, who enjoyed reading and, although she was not particularly religious, joined a choir at one of the Protestant churches.

On the other hand, she also went to see films at the Paissandu, bought clothes at Bibba, the fashion boutique in Ipanema, and consumed large quantities of whisky at Lama's. She went out every night and would often not get home until dawn, her legs unsteady. 'My drug was alcohol,' she confessed years later. 'I simply loved alcohol.'

It was growing dark by the time coffee was being served at the end of Christmas lunch in the Oiticica household. Paulo had had his eye on Chris since he arrived and, even though she was going out with someone else, he decided to use his cousin Sérgio Weguelin, who was also present, to find out whether or not she was doing anything that evening. When it was time to leave, he asked his cousin to invite her to go with them to see Woody Allen's latest hit, *Manhattan*. She was taken by surprise and didn't know what to say. The next thing she knew, she was alone in the cinema with Paulo, not watching *Manhattan*, which was sold out, but a re-run of *Airport*, which had been released almost ten years earlier.

Paulo behaved like a true gentleman throughout the film, and didn't even try to hold Chris's hand. When they left, they found the square outside the cinema full of jugglers, fortune-tellers, tarot readers, chiromancers, fire-eaters and, of course, several religious choirs each singing a different hymn. They walked along until they came to a fake Indian sitting in front of a wicker basket in which was coiled a terrifying reptile 6 metres in length. It was an enormous anaconda, a non-poisonous snake that was, however, capable of asphyxiating an ox or a human, swallowing it whole and spending weeks digesting the remains of its prey.

With a mixture of fear and disgust for the creature the couple went up to the Indian. As naturally as if he were merely asking the time, Paulo said to Chris: 'If I kiss the snake on the mouth will you kiss me on the mouth?'

She couldn't believe what she was hearing. 'Kiss that monster? Are you mad?'

When she realized that he was serious, she accepted the dare. 'Fine: if you kiss the snake, I'll kiss you on the mouth.'

To her astonishment and to that of the Indian and all the bystanders, Paulo stepped forward, grabbed the head of the snake in both hands and kissed it. Then, in front of dozens of wide-eyed spectators, he turned, took Chris in his arms and gave her a long, movie-style kiss on the lips, a kiss that was greeted with a round of applause by those present. Paulo got more than a kiss. A few hours later, the two were sleeping together in his apartment.

On the last day of the year – having first consulted the I Ching – he invited her to spend New Year with him in the sixth of the properties he owned, a small, pleasant summer house he had just bought in the seaside resort of Cabo Frio. The little white chalet, with red windows and a thatched roof, was exactly the same as the other seventy-four in a condominium called Cabana Clube designed by Renato Menescal, the architect brother of Paulo's friend Roberto. On their way there, Paulo told Christina that the previous night he had dreamed of a voice that kept saying over and over: 'Don't spend New Year's Eve in the cemetery.' Since neither could work out what this meant, and since they had no plans to see in the New Year in a cemetery, the matter was forgotten.

Immediately after they arrived in Cabo Frio, they both sensed a strange atmosphere in the house, although they were unable to pinpoint what it was. It wasn't something they could smell or see; it was what Paulo would call negative energy. As night fell, they began to hear noises, but couldn't work out where they were coming from – it sounded as though some creature, human or animal, was dragging itself through the rooms, but apart from the two of them there was no one else there. Feeling both intrigued and frightened, they went out for dinner.

In the restaurant, they told the waiter about these strange occurrences and were given an explanation that made their hair stand on end: 'Are you staying at the Cabana Clube? There used to be an Indian cemetery there. When they were building the foundations, they found the bones of hundreds of Indians, but built the houses on top of them anyway. Everyone in Cabo Frio knows that it's haunted.'

So that was what the warning in Paulo's dream had meant. Paulo and Chris stayed in a hotel that night and didn't go back to the house until the next morning, and even then, they only went to collect their clothes. A few weeks later, the chalet was sold for the same US$4,000 it had cost a few months earlier.

No ghosts darkened their relationship, however. After breaking up with her boyfriend during the first days of the New Year, Chris moved into Paulo's apartment, with all her clothes, furniture and personal possessions, including the easel she needed for her work as an architect. There they began a partnership which, though it has never been formalized, has remained solid ever since.

The start of their life together was not easy, though. As preoccupied as Paulo was with interpreting signs, Chris was most upset to find in the apartment a biography of Count Dracula open on a Bible lectern. It was not that she had anything against vampires or vampirologists – she even liked films on the subject – but she was appalled that a sacred object should be used as a joke, something which she believed would attract negative energies into the house. She was so shocked that she went out into the street and from the first available public telephone called the Baptist pastor who used to counsel her and told him what she had seen. They prayed together over the phone and, before returning to the apartment, Chris thought it prudent to go into a church. She only calmed down when Paulo explained that his interest in vampirology had absolutely nothing to do with satanism, OTO or Aleister Crowley, saying: 'The myth of the vampire existed a hundred years before Christ. I haven't had any contact with anyone involved in the dark arts for years.'

In fact, he hadn't had anything to do with Marcelo Motta's satanists since 1974, but he continued to appear publicly here and there as a specialist on the work of Aleister Crowley. Indeed, some months later he wrote a long article on the English occultist in *Planeta*, which was illustrated with drawings by Chris. Their relationship went through further rocky times before it finally settled down. Paulo was still racked with doubt: was Chris really the 'marvellous companion' he had been waiting for? He feared that deep down the two were only together for the same, unspoken reason, what he called 'the paranoiac desire to escape solitude'. However, even while he was saying that he was afraid of falling in love with her, he broke out in a cold sweat at the thought of losing her. 'We had our first serious argument a few days ago, when she refused to go to Araruama with me. Suddenly I was terrified to think how easily I could lose Chris. I did everything to get her and have her close. I like her, she brings me peace, calm, and I feel that we can try and build something together.'

These ups and downs at the start of their life together did not stop them celebrating their partnership unofficially. On 22 June 1980, a dreary Sunday, they blessed their union with a lunch for their parents, relatives and a few friends in the apartment where they were living. Christina took charge of the hippie-style decorations and on each invitation she wrote a psalm or proverb illustrated with a drawing. Chris's eclectic interest in religion seems to have helped the couple's relationship. When they met, she was already a specialist in tarot, on which she had read numerous books, and, even though she didn't consult the I Ching as often as Paulo, she knew how to interpret its predictions. When Paulo read *The Book of Mediums* by Allan Kardec, the couple decided to see if they could be mediums. Just as Cissa had been a guinea pig in the experiment with LSD, now Paulo was trying to get Chris to write down messages from the Beyond. He wrote: 'I have performed a few experiments. We began last week, when I bought the book. Chris has acted as a medium, and we have achieved some elementary communications. I've found this all very troubling. My concept of things has changed radically since I arrived scientifically at the conclusion that spirits do exist. They exist and are all around us.' Much later, Chris confirmed that the experiment had worked. 'I'm sure that a table really did move,' she recalls, 'and I also wrote down some texts that were dictated to me.'

The suspicion that she might have powers as a medium continued to grow from the moment when she was gripped by strange, inexplicable feelings of dread whenever she went into the bathroom of their apartment. They were odd sensations which she herself had difficulty understanding and of which she never spoke to anyone. More than once it entered her mind to turn on the gas for the shower, seal up the exits and kill herself. On the afternoon of Monday, 13 October, she left her easel and went into the bathroom. This time the desire to kill herself seemed uncontrollable, but fearing that death by asphyxiation might be very slow and painful she decided to turn to medication. She calmly took a taxi to her parents' house in Jardim Botânico, where she knew she would find the tranquillizers that her mother took regularly – Somalium, she recalls, or Valium in Paulo's version of events. Whatever the name of the medication, the fact is that she emptied a whole pack into her mouth, wrote a short note to Paulo and collapsed on the bed.

When he arrived home and Chris wasn't there, Paulo went to her parents' apartment, where they both often used to have dinner, and found Chris unconscious on the bed and, beside her, as well as the note, an empty pack of Valium. With the help of Chris's mother, who had just arrived, he managed to get her to the lift, having first made Chris put her finger down her throat and vomit up what she could. Outside, they stopped the first taxi that passed and went to the St Bernard clinic in Gávea, where the doctors pumped out her stomach. Once recovered, hours later, she was well enough to go home.

While she was sleeping and having spoken to her about what happened, Paulo kept asking himself where those strange emanations in the bathroom came from. With the question still going round and round in his head, he went downstairs to talk to the porter, tell him what had happened to Chris and see if he had an answer to the mystery. The man said: 'The last person who lived in that apartment, before you, was an airline captain who gassed himself in the bathroom.' When he went back upstairs and told Chris the story, she didn't think twice: despite having been in hospital only a few hours earlier, she got up, collected together a change of clothes for them both, as well as other personal items, threw everything into a suitcase and announced: 'We're going to my mother's house. I never want to set foot in this apartment again.'

Neither of them did, not even to move house. They spent a little more than a month with Chris's parents, long enough for work on the seventh property Paulo had bought to be completed so that they could move in there. This was a ground-floor apartment with a lovely garden and one particularly priceless feature: it was in the same building as Lygia and Pedro's apartment. He could only have felt more emotionally secure if he were actually living with his parents.

Chris's rules regarding Paulo's sexual excesses always prevailed, but they were still far from being an average couple. One day, for example, Paulo suggested that they should both try an experiment that had its origins in the Middle Ages, and to which he gave the grand name of 'a reciprocal test of resistance to pain'. Chris agreed, although she knew what was involved: stark naked, they began to whip each other with a thin bamboo cane. They took it in turns to beat the other on the back, the blows growing harder and harder, until they reached the limit of physical endurance. This occurred only when they were both bleeding from their wounds.

Their relationship gradually began to settle down. The first two years passed without anything untoward disrupting their life together. Encouraged by her partner, Chris began to paint again, something she had given up four years earlier, while Paulo began to direct so-called TV specials. Not that they needed money to live on. Besides the forty-one songs he had written with Raul Seixas, in the past few years, Paulo had written more than a hundred lyrics – originals or versions of foreign hits – for dozens of different artists. This meant that the royalties continued to flow into his bank account. He tried to keep busy, however, fearing that idleness would lead him into depression again. Besides the TV specials, he gave talks and took part in round-table discussions on music and, occasionally, on vampirism. But the cure only worked for a while, because even when he was fully occupied, he would still suffer occasional anxiety attacks.

When this occurred, as it did at the end of 1981, he continued to give vent to his feelings in his diary:

> These last two days, I missed two appointments, on the pretext that I was having a tooth extracted. I'm completely confused as to what to do. I can't even be bothered to write a short press release that would bring in a tiny amount of money. The situation inside me is this. I can't even write these pages and this year, which I was hoping would be better than last, has turned out precisely as I described above. Oh, yes: I haven't had a bath for the last few days.

The crisis appears to have hit him so badly that he even changed his behaviour regarding something that had always been very dear to him – money: 'I haven't paid attention to anything, including one of the things that I really like: money. Just imagine, I don't know how much is in my bank account, something I've always known down to the minutest detail.

I've lost interest in sex, in writing, in going to the cinema, in reading, even in the plants I've been tending so lovingly for so long and that are now dying because I only water them sporadically.'

If he had lost interest in both money and sex, things were very bad indeed, and so he did what he always did in such situations – he went back to Dr Benjamim, visiting him once a week. Whenever he felt like this, he would always ask Chris the same question: 'Am I on the right path?' And so, at the end of 1981, she made a suggestion that struck a chord in his nomadic soul: why not just leave everything and go off travelling with no fixed destination and no date set for their return? Her instincts told her that this was the right path. Years later, Chris would recall: 'Something was telling me that it would work. Paulo trusted my instinct and decided to drop everything.' Determined to 'search for the meaning of life', wherever it might be, he asked permission to leave his unpaid post with TV Globo, bought two air tickets to Madrid – the cheapest he could find – and promised that he and Chris would return to Brazil only when the last cent of the US$17,000 he took with him had run out.

Unlike all Paulo's other trips, this one, which was to last eight months, was made without any forward planning. Although he took more than enough for a comfortable trip, with no need to cut corners, he was never one to squander money. He chose Iberia, the airline that not only offered the cheapest flights but added in a free night in a hotel in Madrid. From Spain he and Chris went on to London at the beginning of December 1981, where they rented the cheapest car available, a tiny Citroën 2CV. In London, they also established the first rule of the trip: neither should carry more than 6 kilos of luggage. This meant sacrificing the heavy Olivetti typewriter that Paulo had taken with him; this was shipped back to Brazil.

While pondering what direction to take, Paulo and Chris remained in London until the middle of January 1982, when they took to the road, determined to visit two places: Prague, where he wanted to make a promise to the Infant Jesus, and Bucharest, the capital of Romania and birthplace, 550 years earlier, of the nobleman Vlad Tepeş, who was the inspiration behind Bram Stoker's creation: the most famous of all the vampires, Count Dracula. On the afternoon of Tuesday, 19 January, they arrived in Vienna frozen to the bone, after almost a day travelling the 1,200 or so kilometres separating London from the capital of Austria. Their modest 2CV had no heater, which meant that they had to travel wrapped in woollen blankets in order to withstand the low winter temperatures. The stop in Vienna was so that they could obtain visas for Hungary, which they would have to cross in order to reach Romania.

Once this was done, they went to the Brazilian embassy, where Chris needed to sort out a small bureaucratic matter. Paulo waited for her out in the street, smoking and walking up and down. Suddenly, with a sound like a bomb, a vast sheet of ice several metres long slid off the roof of the building five storeys above and crashed on to the street, ripping open the bodywork of a car that was parked only a few centimetres from where Paulo was standing. He had been that close to death.

After spending the night in Budapest, they left for the capital of Yugoslavia, where they decided to stay for three days. Not that Belgrade held any special attraction, but they couldn't face getting back into the freezing Citroën. The car had become such a problem that they decided to hand it back to the rental company. With the help of the hotel manager they found a real bargain: the Indian embassy was selling a light-blue Mercedes – nine years old, but in good condition – for a mere US$1,000. Although well used, it had a 110-horse-power engine and was equipped with an efficient heating system. This would be the only large expense of the trip. For advice on hotels, restaurants and places to visit, they relied on *Europe on 20 Dollars a Day*.

Now that they had a proper car, the 500 kilometres between Belgrade and Bucharest, the couple's next destination, could be done in one day. However, precisely because they now had a fast, comfortable car, they chose to take a more roundabout route. Having crossed Hungary and part of Austria, driving a little more than 1,000 kilometres, they arrived in Prague, where Paulo was to make the promise to the Infant Jesus that he would honour almost twenty-five years later. It was only then that they turned towards Romania, which meant another 1,500 kilometres. For anyone not in a hurry or concerned about money, this was wonderful.

During this criss-cross journey across Central Europe, chance placed another destination in their path. It was not until a few weeks after buying the Mercedes that Paulo discovered that the car had originally come from the old Federal Republic of Germany (or West Germany) and that the change of ownership had to be registered at the licensing authority in Bonn, the then capital of West Germany. Travelling from Bucharest to Bonn meant a journey of almost 2,000 kilometres, a distance that now held no worries for them. Two days after leaving the capital of Romania, the blue Mercedes was crossing the frontier into West Germany. From Bucharest to Munich, the first German city they went through, the odometer showed that they had driven 1,193 kilometres. Munich was completely covered in snow, it was almost midday and since neither of the travellers was hungry, instead of lunching there, they decided to stop in Stuttgart, about 200 kilometres farther on. Minutes after passing through Munich, the capital of Bavaria, Paulo turned the car off the road into an avenue of bare trees with a sign written in German: 'Dachau Konzentrationslager'. It had long been in his mind to visit the sadly famous Nazi concentration camp in Dachau – since he was a boy he had been a passionate reader of books and stories about the Second World War – but little did he imagine that this visit, which lasted only a few hours, would radically change his life.

CHAPTER 21

First meeting with Jean

ALTHOUGH HE WOULD NOT PUBLISH his first real book until 1987, Paulo Coelho the author was born on 23 February 1982 at the age of thirty-five in Dachau concentration camp in Germany. Five days earlier, he had had a strange experience in Prague. Immediately after making his promise to the Infant Jesus of Prague, he had gone out with Chris for a walk round the city which, like almost all of Central Europe, was covered in snow and with below-zero temperatures. They crossed the river Vltava by the imposing Charles Bridge. One end of the bridge is in the Old City; the other comes out into the Street of Alchemists where, according to legend, lies the entrance to hell through which, naturally, Paulo was determined to go. The object of his interest was a medieval dungeon, which had been opened to the public some years before. In order to get in, he and Chris had to wait until the place had emptied of an enormous group of Soviet recruits – who appeared to be there as tourists.

Minutes after going through the doors of the dark dungeon and entering the cells, Paulo felt as though the ghosts from which he had believed himself to be free were reviving – the electroshock therapy, his supposed meeting with the Devil, his imprisonment by the Dops, his abduction, his cowardly betrayal of Gisa. From one moment to the next, all those events seemed to rise up, as though they had only just happened. He began to sob convulsively and Chris led him away. The gloomy surroundings had reawakened memories that threatened to propel him into a fit of deep depression, and he was thousands of kilometres from the security provided by his parents, Dr Benjamim's consulting rooms or Roberto Menescal.

This time, the origins of his torment were not metaphysical but all too real and visible on the pages of the newspapers and on the TV news: dictatorships, the state oppression of people, wars, abductions and clandestine imprisonments, which appeared to be sweeping the planet. Civil war was to claim almost 80,000 lives in the tiny state of El Salvador. In Chile, the savage dictatorship of General Pinochet was about to celebrate ten years of its existence and appeared to be as firmly entrenched as ever. In Brazil, the military dictatorship seemed exhausted, but there was still no guarantee that democracy was within reach. This was the worst possible state of mind in which to visit the site of a Nazi concentration camp, but this was precisely how Paulo was feeling when he parked the Mercedes in the visitors' car park in Dachau.

Dachau was the first camp built by the Third Reich and was the model for the remaining fifty-six scattered across ten European countries. It operated from 1933 until April 1945, when its gates were opened by the Allied troops. Although it was planned to house 6,000 prisoners, on the day of its liberation there were more than 30,000. During that tragic period, about 200,000 people of sixteen nationalities were taken there. Although the majority were Jews, there were also communists, socialists and others opposed to Nazism, as well as Gypsies and Jehovah's Witnesses. For reasons as yet unknown, the gas chamber in Dachau was never put to use, which meant that any prisoners who were condemned to death had to be taken by bus to Hartheim Castle, halfway between the camp and Linz, in Austria, which had been transformed into a centre of mass execution. The first surprise for Paulo and Chris as they went through the entrance gates of Dachau was that there was absolutely no one there. It was understandable that the freezing wind might have kept away the tourists, but they didn't see any porters, guards or officials who could give them any information. They were – or they appeared to be – alone in that enormous

180,000-square-metre rectangle surrounded on all sides by walls and empty watch towers. Paulo had not yet gotten over the dark thoughts that had assailed him in Prague some days before, but he didn't want to miss the opportunity of visiting one of the largest Nazi concentration camps. They followed the arrows and took the suggested route for visitors – the same as that taken by the prisoners. They went into the reception area, where the newly arrived prisoners would receive their uniforms, have their heads shaved and be 'disinfected' in a collective bath of insecticide. Then they walked down the corridors lined by cells, in which they saw the hooks attached to the ceiling beams from which the prisoners were hung by their arms during torture sessions; then they went into the sheds where, until the end of the war, bunk beds were stacked three or four high and where the prisoners slept like animals, packed into wooden cages. In total silence, their horror only grew with each new revelation.

Although Paulo was clearly upset, he saw the concentration camps as a tragedy of the past, part of the Nazism that was defeated in a war that had ended even before he was born. However, in the room set aside for the relatives of the dead to pay their respects, he felt that the emotions aroused in Prague were returning. The cards pinned on bunches of fresh flowers that had been put there only a few days earlier were living proof that Dachau was still an open wound. The 30,000 dead were not meaningless names taken from books, but human beings whose cruel deaths were recent enough still to awaken the grief of widows, children, brothers and sisters.

Paulo and Chris returned to the open area of the camp feeling overwhelmed. They walked along an avenue of bare trees whose branches looked like bony claws reaching for the sky. In the north part of the camp there were three small religious buildings – Catholic, Protestant and Jewish – beside which a fourth – Russian Orthodox – was to be built in the 1990s. The couple walked straight past these buildings, following a sign indicating the most chilling place in Dachau: the crematorium. At that point, they noticed a radical change in the landscape. Unlike the barren camp itself, which is a lunar landscape of grey stones with not a hint of greenery, the path leading to the crematorium passes through a small wood. Even in the hardest of winters this is covered by vegetation of tropical exuberance, with gardens, flowers and pathways between rows of shrubs. Planted in a clearing in the middle of the wood is a modest, rustic, red-brick building, which can only be distinguished from a traditional family house by the chimney, which seems disproportionately large. This was the crematorium oven, where the bodies of more than thirty thousand prisoners would have been burnt after their execution or death from starvation, suicide or illness, such as the typhoid epidemic that devastated the camp a few months before its liberation.

His experience in the medieval prison in Prague was still very clear in Paulo's mind. He saw all eight red-brick ovens and the metal stretchers on which the bodies would have been piled for incineration, and he stopped in front of a peeling door on which one word was written: 'Badzimmer'. This was not an old bathroom, as the name indicated, but the Dachau gas chamber. Although it was never used, Paulo wanted to feel for himself the terror experienced by millions in the Nazi extermination camps. He left Chris alone for a moment, went into the chamber and shut the door. Leaning against the wall, he looked up and saw, hanging from the ceiling, the fake showerheads from which the gas would be released. His blood froze and he left that place with the stench of death in his nose.

When he stepped out of the crematorium he heard the small bell of the Catholic chapel chiming midday. He went towards that sound and as he re-entered the harsh grey of the camp, he saw an enormous modern sculpture, which recalled Picasso's *Guernica*. On it was written in several languages 'Never again!' As he read the two words on entering the small church, a moment of peace came to him, as he was to remember many years later: 'I'm entering the church, my eye alights on that "Never Again!" and I say: Thank God for that! Never again! Never again is that going to happen! How good! Never again! Never again will there be that knock on the door at midnight, never again will people just disappear. What joy! Never again will the world experience that!'

He went into the chapel feeling full of hope and yet in the short space of time between lighting a candle and saying a quick prayer, he suddenly felt overwhelmed again by his old ghosts. In a moment, he went from faith to despair. As he crossed the frozen camp, a short way behind Chris, he realized that the 'Never again!' he had just read was nothing more than a joke in several languages:

> I said to myself: what do they mean 'Never again!'? 'Never again', my eye! What happened in Dachau is still happening in the world, on my continent, in my country. In Brazil, opponents of the regime were thrown from helicopters into the sea. I myself, on an infinitely smaller scale, lived for several years in a state of paranoia after being the victim of that same violence! I suddenly remembered the cover of *Time* with the killings in El Salvador, the dirty war waged by the Argentine dictatorship against the opposition. At that moment, I lost all hope in the human race. I felt that I had reached rock bottom. I decided that the world is shit, life is shit, and I'm nothing but shit for having done nothing about it.

While he was thinking these contradictory thoughts, a sentence began going round and round in his head: 'No man is an island.' Where had he read that? Slowly, he managed to rebuild and recite to himself almost the entire passage: 'No man is an island entire of itself; every man is a piece of the continent, a part of the main; if a clod be washed away by the sea, Europe is the less, as well as if a promontory were, as well as if a manor of thy friends or of thine own were; any man's death diminishes me, because I am involved in mankind ...' For a moment he could not remember the rest, but when he did, it seemed to have opened all the doors of his memory: 'and therefore never send to know for whom the bell tolls; it tolls for thee'. It was from one of John Donne's *Meditations*, from which Ernest Hemingway took the title for his novel. What happened in the following minutes is something that will remain for ever cloaked in mystery; indeed Paulo himself, on one of the few occasions when he has been urged to describe what occurred, became so emotional that he wept copiously: 'We were in the middle of a concentration camp, Chris and I, alone, absolutely alone, without another living soul around! At that moment I heard the sign: I felt that the bells of the chapel were ringing for me. That's when I had my epiphany.'

According to him, the revelation in Dachau took the form of a beam of light, under which a being of human appearance apparently told him something about possibly meeting again in two months' time. This message was given not in a human voice but, as Paulo himself put it, 'in a communication of souls'. Even the most sceptical would perhaps agree that something took place in Dachau, so radical was the change in Paulo's life from that day on. When he reached the car park, he wept as he told Chris what he had just experienced, and the first, horrifying suspicion fell on the OTO. What if what he had seen minutes earlier were the reincarnation of the Beast? Had the ghosts of Crowley and Marcelo Motta returned to frighten him eight years on? When they reached Bonn, six hours later, Paulo settled on the most rational explanation: he would consider the vision as a delirium, a brief hallucination provoked by the fear and tension he was feeling.

The couple planned to stay in Bonn just long enough to sort out the paperwork for the car and to meet Paula, a niece who had been born a few months earlier. Since they were staying at the home of Chris's sister, Tânia, and so were free of hotel expenses, they decided to extend their stay to a week. In early March, the couple set off once again, this time to cover the 250 kilometres between them and the liberal city of Amsterdam, which had so enchanted Paulo ten years earlier.

They stayed in the Hotel Brouwer, on the edge of the Singel Canal, where they paid US$17 a day for bed and breakfast. In a letter to his parents Paulo talked of the pot shops, 'cafés where you can freely buy and smoke drugs that are considered soft, like hashish and cannabis, although cocaine, heroin, opium and amphetamines, including LSD, are prohibited', and he took the opportunity to add a subtle apology for the liberalization of the drugs: 'This doesn't mean that the Dutch youth are drugged all the time. On the contrary, government statistics show that there are far fewer drug addicts here, proportionally speaking, than in the USA, Germany, England and France. Holland has the lowest rate of unemployment in the whole of Western Europe, and Amsterdam is the fourth largest commercial centre of the world.'

It was in this liberal atmosphere, where the two smoked cannabis until they got tired of it, that Chris tried LSD for the first and only time. Paulo was so shocked by the devastating effects of heroin on its users – zombies of various nationalities wandered the streets of the city – that he wrote two articles for the Brazilian magazine *Fatos&Fotos* entitled 'Heroin, the Road of No Return' and 'Amsterdam, the Kiss of the Needle'. His relationship with this underworld, however, was strictly professional, that of an investigative reporter. Judging by the letters he sent to his father, their European tour was a hippie journey in appearance only: 'We haven't deprived ourselves of anything, lunching and dining every day. And although we have a very thirsty child to support (the 110-horse-power Mercedes), we go to cinemas, saunas, barbers, nightclubs and even casinos.'

There seemed to be no end to the good life. After several weeks in the city, Paulo became bored by so much cannabis. He had tried varieties from places as far away as the Yemen and Bolivia. He had smoked blends of every strength and experimented with plants that had won prizes in the Cannabis Cup, the marijuana world cup which was held once a year in Amsterdam. He had even tried a new product called skunk – cannabis grown in a hot house and fed with fertilizers and proteins. And it was there, in that hippie paradise, that Paulo discovered that the plant had nothing more to offer him. He was, he said, 'fed up' with its repetitious effects. He repeated the oath he had made eight years earlier in New York regarding cocaine: he would never again smoke cannabis.

He was explaining all this to Chris in the hotel café when he felt a cold shiver run through him, just as he had in Dachau. He glanced to one side and saw that the shape he had seen in the concentration camp had taken physical form and was there having tea at a table nearby. His first feeling was one of terror. He had heard of societies which, in order to preserve their secrets, would pursue and even kill those who had left. Was he being followed by people belonging to a satanist group from the other side of the world? He suddenly remembered the lesson he had learned during those PE classes in Fortaleza de São João: to avoid unnecessary pain, confront the fear straight away.

He looked at the stranger – a man in his forties of European appearance, in jacket and tie – and summoned up his courage to address him in English in a deliberately hostile way: 'I saw you two months ago in

Dachau and I'm going to make one thing clear: I have not, nor do I wish to have, anything to do with occultism, sects or orders. If that's why you're here, then you've had a wasted journey.'

The man looked up and reacted quite calmly and, to Paulo's surprise, he replied in fluent Portuguese, albeit with a strong accent: 'Don't worry. Come and join me so that we can talk.'

'May I bring my partner?'

'No, I want to talk to you alone.'

Paulo made a sign to Chris to reassure her that everything was all right. Then he went and sat at the other man's table and asked: 'Talk about what?'

'What's all this about a concentration camp?'

'I thought I saw you there two months ago.'

The man said that there must be some confusion. Paulo insisted: 'I'm sorry, but I think that we met in February in the concentration camp at Dachau. You don't remember?'

The man then admitted that Paulo might have seen him, but that it could also have been a phenomenon known as 'astral projection', something Paulo knew about and to which he had referred many times in his diary. The man said: 'I wasn't at the concentration camp, but I understand what you're saying. Let me look at the palm of your hand.' Paulo cannot remember whether he showed him his left or his right hand, but the mysterious man studied it hard and then began to speak very slowly. He did not seem to be reading the lines on his hand; it was more as if he were seeing a vision: 'There is some unfinished business here. Something fell apart around 1974 or 1975. In magical terms, you grew up in the Tradition of the Serpent, and you may not even know what the Tradition of the Dove is.'

As a voracious reader of everything to do with magic, Paulo knew that these traditions were two different routes leading to the same place: magical knowledge, understood as the ability to use gifts that not all humans succeed in developing. The Tradition of the Dove (also known as the Tradition of the Sun) is a system of gradual, continuous learning, during which any disciple or novice will always depend on a Master, with a capital 'M'. On the other hand, the Tradition of the Serpent (or Tradition of the Moon) is usually chosen by intuitive individuals and, according to its initiates, by those who, in a previous existence, had some connection with or commitment to magic. The two routes are not mutually exclusive, and candidates to the so-called magical education are recommended to follow the Tradition of the Dove once they have followed that of the Serpent.

Paulo began to relax when the man finally introduced himself. He was French, of Jewish origin, worked in Paris as an executive for the Dutch multinational Philips and was an active member of an old, mysterious Catholic religious order called RAM which stood for Regnus Agnus Mundi – Lamb of the Kingdom of the World – or 'Rigour, Adoration and Mercy'. He had gained his knowledge of Portuguese from long periods spent in Brazil and Portugal working for Philips. His real name – which could be 'Chaim', 'Jayme' or 'Jacques' – has never been revealed by Paulo, who began to refer to him publicly as 'the Master', 'Jean' or simply 'J'.

In measured tones, Jean said that he knew Paulo had started out along the road towards black magic, but had interrupted that journey. He said: 'If you want to take up the road to magic again and if you would like to do so within our order, then I can guide you. But, once you have made the decision, you will have to do whatever I tell you without argument.'

Astonished by what he was hearing, Paulo asked for time to reflect. Jean was uncompromising: 'You have a day to make your decision. I shall wait for you here tomorrow at the same time.'

Paulo could think of nothing else. While he had felt great relief at leaving the OTO and rejecting the ideas of Crowley, the world of magic, as opposed to black magic, continued to hold an enormous fascination for him. He recalled later: 'Emotionally I was still connected to it. It's like falling in love with a woman, and sending her away because she really doesn't fit in with your life. But you go on loving her. One day she turns up in a bar, as J did, and you say: "Please, go away. I don't want to see you again, I don't want to suffer again."'

Unable to sleep, he spent all night talking to Chris, and it was dawn when he finally made up his mind. Something was telling him that this was an important moment and he decided to accept the challenge, for good or ill. Some hours later, he met for the second (or was it the third?)

time the mysterious man who from that moment was to be his Master – always with a capital M. Jean explained to Paulo what the first steps towards his initiation would be: on the Tuesday of the following week he was to go to the Vikingskipshuset, the Viking Ship Museum in Oslo.

'Go to the room where you will find three ships called the *Gokstad*, *Oseberg* and *Borre* on display. There someone will hand you something.'

Not quite understanding what he was being asked to do, Paulo wanted to know more. 'But what time should I be at the museum? How will I recognize the person? Is it a man or a woman? What will they give me?'

As Jean stood up, leaving a few coins on the table in payment for the cup of tea he had drunk, he satisfied only a part of Paulo's curiosity: 'Be in the room when the museum opens its doors. The other questions need no answer. You will be told when we are to see each other again.' And then he vanished, as if he had never existed – if indeed he ever did exist. Whether real or supernatural, one thing was certain: he had left his new disciple a task that would begin with a journey of almost 1,000 kilometres to the capital of Norway, a city Paulo had never been to before. They drove there through the snow via Holland, Germany and Denmark. On the appointed day, Paulo woke early, worried that he might arrive late and fearing that any queues and groups of tourists at the museum might delay him. The publicity leaflet from the museum, which he had picked up in the lobby of the hotel, informed him that the doors opened at nine in the morning, but he set off a whole hour earlier. Situated on the Bygdøy Peninsula, ten minutes' drive from the centre of the city, the Vikingskipshuset is a large yellow building in the shape of a cross, with no windows and a pointed roof. It was only when he arrived that Paulo realized he had misunderstood the opening hours. The museum was open from nine in the morning until six in the evening during the high season, but from October to April, the doors only opened at eleven. He spent the time reflecting on the decision he had just taken. 'I had tried everything in order to realize my dream to be a writer, but I was still a nobody,' Paulo was to recall later. 'I had abandoned black magic and the occult sciences when I discovered that they were of no help to me at all, so why not try the route Jean was suggesting?'

At eleven on the dot, he joined the half-dozen Japanese tourists who were also waiting and followed the arrows to the room with high, curved walls like a church nave, where the *Gokstad*, *Oseberg* and *Borre* were displayed. There was only one other person there – a pretty blonde woman of about forty, who seemed to be absorbed in reading a plaque on one of the walls. When she heard his footsteps, she turned, revealing that she was holding something long, like a walking stick or a sword. She said nothing, but walked towards him, took a silver ring bearing the image of an ouroboros – the snake that devours its own tail – from the ring finger of her left hand and placed it on the middle finger of his left hand. She then traced an imaginary circle on the floor with the stick or sword, indicating that Paulo should stand inside it. Then, she made a gesture as if pouring the contents of a cup into the circle. She moved her right hand across Paulo's face without touching it, indicating that he should shut his eyes. 'At that moment I felt that someone had liberated stagnant energies,' he said years later, 'as though the spiritual floodgate of a lake had been opened, allowing fresh water to enter.' When he opened his eyes again, the only sign left by the mysterious woman was the strange ring, which he would wear for the rest of his life.

Paulo would only be in contact with Jean again much later, when he returned to Brazil. At the end of April 1982, he was supposed to return to his job with TV Globo, but after discussing it at length with Chris, he decided not to return to work but to remain in Europe. They had more than enough money to allow them to stay for another three months in Amsterdam.

And so it wasn't until the middle of July that they drove the 1,900 kilometres from Amsterdam to Lisbon – a journey of three days – from where they would take a plane to Brazil. However, the first visible change in Paulo Coelho's behaviour following his meeting with his Master took place on European soil. Only some supernatural force could have persuaded someone as careful with money as he was to donate the Mercedes to a charitable institution, the Sisterhood of the Infant Jesus for the Blind, rather than selling it and pocketing the thousand dollars.

CHAPTER 22

Paulo and Christina – publishers

WHEN THEY ARRIVED IN RIO, reinvigorated by their eight long months in Europe, Paulo and Chris settled back into the ground-floor apartment in Rua Raimundo Correia, in which her parents had been living since their departure. He began his initiation tasks. These so-called ordeals, which would lead to his being admitted to RAM, would arrive in either a letter or a phone call from Jean. The first of these, 'the ritual of the glass', involved a short ceremony that he was to perform alone each day for six months, always at the same hour. He had to fill a glass that had never been used with water, and place it on the table. He then had to open the New Testament at any page, read out loud a paragraph at random and drink the water. The passage he had read was to be marked with the date of the reading. If, on the following days, he alighted on the same text, then he should read the following paragraph. If he had read that one too, then he was to find another that had not been previously read. Paulo chose the early morning as the best time to perform this penance, so that it would not clash with anything else. And since no specific instruction had been given as to the size or shape of the glass, he bought a small shot glass, which could, if necessary, be discreetly carried around with a copy of the New Testament.

Fortunately, none of the trials demanded by Jean prevented him from leading a normal life. Money continued to be no problem, but his partnership with Raul had clearly fallen out of fashion. Their records continued to sell, but royalties from the recording company were not pouring in as they had before. Although a regular income from the five apartments he rented out guaranteed a comfortable lifestyle, his lack of activity was likely to propel him once more into depression. Therefore the best thing to do would be to find some more work as soon as possible.

A year before his trip to Europe, Paulo had persuaded Chris that she should start a company, Shogun Editora e Arte Ltda, which was primarily created for tax purposes to cover the architectural work she was doing, but which also meant that they both had business cards, letterheads and envelopes stating that they were a legal entity. In addition, as he said, when the time came for him to write his books, why not publish them himself? On returning to Brazil, he decided to put this idea into action and rented two rooms in a building on Rua Cinco de Julho in Copacabana, two blocks from the apartment where they lived. Although it managed to grow and even to bring in some income, Shogun was never more than a small family firm whose day-to-day business was handled by its two owners, with the accounts done by Paulo's father, who had just retired. They had only one paid employee – an office boy.

Less than three months after their return to Brazil, in October 1982, the publishing house launched its first book: *Arquivos do Inferno* [*Archives of Hell*], a collection of sixteen texts written by the proprietor, Paulo Coelho. On the cover was a picture of the author sitting cross-legged in front of a typewriter, holding a cigarette and apparently deep in thought, while beside him are two young women with bare breasts: one was Chris, and the other was Stella Paula, his old colleague from his Crowley witchcraft days. In the photo she had such long hair that it not only covered most of her breasts but fell below her waist. Although it was little more than a booklet (it was only 106 pages long), *Arquivos do Inferno* was certainly a record-breaker in terms of prefaces, forewords and notes on the inside flaps. The preface, entitled 'Preface to the Dutch Edition', was signed by the pop genius Andy Warhol (who, as Paulo confessed years later, never read the book):

I met Paulo Coelho at an exhibition of mine in London, and discovered in him the kind of forward-looking nature one finds in very few people. Rather than being a literary man in search of clever ideas, he coolly and accurately touches on the concerns and preoccupations of the present time. Dear Paulo, you asked for a preface to your book. I would say that your book is a preface to the new era that is just beginning, before the old one has even ended. Anyone who, like you, strides forward, never runs the risk of falling into a hole, because the angels will spread their cloaks out on the ground to catch you.

The second was written by Jimmy Brouwer, the owner of the hotel where the couple had stayed in Amsterdam; the third by the journalist Artur da Távola, Paulo's colleague at Philips; the fourth by the psychiatrist Eduardo Mascarenhas, who at the time was the presenter of a television programme and a Member of Parliament; and the fifth by Roberto Menescal, who was one of the book's two dedicatees, the other being Chris. Nothing about the book quite fits. According to the cover, it was supposedly a co-edition by Shogun with a Dutch publisher, the Brouwer Free Press, a firm that apparently never existed. A press release distributed by Shogun confused things still more by stating that the book had been published abroad, which was not true: 'After its successful launch in Holland, where it was acclaimed by critics and public alike after only two months in the shops, *Arquivos do Inferno*, by Paulo Coelho, will be in all the bookshops in Brazil this month.' The information given about the author's previous works muddied the waters still further, including as it did something entitled *Lon: Diário de um Mago*, which had apparently been published by Shogun in 1979, even though the firm did not exist at that time and *Diário de um Mago* (translated as *The Pilgrimage* in English) wasn't published until 1987. On one of the few occasions, years later, when he spoke about the matter, Paulo gave a strange explanation: 'It can only have been a prophecy.' On the imprint page, in tiny print, is another peculiarity: '300 copies of the first editions in Portuguese and Dutch will be numbered and signed by the author and sold at US$350 each, the money to be donated to the Order of the Golden Star.'

The book did not contain a single chapter or essay that dealt with the theme mentioned in the title – hell. The sixteen texts are a jumble of subjects arranged in no particular order, covering such disparate matters as the proverbs of the English poet William Blake, the rudiments of homoeopathy and astrology, and passages from manuscripts by a certain Pero Vaz and from Paulo's own works, such as 'The Pieces':

It is very important to know that I have scattered parts of my body across the world. I cut my nails in Rome, my hair in Holland and Germany. I saw my blood moisten the asphalt of New York and often my sperm fell on French soil in a field of vines near Tours. I have expelled my faeces into rivers on three continents, watered some trees in Spain with my urine and spat in the English Channel and a fjord in Oslo. Once I grazed my face and left some cells attached to a fence in Budapest. These small things – created by me and which I shall never see again – give me a pleasant feeling of omnipresence. I am a small part of the places I have visited, of the landscapes I have seen and that moved me. Besides this, my scattered parts have a practical use: in my next incarnation I am not going to feel alone or unprotected because something familiar – a hair, a piece of nail, some old, dried spit – will always be close by. I have sown my seed in several places on this earth because I don't know where I will one day be reborn.

The most striking feature of the book is the second chapter, entitled 'The Truth about the Inquisition'. Paulo makes it clear that this was not written by him, but was dictated by the spirit of Torquemada, the Dominican friar who was in charge of the trials held by the Holy Office in Spain at the end of the fifteenth century. As though wanting to clear himself of any responsibility for its content, the author explains that not only the spelling and the underlinings but also 'some syntactical errors' were retained exactly as dictated by the spirit of the Grand Inquisitor. The eight pages of the chapter are filled with celebrations of torture and martyrdom as instruments in the defence of the faith:

It is therefore most just that the death penalty be applied to those who obstinately propagate heresy and so ensure that the most precious gift of man, Faith, is lost for ever!

[…] Anyone who has the right to command also has the right to punish! And the authority that has the power to make laws also has the power to ensure that those laws are obeyed!

[…] Spiritual punishment is not always enough. The majority of people are incapable of understanding it. The Church should, as I did, have the right to apply physical punishment!

Apparently wanting to attribute a scientific character to this psychic writing, Paulo ends the text with a curious parenthetical observation: '[After these words, no other communication was made by what called itself the "spirit of Torquemada". As it is always important to note the conditions in which a transmission was made – with a view to future scientific investigations – I recorded the ambient temperature (29°C), the atmospheric pressure (760 mmHg), weather conditions (cloudy) and the time the message was received (21h15m to 22h07m)].'

This was not the first occasion on which Paulo had shown an interest in the Holy Office of the Inquisition. In September 1971, he had thought of writing a play on the subject and during his research he came across a book by Henrique Hello, published by Editora Vozes in 1936 and reprinted in 1951, the title of which was *The Truth about the Inquisition*. The ninety-page text is a long peroration in defence of the objectives and methods used by the Inquisition. Part had been quoted in the preface to *O Santo Inquérito* [*The Holy Inquisition*], written in 1966 by the playwright Dias Gomes. When he finished reading it, Paulo had concluded ironically: 'I set to work on the play about the Inquisition. It's an easy play. It simply plagiarizes what someone called Henrique Hello said about it. No, it doesn't plagiarize, it criticizes. The guy wrote a book called *The Truth about the Inquisition* in favour of the Inquisition!'

Probably because of his imprisonment and abduction in 1974, Paulo held back from criticizing the author and simply transcribed his words. A comparison between the content of *Arquivos do Inferno* and the 1936 publication shows that if it was in fact an example of psychic writing, the spirit that dictated 'The Truth about the Inquisition' was that of Henrique Hello and not Torquemada, since 95 per cent of the text is simply copied from Hello's work.

None of this, however, surpasses the extraordinary piece of information the author gives at the beginning of 'The Truth about the Inquisition'. He states there that the automatic writing had occurred 'on the night of 28 May 1974'. The fact is that, between 21.15 and 22.07 on the night of 28 May 1974, Paulo was lying handcuffed on the floor of a car with his head covered by a hood and was being driven to the buildings of the DOI-Codi. It is hard to believe that the prison guards of one of the most violent prisons of the Brazilian dictatorship would have allowed a prisoner to write such an essay, even though it was a treatise in praise of torture. The author seems to have realized that *Arquivos do Inferno* would not stand up to scrutiny, and once the first, modest print run had sold out, he did not publish it again. When he had become an international name, the work was mentioned discreetly on his website: 'In 1982 he published his first book, *Arquivos do Inferno*, which made no impact whatsoever.'

A quarter of a century after this major failure, *Arquivos* became a rarity sought by collectors in auctions on the Internet with starting prices of about US$220, as though Paulo's initial fantasy were finally coming to fruition.

The lack of success of Shogun's debut book acted as an important lesson, since it made it clear that this was an undertaking requiring a professional approach. Determined to do things properly, Paulo took over the management of the business, and his first step was to take a seven-week correspondence course on financial planning. The course seems to have borne fruit, since in 1984, two years after it was set up, Shogun was ranked thirty-fourth among Brazilian publishers listed in the specialist magazine *Leia Livros*, rivalling traditional publishing houses such as Civilização Brasileira and Agir, and even Rocco (which some years later would become Paulo's publisher in Brazil). Shogun rented stands at book fairs and biennials and had a backlist of more than seventy titles.

Among the authors published, besides the proprietors themselves, there were only two well-known names, neither of whom was exactly a

writer: the rock singer Neusinha Brizola, the daughter of the then governor of Rio, Leonel Brizola (*O Livro Negro de Neusinha Brizola* [*The Black
Book of Neusinha Brizola*]), and the ever-present 'close enemy', Raul
Seixas (*As Aventuras de Raul Seixas na Cidade de Thor* [*Raul Seixas'
Adventures in the City of Thor*]). Shogun's success was, in fact, due to
hundreds and thousands of anonymous poets from all over Brazil who,
like the owner of Shogun, had dreamed for years of one day having a
book of their poetry published. In a country where hundreds of young
authors were desperate to publish, Shogun came up with the perfect solution: the 'Raimundo Correia Poetry Competition'.

Paulo placed small advertisements in newspapers and left flyers at
the doors of theatres and cinemas, inviting unpublished poets from across
Brazil to take part in the competition, which had been named after the
street in which Paulo and Chris lived, in turn named after an influential
Brazilian poet who had died in 1911. The rules were simple. The competition was open to poems written in Portuguese by 'authors, whether
amateur or professional, published or not, and of any age'. Each person
could submit up to three poems of a maximum length of two pages
double-spaced, and a 'committee of critics and experts of high standing'
(whose names were never revealed) would select those to be included in
an anthology to be published by Shogun. Those selected would receive a
contract under which they committed themselves to paying US$175, for
which they would receive ten copies. To the couple's surprise, one of the
competitions received no fewer than 1,150 poems, of which 116 were
selected for a book entitled *Poetas Brasileiros*. The publishers ran no financial risk at all, because the work was published only after the authors had
paid up. Each contributor would receive, along with the books, a certificate produced by Shogun and signed by Chris, and a handwritten note
from Paulo:

Dear So and So,
    I have received and read your poems. Without going into the
merits of the material – which, as you yourself know, is of the highest quality – I should like to compliment you on not having let your
poems stay in a drawer. In today's world, and during this particularly

exceptional period of History, it is necessary to have the courage to make one's thoughts public.

Once again my congratulations,

Paulo Coelho

What at first sight had appeared to be an amateur enterprise turned out to be very good business indeed. When the couple sent off the last package of books in the post, Shogun had earned the equivalent of US$187,000. The success of an apparently simple idea encouraged Paulo and Chris to repeat the project on a larger scale. A few weeks later, Shogun announced competitions to select poems to be published in four new anthologies, entitled *Poetas Brasileiros de Hoje*, *A Nova Poesia Brasileira*, *A Nova Literatura Brasileira* and *Antologia Poética de Cidades Brasileiras*. In order to motivate those who had been rejected in the first anthology, Chris sent each of them an encouraging letter in which she explained that the number of poems to be awarded the prize of publication was to rise from 116 to 250:

Rio de Janeiro, 29 August 1982

Dear Poet,

A large number of the works that failed to be placed in the Raimundo Correia Poetry Competition were of very high quality. Therefore, although we are forced to restrict the number of winning poems to 250, we have decided to find a solution for those poems which, either because they did not comply with the rules or because they were not selected by the Committee of Judges, were not included in the Anthology.

The book *Poetas Brasileiros de Hoje* – another Shogun publication – is to be published this year. We would love one of your poems to be included in this anthology. Each of the authors will pay the amount stated in the attached agreement and, in exchange, will receive ten copies of the first edition. This means that, for each copy, you will be paying only a little more than you would pay for a weekly news magazine, and you will be investing in yourself, increasing the sphere of influence of your work and, eventually, opening doors to a fascinating career.

As stated in the attached agreement, Shogun will send copies of *Poetas Brasileiros de Hoje* to the best-known literary critics in the country, and publicity material will be sent to more than two hundred important newspapers and magazines. Copies of the first edition will also be donated to state and municipal libraries, thus ensuring that thousands of readers will, over the years, have access to your poetry.

Lord Byron, Lima Barreto, Edgar Allan Poe and other great names in Literature had to finance the publication of their own books. Now, with this system of sharing the costs, it is possible to produce the book quite cheaply and for it to be read and commented upon throughout the country. In order to take part in *Poetas Brasileiros de Hoje*, all you have to do is fill in the attached agreement, sign it and send it with the stated amount to Shogun.

If you have any questions, please write to us.

Christina Oiticica

The Shogun anthologies grew in popularity, and poets of every sort sprang up in every corner of the country. On the evenings when the diplomas and other awards were handed out, there were so many present that the publisher was forced to hire the Circo Voador in Lapa, one of the newest venues in Rio, to accommodate the winning bards and their guests. Chris also organized public events, usually held in busy places, where the authors would recite their prize-winning poetry to passers-by, who would stop, genuinely interested, to listen to the poetry. There was, of course, always some problem, such as those who took a long time to pay or the poet who wrote a letter of protest to the *Jornal do Brasil*:

> I took part in the Fifth Raimundo Correia Poetry Competition and was awarded a prize for my poem 'Ser humano'. In order for my poem to be published, I had to pay a fee of Cr$380,000 in four instalments, for which I would receive ten copies of the book. When I paid the final instalment, I received the books. When I saw them and opened them, I was so disappointed that I didn't even want to read them. I realized, then, that I had fallen for a confidence trick.

The book uses very old-fashioned typography, and the design itself is one of the worst I've ever seen, muddled and ugly. It is Shogun's philosophy that he who does not pay is not published. I know of several people who were excluded because they couldn't pay all the instalments. 116 poets were published. By my calculations, Shogun have made a total of Cr$44 million, and have the right to use our money as they wish from the very first instalment.

Considering the amount we paid, we deserved something better. I work in the field of graphic design myself, and so feel able to make these criticisms. I wouldn't give the book away as a present or even sell it to my worst enemy.

Rui Dias de Carvalho – Rio de Janeiro

A week later, the *Jornal do Brasil* published Shogun's reply in which the director Christina Oiticica stated that the printers who produced their books were the same as those who worked for such publishing giants as Record and Nova Fronteira. As for making money from the anthology, she responded by saying that this was used to finance projects that would never interest large publishers, such as *Poesia na Prisão* (a competition held among prisoners within the Rio de Janeiro prison system), without depending upon public funds: 'We do not beg for support from the state for our cultural activities. We are independent and proud of the fact, because all of us – publishers and poets – are proving that it is possible for new artists to get their work published.'

The complaints did not seem to be shared by other authors published by Shogun. Many years later, the poet Marcelino Rodriguez recalled proudly in his Internet blog seeing his 'Soneto Eterno' included in the publisher's anthology: 'My first literary venture was produced by Shogun, owned by Paulo Coelho (who is now our most important writer, although many "academics" do not recognize his worth, perhaps because they do not understand the content of his work) and Christina Oiticica, who is a highly talented artist (I still haven't forgotten the smile she gave me when I visited the office once).'

The fact is that, as well as encouraging young authors, the project proved to be a successful business enterprise. By organizing four anthologies a year, Shogun could earn some 160 million cruzeiros a year. Between 1983 and 1986, there was a boom in anthologies and poetry competitions, and so these sums may have been even greater, particularly when Shogun doubled the number of prize-winners. At the age of nearly forty, Paulo's life finally seemed to be working out. Chris was proving to be a wonderful partner – their relationship grew more solid by the day – and business was flourishing. All that was needed to complete his happiness was to realize his old dream of becoming a world-famous writer. He continued to receive spiritual guidance from Jean, but this did not prevent him from reading about and entering into public debates on esoteric subjects and indulging his old curiosity for vampirism. It was as a vampirologist that, in 1985, he accepted an invitation to give a talk in the largest conference centre in the city, Riocentro, which was holding the first Brazilian Esoteric Fair, an initiative by the guru Kaanda Ananda, the owner of a shop selling esoterica in the Tijuca district in Rio, who had invited Paulo to open the meeting with a talk on vampirism.

When he arrived on the afternoon of Saturday, 19 October, Paulo was greeted by the reporter Nelson Liano, Jr, who had been selected by the Sunday magazine of the *Jornal do Brasil* to interview him. Although he was only twenty-four, Liano had worked on the main Rio publications and, like Paulo, had experimented with every type of drug. If there is such a thing as love at first sight between esoterics, this is what happened between Paulo and Liano. Such was their reciprocal delight in each other's company that their conversation ended only when Kaanda Ananda told them for the third time that the auditorium was full and that an impatient public was waiting for Paulo. The two exchanged phone numbers and took their leave of each other with a warm embrace. While Paulo went into the auditorium, Liano headed off to have a coffee with his friend Ernesto Emanuelle Mandarino, the owner of the publishing house Editora Eco.

Eco was a small publishing house founded in the 1960s. Although it was unknown in intellectual circles, during its twenty years in existence, it had become a reference point for anyone interested in umbanda and candomblé (the Brazilian forms of voodoo), magic, etc. Over coffee with Mandarino, Liano told him that he had just interviewed a vampirologist.

'The guy's called Paulo Coelho and he trained in vampirism in England. He's talking at the moment to a packed auditorium of people on the subject. Don't you think it might make a book?'

Mandarino opened his eyes wide: 'Vampirism? It sounds like something out of the movies. Would a book like that sell? When he finishes his talk bring him over here to the stand for a coffee.'

Minutes after being introduced to Paulo, Mandarino told him point-blank: 'If you write a book on vampirism, Eco will publish it.'

Paulo replied: 'I'll do it, if Nelson Liano will write it with me.'

Mandarino was astonished: 'But Nelson told me that you had only just met!'

Paulo chuckled: 'That's true, but we're already life-long friends.'

The deal was done. The two left, having agreed to write a book entitled *Manual Prático do Vampirismo* [*Practical Manual on Vampirism*]. The work was to be arranged in five parts, the first and fifth to be written by Paulo, the second and fourth by Liano and the third divided between the two. Paulo and Chris wondered afterwards whether it wouldn't be better if Shogun published the book, but they were dissuaded from this idea by Liano, who felt that only a publisher of Eco's standing would be able to market such a book, whereas Shogun's speciality was poetry anthologies. On the assumption that it would be a best-seller, Paulo demanded changes to Eco's standard contract. Concerned about inflation, he asked to receive monthly rather than quarterly accounts. Even though Liano was going to write half the book and edit the final text, Paulo asked Mandarino's secretary to add this clause at the bottom of the contract: 'Only the name Paulo Coelho will appear on the cover, with the words "Edited by Nelson Liano, Jr." on the title page under the title.'

In effect, Liano was going to write half the book and edit the whole thing, but was to appear only as its coordinator (and this only on the inside pages). And, following a final addendum suggested by Paulo, he was to receive only 5 per cent of the royalties (0.5 per cent of the cover price of the book), the remaining 95 per cent going to Paulo. As though anticipating that this was going to be the goose that laid the golden egg, Mandarino patiently accepted his new author's demands and since Liano also made no objections, they signed the contract a week after their first meeting.

However, only Liano handed in his chapters on the agreed date. Saying that he had too much work at Shogun, Paulo had not written a single word of his part. Time went on, and still the text did not appear. It was only after much pressure and when he realized that all deadlines had passed that Paulo finally handed his text to Eco. At the last minute, perhaps feeling that he had been unfair to his partner, he allowed the inclusion of Liano's name on the cover, but in small print, as though he were not the co-author but only an assistant.

The launch of the *Manual*, with waiters serving white wine and canapés, was held in the elegant Hotel Glória, in front of which, eleven years earlier, Paulo had been seized by the DOI-Codi. The cover, designed by Chris, bore the title in gothic characters over a well-known photograph of the Hungarian-American actor Béla Lugosi who, in 1931, had become world-famous when he played Count Dracula in the Tod Browning film. The texts covered subjects ranging from the origins of vampirism to the great 'dynasties' of human bloodsuckers, which were divided into the Romanian, British, German, French and Spanish branches. One chapter explained how to recognize a vampire. At social gatherings this could be done by observing certain habits or gestures. For example, if you come across a person with a particular liking for raw or undercooked meat, who is also studious and rather verbose, you should be on your guard: he could be a true descendant of the Romanian Vlad Tepeş. It would be even easier, the *Manual* explained, to know whether or not you were sleeping with a dangerous bloodsucker because vampires don't move their pelvis during the sexual act and the temperature of their penis is many degrees below that of ordinary mortals.

The *Manual* concealed some even greater mysteries. None of the guests in the lobby of the Hotel Glória could know that, although his name appeared in larger print than Liano's on the cover, Paulo had not written a single word, a single syllable, of the 144 pages of the *Manual*. The author never revealed that, under pressure of the deadline and disinclined to keep his part of the agreement, he had secretly taken on someone else to write his parts of the book.

His choice fell on a strange man from Minas Gerais, Antônio Walter Sena Júnior, who was known in the esoteric world as 'Toninho Buda' or

'Tony Buddha', a somewhat inappropriate name for a very skinny man who never weighed more than 55 kilos. He had graduated in engineering at the Universidade Federal in Juiz de Fora, where he still lived, and had met Paulo in 1981 during a debate on vampirism at the Colégio Bennett in Rio. He had studied subjects such as magic and the occult, had closely followed the career of Paulo and Raul Seixas, and dreamed of resurrecting the old Sociedade Alternativa. He felt greatly honoured at the thought of seeing his name alongside that of Paulo Coelho in a book and he accepted the task in exchange, as he said later, 'for the price of lunch in a cheap restaurant in Copacabana'. He wrote all the chapters that Paulo was supposed to write.

On 25 April 1986, Toninho Buda was recovering after being run over some weeks earlier. He was shocked to read in a column in the *Jornal do Brasil* that Paulo Coelho would be signing his new book, *Manual Prático do Vampirismo*, that evening in the Hotel Glória. He thought it rude that he hadn't been invited to the launch, but preferred to believe that the invitation had not arrived on time. Still walking with the aid of a stick, he decided to go to the launch of a book that was, after all, also his. He went to the bus station, took the bus and, after two hours on the road, arrived in Rio de Janeiro as night was falling. He crossed the city by taxi and hobbled up the four white marble steps at the main entrance of the Hotel Glória. It was only then that he realized that he was the first to arrive: apart from the employees of the publishing house, who were stacking books on a stand, there was no one else there, not even the author.

He decided to buy a copy – as well as receiving no invitation he hadn't even been sent a complimentary copy – and sat in an armchair at one end of the room to enjoy his creation in peace. He admired the cover, ran his eyes over the first pages, the frontispiece, the two flaps, but his name did not appear anywhere in the book, of which half had been entirely written by him. He was about to take a taxi back to the bus station when he saw Paulo enter, smiling, with Chris, Liano and Mandarino.

At that moment, he decided that he wasn't going to waste the journey and so he gave vent to his feelings: 'Dammit, Paulo! You didn't even put my name on the book, man, and that was the only thing I asked for! The only thing I asked for, man!'

Paulo pretended not to understand, asked to see a copy of the *Manual*, flipped quickly through it and said regretfully: 'It's true, Toninho. They didn't add your name. But I promise you: I'll ask for a special stamp to be made and we'll stamp the whole of the first edition. I'll correct it in the next edition, but with this one, we'll stamp every book. Forgive me.'

Although deeply upset, Toninho Buda didn't want to ruin Paulo's evening and felt it best to end the conversation there: 'Paulo, I'm not an idiot. Don't talk to me about a stamp, man. Go off to your launch, where there are loads of people wanting your autograph. Go on and I'll just leave.'

Toninho swallowed the insult in the name of a higher ambition: to get Paulo interested in reinstituting the Sociedade Alternativa. His strategy was a simple one: to use public debates and popular demonstrations to gain the attention of the media and public opinion. Some months earlier, he had written a long letter to Paulo from Juiz de Fora suggesting 'public actions' by the group, among which he suggested rushing on to the stage of the first international rock concert in Rio on the night when stars such as Whitesnake, Ozzy Osbourne, the Scorpions and AC/DC were performing. Toninho's plan was to seize the microphone and start talking about the Sociedade Alternativa: 'This will depend almost entirely on you and your contacts in Rio. I'm prepared to go there myself. If you agree, you can start to work on things, but please don't forget to keep me informed as to how it's going.'

In January 1986, some months after the book signing, the threesome had taken part in an event in Rio. They decided to use a protest by inhabitants of the South Zone against the decision of the Prefecture to close a public park in order to announce the launch of a newspaper, *Sociedade Alternativa*, the first draft of which had been designed entirely by Toninho. It was he who enrolled with the organizers of the demonstration in order to get his message heard. As soon as his name was called, he went up to the improvised rostrum in suit and tie and in front of the television cameras began to read what he had entitled 'Manifesto Number 11'. It was an entire page of statements such as 'Free space, everyone should occupy their space'; 'Time is free, everyone has to live in their time'; and 'The artistic class no longer exists: we are all writers, housewives, bosses and employees, radicals and conservatives, wise and mad'. It wasn't the content that mattered though, but the manner of his performance. As Toninho Buda read out each sentence, paragraph or thought, Chris carefully and silently cut off a piece of his clothing: first his tie, then a sleeve of his suit, then a leg of his trousers, then another sleeve, a collar, another sleeve ... When he pronounced the final sentence (something like 'The great miracle will no longer be being able to walk on water, but being able to walk on the earth') he was completely naked, without a square centimetre of cloth on his body.

That night, when they were all celebrating the repercussions of their 'public action' in the park, Paulo was still muttering about the need to do something even more scandalous, with greater impact. However, Chris and Paulo were flabbergasted when Toninho told them that what he hoped to do would, in his words, 'leave the Sociedade Alternativa engraved for ever in the memory of millions of Brazilians': neither more nor less than blowing the head off the statue of Christ the Redeemer. He explained the plan to explode the monument's 3.75-metre-high, 30-ton head, a monument which, in 2007, would be named one of the seven new wonders of the modern world. Any normal person would have thrown such a madman out of the house, but Paulo didn't do that. On the contrary, he simply said: 'Go ahead.'

This was what Toninho wanted to hear. 'Just imagine the population of Rio de Janeiro waking up one morning and seeing Christ there, without his head and with that great mound of twisted iron struts sticking out of his neck towards the indigo sky! Think of the Pope's edict for making amends, the crowds climbing up Corcovado looking for pieces to keep as a relic. Imagine that! The Church collecting tithes for the miracle of its reconstruction! That's when we would go in singing "Viva, Viva, Viva a Sociedade Alternativa!" and distributing the first edition of our newspaper with the hot news on the dreadful episode ...'

This was a heresy too far, particularly for someone who was in the process of reconciliation with the Church, and Paulo preferred to bring the conversation to a close and never return to the subject. As Toninho would only find out months later, Paulo was very close to being admitted as a Master of RAM, the religious order to which Jean had introduced him. His first failed attempt to acquire this rank in the secret organization had occurred in January that year. Taking advantage of a business trip to Brazil, Jean had appointed 2 January 1986 as the date for a secret ceremony during which Paulo would receive a sword, the symbol of his ordination as a Master. The site for this was to be the summit of one of the mountains in Mantiqueira, on the frontier between Minas Gerais and Rio de Janeiro, next to one of the highest points in Brazil, the peak of Agulhas Negras. As well as Jean and Paulo, Chris, a hired guide and another man who was to be initiated into the order were also to be there. The sole instruction Paulo had received was to take with him the old sword that he had been using for years in his esoteric exercises.

As Paulo himself describes in the prologue to *The Pilgrimage*, they all met around a bonfire and the ceremony began when Jean pointed a brand-new sword, which he had not yet removed from its sheath, towards the sky, saying: 'And now before the sacred countenance of RAM, you must touch with your hands the Word of Life and acquire such power as you need to become witness to that Word throughout the world!' After digging a long, shallow hole with his bare hands, Paulo received from Chris his old sword, which was to be buried there, and in a tremulous voice, he pronounced the words of the ritual. As he finished, he saw that Jean was placing the new sword on top of the hole.

He then goes on to say that they were all standing with their arms outstretched when something happened. 'The Master, invoking his power, created a strange light that surrounded us; it didn't illuminate, but it was clearly visible, and it caused the figures of those who were there to take on a colour that was different from the yellowish tinge cast by the fire.' The high point, not just of the ceremony but of the whole long day, was approaching. Still not believing what he was experiencing, he heard the words Jean was saying while he made a slight cut on his forehead with the point of the blade of the new sword: 'By the power and the love of RAM, I anoint you Master and Knight of the Order, now and for all the days of your life. R for Rigour, A for Adoration, and M for Mercy; R for *regnum*, A for *agnus*, and M for *mundi*. Let not your sword remain long in its scabbard, lest it rust. And when you draw your sword, it must never be replaced without having performed an act of goodness, opened a path or tasted the blood of an enemy.' Paulo was not shaking quite so much and, for the first time since he had arrived, he felt relief. When his hand touched the sword that Jean had laid down on the ground, he would finally be a magus.

At that moment, someone stepped roughly on the fingers of his right hand, which he had just reached out to touch the sword. He looked up and saw that the foot that had almost maimed him was Jean's. Furious, the Frenchman snatched up the sword, replaced it in its scabbard and gave it to Chris. Paulo realized then that the strange light had disappeared and that Jean was looking at him coldly, saying: 'You should have refused the sword. If you had done so, it would have been given to you, because you would have shown that your heart was pure. But just as I feared, at the supreme moment, you stumbled and fell. Because of your avidity you will now have to seek again for your sword. And because of your pride you will have to seek it among simple people. Because of your fascination with miracles, you will have to struggle to recapture what was about to be given to you so generously.'

The ceremony ended miserably. Alone in the car on the return to Rio de Janeiro, Paulo and Chris remained silent for a long time, until Paulo was unable to restrain his curiosity and asked her what the Master had said to her. Chris tried to reassure him, saying that she was sure he would get the sword back. She had received precise instructions from Jean as to where she was to hide the sword so that Paulo could try to regain it.

Still more troubled, he wanted to know what place had been chosen as the hiding place, but she was unable to reply precisely: 'He didn't explain very well. He just said that you should look on the map of Spain for a medieval route known as the Road to Santiago.'

CHAPTER 23

The road to Santiago

WHEN HE ENQUIRED AT TRAVEL AGENCIES, Paulo discovered that in 1986, there was hardly any interest in the so-called Road to Santiago. Each year, fewer than 400 pilgrims ventured along the 700 inhospitable kilometres of the mystical route between St-Jean-Pied-de-Port, in the south of France, and the cathedral in Santiago de Compostela, the capital of Galicia, in the northwest of Spain. From the first millennium of Christianity onwards, this road had been taken by pilgrims seeking the supposed tomb of the Apostle James. All Paulo needed to do was to pluck up the courage and leave. Instead, he handed over the day-to-day management of Shogun to Chris, while he spent his days at home filling pages and pages of diaries with a constant lament: 'I haven't felt this angry for a long time. I'm not angry at Jesus, but at myself for not having sufficient willpower to realize my dreams.'

He felt that he lacked the strength he needed and frequently said that he felt like becoming an atheist. However, he never lost sight of the commitment he had made to Jean. Since, though, he seemed determined to put off the trip for ever, it fell to Chris to take the initiative. Without telling him, at the end of July she went to a travel agency, bought two tickets and came home to announce: 'We're going to Madrid.'

He tried to put off their departure yet again, saying that the publishing house couldn't function on its own and that the business about him finding the sword, which Chris was to hide somewhere on a 700-kilometre-long road, seemed utter madness: 'Has my Master set me an impossible task, do you think?'

Chris, however, was determined: 'You've done nothing for the last seven months. It's time to fulfil your commitment.'

So at the beginning of August 1986, they landed in Barajas international airport in Madrid, where skinny Antônio Walter Sena Júnior, the same Toninho Buda who had dreamed of blowing off the head of Christ the Redeemer, was waiting for them.

Once Paulo had made the decision to follow the Road to Santiago, he had taken on Toninho as his assistant and, since then, had started to refer to him as 'slave'. Toninho had barely recovered from his frustration over the *Manual Prático do Vampirismo* and was setting up a macrobiotic restaurant in Juiz de Fora when he received Paulo's proposal, in which Paulo made it clear that this wasn't an invitation to travel together but an employment contract.

When he learned the details of the proposal over the telephone, Toninho had a surreal conversation with his friend – surreal because this was to be paid slavery.

'But what you're suggesting is slavery!'

'Exactly. I want to know if you'll agree to be my slave for the two months I'll be in Spain.'

'But what am I going to do there? I haven't got a penny to my name, I've never been outside Brazil, I've never been on a plane.'

'Don't worry about money. I'll pay your fare and give you a monthly salary of 27,000 pesetas.'

'How much is that in dollars?'

'It must be about US$200, which is a fortune if you take into account that Spain is the cheapest country in Europe. Do you accept?'

Aged thirty-six, single and with no responsibilities, Toninho saw no reason to refuse: after all, it wasn't every day that someone invited him to go to Europe, regardless of what he would have to do when he got there. And if things didn't work out, all he had to do was take the plane back. But it was only when he arrived in Rio, with his bags packed, and read the contract drawn up by Paulo that he discovered that things were not quite like that. In the first place, while Paulo and Chris were taking an Iberia flight that included a free night in a hotel, Paulo had bought him a much cheaper flight on the ill-fated Linhas Aéreas Paraguaias. Apart from the risks involved in flying with a company that was hardly a world champion in safety, he had to go to Asunción, in Paraguay, in order to get the plane to Madrid. In addition, the ticket could not be exchanged and could be used only on the specified dates, which meant that, whatever happened, he could not return to Brazil until the beginning of October, two months later. The contract, grown yellow over time and lost at the bottom of a trunk in Rio de Janeiro, shows how draconian were the conditions Paulo imposed on his slave, who is referred to here as 'Tony':

Agreements

1   If Tony sleeps in my room, he will only do so when it is time to sleep, since I will be working there day and night.

2   Tony will receive an allowance of US$200 a month which will be reimbursed to him when he returns to Rio, but this is not obligatory.

3   Should my room or apartment be occupied by someone else, Tony will sleep elsewhere at his own expense.

4   Any visits I want to make and for which I require Tony's company will be at my expense.

5   Tony will not make the journey with me and Chris. He will wait for us in Madrid.

6   Tony has been advised of the following items:

6.1 That the air ticket does not allow him to change the date of his return;

6.2 That it is illegal for him to work in Spain;

6.3 That, apart from his monthly allowance of US$200, he will have to find money himself;

6.4 That if he changes his return date he will have to pay the equivalent of a normal fare (US$2080) to be discounted from the US dollars already paid for the non-refundable ticket.

1 August 1986
Antônio Walter Sena Júnior
Paulo Coelho

On reading these monstrous requirements, Toninho Buda considered
returning to Minas Gerais, but the desire to know Europe won out and so
he had no alternative but to sign the agreement. Since their respective
flight times did not coincide, he took a flight the day before Paulo and
Chris on a journey that started badly. On arriving in Madrid, without
knowing a word of Spanish, he spent three hours trying to explain to the
authorities how he was planning to stay sixty days in Spain with the four
10-dollar notes in his wallet. He found himself in the humiliating position
of being undressed and interrogated before, finally, being allowed to go.
On the following day, Tuesday, 5 August, he was once again at Barajas
airport, awaiting the arrival of his boss. Toninho had found somewhere to
stay with an old blind woman who hated Brazil (a 'country full of shame-
less hussies', she would mutter) and who would lock the front door at
eleven at night, after which whoever was still out in the street slept in the
street. The only advantage of Doña Cristina Belerano's boarding house
was the price – a paltry 600 pesetas (US$7 in today's terms) a day, which
included a modest breakfast. Chris and Paulo spent only the first night
together in Madrid: the following day Chris rented a car and went off to
hide Paulo's sword in the place indicated by Jean.

It was suffocatingly hot in the Spanish capital on 7 August 1986, when
Paulo left the city in a hired car. He drove about 450 kilometres north,
crossed the frontier with France and left the car at a branch of the hire
firm in Pau, where he spent two nights. On the Sunday morning, 10 August,
he took a train to the Pyrenees and there wrote what was to be the final
note in his diary before returning from his pilgrimage:

11h57 – S.-Jean-Pied-de-Port
A fiesta in town. Basque music in the distance.

Immediately below, on the same page, was a stamp on which one can
read an inscription in Latin – 'St. Joannes Pedis Portus' – beside which

there is a handwritten note in French signed by someone called 'J.', whose surname looks something like 'Relul' or 'Ellul':

Saint-Jean-Pied-de-Port
Basse-Navarre
Le 10 Août 1986
J.........

Could this initial J be for Jean? As is usually the case whenever someone tries to cross the frontier of his mystical world by asking too many questions, Paulo Coelho neither confirms nor denies this. Everything indicates that Jean was the person in St-Jean-Pied-de-Port (presumably, as the official representative of the religious order RAM) to ensure that his disciple really was beginning the ordeal imposed on him.

Paulo's pilgrimage would end in the Spanish city of Cebrero, where he found the sword and broke off his journey. An episode in which a taxi driver claimed that Paulo had in fact made the journey in the back of his comfortable, air-conditioned Citroën, and was proved by a Japanese television company to have been lying, led Paulo to include in the preface to the subsequent editions of *The Pilgrimage* a short piece in which he invites the reader to believe whichever version he prefers, thus only increasing the mystery surrounding the journey:

I've listened to all kinds of theories about my pilgrimage, from me doing it entirely by taxi (imagine the cost!) to my having secret help from certain initiating societies (imagine the confusion!).

My readers don't need to be sure whether or not I made the pilgrimage: that way they will seek a personal experience and not the one I experienced (or didn't).

I made the pilgrimage just once – and even then I didn't do the whole thing. I finished in Cebrero and took a bus to Santiago de Compostela. I often think of the irony: the best-known text on the Road at the end of this millennium was written by someone who didn't follow it right to the end.

The most important and mysterious moment of the whole journey, which is not revealed until the end of the book, occurred when Paulo was nearing Cebrero, some 150 kilometres from Santiago. At the side of the road, he came across a solitary lamb, still unsteady on its feet. He began to follow the animal, which plunged off into the undergrowth until it reached a little old church built beside a small cemetery at the entrance to the town, as he describes in the book:

> The chapel was completely lit when I came to its door. [...] The lamb slipped into one of the pews, and I looked to the front of the chapel. Standing before the altar, smiling – and perhaps a bit relieved – was the Master: with my sword in his hand.
>
> I stopped, and he came toward me, passing me by and going outside. I followed him. In front of the chapel, looking up at the dark sky, he unsheathed my sword and told me to grasp its hilt with him. He pointed the blade upward and said the sacred Psalm of those who travel far to achieve victory:
>
> 'A thousand fall at your side and ten thousand to your right, but you will not be touched. No evil will befall you, no curse will fall upon your tent; your angels will be given orders regarding you, to protect you along your every way.'
>
> I knelt, and as he touched the blade to my shoulders, he said:
>
> 'Trample the lion and the serpent. The lion cub and the dragon will make shoes for your feet.'

Paulo tells how at the exact moment when Jean finished speaking, a heavy summer shower began to fall. 'I looked about for the lamb, but he had disappeared,' he wrote, 'but that did not matter: the Water of Life fell from the sky and caused the blade of my sword to glisten.' Like a child celebrating some form of rebirth, Paulo returned to Madrid, moved into a pleasant furnished flat in the elegant Alonso Martínez district, and gave himself over body and soul to the city's vibrant lifestyle. Until October, he could count on the assistance of Toninho Buda – whom he referred to in his diary as 'the slave', or simply 'the sl.' – but he soon realized that he had chosen the wrong man to be his servant. While Paulo had become a sybarite eager to drain Madrid's night-life to the last drop, Toninho turned out to be a radical vegetarian who would eat only minute portions of macrobiotic food and drink no alcohol. Nor could he spend his evenings with his boss, since he had to be back at Doña Cristina's boarding house by eleven, when the night in Madrid had barely begun. He also complained with increasing frequency that his salary was not enough to live on. On one such occasion, they had a bitter argument.

'Paulo, the money isn't enough even for me to buy food.'

'I think you'd better read our contract again. It's says there that if the pay isn't enough, then you have to earn some extra money yourself.'

'But Paulo, the contract also says that it's forbidden for foreigners to work here in Spain!'

'Don't be so stupid, slave. Other people manage to get by. It's not as if you were crippled or anything, so do something!'

Toninho had no option. When he was down to his last penny, he took his guitar, which he had brought with him from Brazil, chose a busy underground station, sat on the floor and began to sing Brazilian songs. Beside him was a cap waiting for the coins and, more rarely, notes thrown in by passers-by. He could never stay long in the same place before being moved on, but an hour's singing would usually bring in 800–1,000 pesetas (US$9–11), which was enough to buy a plate of food and pay for his board and lodging. Another way of earning money was by using his rudimentary knowledge of Asian massage, in particular shiatsu, which wouldn't require him to speak Spanish or any other language. The cost of putting an advertisement in one of the Madrid newspapers was prohibitive, but with the help of a friend, he managed to find a kind soul willing to print a number of cards on which he offered to perform therapeutic massage for 'back, muscular pain, insomnia, tiredness, stress, etc'. On the day when the cards were ready, he stuck a copy in his diary and wrote above it:

Thursday, 25 Sep 86
I woke late, but went for a run in the Retiro Park. I had diarrhoea when I got back and felt very weak. Paulo phoned me, and I told him that it was going to take a miracle for them to keep me here ... I had

the business card made to hand it out in strategic places in Madrid, but I'm the one who needs a massage! I need to get stronger. The tension is killing me.

Given Paulo's indifference to the sufferings of his 'slave', Toninho returned to Brazil at the beginning of October without saying goodbye.

All Paulo wanted to do was enjoy himself. He would lunch and dine in good restaurants, he would go to cinemas and museums, and he found himself giving way to two new passions: bullfights and pinball machines. With the latter, he would usually stop playing only once he had broken the record set by the previous player. He gradually became such an aficionado of bullfights that he would travel for hours by train to see a particular fighter in action. If there were no bullfights, he would spend his afternoons standing in bars full of adolescents, eyes glued to the illuminated screen of the pinball machine. He even joined a course to learn how to play the castanets.

It did not take long, though, for him to fall once more into depression. He had US$300,000 in the bank and five apartments bringing in a regular income, he was in a stable relationship and he had just received the sword of a Master or Magus, but he was still unhappy. In spite of the busy life he was leading, he found time to fill more than five hundred pages of his diary between September and January, when he was due to return to Brazil. Most of these pages repeated for the umpteenth time the monotonous complaint he had been making for the last twenty years, which had now become a tearful mantra: 'I'm still not an established writer.'

At the end of October, Chris came to Madrid for a few weeks and rubbed more salt into his wounds. One day, when Paulo was saying how prolific Picasso was, she said: 'Look, Paulo, you have as much talent as he has, but since we got together six years ago, you haven't produced anything. I've given and I'll continue to give you all the support you need. But you have to have a concrete objective and pursue it tenaciously. That's the only way you'll get where you want to be.'

When Chris returned to Brazil at the beginning of December, Paulo was in an even worse mental state than before. He was lamenting the fact that he had lost the ability to tell 'even stories about myself or my life'. He found his diary 'boring, mediocre and empty', but eventually recognized that, if he did, this was his own fault: 'I haven't even written here about the Road to Santiago. Sometimes I think about killing myself because I'm so terrified of things, but I have faith in God that I shall never do that. It would be exchanging one fear for a greater fear. I've got to get away from the idea that writing a book would be an important thing to do in Madrid. Perhaps I could dictate a book to someone.'

In the middle of December, Chris phoned to say that she could no longer stand working with Pedro: 'Paulo, your father is being very difficult. I need you to come back here straight away.'

Pedro Queima Coelho did not agree with the expenses that the publishing house incurred in advertising, and this created permanent friction between him and Chris. The phone call was an ultimatum for Paulo to start the countdown and think about returning, with or without his book. He handed over this final responsibility to God, begging in his diary for the Creator to give him a sign when the time came to start writing.

Some days later, one icy Tuesday morning, he left early to go for a walk in the Retiro Park. When he returned home, he went straight to his diary and wrote: 'I had hardly gone any distance when I saw the particular sign I had asked God for: a pigeon feather. The time has come for me to give myself entirely to that book.'

In biographies and on official websites, *The Pilgrimage* is described as having been written in Rio during the Carnival of 1987, but there are clear indications in the author's diary that he began to write the first lines of the book when he was still in Spain. A day after receiving what he believes to have been a sign from heaven he wrote:

15/12 – I can't write this book as though it were just any book. I can't write this book just to pass the time, or to justify my life and/or my idleness. I have to write this book as though it were the most important thing in my life. Because this book is the beginning of something very important. It's the beginning of my work of indoctrination in RAM and that is what I must devote myself to from now on.

18/12 – I wrote for an hour and a half. The text came easily, but there are lots of things missing. It seemed very implausible, very

Castaneda. Using the first person worries me. Another alternative would be an actual diary. Perhaps I'll try that tomorrow. I think the first scene is good, so I can make variations on that theme until I find the right approach.

The miracle was apparently taking place.

CHAPTER 24

The Alchemist

PAULO'S FIRST MOVE when he returned to Brazil was to persuade his father to leave Shogun so that Chris could work in peace, which he managed to do without causing any resentment. During his absence, she had dealt very competently with the firm's business, and knowing that Chris was looking after the firm as well as or even better than he could was a further inducement for Paulo to dedicate himself entirely to the book. He was still full of doubts, though. Was he really just writing a book about his pilgrimage? Weren't there enough books on that topic? Why not abandon the idea and try writing something else, such as a *Manual of Practical Magic*? And whatever the subject, should the book be published by Shogun or given to Eco, as had been the case with *Manual Pratico do Vampirismo*?

These uncertainties lasted until 3 March 1987, a Tuesday during Carnival. That day Paulo sat down in front of his typewriter, determined to leave the apartment only when he had put the final full stop on the last page of *The Pilgrimage*. He worked frenetically for twenty-one days, during which time he did not set foot outside the house, getting up from his chair only to eat, sleep and go to the toilet. When Chris arrived home on the twenty-fourth, Paulo had a package in front of him containing

200 pages ready to be sent to the printer. The decision to have Shogun publish it was growing in his mind and he even put some small classified ads in the Saturday edition of *Jornal do Brasil* announcing: 'It's on its way! *The Pilgrimage* – Editora Shogun.'

The person who once again dissuaded him from the idea of being at once author and publisher was the journalist Nelson Liano, Jr, who advised him to knock on Ernest Mandarino's door. Paulo thought about it for a few days, and it wasn't until mid-April that he signed the contract for the first edition of *O Diário de um Mago*, or *The Pilgrimage*, standing at the counter of a small bar next to the publisher's office in Rua Marquês de Pombal.

The contract contains some odd things. First, Paulo demanded that, instead of the usual five- or seven-year contract, he should have a contract that would be renewed with every edition (the first had a print run of 3,000 copies). He did not, as he had with *Manual Prático do Vampirismo*, ask for monthly rather than quarterly accounts, but accepted what he was offered, even though inflation in Brazil had reached almost 1 per cent a day. The other strange thing is that at the foot of the contract the author put in an apparently meaningless addendum – which would, however, prove to be prophetic: 'Once the book has sold 1,000 (one thousand) copies, the publisher will be responsible for the costs of producing the book in Spanish and English.' If, among his gifts, Paulo had had the ability to predict the future, he could have taken the opportunity to make it Mandarino's responsibility to produce versions not only in English and Spanish but also in the other forty-four languages into which *The Pilgrimage* would subsequently be translated, among them Albanian, Estonian, Farsi, Hebrew, Hindi, Malay and Marathi.

Although sales got off to a very slow start, they soon overtook all of Eco's other titles. Years later, when he was retired and living in Petrópolis, 70 kilometres from Rio de Janeiro, Ernesto Mandarino was to recall how much of this success was due to a virtue that few authors possess – a desire to publicize the book: 'Authors would leave the finished manuscript with the publisher and do nothing to publicize their work. Paulo not only appeared in all the media, newspapers, radio and television, but gave talks on the book wherever he was asked.'

On the advice of his friend the journalist Joaquim Ferreira dos Santos, Paulo took an initiative rare even among established authors: at his own expense he employed the twenty-year-old journalist Andréa Cals to work exclusively on publicizing the book in the media. The salary was modest – 8,000 cruzados a month, the equivalent in 1987 of about US$400 – but he offered a tempting bonus. Should the book sell 20,000 copies by the end of 1987, Andréa would get a return flight from Rio to Miami. The contract also included the publicity for an exhibition of art by Chris entitled 'Tarô', and if all twenty-two works on show were sold before the exhibition closed, Andréa would earn a further 5,000 cruzados. Meanwhile, Paulo and Chris printed flyers about *The Pilgrimage*, which they themselves handed out nightly in cinema, theatre and stadium queues.

All this was an attempt to make up for the resistance of large media companies to give space to something as specific as *The Pilgrimage* – which seemed to be of interest only to the shrinking underground press. Andréa recalls trying in vain to get a copy of *The Pilgrimage* included in *Mandala*, a TV soap being shown by Globo and whose theme was in some ways similar to that of the book, but it was down to her hard work that the book got its first mention in one of the major newspapers. Beside the very brief mention in the *Jornal do Brasil* was a photo of the author who, at Joaquim's suggestion, was wearing a black cape and holding a sword. The picture caught the attention of the producers of *Sem Censura*, a chat show that went out every afternoon on the national television network Educativa, to which Paulo was invited.

In response to a question from the presenter, Lúcia Leme, and in front of millions of television viewers, Paulo revealed for the first time in public the secret that had been known only to a few friends and his diary: yes, he was a magus and among his many powers was that of making it rain. The strategy worked. The reporter Regina Guerra, from the newspaper *O Globo*, saw the programme and suggested to her boss an interview with this new individual on the Rio cultural scene: the writer who could make it rain. Her boss thought it all complete nonsense, but when his young reporter persisted, he gave in. The result was that, on 3 August, the cultural section of the newspaper devoted its entire front page to Paulo Coelho, who was given the title of 'the Castaneda of Copacabana'. In a sequence of photos, he appears among the leaves of his garden wearing the same black cloak and dark glasses and holding a sword. The text preceding the interview seems made to order for someone claiming to have supernatural powers:

> The thick walls of the old building mean that the apartment is very quiet, in spite of the fact that it's in one of the noisiest parts of the city – Copacabana, Posto Quatro. One of the bedrooms acts as a study and opens on to a miniature forest, a tangle of bushes, climbing shrubs and ferns. To the question – 'Are you a magus?' Paulo Coelho, who has just launched *The Pilgrimage*, his fifth book, replies with another: 'Is it windy outside?'
>
> A glance at the dense leaves is enough to make one shake one's head and murmur a casual 'No', implying that it really doesn't matter if there's a breeze outside or not: 'Right, take a look' – he remains as he was, seated on a cushion and leaning against another, doing nothing.
>
> First, the tip of the highest leaf of a palm tree starts to sway gently. In the next instant, the whole plant moves, as does all the vegetation around. The bamboo curtain in the corridor sways and clicks, the reporter's notes fly off her clipboard. After one or two minutes, the wind stops as suddenly as it began. There are a few leaves on the carpet and a question: was it coincidence or is he really a magus who knows how to summon up the wind? Read on and find out more.

Apart from *O Globo*, the only other coverage the rain-making author received was in *Pasquim* and the magazine *Manchete*. He was always friendly and receptive towards journalists, posing in a yoga position and allowing himself to be photographed behind smoking test tubes and putting on or removing his cloak and sword according to the demands of his clients. The barriers began to fall. His telephone number was soon in the diaries of social columnists, among them his friend Hildegard Angel, and he was often reported as having been seen dining in such-and-such a restaurant or leaving such-and-such a theatre. For the first time Paulo could feel the wind of fame in his face – something he had never experienced even at the height of his musical success, since, at the time, the star of the partnership was Raul Seixas. This media exposure did increase the sales of the book, but *The Pilgrimage* still seemed far from becoming a best-seller.

In order to try and capitalize on his new-found 'almost-fame', as he himself called it, Paulo and the astrologer Cláudia Castelo Branco, who had written the preface to *The Pilgrimage*, joined forces with the specialist travel firm Itatiaia Turismo to organize a spiritual package holiday named 'The Three Sacred Roads', which were to be Christianity, Judaism and Islam. Those interested would be guided by Paulo and Cláudia on a journey that would start in Madrid and end in Santiago de Compostela, via a zigzag route through Egypt (Cairo and Luxor), Israel (Jerusalem and Tel Aviv), France (Lourdes) and then back to Spain (Pamplona, Logroño, Burgos, León, Ponferrada and Lugo). Whether it was the fault of the dreadful advertisement published in the newspapers (which did not even say how long the excursion would last) or the high price of the package (US$2,800), they received not a single enquiry. However, although it produced no results, the project had cost them both time and money, and in order to pay them for their work, the agency gave them a half-price trip to the Middle East, one of the places suggested for the failed magical mystery tour.

Paulo and Cláudia set off on 26 September with Paula, Chris's mother, but as soon as they arrived in Cairo, he decided to continue alone with Paula. On their second day in the Egyptian capital, he hired a guide named Hassan and asked him to take them to the Moqattam district, in the southwest of the city, so that he could visit the Coptic monastery of St Simon the Shoemaker. From there they crossed the city by taxi, and night was falling when, after driving through an enormous slum, they reached the sandy fringe of the largest desert on the planet, the Sahara, a few hundred metres from the Sphinx and the famous pyramids of Cheops, Chephren and Mykerinos. They left the taxi and continued their journey to the pyramids on horseback (Paulo was frightened of falling off a camel, the only other available means of transport from there on). When they drew near, Paulo decided to proceed on foot, while Hassan looked after the horses and read the Koran. Paulo says that, near one of the illuminated monuments, he saw a woman in the middle of the desert wearing a chador and carrying a clay pot on her shoulder. This, according to him, was very different from what had occurred in Dachau. 'A vision is something that you see and an apparition is something almost physical,' he explained later. 'What happened in Cairo was an apparition.' Although used to such phenomena, he found what he had seen strange. He looked at the endless stretch of sand surrounding him on that moonlit night and saw no one else apart from Hassan, who was still reciting sacred verses. As the shape approached Paulo, it disappeared as mysteriously as it had appeared. However, it left such a strong impression that, months later, he could reconstruct the apparition in detail when describing it in his second book.

When he flew back to Brazil some weeks later, he received the first major news regarding his career while still on the plane. The stewardess handed him a copy of *O Globo* from the Saturday before, and he placed the folded newspaper on his lap, closed his eyes, meditated for a moment and only then opened the paper at the arts section – and there was *The Pilgrimage* on that week's best-sellers' list. Before the end of the year, he would sign contracts for five new editions of the book, the sales of which went on to exceed 12,000 copies. This success encouraged him to enter *The Pilgrimage* for the Prêmio Instituto Nacional do Livro, an award supported by the Ministry of Education for published novels. The jury that year was to meet in Vitória, the capital of Espírito Santo, and its members were the poet Ivan Junqueira, the writer Roberto Almada, and the journalist Carlos Herculano Lopes. *The Pilgrimage* didn't even appear on the list of finalists and only got Junqueira's vote. 'The book was unusual for us, because it mixeu reality with fantasy,' the poet recalled later. 'For me personally it was interesting in that I like travel literature very much and also this kind of half-ghost-story.'

Immediately after the results were announced, Paulo suffered yet another disappointment. The magazine *Veja* had published a long report on the boom in esoteric books in Brazil and made no mention of *The Pilgrimage*. This was such a hard blow that Paulo once again thought of giving up his career as a writer. 'Today I seriously thought of abandoning everything and retiring,' he wrote in his diary. Weeks later, however, he seemed to have recovered from those two setbacks and returned to the I Ching, already with an idea for a new book. He wrote a question in his diary: 'What should I do to make my next book sell 100,000 copies?' He threw the three coins on the table and stared in delight at the result. Usually vague and metaphorical in its responses, the Chinese oracle was, according to Paulo, astonishingly clear: 'The great man brings good luck.'

That piece of good luck – the new book – was already in his head. The next work by Paulo Coelho was to be based on a Persian fable that had also inspired the Borges story 'Tale of the Two Dreamers', published in 1935 in *A Universal History of Infamy*. It is the tale of Santiago, a shepherd who, after dreaming repeatedly of a treasure hidden near the Egyptian pyramids, resolves to leave the village where he was born in search of what the author calls a 'personal legend'. On the journey to Egypt Santiago meets various characters, among them an alchemist, and at each meeting he learns a new lesson. At the end of his pilgrimage he discovers that the object of his search was in the very village he had left. Paulo had also chosen the title: *O Alquimista*, or *The Alchemist*. It's odd to think that a book that would become one of the greatest best-sellers of all time – at the beginning of 2000 it had sold more than 35 million copies – started out as a play that would combine Shakespeare and the Brazilian humourist Chico Anysio, as the author recorded in his diary in January 1987:

> Menescal and [the actor] Perry [Salles] called me asking me to write a play for one actor alone on the stage. By coincidence, I was watching *Duel* on video, which is a film about a man alone.
>
> I had an idea: a large laboratory in which an old man, an alchemist, is searching for the philosopher's stone, for wisdom. He wants to discover what man can achieve through inspiration. The alchemist (perhaps that would be a good title) recites texts by Shakespeare and by Chico Anysio. He will perform songs and hold dialogues with himself, playing more than one character. He could be an alchemist or a vampire. I know through personal experience that vampires really excite the human imagination, and it's some time

since I've seen anything that combines horror and humour on the stage.

But, like Faust, the alchemist realizes that knowledge lies not in books but in people – and the people are in the audience. In order to get them in the mood, he gets them to chant or sing something all together. Perry would be the alchemist, in the role of the discoverer. Again, I stress that this must all be done with great good humour.

This sketch never became a play, but went on to become a novel. Paulo knew the story so intimately that when it came to writing the book, it took him only two weeks to produce 200 pages. At the beginning was a dedication to Jean, to whom Paulo gave the privilege of being the first to read the original manuscript:

For J.,
An alchemist who knows and uses the secrets of the Great Work.

When *The Alchemist* was ready for publication in June 1988, sales of *The Pilgrimage* had exceeded 40,000 copies and it had spent nineteen uninterrupted weeks in the main best-seller lists of the Brazilian press. The sublime indifference with which the media had treated it gave a special savour to Paulo's success, a success that was entirely down to the book itself and to the guerrilla warfare that Paulo, Chris and Andréa Cals had engaged in to publicize it. The I Ching, as interpreted by Paulo, recommended that he renew his contract with Andréa, but since she had taken on other work and he required her to devote herself entirely to him, her responsibilities were transferred to Chris.

She and Paulo adopted the same tactics for *The Alchemist* as had been used for the first book: the couple once again distributed flyers at the doors of theatres, bars and cinemas, visited bookshops and presented booksellers with signed copies. With his experience of the record industry, Paulo brought to the literary world a somewhat reprehensible practice – the *jabaculê*, a payment made to radio stations to encourage them to make favourable comments about a record, or in this case, a book.

Evidence of this can be found in spreadsheets – *certificados de irradiação* – sent to him by O Povo AM-FM, the most popular radio station in Fortaleza, Ceará. These show that during the entire second half of July, *The Alchemist* was mentioned three times a day in programmes presented by Carlos Augusto, Renan França and Ronaldo César, who were, at the time, the station's most popular presenters.

Paulo and Chris knew that they were in a world where anything goes – from sending signed copies to the grandees of the Brazilian media to becoming a full-time speaker, albeit unpaid. He had eight themes for organizers of talks to choose from: 'The Sacred Paths of Antiquity'; 'The Dawn of Magic'; 'The Practices of RAM'; 'The Philosophy and Practice of the Occult Tradition'; 'The Esoteric Tradition and the Practices of RAM'; 'The Growth of the Esoteric'; 'Magic and Power'; and 'Ways of Teaching and Learning'. At the end of each session, the audience could buy signed copies of *The Pilgrimage* and *The Alchemist*, and it was, apparently, very easy to get people to come and listen to him. Paulo's diary at the time shows that he spoke frequently at theatres and universities, as well as in country hotels and even people's homes.

However, this campaign produced slow results and the effects on sales of *The Alchemist* took time to appear. Six weeks after its launch, a few thousand copies had been sold – a vast number in a country like Brazil, it's true, but nothing when compared with the success of *The Pilgrimage* and far fewer than he had planned: 'Up to now', he wrote, 'the book hasn't reached 10 per cent of the goal I set myself. I think what this book needs is a miracle. I spend all day by the telephone, which refuses to ring. Why the hell doesn't some journalist call me saying that he liked my book? My work is greater than my obsessions, my words, my feelings. For its sake I humiliate myself, I sin, I hope, I despair.'

With *The Pilgrimage* still high in the best-seller lists and *The Alchemist* heading in the same direction, it had become impossible to ignore the author. A great silence had greeted the publication of the first book, but the launch of *The Alchemist* was preceded by full-page articles in all the main Brazilian newspapers. And because most of the press had totally ignored *The Pilgrimage* on its publication, they felt obliged to rediscover it following the success of *The Alchemist*. However, most restricted themselves to printing an article on the author and a summary of the story. The journalist and critic Antônio Gonçalves Filho, in *Folha de São Paulo*, was the first to publish a proper review. He commented only that *The Alchemist* was not as seductive a narrative as *The Pilgrimage* and that the story adopted by the author had already been the subject of a considerable number of books, plays, films and operas, something that Paulo himself had commented on in his preface to the book.

'This is why *The Alchemist*, too, is a symbolic text. In the course of the book I pass on everything I have learned. I've also tried to pay homage to great authors who managed to achieve a Universal Language: Hemingway, Blake, Borges (who also used the Persian story for one of his tales) and Malba Tahan, among others.'

In the second half of 1988, Paulo was just wondering whether to move to a larger, more professional publisher than Eco, when he was set yet another trial by Jean. He and Chris were to spend forty days in the Mojave Desert in southern California. A few days before they were due to leave, he had an unsettling phone conversation with Mandarino, the owner of Eco, who, although he was still enthusiastic about *The Pilgrimage*, did not believe that *The Alchemist* would enjoy the same success. The best thing to do would be to postpone the trip and try to resolve the problem immediately, but Master J would not be moved. And so in the middle of September, Paulo and Chris found themselves practising the spiritual exercises of St Ignatius Loyola in the extreme heat of the Mojave Desert, which could reach 50°C. Four years later, he wrote *As Valkirias* [*The Valkyries*], which was based on this experience.

At the end of October, they returned to Rio. Paulo wanted to resolve his difficulties with Eco immediately, but leaving the small publishing house without having anywhere else to go was not a good idea. One night, wanting to forget these problems for a while, he went with a friend to a poetry recital that was being held in a small fashionable bar. During the entire evening, he had the strange feeling that someone in the audience behind him was staring at him. It was only when the evening came to an end and the lights went up that he turned and caught the fixed gaze of a pretty dark-haired young girl in her early twenties. There was no apparent reason for anyone to look at him like that. At forty-one, Paulo's close-cropped hair was almost entirely white, as were his moustache and goatee. The girl was too pretty for him not to approach her.

He went up to her and asked straight out: 'Were you by any chance looking at me during the reading?'

The girl smiled and said: 'Yes, I was.'

'I'm Paulo Coelho.'

'I know. Look what I've got here in my bag.'

She took out a battered copy of *The Pilgrimage*.

Paulo was about to sign it, but when he heard that it belonged to a friend of hers, he gave it back, saying: 'Buy your own copy and I'll sign it.'

They agreed to meet two days later in the elegant old Confeitaria Colombo, in the centre of the city, so that he could sign her book. Although his choice of such a romantic venue might seem to indicate that he had other intentions, this was not the case. He arrived more than half an hour late, saying that he couldn't stay long because he had a meeting with his publisher, who had just confirmed that he was not interested in continuing to publish *The Alchemist*. So that they could talk a little more, Paulo and the girl walked together to the publisher's office, which was ten blocks from the Colombo.

Her name was Mônica Rezende Antunes, and she was the twenty-year-old only daughter of liberal parents whose sole demand had been that she take a course in classical ballet, which she abandoned almost at once. When she met Paulo, she was studying chemical engineering at the Universidade Estadual do Rio de Janeiro. What Mônica remembers most vividly about that meeting was that she was 'dressed ridiculously': 'Imagine going to discuss contracts with your publisher in the company of a girl in tiny shorts, a flowery blouse and hair like a nymphet!'

Mônica ended up being a witness to the moment when Mandarino at Eco decided not to continue to publish *The Alchemist*. He didn't believe that a work of fiction such as this could have the same degree of success as a personal narrative like *The Pilgrimage*. Although she had read only *The Pilgrimage*, Mônica couldn't understand how anyone could reject a book by an author who had made such an impact on her. Perhaps in an attempt to console himself, Paulo gave her a not very convincing explanation for what might be Ernesto Mandarino's real reason: with annual inflation in the country running at 1,200 per cent it was more profitable to put his money in financial deals than to publish books that ran the risk of not selling. The two of them walked on together a little farther, exchanged telephone numbers and went their different ways.

A few days later, before Paulo had decided what to do with the rights to *The Alchemist*, he read in a newspaper column that Lya Luft would be signing her book of poetry, *O Lado Fatal* [*The Fatal Side*], at a cocktail party given by her publisher, Paulo Roberto Rocco. Paulo had been keeping an eye on Editora Rocco for some time. It had only been in existence for just over ten years, but its catalogue already included heavyweights like Gore Vidal, Tom Wolfe and Stephen Hawking. When Paulo arrived, the bookshop was crammed with people. Squeezing his way past waiters and guests, he went up to Rocco, whom he knew only from photographs in newspapers, and said:

'Good evening, my name's Paulo Coelho, we don't know each other but ...'

'I already know you by name.'

'I wanted to talk to you about my books. I've a friend, Bona, who lives in the same building as you and had thought of asking her to give a dinner so she could introduce us.'

'You don't need to ask anything of anyone. Come to my office and we'll have a coffee and talk about your books.'

Rocco arranged the meeting for two days later. Before making a decision, though, Paulo turned to the I Ching to find out whether or not he should hand *The Alchemist* to a new publisher, since Rocco had clearly shown an interest. From what he could understand from the oracle's response, it seemed that the book should be given to the new publisher only if he agreed to have it in the bookshops before Christmas. This was a highly convenient interpretation since, as any author knows, Christmas is the best time of the year for selling books. As he was about to leave to meet Rocco, the phone rang. It was Mônica, whom he invited to go along with him.

After a brief, friendly conversation with Rocco, Paulo left copies of *The Pilgrimage* and *The Alchemist* with him. The publisher thought it somewhat strange that Paulo should want him to publish the book so quickly, but Paulo explained that all he had to do was buy the camera-ready copy from Eco, change the name of the publisher and put the book on the market. Rocco said that he would think about it and would reply that week. In fact, two days later, he called to say that the new contract was ready for signature. Rocco was going to publish *The Alchemist*.

CHAPTER 25

The critics' response

REJECTED BY MANDARINO, *The Alchemist* became one of the most popular gifts not only that Christmas but on many other Christmases, New Years, Easters, Carnivals, Lents and birthdays in Brazil and in more than a hundred other countries. The first edition to be launched by his new publisher sold out within a few days, creating a most unusual situation: an author with two books in the best-seller lists, one, *The Alchemist*, fiction and the other, *The Pilgrimage*, non-fiction. *The Alchemist* never stopped selling.

The phenomenon that the book became in the hands of Rocco encouraged Paulo to take *The Pilgrimage* from Eco as well and give it to his new publisher. Needing a pretext for such a change, he began to make demands on his old publisher. The first of these was an attempt to protect his royalties from the erosion caused by an astonishing 1,350 per cent annual rate of inflation: instead of quarterly payments (a privilege accorded to very few authors), he wanted Mandarino to make them weekly, which he agreed to do even though it was against market practice. Taking advantage of Mandarino's infinite patience (and his clear interest in retaining the book), Paulo then added two clauses hitherto unknown in Brazilian publishing contracts: daily monetary correction, linked to one of the mechanisms that existed at the time, and the use of a percentage of gross sales for marketing the book. These tactics seemed to be of particular interest to Mônica Antunes, who now went everywhere with Paulo. At the beginning of 1989, she told him over dinner in a pizzeria in Leblon that she was thinking of giving up her degree course at the university (she had just finished her second year in chemical engineering) and moving abroad with her boyfriend, Eduardo. The author's eyes lit up, as if he had just seen a new door opening, and he said: 'Great idea! Why don't you go to Spain? I've got various friends there who can help you. You could try to sell my books. If you succeed, you'll get the 15 per cent commission every literary agent earns.'

When she told her boyfriend about this, he discovered that the company for which he was working had a factory in Barcelona and it appeared, at first glance, that it would be fairly easy to get a transfer there, or at least a paid placement for a few months. Mônica, meanwhile, had learned that some of the most important Spanish publishers had their headquarters in Barcelona.

In the last week of May 1989, Mônica and Eduardo arrived in Madrid, where they stayed for three weeks before going on to Barcelona. During their first year in Spain, Mônica and Eduardo lived in an apartment in Rubí, just outside Barcelona. At book fairs they would go to all the stands collecting publishers' catalogues and would then spend the following days sending each a small press release offering the Spanish language rights to *The Alchemist* and other foreign language rights to publishers in other countries for *The Pilgrimage,* which had been taken on and translated by the Bolivian agency H. Katia Schumer and published in Spanish by Martínez Roca.

Meanwhile, in Brazil *The Pilgrimage* and *The Alchemist* remained at the top of the best-seller lists. Although Mandarino had accepted all the author's demands, at the end of 1989, he received a visit from Paulo Rocco, who brought bad news. For an advance of US$60,000, his company had acquired the publication rights to *The Pilgrimage.* Nearly two decades later, Ernesto Mandarino still cannot hide the hurt caused by the author on whom he had gambled when he was still a nobody: 'New editions were continuing to come out – to the envy of other publishers. When he visited me, Rocco said that he was offering Paulo Coelho an advance of US$60,000. I said that if that was what he wanted, there was nothing I could do, as the contracts were renewable after each edition. After twenty-eight editions of *The Pilgrimage* he left us. That really hurt. Almost as hurtful was the fact that, in interviews and articles, he never mentioned that he began with us.'

Bad feelings apart, Mandarino recognizes the importance of the author not only in the publishing world in Brazil but also in Brazilian literature: 'Paulo Coelho made books into a popular consumer product. He revolutionized the publishing market in Brazil, which used to limit itself to ludicrously small runs of 3,000 copies. With him the market grew. Paulo Coelho brought respect for books in Brazil and for our literature in the world.'

In a very small publishing market such as that in Brazil, it was only natural that large publishers should feel interested in an author who, with only two titles to his name, had sold more than five hundred thousand copies. Despite the Olympian indifference of the media, his books vanished from the bookshop shelves and thousands crowded into auditoriums across the country, though not to listen to the usual promotional rubbish. Readers seemed to want to share with the author the spiritual experiences he wrote of in his works. Paulo's talks were incredibly popular, and scenes such as that in the Martins Pena auditorium in Brasília – when it was necessary to put up loudspeakers outside the 2,000-seater auditorium for those arriving late – were not uncommon. One interview which he gave to the journalist Mara Regea, of Rádio Nacional de Brasília, had to be repeated three times at the request of listeners wanting to hear him talk for an hour and a half on alchemy and mysticism. Such enthusiasm was repeated across the country. In Belo Horizonte, the 350-seat Banco do Desenvolvimento de Minas Gerais auditorium wasn't large enough for the almost one thousand people who turned up to hear him, forcing the young Afonso Borges, the organizer of the event, to place televisions in various parts of the building so that no one would miss the author's words.

When the press woke up to this phenomenon, it seemed confused and at a loss to explain his overwhelming success. Reluctant to judge the literary content of the books, the newspapers preferred to regard them as yet another passing marketing phenomenon. In the opinion of a large number of journalists, the author Paulo Coelho was nothing more than a fad, like the hula hoop, the twist and even the lyricist Paulo Coelho and his Sociedade Alternativa. Since *O Globo* had called him 'the Castaneda of Copacabana' on the front page of its arts section two years earlier, the media had practically forgotten him. It was only when his books reached the top of the best-seller lists and the newspaper *O Estado de São Paulo* learned that *The Pilgrimage* and *The Alchemist* had sold more than half a million copies that the critics took note of the fact that two years was a long time for something that was merely a fad. The man with the prematurely white hair who talked about dreams, angels and love seemed to be here to stay, but it took a while for the press to understand this.

He did not appear prominently in the newspapers again until October 1989, in a full-page feature in the arts supplement of *O Estado de São Paulo*, which was divided into two parts. The first was a profile written by Thereza Jorge on the author's career in rock music. At the end, she stated unequivocally: 'But it is in literature that Coelho has clearly found his place.' However, proof that opinions on his work were divided appeared on that same page, in the form of a twenty-line item signed by Hamilton dos Santos. He summarized Paulo's work as 'a cloying synthesis of teachings drawn from everything from Christianity to Buddhism'. As the author himself confessed, this was 'the first real blow' that he had received from a critic: 'I just froze when I read it. Absolutely froze. It was as though the person who wrote it was warning me about the price of fame.'

Even the monthly literary tabloid *Leia Livros*, a cult publication edited by Caio Graco Prado, found itself bowing to the sheer force of numbers. On the cover of the December 1989 edition, Paulo appeared with sword in hand, hair bristling and gazing Zen-like into infinity. The treatment meted out to him by *Leia Livros*, however, was no different from the approach normally adopted by other members of the press. Of the twelve pages of the article, eleven were taken up with a detailed profile of the author, with no evaluation of his work. The actual review, signed by Professor Teixeira Coelho of the University of São Paulo, occupied only half a page. The average Brazilian – as one presumes most readers of *The Pilgrimage* and *The Alchemist* were – might have had difficulty in understanding whether Paulo was being praised or insulted, so convoluted was the reviewer's language:

> The time when vision, imagination, the non-rational (albeit with its own rationality) were considered an integral part of the real and came 'from above'; it was just a mental habit. This norm defined a cultural paradigm, a way of thinking and knowing about the world. This paradigm was replaced by the new rationalist paradigm of the eighteenth century. Today, it is this paradigm that appears to be (temporarily) exhausted. The Paulo Coelho phenomenon is a symbol of the decadence of this paradigm and implies a distrust of rationalism as we have known it over the last two centuries.
>
> [...] I prefer to see in the sales success of Paulo Coelho's works the primacy of the imagination, which continues to exert its power in different forms (religions, 'magic', 'alternative' medicine and sex, the poetic road to knowledge), forms that old-fashioned emblematic Cartesian thinking would designate as 'irrational'.
>
> [...] Within the Paulo Coelho genre, Lawrence Durrell with his 'Avignon Quintet' is a better writer, and Colin Wilson more intellectual. However, such judgements are superfluous.

While the press was racking its brains as to how to understand the phenomenon, it continued to grow. In a rare unguarded moment – especially when it came to money – Paulo revealed to the *Jornal da Tarde* that the two books had so far earned him US$250,000. It may well have been more. Assuming that the amounts he and Rocco disclosed were true, the 500,000 copies sold up until then would have brought him at least $350,000 in royalties.

With two best-sellers, a new publisher, hundreds of thousands of dollars or more invested in property and his international career showing signs of taking off, Paulo was summoned by Jean to fulfil another of the four sacred paths that initiates to RAM must follow. After the Road to Santiago, he had performed a further penance (the trip to the Mojave Desert), but there was still the third and penultimate stage, the Road to Rome. The fourth would be the road towards death. The so-called Road to Rome was merely a metaphor, since it could be followed anywhere in the world, with the added advantage that it could be undertaken by car. He chose Languedoc, on the edge of the Pyrenees in southwestern France, where a Christian religious sect, Catharism or Albigensianism, had flourished in the twelfth and thirteenth centuries, only to be stamped out by the Inquisition. Another peculiarity of the Road to Rome was that the pilgrim must always follow his dreams. Paulo thought this too abstract and asked for more information, but the reply was less than illuminating: 'If you dream of a bus stop during the night, the following morning go to the nearest bus stop. If you dream of a bridge, your next stop should be a bridge.'

For a little more than two months he wandered through the valleys and across the mountains and rivers of what is one of the most beautiful regions of Europe. On 15 August he left the Hotel d'Anvers in Lourdes, where he had been staying, and continued on towards Foix, Roquefixade, Montségur, Peyrepertuse, Bugarach and dozens of other tiny villages which were, in the majority of cases, no more than a handful of houses. Since Jean had made no restrictions on the matter, Paulo travelled part of the route in the company of Mônica, who skipped work in Barcelona for a week in order to go with him.

On the evening of 21 August 1989, when they reached Perpignan, he used a public phone to call Chris in Brazil, because he was missing her. Chris told him that his ex-partner Raul Seixas had died in São Paulo from pancreatitis, brought on by alcoholism.

This was an enormous loss for Paulo. After not seeing one another for several years, he and Raul had met up again four months earlier in Rio de Janeiro during a show Raul was giving in Canecão, which would prove to be one of his last. It was not a reconciliation, since they had never quarrelled, but it was an attempt on the part of Raul's new musical partner, the young rock star Marcelo Nova, to bring them back together again. During the show, Paulo was called up on to the stage to sing the chorus 'Viva! Viva! Viva a Sociedade Alternativa!' with the band. According to his ex-slave Toninho Buda, the author sang with his hands in his pockets, 'because he was being forced to sing Crowley's mantra in public and had to keep his fingers crossed'. Parts of the show were filmed by an amateur fan and put on the Internet years later. They show a shaky Raul Seixas, his face puffy and with all the appearance of someone ruined by drink.

The last work the two had done together was the LP *Mata Virgem*, which had been recorded long ago, in 1978. In 1982 the Eldorado label, based in São Paulo, tried to revive the duo with a new album, but as a Rio journalist put it, they both seemed to be 'inflicted by acute primadon-naitis': Paulo lived in Rio and Raul in São Paulo, and both refused to travel to where the other was in order to start work. Solomon-like, Roberto Menescal suggested a solution. He had been invited to produce the record and suggested meeting exactly halfway between the two cities in the Itatiaia national park. They arrived at the Hotel Simon on a Sunday, and when Paulo woke early on the Monday, before even having a coffee, he left a note under the door of Raul's room: 'I'm ready to start work.' Raul didn't even show his face. The same thing happened again on Tuesday. On the Wednesday, the owner went to Paulo, concerned that Raul had been shut up in his room for three days, drinking and not even touching the sandwiches he had ordered by phone. Any hope of reuniting the duo who had revolutionized Brazilian rock music died there and then.

Six days after the news of the death of his 'close enemy', still shaken and still on the Road to Rome, Paulo had what he describes as another extrasensory experience. He was heading for one of the small towns in the region where he was to take part in the so-called ritual of fire, during which invocations are made in the light of a bonfire. On the way, he says, he felt the presence beside him of no less a person – or thing – than his guardian angel. It wasn't a tangible or audible being, nor even an ecto-plasm, but a being whose presence he could clearly feel and with whom he could only communicate mentally. According to his recollection, it was the being that took the initiative, and a non-verbal dialogue took place.

'What do you want?'

Paulo kept his eyes on the road and said: 'I want my books to be read.'

'But in order for that to happen you're going to have to take a lot of flack.'

'But why? Just because I want my books to be read?'

'Your books will bring you fame, and then you're really going to get it in the neck. You've got to decide whether that really is what you want.'

Before disappearing into the atmosphere, the being said to him: 'I'm giving you a day to think about it. Tonight you will dream of a particular place. That's where we shall meet at the same time tomorrow.'

In the hotel where he was staying in Pau, he dreamed of a small 'tram' taking passengers to the top of a very high mountain. When he woke the following morning, he learned at reception that one of the city's attractions was precisely that: a cable car, the Funiculaire de Pau, which set off only a few metres from the hotel, next to the railway station. The hill where the dark-green cable car let off its thirty or so passengers every ten minutes was not as high as the one in his dream, but there was no doubt that he was on the right route. When it was getting dark, more or less twenty-four hours after the apparition of the previous day, Paulo joined a short queue and minutes later, reached a terrace surrounded by fountains – the Fontaine de Vigny, where he had an amazing view of the lights in the city coming on. The writer recalls clearly not only the date – 'It was 27 September 1989, the feast-day of Cosmos and Damian' – but also what he said to the apparition: 'I want my books to be read. But I want to be able to renew my wish in three years' time. Give me three years and I'll come back here on 27 September 1992 and tell you whether I'm man enough to continue or not.'

The seemingly interminable seventy days of the pilgrimage were drawing to a close, when one night, following the 'ritual of fire', a fair-skinned, fair-haired young woman went up to him and began a conversation. Her name was Brida O'Fern, and she was a thirty-year-old Irish woman who had reached the rank of Master in RAM and, like him, was following the Road to Rome. Brida's company proved to be not only a pleasant gift that would alleviate his weariness as he completed the pilgrimage, for Paulo was so delighted by the stories she told him that he decided to base his third book on her, which, like her, would be called *Brida*. Writing about the Road to Rome could come later.

Once he had completed the trial set by Jean, he set about writing *Brida*, using a method he would continue to use from then on: he would ponder the subject for some time and then, when the story was ready, write the book in two weeks. The novel tells the story and adventures of the young Brida O'Fern, who, at twenty-one, decides to enter the world of magic. Her discoveries start when she meets a wizard in a forest 150 kilometres from Dublin. Guided by the witch Wicca, she starts her journey and, after completing all the rituals, finally becomes a Master in RAM. In the very first pages the author warns his readers:

> In my book *The Diary of a Magus*, I replaced two of the practices of RAM with exercises in perception learned in the days when I worked in drama. Although the results were, strictly speaking, the same, I received a severe reprimand from my Teacher. 'There may well be quicker or easier methods, that doesn't matter; what matters is that the Tradition remains unchanged,' he said. For this reason, the few rituals described in *Brida* are the same as those practised over the centuries by the Tradition of the Moon – a specific tradition, which requires experience and practice. Practising such rituals without guidance is dangerous, inadvisable, unnecessary and can greatly hinder the Spiritual Search.

Encouraged by the success of *The Pilgrimage* and *The Alchemist*, Rocco, when he learned that Paulo had a new book on the boil, took the initiative and offered him US$60,000 for *Brida*. Although the amount offered was high by Brazilian standards, it certainly didn't break any records (a few months earlier Rocco had paid US$180,000 for the right to publish Tom Wolfe's novel *The Bonfire of the Vanities*). What was so different was the way in which Paulo proposed that the money should be divided up, a method he would continue to use in almost all negotiations over his future publications in Brazil: US$20,000 would be spent by the publisher on promotion and advertising; a further US$20,000 would be used to cover the journeys he would have to make within Brazil to promote the book; and only US$20,000 would go to him as an advance against royalties. The biggest surprise, which was kept secret by the publisher until a few days before its launch during the first week of August 1990, was that the first edition of *Brida* would have a print run of 100,000 copies – a run surpassed among Brazilian authors only by Jorge Amado, whose novel

Tieta do Agreste [translated as *Tieta, the Goat Girl*] was launched in 1977 with an initial print run of 120,000 copies.

The angel Paulo met near Pau was absolutely right when he predicted that the author would be massacred by the critics. *The Pilgrimage* and *The Alchemist* had been treated fairly gently by the press, but when *Brida* was launched, the critics appeared to want blood. Merciless and on many occasions almost rude, the main newspapers in Rio and São Paulo seemed determined to demolish him:

> The author writes very badly. He doesn't know how to use contractions, his use of pronouns is poor, he chooses prepositions at random, and doesn't know even simple things, like the difference between the verbs 'to speak' and 'to say'.
>
> (Luiz Garcia, *O Globo*)

> In aesthetic terms, *Brida* is a failure. It is an imitation of Richard Bach's tedious model seasoned with a little Carlos Castaneda. Paulo Coelho's book is full of stereotypes.
>
> (Juremir Machado da Silva, *O Estado de São Paulo*)

> What he should perhaps announce more boldly is that he can make it rain. For that is precisely what Paulo Coelho does – on his own garden.
>
> (Eugênio Bucci, *Folha de São Paulo*)

> . . . one of those books which, once you've put it down, you can't pick up again.
>
> (Raul Giudicelli, *Jornal do Commercio*)

The insults came from all sides, not only from newspapers and magazines. A few days after the launch of *Brida*, the author was interviewed on a popular Brazilian television chat show, *Jô Soares Onze e Meia*, which was broadcast nationally by SBT. Although they were friends and had worked together on the soft-porn movie *Tangarela, a Tanga de Cristal*, the presenter joined the attack on Paulo Coelho and opened the programme with a list of dozens of errors he had discovered in *The Alchemist*. The interview provoked a parallel squabble. Two days later, the Rio newspaper *O Dia* carried a note in the column written by Artur da Távola, Paulo's ex-colleague in the working group at Philips and someone who had contributed a preface to *Arquivos do Inferno*, entitled 'Credit where credit's due, Jô':

> Although we weren't given due credit – he did, after all, go into the studio with a fax of the article published in this paper listing the eighty-six [grammatical] mistakes found in *The Alchemist*, requested from us by the producers of their programme on SBT – Jô Soares interviewed the writer Paulo Coelho the day before yesterday going on about the errors overlooked by Editora Rocco.
>
> The magus justified the publisher's editorial laxity by stating that all the errors had been made on purpose. 'They're codes,' said Paulo Coelho. 'If they weren't, they would have been corrected in later editions.'

There remained, however, a faint hope that someone in the media might read his books with the same unprejudiced eyes as the thousands of people who were flocking to bookshops across the country looking for one of his three books. Perhaps it would be Brazil's most widely read and influential weekly, *Veja*, which had decided to put him on its next cover? After giving a long interview and posing for photographs, the writer waited anxiously for Sunday morning, when the magazine would arrive on the news-stands in Rio. The first surprise was seeing the cover, where, instead of his photo, he found the image of a crystal ball under the title 'The Tide of Mysticism'. He quickly leafed through the magazine until he came to the article, entitled 'The All-High Wizard' and illustrated with a photograph of him in a black cloak and trainers and holding a crook in his hand. He began to skim-read, but needed to go no farther than the tenth line to realize that the journalist (the article was unsigned) was using heavy artillery fire: *Brida*, *The Pilgrimage* and *The Alchemist* were all classed as 'books with badly told metaphysical stories steeped in a vague air of mysticism'. In the following six pages, the bombardment continued with the same intensity, and hardly a paragraph went by that did not contain some criticism, gibe or ironic remark: 'crazy superstitions'; 'it's impossible to know where genuine belief ends and farce begins'; 'yet another surfer on the lucrative wave of mysticism'; 'he pocketed US$20,000 as an advance for perpetrating *Brida* and is already thinking of charging for his talks'; 'surely the worst of his books'; 'pedestrian fiction'. Not even his faith was spared. Referring to the religious order to which he belonged, *Veja* stated that Regnum Agnus Mundi was nothing more than 'an assemblage of Latin words that could be translated approximately as Kingdom of the Lamb of the World'. Despite the hours of interviewing time he had given them, only one sentence was used in its entirety. When he was asked what was the reason for his success, he had replied: 'It's a divine gift.'

The author reacted by writing a short letter to *Veja*, saying: 'I should like to make just one correction to the article "The All-High Wizard". I do not intend to charge for my talks to the public. The remainder came as no surprise: we are all idiots and you are very intelligent.' He sent a long article to the journalist Luiz Garcia of *O Globo*, which was published under the headline 'I am the Flying Saucer of Literature', and in which for the first time Paulo complained about the treatment he had received from the media:

> At the moment I am the flying saucer of literature – regardless of whether or not you like its shape, its colours and its crew. So I can understand the astonishment, but why the aggression? For three years the public has been buying my books in ever greater numbers and I really don't think I could fool so many people in so many age groups and from all social classes at the same time. All I've done is try to show my truth and the things in which I sincerely believe – although the critics haven't even spared my beliefs.

The author of the review replied on the same page, at the end of which he adopted as abrasive a tone as he had before: 'Resigned to the fact that he will continue, as he says in his all too mistakable style, to "fight the good fight", I would simply advise him not to persist with his thesis that writing simply and writing badly are the same thing. It does him no favours.'

Fortunately for Paulo, the bacteria of the critics' remarks did not infect sales. While the journalists, magnifying glass in hand, searched for misused verbs, doubtful agreements and misplaced commas, the readers kept buying the book. A week after it went on the market, *Brida* topped the best-seller lists throughout the country, bringing the author a new record, that of having three books simultaneously in the national best-seller lists. The popular phenomenon that Paulo Coelho had become meant that public figures, intellectuals and artists had to have an opinion about him. Curiously enough, to judge by the statements in various newspapers and magazines of the time, while the critics may have been unanimous, the world of celebrities seemed divided:

He's a genius. He teaches that enlightenment doesn't lie in complicated things.

(Regina Casé, actress)

Who? Paulo Coelho? No, I've never read anything by him. But it's not because I'm not interested. It's just that I'm completely out of touch.

(Olgária Matos, philosopher and professor
at the University of São Paulo)

The Alchemist is the story of each of us as individuals. I found the book very illuminating, in fact I recommended it to my family.

(Eduardo Suplicy, economist and politician)

I read and there was light. The narrative explores intuition and flows as naturally as a river.

(Nelson Motta, composer)

I found both books very enlightening. I understood things in them that are very hard to explain.

(Técio Lins e Silva, lawyer and politician)

I've read *The Pilgrimage*, but I prefer the lyrics he wrote in partnership
with Raul Seixas.

(Cacá Rosset, theatre director)

It's all extraordinarily enlightening. He converses with the mystery.

(Cacá Diegues, film director)

In spite of the critics' bile, a year after its launch, *Brida* had been through
fifty-eight editions and continued to top all the best-seller lists with sales
which, combined with those of the previous books, were edging towards
the one million mark, something very few Brazilian authors had achieved
up to then. Encouraged by his success, Paulo was preparing to write a
non-fiction book, a real bombshell that he intended to be in the shops in
1991. It was an autobiographical book that would describe his adventures
with Raul Seixas in the world of black magic and satanism – including, of
course, the 'black night', when he believed that he had come face-to-face
with the Devil. He usually gave Chris the text to read only when he had
finished the book, but this time he handed it to her a chapter at a time.
While Paulo spent his days bent over his computer, she was electrified by
what she was reading. When he was already on page 600, though, she
gave him a piece of harsh advice.

'Paulo, stop writing that book.'

'What!'

'I love the book. The problem is that it's all about Evil. I know Evil is
fascinating, but you can't go on writing it.'

He tried to talk her out of this crazy idea 'first, with arguments and
then by kicking anything that happened to be near': 'You're mad, Chris!
You might have told me that on page 10, not page 600!'

'OK, I'll tell you the reason for my concerns: I looked at Our Lady of
Aparecida, and she said that you can't write this book.' (She was referring to the black patron saint of Brazil.)

After much discussion, Chris's point of view won the day, as usually
happened. When he decided that the wretched work would die, unpublished, Paulo printed out one version of the book and then deleted all
traces of it from his computer.

He arranged to have lunch with his publisher, Paulo Rocco, in the elegant Portuguese restaurant Antiquarius, in Leblon, and put the great thick tome on the table, saying: 'Here's the new book. Open it at any page.'

Rocco, out of superstition, normally never read any of Paulo's original texts before sending them off to the printer; this time, though, he thought that he should do as the author suggested. He opened the typescript at random and read the page, and when he finished, Paulo said: 'Besides myself and Christina, you will have been the only person to read any part of this book, because I'm going to destroy it. The only reason I'm not asking the waiter to flambé it right here and now is because I don't want the negative energy to turn to fire. I've already deleted it from my computer.'

After lunch, Paulo went alone to Leblon beach, looking for somewhere to bury the book for good. When he saw a rubbish truck chewing up the contents of the litter bins outside the buildings along the seafront, he went up to it, threw the package containing the original into the rotating drum and, in a matter of seconds, the book that would never be read had been utterly destroyed.

CHAPTER 26

Success abroad

DESTROYING A BOOK laden with so much negative energy may have saved Paulo from future metaphysical problems, but it presented him and his publisher with a new problem: what to launch in 1991 in order to capitalize on the phenomenal success of the three previous best-sellers. Paulo suggested to Rocco that he adapt and translate into Portuguese a small book, little more than a pamphlet, containing a sermon given in England in 1890 by the young Protestant missionary Henry Drummond: *The Greatest Thing in the World*, based on St Paul's letter to the Corinthians in which the author talks of the virtues of patience, goodness, humility, generosity, kindness, surrender, tolerance, innocence and sincerity as manifestations 'of the supreme gift given to Humanity: love'. It was given the new title of *The Supreme Gift* [*O Dom Supremo*] and despite being published with little fuss and almost entirely ignored by the media, in a matter of weeks, *The Supreme Gift* had entered the best-seller lists, where his other three books, *The Pilgrimage*, *The Alchemist* and *Brida*, had become permanent fixtures.

Its success did not, however, appear to satisfy the author. In the long run, this was not a work of his own but a translation produced in order to fill a gap. Paulo decided on a story that had been in his mind since 1988: his adventure with Chris in the Mojave Desert. The task that had been entrusted to him by Jean, Paulo says, was precise: he and Chris were to spend forty days in the Mojave Desert, one of the largest of the American national parks. The desert is known for its hostile climate and its unique geological formations, notably the Valley of Death; it is a place where the rivers and lakes disappear for half the year, leaving behind only dried-up beds. In order to fulfil the trial set by the Master – to find his guardian angel – the writer would have to employ a guide in the immense desert that stretches across California, Nevada, Utah and Arizona. The person chosen by Jean was Took.

On 5 September 1988, the couple landed at Los Angeles airport, where they hired a car and drove south towards the Salton Sea, a saltwater lake 50 kilometres long and 20 wide. After hours of driving, they reached one of those half-abandoned gas stations that are so common in films about the American West. 'Is it far to the desert?' Paulo asked the girl who was working the pump. She said no, they were about 30 kilometres from the small town of Borrego Springs, on the edge of the desert, and gave them some important advice: not to turn on the air-conditioning when the car was stationary, to avoid overheating the engine; to put four gallons of water in the boot; and not to leave the vehicle should anything unforeseen happen. Paulo was astounded to learn that the desert was so close: 'The climate there was comfortable and the vegetation was a luxuriant green. I found it hard to believe that a fifteen-minute drive away everything would change so radically, but that is precisely what happened: as soon as we crossed a chain of mountains the road began to descend and there in front of us lay the silence and the immensity of the Mojave.'

During the forty days they spent camping or, when they could, staying in hotels, Paulo and Chris lived with the historical remnants that form part of the legend of the desert: abandoned gold mines, the dusty carcasses of pioneers' wagons, ghost towns, hermits, communities of hippies who spent the day in silent meditation. Besides these, the only living beings they came across were the so-called Mojave locals: rattle snakes, hares and coyotes – animals that come out only at night in order to avoid the heat.

The first two weeks of the forty days were to be spent in total silence, with the couple not being allowed to exchange so much as a 'good morning'. This period was to be entirely devoted to the spiritual exercises of St Ignatius Loyola. These exercises, which were approved by the Vatican in 1548, are the fruit of the personal experience of the founder of the Society of Jesus. It is a spirituality that is not to be preached about or intellectualized but experienced. 'It is through experience that the mystery of God will be revealed to each person, in a singular, individual form,' the manuals produced by the Jesuits explain, 'and it is this revelation that will transform your life.' St Ignatius' aim was that each individual practising these exercises should become a contemplative during this time, 'which means seeing in each and every thing the figure of God, the presence of the Holy Trinity constructing and reconstructing the world'. And that was what Paulo and Chris did during the first two weeks, offering up prayers and reflections in their search for God.

One night, a week after their arrival, they were sitting immersed in this atmosphere of spirituality, beneath a sky filled with millions of stars, when a great crash shattered the peace and silence, immediately followed by a second, and then another and another. The deafening noise was coming from the sky and was caused by gigantic balls of fire exploding and breaking up into thousands of coloured fragments, briefly illuminating the entire desert. It took a few seconds for them to be convinced that this was not Armageddon: 'Startled, we saw brilliant lights falling slowly from the sky, lighting up the desert as if it were day. Suddenly, we began to hear crashes around us: it was the sound of military planes breaking the sound barrier. Illuminated by that phantasmagorical light, they were dropping incendiary bombs somewhere on the horizon. It was only the next day that we learned that the desert is used for military exercises. It was terrifying.'

At the end of those first two weeks of spiritual practices, and still following the instructions given by Jean, they finally reached Took's old trailer, permanently parked near Borrego Springs. Both Paulo and Chris were surprised to see that the powerful paranormal to whom Jean had referred was a young man of twenty. Guided by the young magus, Paulo was to travel through dozens of small towns on the frontier between the United States and Mexico until he met a group known in the region as the 'Valkyries'. These were eight very attractive women who wandered through the towns of the Mojave dressed in black leather and driving powerful motorbikes. They were led by the eldest of the eight, Valhalla, a former executive of Chase Manhattan Bank, who, like Paulo and Took, was also an initiate in RAM. It was through contact with her that, on the thirty-eighth day of their journey, Paulo – without Chris this time – came across a blue butterfly and a voice which, he says, spoke to him. After this, the author states, he saw his angel – or at least the materialization of part of his angel: an arm that shone in the sunlight and dictated biblical words which he wrote down, shaking and terrified, on a piece of paper. Trembling with emotion, he could not wait to tell Chris what he had experienced and to explain that 'seeing the angel was even easier than talking to it'. 'All you had to do was to believe in angels, to need angels, and there they were, shining in the morning light.'

To celebrate the event, Paulo drove into the desert with Chris and Took to a village known as Glorieta Canyon. After walking across an area of barren, stony ground, the author stopped in front of a small grotto. Then he took bags of cement and sand and a flagon of water from the boot of the car and began to prepare some mortar. When it was the right consistency, he covered the floor of the grotto with the cement and, before the mixture began to harden, he affixed a small image of Our Lady of Aparecida, which he had brought with him. At the foot of the image he wrote in the still-wet cement the following words in English: 'THIS IS THE VIRGIN OF APARECIDA FROM BRAZIL. ASK FOR A MIRACLE AND RETURN HERE.' He lit a candle, said a quick prayer and left.

On his return to Brazil, Paulo was to spend three more years pondering those events in the Mojave Desert. It was only at the end of 1991, when he felt that the typescript he had destroyed required a replacement, that he decided to write *The Valkyries*. According to the records of his computer's word-processing program, he typed the first words of the book at 23.30 on 6 January 1992. After seventeen uninterrupted days of work, as had become his custom, he typed the final sentence of the 239th and final page of the work: 'And only then will we be able to understand stars, angels and miracles.'

On 21 April, when the book had gone through all the editorial processes and was ready to be printed, Paulo sent a fax from his apartment in Rio to Editora Rocco saying that Jean was not suggesting but 'ordering' and 'demanding' changes to the text:

> Dear Rocco:
>
> Half an hour ago, I received a phone call from J. (the Master), ordering me to delete (or change) two pages in the book. These pages are in the middle of the book and refer to a scene called 'The ritual that demolishes rituals'. He says that in the scene I must not describe things exactly as they happened, that I should use allegorical language or break off the narrative of the ritual before I reach the forbidden part.
>
> I have decided to opt for the second alternative, but this is going to mean me doing some rewriting. I will make these changes over the holiday, but I was anxious to let you know this. You can send someone to collect the following on Thursday:
>
> – the changes demanded by my Master;
>
> – the new 'Author's Note'
>
> If I can't manage this, I'll send you another fax, but my Master said that I was to contact the publisher immediately and that's precisely what I'm doing (even though I know that today is a holiday).
>
> Paulo Coelho

Besides Jean, the author and Paulo Rocco, no one would ever know what the censored passages contained. The removal of those passages doesn't in any way appear to have compromised the success of *The Valkyries*. Less than twenty-four hours after the book's launch in August 1992, 60,000 copies of the initial 120,000 print run had vanished from the book-shop shelves. A fortnight later, *The Alchemist* lost its number one spot in the best-seller lists, where it had remained for 159 consecutive weeks, to give way to *The Valkyries*. The author was breaking one record after another. With *The Valkyries*, he became the first Brazilian to have no fewer than five books in the best-seller lists. Besides the new launch, there were *The Alchemist* (159 weeks), *Brida* (106 weeks), *The Pilgrimage* (68 weeks) and *The Supreme Gift* (19 weeks) – something which had only been bettered at the time by Sidney Sheldon. What most caught the attention of the press, apart from the astonishing sales figures, were the details of the author's contract with Rocco. One newspaper stated that Paulo was to receive 15 per cent of the cover price of the book (as opposed to the usual 10 per cent), while another revealed that he would have a bonus of US$400,000 when sales passed the 600,000 mark. A third speculated about the money spent by the publisher on publicity and said that, in order to protect himself against inflation, the author had demanded payments every fortnight. The *Jornal do Brasil* stated that in the wake of the success of *The Valkyries* the market would be 'inundated with plastic knickknacks with the inscription "I believe in angels", posters announcing that "the angels are among us" and china replicas of the author, complete with goatee, as well as 600 shirts with a company logo and the Archangel Michael'. One Rio columnist said that the author had supposedly turned down a payment of US$45,000 to appear in an advertisement for an insurance company in which he would say: 'I believe in life after death, but, just in case, get some insurance.' A further novelty was that, from then on, Paulo was also able to influence the cover price of the book – an area in which, generally speaking, authors do not become involved. Concerned to keep his work accessible to those with less buying power, he went on to set a ceiling price for his books which, in the case of *The Valkyries*, was US$11.

Once the initial interest in numbers, records and figures had passed, the criticisms started to pile in, couched in much the same terms as the reviews of his earlier books:

> The literary mediocrity of *The Valkyries* does at least have one positive effect. It could have been thrilling, but is, in fact, dull, and is, therefore, easier to read.
>
> (*Folha de São Paulo*)

> In terms of literature, if one understands by that the art of writing, *The Valkyries* is generously endowed with the same qualities as Coelho's previous books, namely, none at all.
>
> (*Veja*)

Paulo Coelho's books, and *The Valkyries* is no exception, do not stand out for their stylistic excellence. Plot-line apart, the books consist of crudely constructed sentences that appear to have been taken from a school composition.

(*O Estado de São Paulo*)

In the midst of this bombardment, however, the newspapers had quietly let it be known that the Ministry of Education in Rio wanted to use Paulo Coelho's works as a means of getting students to read. The two reactions to the idea, both published in the *Jornal do Brasil*, were even harsher than the words of the critics. In the first of these, entitled 'Stupidities', the journalist Roberto Marinho de Azevedo said that he was astounded and accused the ministry of 'feeding these innocents with eighth-hand mysticism written in sloppy Portuguese'. Even worse was the illustration accompanying the article, a caricature of a student with the ears of a donkey holding a copy of *The Pilgrimage*. Having published four books and become one of the greatest literary successes of all time in Brazil, Paulo could count on the fingers of one hand the positive reviews he had received. Unable to offer readers an explanation as to why an author whom they considered mediocre was so successful, the media flailed around for answers. Some preferred to put it all down to publicity, but this left one question unanswered: if it was so simple, why didn't other authors and publishers adopt the same formula? When she was travelling in Brazil before the launch of *The Valkyries*, Mônica Antunes was sought out by the *Jornal do Brasil* and asked the same old question: to what do you attribute Paulo Coelho's success? She replied with the prophetic words: 'What we are witnessing is only the start of a fever.'

Another argument used to explain his success – the low cultural level of Brazilians, who are little used to reading – was soon to be demolished by the arrival of Paulo's books in the two most important publishing markets, America and France. This began in the United States at the end of 1990. Paulo was staying in Campinas, 100 kilometres from São Paulo, preparing for a debate on his book *Brida* with students at the Universidade Estadual de Campinas (Unicamp), when the telephone rang. On the other end of the line was Alan Clarke, a man in his fifties, owner of the Gentleman's Farmer, a five-room bed-and-breakfast hotel in the small town of West Barnstable, in Massachusetts. Speaking fluent Portuguese, Clarke explained that during his free time, he worked as a certified translator and had worked for some years in Brazil as an executive with ITT, which dominated the telecommunications industry in a large part of the world until the end of the 1980s. He had read and enjoyed *The Pilgrimage* and was offering to translate it into English.

Paulo knew that the American market could be a springboard to the rest of the world, but he was not excited by the idea and said: 'Thank you for your interest, but what I need is a publisher in the United States, not a translator.'

Clarke was not put off: 'All right, then, can I try and find a publisher for the book?'

Sure that the conversation would lead nowhere, Paulo agreed. Never having worked before on a literary project, Alan Clarke translated the 240 pages of *The Pilgrimage* and set off with his English translation under his arm. After hearing the word 'No' twenty-two times, he came across someone who was interested. All his efforts had been worth it, because the publisher was none other than HarperCollins, at the time the largest in the United States. It was not until 1992, when Paulo was launching *The Valkyries* in Brazil, that *The Pilgrimage*, under the title *The Diary of a Magician*, was published (the title was changed much later). Days and weeks went by and it became clear that the book was never going to be a blockbuster. 'The book simply didn't happen,' the author recalls. 'It got no media coverage and was practically ignored by the critics.'

However, this lack of success did not dishearten his agent-cum-translator. Some months after its launch, Clarke took his translation of *The Alchemist* to HarperCollins, and the book won the hearts of all the professional readers invited to give their opinion as to whether or not to launch it on the American market. HarperCollins' enthusiasm for the book can be judged by the size of the initial print run: 50,000 hardback copies. HarperCollins' instincts were shown to be right: in a few weeks, the book was in the best-seller lists of important newspapers such as the *Los*

Angeles Times, the *San Francisco Chronicle* and the *Chicago Tribune*. The hardback version was so successful that the publisher didn't put the paperback version on the market until two years later.

The explosion of *The Alchemist* opened doors to markets of which the author had never even dreamed. Published in Australia immediately after its publication in the United States, *The Alchemist* was acclaimed by the *Sydney Morning Herald* as 'the book of the year'. The newspaper stated that it was 'an enchanting work of infinite philosophical beauty'. Australian readers seemed to agree, since weeks after arriving in the bookshops it was number one on the *Herald*'s own best-seller list. However, Paulo was dreaming of greater things. He knew that recognition as an author would come not from New York or Sydney but from the other side of the Atlantic. His dream was to be published, and above all read, in France, the land of Victor Hugo, Flaubert and Balzac.

At the beginning of 1993, during a short trip to Spain, Paulo was asked by the agent Carmen Balcells if she could represent him. The owner of the most respected literary agency in Europe, Balcells counted among her authors Mario Vargas Llosa and Gabriel García Márquez. Her request was a huge temptation, especially since, unlike most literary agents, among them Mônica Antunes, who received 15 per cent, the agency took only 10 per cent of its authors' royalties.

Paulo had been concerned for some time about his and Mônica's complete lack of experience in the foreign publishing world. Neither of them had the necessary contacts. He was worried that Mônica would waste her youth on trying to sell his work abroad, a venture that had so far lasted four years and brought no real results. 'It was my duty to tell her that she could never make a living working solely as my international agent,' the author recalled some time later. 'For her to be able to live well I would have to sell millions of books abroad, and that wasn't happening.' They needed to have a talk. After giving the matter serious thought, he invited her for a coffee in a small bar in Barcelona and came straight to the point. More than a dialogue, their conversation was a kind of tense verbal arm-wrestle.

'You know who Carmen Balcells is, don't you?'

'Yes.'

'Well, she sent me this letter proposing that her agency represent me. You're investing in someone you believe in, but let's be realistic: we're not getting anywhere. This business needs experience; it's a serious gamble.'

Mônica did not appear to understand what she was hearing, but Paulo went on: 'Let's accept that our work hasn't, as we hoped, borne fruit. There's nothing wrong with that. It's my life that's at stake, but I don't want you also to sacrifice yours in search of a dream that seems impossible.'

She could hardly believe what she was hearing.

'So, realistically speaking, what do you think about us terminating our professional relationship? If I want to go to Carmen Balcells now, I will. I'll pay you for all the years of work you've put in and I'll get on with my life. But the final decision is up to you. You've invested four years of your life in me, and I'm not going to be the one who gets rid of you. It's just that you have to understand that it would be best for both of us to call a halt. Do you agree?'

'No.'

'What do you mean "No"? I'm going to pay you for the time you've given me, for all your efforts. It's not as if I had a contract with you, Mônica.'

'No way. If you want to get rid of me, you can, but I'm not going to ask to leave.'

'You know who Carmen Balcells is, don't you? You're asking me to say "No" to her? She's going to announce that she is taking me on by filling the Frankfurt Book Fair with posters of my books, and you want me to say "No"?'

'No. I'm saying that you can sack me, if you want. You're free to do as you wish. After all, you made a separate deal with Alan Clarke in the States, didn't you? I think that I could do much better than him.'

Her utter conviction meant that Paulo could go no further. In a second, his dream of posters in Frankfurt and being in the same catalogue as García Márquez and Vargas Llosa had evaporated. He had swapped the elegant offices in central Barcelona occupied by Carmen Balcells and her dozens of employees for Sant Jordi Asociados, which was nothing more than a bookshelf with some cardboard files in the small apartment where Mônica lived.

In September, she plucked up her courage and prepared to face her first big challenge: to try to sell Paulo Coelho at the most important annual meeting of publishers and literary agents, the Frankfurt Book Fair.

At twenty-five, with no experience in the field and afraid of facing this challenge alone, she decided she needed the company of a friend, her namesake Mônica Moreira. The first surprise when she arrived in Frankfurt was the discovery that there wasn't a single hotel room to be found in the city. It hadn't occurred to them to make reservations in advance and so they ended up having to sleep in a youth hostel in a neighbouring town. For the four days that the fair lasted, Mônica worked like a Trojan. Unlike the posters and banners used by Balcells, her only weapon was a modest publicity kit – a brief biography and a summary of the success Paulo's books had enjoyed in Brazil and in other countries. She visited the stands of publishers from all over the world one by one, arranging as many meetings as possible. Her efforts were royally rewarded: by the end of the year, Mônica had sold the rights of Paulo Coelho's books in no fewer than sixteen languages.

The first contract she negotiated in Frankfurt, with the Norwegian publisher ExLibris, also had the virtue of changing her personal life: four years later, in 1997, the owner of ExLibris, Øyvind Hagen, and Mônica decided to marry. In a matter of months, she drew up contracts for the publication of *The Pilgrimage*, *The Alchemist*, or both, not only in Norway but also in Australia, Japan, Portugal, Mexico, Romania, Argentina, South Korea and Holland.

In the same year, 1993, Paulo entered the Brazilian version of *The Guinness Book of Records* after *The Alchemist* had been in *Veja*'s best-seller list for an impressive 208 consecutive weeks. However, there was still no sign from France. Mônica had sent the American version of *The Alchemist* to several French publishers, but none showed any interest in this unknown Brazilian. One of those who turned down Paulo Coelho's books was Robert Laffont, the owner of a traditional, reputable publishing house founded during the Second World War. The indifference with which *The Alchemist* was received was such that a reader's report – so important in deciding the fate of a book – was delegated to the only person in the company who spoke Portuguese, an administrative secretary, who was responsible for the book's rejection.

Destiny, however, seems to have decided that the literary future of Paulo Coelho in France would lie with the Laffont family anyway. At the beginning of 1993, Robert's daughter Anne had left her position as adviser in her father's company to set up her own publishing house, the tiny Éditions Anne Carrière. This was not a hobby to fill her time but a business in which she and her husband, Alain, had invested all their money and for which they still had to beg loans from banks, friends and relatives. The company was not yet three months old when Brigitte Gregory, Anne's cousin and best friend (and one of the investors who had put money into the new publishing house), telephoned from Barcelona, where she was on holiday, to say that she had read the Spanish translation 'of a fascinating book called *El Alquimista*, written by an unknown Brazilian'. Unable to read a word of Spanish or Portuguese, Anne simply relied upon her cousin's opinion (and a quick reading by her son, Stephen, who knew a little Spanish), and asked her to find out whether the publishing rights were held by anyone in France. When she found Mônica, Brigitte learned that *The Alchemist* was coming out in the United States in May and that the agent would send her a copy as soon as it was published.

Anne appeared prepared to put all her energies into the project. Although she offered a mere US$5,000 advance on royalties, to compensate she called upon a top translator, Jean Orecchioni, who had translated the entire works of Jorge Amado into French. Brigitte, who had been the fairy godmother of the publication, did not live long enough to see the success of *The Alchemist* in France: in July, before the book was ready, she died of a brain tumour. Many years later, Anne Carrière dedicated her memoirs to her, *Une chance infinie: l'histoire d'une amitié* (Éditions la Table Ronde), in which she talks about her relationship with Paulo Coelho and reveals the behind-the-scenes story of how he came to be the most successful Latin-American writer in France.

The wheels of the publishing business grind exceedingly slow all over the world, and the launch of the book was pushed forward to March 1994, when Paulo was about to publish his fifth title in Brazil, *Na Margem do Rio*

Piedra eu Sentei e Chorei, or *By the River Piedra I Sat Down and Wept*. Anne was faced by a double problem: how to launch the book of an unknown author published by an equally unknown publishing house? How to make booksellers stop to look at one book among thousands? She decided to produce a special, numbered edition of *The Alchemist*, which would be sent to 500 French booksellers a month before its launch. On the fourth page of the book was a short statement written by her: 'Paulo Coelho is a Brazilian author famous throughout Latin America. *The Alchemist* tells the story of a young shepherd who leaves his homeland to follow a dream: the search for a treasure hidden at the foot of the pyramids. In the desert he will come to understand the language of signs and the meaning of life and, most important of all, he will learn to let his heart speak. He will fulfil his destiny.' On the book's spine was a sentence used by HarperCollins for the launch in the United States: '*The Alchemist* is a magical book. Reading this book is like getting up at dawn and seeing the sun rise while the rest of the world is still sleeping.'

While half the road to success was guaranteed by the booksellers' favourable reception, the other half would be determined by the critics, whose reaction could not have been better. The most important of the French newspapers and magazines, among them *Le Nouvel Observateur* (which, years later, became a harsh critic of the author), carried highly favourable reviews, as Anne Carrière describes in her memoirs:

> With what appears to be a simple tale, Paulo Coelho soothes the hearts of men and makes them reflect upon the world around them. A fascinating book that sows the seeds of good sense in the mind and opens up the heart.
>
> (Annette Colin Simard, *Le Journal du Dimanche*)

> Paulo Coelho is a testament to the virtue of clarity, which makes his writing like a cool stream flowing beneath cool trees, a path of energy along which he leads the reader, all unwitting, towards himself and his mysterious, distant soul.
>
> (Christian Charrière, *L'Express*)

It is a rare book, like an unexpected treasure that one should savour and share.

(Sylvie Genevoix, *L'Express*)

It is a book that does one good.

(Danièle Mazingarbe, *Madame Figaro*)

Written in a simple, very pure language, this story of a journey of initiation across the desert – where, at every step, one sign leads to another, where all the mysteries of the world meet in an emerald, where one finds 'the soul of the world', where there is a dialogue with the wind and the sun – literally envelops one.

(Annie Copperman, *Les Échos*)

The joy of his narrative overcomes our preconceptions. It is very rare, very precious, in the torrid, asphyxiating present day to breathe a little fresh air.

(*Le Nouvel Observateur*)

Now all that was needed was to wait and reap the harvest, and that was not long in coming. The cautious initial print run of 4,000 copies ran out in the bookshops in a matter of days and at the end of April, when 18,000 copies had been sold, *The Alchemist* appeared for the first time on a best-seller list in the weekly *Livres Hebdo*. Intended for the publishing world, this was not a publication for the public at large and the book was given only twentieth place, but, as Mônica had predicted, this was just the start. In May, *The Alchemist* was in ninth place in the most important best-seller list, that of the weekly magazine *L'Express*, where it remained for an incredible 300 consecutive weeks. The book was a success in several countries besides Brazil, but its acclaim in the United States and France would mean that the author would no longer be considered merely a Latin-American eccentricity and would become a worldwide phenomenon.

CHAPTER 27

World fame

WHILE THE WORLD WAS BOWING THE KNEE to Paulo Coelho, the Brazilian critics remained faithful to the maxim coined by the composer Tom Jobim, according to which 'in Brazil someone else's success is felt as a personal affront, a slap in the face', and they continued to belittle his books. The massive success of *The Alchemist* in France seems to have encouraged him to confront his critics. 'Before, my detractors could conclude, wrongly, that Brazilians were fools because they read me,' he declared to the journalist Napoleão Sabóia of *O Estado de São Paulo*. 'Now that my books are selling so well abroad, it's hard to universalize that accusation of stupidity.' Not so. For the critic Silviano Santiago, who had a PhD in literature from the Sorbonne, being a best-seller even in a country like France meant absolutely nothing. 'It's important to demystify his success in France,' he told *Veja*. 'The French public is as mediocre and as lacking in sophistication as the general public anywhere.' Some did not even go to the trouble of opening Paulo's books in order to condemn them. 'I've not read them and I don't like them' was the judgement given by Davi Arrigucci, Jr, another respected critic and professor of literature at the University of São Paulo. However, none of this seemed to matter to Paulo's Brazilian readers, still less his foreign ones. On the contrary. Judging by the numbers, his army of readers and admirers

seemed to be growing in the same proportion as the virulence of his critics. The situation was to be repeated in 1994 when, as well as *By the River
Piedra I Sat Down and Wept*, he launched a 190-page book, *Maktub* – a
collection of the mini-chronicles, fables and reflections he had been
publishing in the *Folha de São Paulo* since 1993.

Just as *The Valkyries* had been inspired by the penance Paulo and
Chris had undertaken in 1988 in the Mojave Desert, in *By the River Piedra
I Sat Down and Wept* Paulo shares with his readers yet another spiritual
experience, the Road to Rome, which he undertook in the south of
France, partly in the company of Mônica Antunes. In the 236 pages of the
book, he describes seven days in the life of Pilar, a twenty-nine-year-old
student who is struggling to complete her studies in Zaragoza in Spain
and who meets up again with a colleague with whom she'd had an adolescent affair. The meeting takes place after a conference organized by the
young man – who remains nameless in the book, as do all the other characters apart from the protagonist. Now a seminarian and a devotee of the
Immaculate Conception, he confesses his love for Pilar during a trip from
Madrid to Lourdes. The book, according to Paulo, is about the fear of
loving and of total surrender that pursues humanity as though it were a
form of original sin. On the way back to Zaragoza, Pilar sits down on the
bank of the river Piedra, a small river 100 kilometres south of the city, and
there she sheds her tears so that they may join other rivers and flow on
out into the ocean.

Centred more upon the rituals and symbols of Catholicism than on
the magical themes of his previous books, *By the River Piedra I Sat Down
and Wept* received unexpected praise from the clergy, such as the
Cardinal-Archbishop of São Paulo, Dom Paulo Evaristo Arns, but there
were no such surprises from the critics. As had been the case with all five
of his previous books, both *Rio Piedra* and *Maktub* were torn apart by the
Brazilian media. The critic Geraldo Galvão Ferraz, of the São Paulo *Jornal
da Tarde*, branded *By the River Piedra I Sat Down and Wept* as 'a poorly
mixed cocktail of mediocre mysticism, religion and fiction, full of clichés
and stereotypical characters who spend the greater part of their time
giving solemn speeches'. The author's approach to what he calls 'the femi-
nine side of God' was ridiculed by another journalist as 'a Paulo Coelho

for girls'. The magazine *Veja* handed the review of *Maktub* to Diogo
Mainardi, who derided certain passages, comparing *Maktub* to a pair of
dirty socks that he had left in his car:

> In truth all this nonsense would mean nothing if Paulo Coelho were
> merely a charlatan who earns a little money from other people's
> stupidity. I would never waste my time reviewing a mediocre author
> if he simply produced the occasional manual of esoteric clichés.
> However, things aren't quite like that. At the last Frankfurt Book Fair,
> the theme of which was Brazil, Paulo Coelho was marketed as a real
> writer, as a legitimate representative of Brazilian literature. That
> really is too much. However bad our writers might be, they're still
> better than Paulo Coelho. He can do what he likes, but he shouldn't
> present himself as a writer. When all's said and done, there's about as
> much literature in Paulo Coelho as there is in my dirty socks.

As on previous occasions, such reviews had no effect whatsoever on
sales. While derided in the pages of newspapers and magazines, *By the
River Piedra I Sat Down and Wept* sold 70,000 copies on the first day, more
than *The Valkyries*. Some weeks after its launch, *Maktub* also appeared in
the best-seller lists. The only difference was that this time, the victim of
the attacks was thousands of kilometres from Rio, travelling through
France with Anne Carrière in response to dozens of invitations for talks
and debates with his growing number of French readers.

Despite the enormous success achieved by the author, Paulo's presence at the Frankfurt Book Fair in 1994, the first in which he had taken
part, had made it clear that preconceptions about his work were not just
the privilege of Brazilian critics but also of his fellow writers. Although the
position of Minister of Culture was, at the time, held by an old friend of
the author's, the diplomat Luiz Roberto do Nascimento e Silva, the brother
of his ex-girlfriend Maria do Rosário, when it came to organizing a party of
eighteen writers to represent Brazilian literature – Brazil was the guest of
honour – Paulo was not included. According to Nascimento e Silva, writers were chosen who were popular with or familiar to German readers.
Paulo's trip, therefore, was paid by Editora Rocco. In order to celebrate the

contracts being signed around the world, his German publisher at the time, Peter Erd, owner of the publishing house of the same name, gave a cocktail party to which he invited all of Paulo's publishers present at the book fair and, naturally enough, all the members of the Brazilian delegation. The party was well attended, but not entirely a success because only two other Brazilian writers were present, and of the other delegation members, only Chico Buarque was polite enough to phone to give his excuses, since he would be giving a talk at the same time. A lone voice, that of Jorge Amado, who was not part of the delegation, spoke out loudly in Paulo's defence: 'The only thing that makes Brazilian intellectuals attack Paulo Coelho is his success.' In spite of this, in 1995, the fever that the British magazine *Publishing News* called 'Coelhomania' and the French media '*Coelhisme*' reached pandemic proportions. Sought out by the French director Claude Lelouch and then by the American Quentin Tarantino, both of whom were interested in adapting *The Alchemist* for the cinema, Paulo replied that the giant American Warner Brothers had got there first and bought the rights for US$300,000. Roman Polanski had told journalists that he hoped to be able to film *The Valkyries*. In May, when Anne Carrière was preparing for the launch of an edition of *The Alchemist* to be illustrated by Moebius, HQ, owners of Hachette and *Elle*, announced that the Elle Grand Prix for Literature that year had been awarded to Paulo Coelho. This caused such a stir that he earned the privilege of being featured in the 'Portrait' section of the magazine *Lire*, the bible of the French literary world.

But the crowning glory came in October. After thirty-seven weeks in second place, *The Alchemist* dethroned *Le Premier Homme*, an unfinished novel by Albert Camus, and went on to head the best-seller list in *L'Express*. Two famous critics compared *The Alchemist* to another national glory, *Le Petit Prince* by Antoine de Saint-Exupéry. 'I had the same feeling when I read both books,' wrote Frédéric Vitoux in his column in the magazine *Le Nouvel Observateur*. 'I was enchanted by the sensibility and the freshness, the innocence of soul.' His colleague Eric Deschot, of the weekly *Actuel*, shared his opinion: 'It is not a sacrilegious comparison, since the simplicity, transparency and purity of this fable remind me of the mystery of Saint-Exupéry's story.'

Paulo received news that he had leapt into first place in *L'Express* while he was in the Far East, where he had gone with Chris to take part in a series of launches and debates with readers. One afternoon, as the *shinkansen*, the Japanese bullet train taking them from Nagoia to Tokyo, was speeding past the snow-covered Mount Fuji, the writer made a decision: when he returned to Brazil, he would change publishers. The decision was not the result of some sign that only he had noticed: it came after a long period of reflection on his relationship with Rocco. Among other disagreements, Paulo was demanding a distribution system that would open up sales outlets other than bookshops, such as newspaper stands and supermarkets, so that his books could reach readers on lower incomes. Rocco had asked for a study by Fernando Chinaglia, an experienced newspaper and magazine distributor, but the plan went no further. On 15 February 1995, the columnist Zózimo Barroso do Amaral published a note in *O Globo* informing his readers that 'one of the most envied marriages in the literary world' was coming to an end.

The other newspapers picked up the scoop and some days later, the entire country knew that, for US$1 million, Paulo Coelho was moving from Rocco to Editora Objetiva, who would publish his next book, *O Monte Cinco*, or *The Fifth Mountain*. This vast sum – more than had ever been paid to any other Brazilian author – would not all go into his pocket, but would be divided up more or less as it had been with Rocco: 55 per cent as an advance on royalties and the remaining 45 per cent to be invested in publicity. This was a big gamble for Roberto Feith, a journalist, economist and ex-international correspondent with the television network Globo, who had taken control of Objetiva five years earlier. The US$550,000 advance represented 15 per cent of the publisher's entire turnover, which came mostly from sales of its three 'big names', Stephen King, Harold Bloom and Daniel Goleman. The experts brought in by the firm were unanimous in stating that if *The Fifth Mountain* were to repeat the success of *By the River Piedra I Sat Down and Wept*, Objetiva would get the US$1 million investment back within a matter of months. Apparently the change caused no resentment on the part of his ex-publisher, for although Paulo had moved to Objetiva, he left with Rocco his entire backlist, the profitable collection of seven books published there since 1989. In fact, a month after announcing the move, Paulo Rocco was among the author's guests at Paulo's traditional celebration of St Joseph's feast day on 19 March.

Inspired by a passage from the Bible (1 Kings 18:8–24), *The Fifth Mountain* tells of the suffering, doubts and spiritual discoveries of the prophet Elijah during his exile in Sarepta in Phoenicia, present-day Lebanon. The city, whose residents were well educated and famous for their commercial acumen, had not known war for 300 years, but it was about to be invaded by the Assyrians. The prophet encounters religious conflicts, and is forced to face the anger both of men and of God. In the prologue, Paulo once again reveals how he interweaves his personal experiences with the themes of his books. When he states that, with *The Fifth Mountain*, he had perhaps learned to understand and live with the inevitable, he recalls his dismissal from CBS seventeen years earlier, which had brought to an end a promising career as an executive in the recording industry:

> When I finished writing *The Fifth Mountain,* I recalled that episode – and other manifestations of the unavoidable in my life. Whenever I thought myself the absolute master of a situation, something would happen to cast me down. I asked myself: why? Can it be that I'm condemned to always come close but never to reach the finishing line? Can God be so cruel that He would let me see the palm trees on the horizon only to have me die of thirst in the desert? It took a long time to understand that it wasn't quite like that. There are things that are brought into our lives to lead us back to the true path of our Personal Legend. Other things arise so we can apply all that we have learned. And, finally, some things come along to *teach* us.

The book was ready to be delivered to Editora Objetiva when Paulo unearthed information on periods in Elijah's life that had not been dealt with in the Scriptures, or, more precisely, about the time he had spent in Phoenicia. This exciting discovery meant that he had to rewrite almost the entire book, which was finally published in August 1996 during the fourteenth São Paulo Book Biennial. The launch was preceded by a huge publicity campaign run by the São Paulo agency Salles/DMB&B, whose owner, the advertising executive Mauro Salles, was an old friend and informal guru on marketing matters, and the book's dedicatee. The campaign included full-page advertisements in the four principal national newspapers (*Jornal do Brasil, Folha de São Paulo, O Estado de São Paulo* and *O Globo*) and in the magazines *Veja-Rio, Veja-SP, Caras, Claudia* and *Contigo*, 350 posters on Rio and São Paulo buses, eighty hoardings in Rio, and displays, sales points and plastic banners in bookshops. Inspired by Anne Carrière's idea, which had worked so well in the French launch of *The Alchemist*, Paulo suggested and Feith ordered a special edition of numbered, autographed copies of *The Fifth Mountain* to be distributed to 400 bookshops across Brazil a week before the ordinary edition reached the public. In order to prevent any disclosure to the press, every recipient had to sign a confidentiality agreement.

The result was proportionate to the effort invested. The books were distributed on 8 August and in less than twenty-four hours 80,000 of the 100,000 copies of the first edition had been sold. Another 11,000 were sold in the week of the Book Biennial, where seemingly endless queues of readers awaited Paulo and where he signed copies for ten hours non-stop. *The Fifth Mountain* had barely been out for two months when sales rose to 120,000 copies, meaning that the publisher had already recouped the US$550,000 advance paid to the author. The remaining US$450,000 that had been spent would be recouped during the following months.

In the case of *The Fifth Mountain*, the critics appeared to be showing signs of softening. 'Let's leave it to the magi to judge whether Coelho is a sorcerer or a charlatan, that's not what matters,' wrote the *Folha de São Paulo*. 'The fact is that he can tell stories that are easily digested, with no literary athletics, and that delight readers in dozens of languages.' In its main competitor, *O Estado de São Paulo*, the critic and writer José Castello did not hold back either. 'The neat, concise style of *The Fifth Mountain* proves that his pen has grown sharper and more precise,' he said in his review in the cultural supplement. 'Whether or not you like his books, Paulo Coelho is still the victim of terrible prejudices – the same [...] which, if you transfer them to the religious field, have drowned the planet in blood.' A week before the launch, even the irascible *Veja* seemed to

have bowed to the evidence and devoted a long and sympathetic article
to him, entitled 'The Smile of the Magus', at the end of which it published
an exclusive excerpt from *The Fifth Mountain*. However, in the middle of
this torrent of praise, the magazine summarized the content of Coelho's
work as 'ingenuous stories whose "message" usually has all the philosophical depth of a Karate Kid film'.

At the following launch, however, when *Manual do Guerreiro da Luz*, or
Manual of the Warrior of Light, came out, the critics returned with renewed
appetite. This was the first of Paulo's books to be published abroad before
coming out in Brazil, and was the result of a suggestion from Elisabetta
Sgarbi, of the Italian publisher Bompiani. Encouraged by the success of
the author's books in Italy, she went to Mônica to see whether he might
have any unpublished work for the *Assagi* collection, which Bompiani had
just created. Coelho had for some time been thinking of collecting together
various notes and reflections recorded over the years into one book, and
this was perhaps the right moment. Some of these had already been
published in the *Folha de São Paulo*, and this led him to stick to the same
eleven-line limit imposed by the newspaper. Using metaphors, symbolism
and religious and medieval references, Paulo reveals to readers his experiences during what he calls 'my process of spiritual growth'. In his view,
the *Manual* was such a fusion between author and work that it became the
'key book' to understanding his universe. 'Not so much the world of magic,
but above all the ideological world,' he says. '*Manual of the Warrior of Light*
has the same importance for me as the *Red Book* had for Mao or the *Green
Book* for Gaddafi.' The term 'Warrior of Light' – someone who is always
actively trying to realize his dream, regardless of what obstacles are placed
in his way – can be found in several of his books, including *The Alchemist*,
The Valkyries and *By the River Piedra I Sat Down and Wept*. And should there
remain any doubts as to its meaning, the home page of the author's then
recently created website took on the task of responding to those doubts:
'This book brings together a series of texts written to remind us that in
every one of us there is a Warrior of Light. Someone capable of listening
to the silence of his heart, of accepting defeats without allowing himself
to be weakened by them and of nourishing hope in the midst of dejection
and fatigue.'

When it was launched in Brazil, the *Manual* was preceded by the success of the book in Italy, but this did not seem to impress the Brazilian critics – not even the *Folha de São Paulo*, which had originally published several of the mini-articles reproduced in the book. In a short, two-column review, the young journalist Fernando Barros e Silva, one of the newspaper's editors, referred to the launch as 'the most recent mystical spasm from our greatest publishing phenomenon' and dismissed the author in the first lines of his article:

> Paulo Coelho is not a writer, not even a lousy writer. There's no point in calling what he does 'subliterature'. That would be praise indeed. His model is more Edir Macedo [the 'bishop' of the Universal Church of the Kingdom of God] than Sidney Sheldon. [...] Having said that, let us turn to the book itself. There is nothing new. The secret, as ever, lies in lining up platitudes so that the reader can read what best suits him. As with the I Ching, this is about 'illuminating' routes, 'suggest-ing' truths by using vague metaphors, sentences that are so cloudy and surrounded by metaphysical smoke that they are capable of saying everything precisely because they say absolutely nothing. [...] Every cliché fits into this successful formula: an ecological and idyl-lic description of nature, allusions to interminable conflicts between good and evil, touches of Christian guilt and redemption – all stitched together in a flat, unpolished language that seems to be the work of an eight-year-old child and is aimed at people of the same mental age. Each time you read Paulo Coelho, even with care and attention, you become more stupid and worse than you were before.

Such reviews only proved to the author the tiresome and repetitive abyss that separated the views of the critics from the behaviour of his readers. As had been the case since his very first book – and as would be the case with the rest – despite being ridiculed in newspapers such as the *Folha de São Paulo*, the *Manual* appeared a few days later in all the best-seller lists. Paulo went on to achieve something that probably no other author ever had: being number one in best-seller lists of both non-fiction (in this case in *O Globo*) and fiction (in the *Jornal do Brasil*). Things were no different in the rest of the world: the *Manual* was translated into twenty-nine languages, and in Italy it sold more than a million copies, becoming, after *The Alchemist* and *Eleven Minutes*, the most successful of the author's books there – and a decade after its launch by Bompiani it still had an average sale of 100,000 copies a year. Its popularity in Italy became such that at the end of 1997, the designer Donatella Versace announced that her collection for 1998 had taken its inspiration from Coelho's book. In France, *The Alchemist* had sold two million copies and *By the River Piedra I Sat Down and Wept* 240,000, which led Anne Carrière to buy the publishing rights to *The Fifth Mountain* for US$150,000. Some months before, the author had been overwhelmed to receive from the French government the title of Chevalier de l'Ordre des Arts et des Lettres. 'You are an alchemist for millions of readers who say that you write books that do good,' the French Minister of Culture, Philippe Douste-Blazy, said as he presented him with the medal. 'Your books do good because they stimulate our power to dream, our desire to seek and to believe in that search.'

Some Brazilians, however, continued to turn their noses up at their compatriot, for whom the red carpet was rolled out wherever he walked. This attitude was made even more explicit at the beginning of 1998, when it was announced that Brazil was to be guest of honour at the 18th Salon du Livre de Paris to be held between 19 and 25 March that year. The Brazilian Minister of Culture, Francisco Weffort, had given the president of the National Library, the academic Eduardo Portela, the task of organizing the group of writers who would take part in the event as guests of the Brazilian government. Following several weeks of discussion, only ten days before the event the press received the list of the fifty authors who were to spend a week in Paris. Exactly as had happened four years earlier in Frankfurt, Paulo Coelho's name was not among those invited. It was a pointless insult by a government that the author had supported. Invited, instead, by his publisher, he spent the afternoon of the opening day signing copies of the French translation of *The Fifth Mountain*, which had an initial run of 250,000 copies (hardly too many for someone who had already sold five million books in France).

In fact, the author had arrived in Paris a week before the Brazilian delegation and been faced with a plethora of interviews with newspapers, magazines and no fewer than six different French television programmes. Finally, on 19 March, to the sound of a noisy Brazilian percussion group, President Jacques Chirac and the Brazilian First Lady, who was representing her husband, President Fernando Henrique Cardoso, officially declared the salon open and, surrounded by a crowd of journalists and security guards, walked along some of the aisles down the centre of the Paris Expo convention centre where the event was being held. At one point, to the dismay of the Brazilian contingent, President Chirac made a point of going over to the Éditions Anne Carrière stand, shook hands with the publisher and, with an enormous smile on his face, warmly embraced Paulo Coelho. He heaped praise on, as it was later discovered, the only Brazilian author he had read and on whom, two years later, he would bestow the Légion d'Honneur – an honour previously given to such international celebrities as Winston Churchill, John Kennedy and even some famous Brazilians, such as Santos Dumont, Pelé and Oscar Niemeyer. Before moving on, Chirac then turned to Anne Carrière, saying: 'You must have made a lot of money with Monsieur Coelho's books. Congratulations!'

The following day, the Salon du Livre de Paris opened to the public and was witness to another world record: an author signing autographs for seven hours non-stop apart from short trips to the toilet or to smoke a cigarette. However, the best was yet to come for Anne Carrière. Some days before the close of the event, she took over the Carrousel du Louvre, an elegant, exclusive gallery beneath the famous Paris museum where shows were held by the famous European fashion houses. There Paulo hosted a banquet to which he invited booksellers, publishers, journalists and famous intellectuals. Throwing down the gauntlet to those who had snubbed him, the host made sure that every member of the Brazilian delegation received a personal invitation to the dinner. One of these was the journalist and writer Zuenir Ventura, who had just published a book entitled, appropriately enough, *Inveja* [*Envy*]. He recalled Paulo's concern that the Brazilians were being well looked after: 'He didn't eat, he went round to every table. Although at the time, he had everyone who mattered in the literary world at his feet, Paulo was exactly the same person as ever. When he came to my table, instead of talking about himself, he wanted to know how my book *Inveja* was going, whether I had any translation offers, whether he could help …'

When it came to the time for toasts, the author asked the band to stop playing for a while so that he could speak. Visibly moved and speaking in good French, he thanked everyone for being there, heaped praise on his Brazilian colleagues and dedicated the evening to one absentee: 'I should like this night of celebration to be an homage from all of us to the greatest and best of all Brazilian writers, my dear friend Jorge Amado, to whom I ask you all to raise your glasses.'

Then, to the sound of Brazilian music, the 600 guests turned the hallowed marble rooms of the Carrousel into a dance floor and danced the samba into the early hours. On their return to the hotel, Paulo had yet another surprise: a special edition of *The Fifth Mountain*, produced for the occasion. Each book in its own velvet case contained the same sentence, written in French and signed by the author: 'Perseverance and spontaneity are the paradoxical conditions of the personal legend.' When Paulo boarded the plane back to Brazil, three weeks after landing in Paris, 200,000 copies of *The Fifth Mountain* had been bought by the French public.

Now firmly and comfortably established as one of the most widely sold authors in the world, Paulo Coelho became an object of interest in the academic world. One of the first essayists to turn his attention to his work was Professor Mario Maestri of the University of Passo Fundo, in Rio Grande do Sul, the author of a study in 1993 in which he had recognized that Coelho's books 'belong by right to the national literary-fictional corpus'. Six years later, however, when he published his book *Why Paulo Coelho Is Successful*, Maestri seems to have been infected by the ill will of literary critics:

> Replete with proverbs, aphorisms and simplistic stories, full of commonplaces and clichés, Paulo Coelho's early fiction nevertheless has an important role in self-help. It allows readers demoralized by a wretched day-to-day existence to dream of achieving happiness swiftly and as if by magic. The worn-out modern esoteric suggests to his readers easy ways – within the reach of all – of taking positive

action in their own lives and in the world, usually in order to gain
material and personal advantage. It is essentially a magical route to
the virtual universe of a consumer society.

The many MA and PhD theses being written throughout the country
confirmed that, apart from a few exceptions, Brazilian universities were
as hostile towards the writer as the Brazilian media. This feeling became
public in a report published in the *Jornal do Brasil* in 1998, in which the
newspaper described the experience of Otacília Rodrigues de Freitas,
literature professor at the University of São Paulo, who had faced fierce
criticism when she defended a doctoral thesis entitled 'A best-seller from
the reader's point of view: *The Alchemist* by Paulo Coelho' – a thesis
considered by her colleagues to be sympathetic towards the author. The
professor told the *Jornal do Brasil* indignantly: 'They said that Paulo
Coelho had paid me to write the thesis, that I was his mistress.'

Indifferent to what academics might think of his work, Paulo was
preparing once again to face the whirlwind of activity that now accompanied the launch of each new book. Set in Slovenia, the story of *Veronika
Decide Morrer*, or *Veronika Decides to Die*, has as its backdrop the romance
between Eduard, the son of a diplomat, and the eponymous heroine who,
after attempting suicide, is placed in a mental asylum by her parents and
subjected to brutal electroshock treatment. The explosive nature of the
book lay in Paulo's revelation that he had been admitted to the Dr Eiras
clinic in Rio during the 1960s on three separate occasions, something he
had never spoken about in public before. By doing so, he was breaking an
oath he had made that he would deal with the subject in public only after
the death of his parents. His mother had died five years earlier, in 1993, of
complications arising from Alzheimer's disease, and he had been unable to
be at her funeral because he received the news while he was in Canada,
working on the launch of *The Alchemist*, and was unable to get back to Brazil
in time. Although his energetic father, Pedro, was not only alive but, as he
appears in the book, 'in full enjoyment of his mental faculties and his
health', *Veronika Decides to Die* exposes in no uncertain terms the violence
to which the author was subjected by his father and his late mother.
'Veronika is Paulo Coelho', the author declared to whoever wanted to listen.

Concerned as always that his books should reach poorer readers, this time he decided to change his launch tactics. He told Objetiva to cut by half the US$450,000 spent on advertising *The Fifth Mountain*, thus allowing a reduction of almost 25 per cent on the cover price. Another move intended to make his work more accessible was a contract with the supermarket chain Carrefour, which included *Veronika* in its promotional package of presents for Father's Day. The book's publication coincided with an intense debate in Brazil about the treatment of people being held in public and private mental asylums. The Senate was discussing a bill drawn up to bring about the gradual eradication of institutions where patients with mental problems were held as virtual prisoners, and during that debate, passages of *Veronika* were read out. On the day on which the vote was to be held and the law ratified, Senator Eduardo Suplicy quoted from a letter he had received from Paulo Coelho in praise of the bill: 'Having been a victim in the past of the violence of these baseless admissions to mental hospitals – I was committed to the Casa de Saúde Dr Eiras in 1965, '66 and '67 – I see this new law not only as opportune, but as absolutely necessary.' Together with the letter the author sent a copy of the records of his admissions to the clinic. Two years later, Paulo was invited to join the team of the International Russell Tribunal on Psychiatry, an institution created by the European Parliament, and in 2003, he was one of the speakers at a seminar on the Protection and Promotion of the Rights of Persons with Mental Health Problems organized by the European Committee on Human Rights.

Veronika broke all Paulo's previous records. What was new was the respectful treatment accorded to the book by the media. Perhaps moved by the shocking revelations contained in the book, the newspapers and magazines devoted pages and pages to accounts of the horror of his three internments.

One of the few dissenting voices was that of a friend of his, the writer and journalist Marcelo Rubem Paiva. Asked by the *Folha de São Paulo* to review *Veronika*, he did so tongue in cheek and even suggested stylistic changes to the text, only to pull himself up short: 'What am I saying? Here I am giving tips to a writer who has sold millions and won commendations and prizes abroad!'

Exactly. To judge by all those sales, prizes and commendations, it would seem that his readers preferred his texts as they were. Immediately following the publication of *Veronika* in Brazil, the journalist and professor Denis de Moraes published an essay entitled *The Big Four*. These were Stephen King, Michael Crichton, John Grisham and Tom Clancy. Moraes used a list of Paulo's achievements and engagements in 1998 to show that the Brazilian already had a foot in that select group of world best-sellers:

He spoke about spirituality at the Economic Forum in Davos, in Switzerland.

He was granted an audience at the Vatican and blessed by Pope John Paul II.

He beat the world record for a book signing at the eighteenth Salon du Livre de Paris with *The Fifth Mountain*, which has sold almost 300,000 copies in France.

He recorded a statement for the documentary *The Phenomenon*, based on his life, for a Canadian/French/American co-production.

His book *Manual of the Warrior of Light* inspired the 1998/1999 Versace collection.

He spent a week in Britain publicizing *The Fifth Mountain*.

On his return to Rio de Janeiro in May, he gave interviews to the Canadian TV5 and to the English newspapers the *Sunday Times* and the *Guardian*.

Between August and October, he undertook engagements in New Zealand, Australia, Japan, Israel and Yugoslavia.

He returned to Rio for interviews with French and German television, before setting off for a series of launches in Eastern Europe (Poland, the Czech Republic, Slovakia, Slovenia and Bulgaria).

Before returning to Brazil for the end-of-year festivities he went to Finland and Russia.

Hollywood wants to adapt four of his books for the cinema.

The French actress Isabelle Adjani is fighting Julia Roberts for the film rights to *By the River Piedra I Sat Down and Wept*.

The Arenas Group, with links to Sony Entertainment, wants to bring *The Valkyries* to the screen, while Virgin is interested in *The Pilgrimage*.

Awarded the Ordem do Rio Branco by President Fernando Henrique Cardoso.

Named special UN envoy for the Spiritual Convergence and Intercultural Dialogue programme.

All this feverish travelling was interrupted only in 2000, when he finished his new book, *O Demónio e a Srta. Prym*, or *The Devil and Miss Prym*. The launch this time was rather different. Firstly, the author decided to stay at home (the book was launched simultaneously in Brazil and other countries), preferring to receive foreign journalists in his new apartment in Copacabana. This was an apartment occupying an entire floor, which he had transformed into a vast bedroom-cum-sitting room, for which he had paid about US$350,000 and from where he enjoyed a wonderful view of Brazil's most famous beach. The idea of asking journalists to come to him had arisen some weeks earlier, when the North American television network CNN International recorded a long interview with him that was shown in 230 countries.

During the weeks that followed, at the invitation of his agent, teams from all the major newspapers and television stations began to arrive in Rio from Germany, Argentina, Bolivia, Chile, Colombia, Ecuador, Spain, France, Greece, England, Italy, Mexico, Portugal and the Czech Republic. Many used the trip to Brazil to file reports on Rio de Janeiro as well, and Mônica commented: 'That amount of publicity would have cost the Prefecture of Rio a fortune.' The other unusual thing about the launch in Brazil was the choice of venue. Coelho preferred to hold it in the Brazilian Academy of Letters. You didn't have to be very sharp to guess what this choice meant: Paulo Coelho, who had been so mistreated by Brazilian critics, clearly had his eye on a seat in the Olympus of Brazilian literature.

CHAPTER 28

Becoming an 'immortal'

THE DEVIL AND MISS PRYM was not the book Coelho had wanted to publish at the turn of the millennium. He had written a novel about sex, which had been carefully checked by Mônica and a friend of the author, the theologian and ex-impresario Chico Castro Silva, but it did not survive Chris's reading of it, and, as with his book on satanism, she refused to give it her approval.

This was not the first time he had been down this route. At the end of the 1980s, a little after publishing *The Alchemist* in Brazil, he had tried to write a book in which he treated sex with a starkness rarely found in literature. Between January and March 1989, he produced a 100-page novel telling the story of a man who is identified simply as 'D.', with the book being given the provisional title *A Magia do Sexo, A Glória de Deus* [*The Magic of Sex, The Glory of God*] or, simply, *Conversas com D.* [*Conversations with D*].

Tormented by doubts about his sexuality, the main character is only able to find sexual satisfaction with his wife, but has terrible dreams in which he sees his mother naked and being abused by several men who, having raped her, urinate over her. What troubles the forty-year-old D. is not just the nightmare in itself but also the fact that witnessing this violence gives him pleasure. Lost in the midst of these terrible fantasies,

D. starts to tell his problems to a friend, who becomes the narrator of the plot. The two meet every evening for a beer. As he describes his innermost secrets and insecurities, D. ends up confessing that, although he is not homosexual, he experiences enormous pleasure when dreaming that he is being raped by men ('I like the humiliation of being on all fours, submissive, giving pleasure to the other man'). Coelho never finished *Conversas com D.*, and it ends without one knowing what fate the author will choose for the central character – whose story bears a certain resemblance to his own. The book ended up in the trunk full of diaries that Coelho had said should be burned after his death.

The Devil and Miss Prym arose from a visit Coelho made to the French town of Viscos, on the Spanish frontier. In the main square, he saw a strange sculpture in which the water flowed out of a sun and into the mouth of a toad, and, however much he quizzed the inhabitants, no one could explain to him the significance of this odd creation. The image remained in his head for months, until he decided to use it as a representation of Good and Evil. With *The Devil and Miss Prym*, Coelho was completing a trilogy that he called 'And on the Seventh Day', which began with *By the River Piedra I Sat Down and Wept* (1994) and was followed by *Veronika* (1998). According to him, 'they are three books that describe a week in the life of normal people who suddenly find themselves confronted by love, death and power'.

The story takes place in a small imaginary village of 281 inhabitants, all of whom are believed to be extremely honest. The village routine is interrupted by the arrival of Carlos, a foreigner who is at once identified by the widow Berta, the eldest of the inhabitants, as someone bringing evil to their peaceful town, i.e., the Devil. The stranger stays in a hotel where the only single woman in town, Chantal Prym, works in the snack bar. Miss Prym is an orphan and rather frowned on by the other inhabitants, and she is chosen by the visitor as an instrument to test their honesty. Presenting himself as a businessman who has lost his wife and two daughters to a dreadful crime, the mysterious Carlos offers the young woman the chance to become rich and leave the tedious life of the town. In exchange, she must help him to convince the local inhabitants to take part in a macabre competition: if, within a week, someone can commit the motiveless murder of at least one local inhabitant, the town will receive ten bars of gold which he has hidden in a secret place. The book deals with the conflicts generated by this extraordinary offer and concludes by identifying the possible simultaneous existence within every human soul of a personal angel and a personal devil.

In March 2000, after delivering *The Devil and Miss Prym* to Editora Objetiva, Paulo took a plane to Paris in time to see the start of the huge publicity campaign organized by Anne Carrière for the launch of *Veronika Decides to Die*. On a cold, grey Monday morning, along with the millions of Parisians and tourists who daily cross the city, he was shown a number 87 bus bearing a gigantic close-up of his face printed against a blue back-drop, announcing that *Veronika* was in all the bookshops. The number 87 buses departed from Porte de Reuilly, to the east of the capital, and trav-elled some 30 kilometres through the streets until reaching their final stop in Champs de Mars, having passed through some of the busiest areas of Paris, such as Gare de Lyon, the Bastille and St Germain-des-Près. The same scene was being repeated in fourteen other French cities. This time, however, the publicity campaign did not produce the hoped-for results. The reaction of French readers was lukewarm, perhaps because they found it odd to see a book being advertised like soap or toothpaste. Although it sold more than the previous books, the sales of *Veronika* in France were below expectations. Even so, the book was warmly received by the French press, including *L'Express* and the serious and conservative *Figaro*, one of the most influential newspapers in the country. At the same time, although without the same fanfare, *Veronika* was beginning to arrive in bookshops in Taiwan, Japan, China, Indonesia, Thailand and the United States.

The globalization of his literary success was finally introducing the author to another circle – the international jet set. As he had been doing since 1998, Coelho had taken part in the World Economic Forum some weeks earlier. The forum is an organization created in 1971 by the profes-sor and economist Klaus Schwab and every year it brings together in Davos the elite of world politics and economics (at Schwab's invitation, the author has been a member of the Schwab Foundation since 2000). The most important guest at the 2000 meeting, the American President

Bill Clinton, had been photographed some months earlier clutching a copy of *The Alchemist* as he stepped out of a helicopter in the gardens of the White House. On hearing that Paulo was in Davos as well, Clinton took the opportunity to meet him. 'It was my daughter Chelsea who gave me the book – in fact she ordered me to read it,' the President joked. 'I liked it so much that I gave it to Hillary to read as well,' he went on, ending the meeting with an invitation that would not in fact be followed up: 'Let me know if you're visiting the United States. If I'm home, my family and I would love to have you over for dinner.' Seven years later, in 2007, at the request of Hillary Clinton's team, Paulo produced a text in support of her candidature for nomination for the presidency of the United States.

The meeting in Davos in 2000 and in subsequent years meant that he could personally meet some of his most famous readers – such as the former Israeli prime minister and winner of the Nobel Peace Prize, Shimon Peres, the American actress Sharon Stone and the Italian author Umberto Eco – and could mingle with such world-famous names as Bill Gates and political leaders such as the Palestinian Yasser Arafat and the German Gerhard Schroeder. Interviewed during one of the 'literary teas' held during the forum, Umberto Eco revealed that he had read Paulo's works, saying: 'My favourite book by Paulo Coelho is *Veronika*. It touched me deeply. I confess that I don't like *The Alchemist* very much, because we have different philosophical points of view. Paulo writes for believers, I write for those who don't believe.'

In the second half of 2000, the 'fever' predicted by Mônica Antunes ten years earlier had spread through all the social, economic and cultural classes regardless of race, sex or age, far less ideology. Some months before, the author had been appalled to read in the English newspaper the *Guardian* that *The Alchemist* and *The Fifth Mountain* were the favourite bedside reading of the Chilean ex-dictator Augusto Pinochet, who was at the time being held in England at the request of the Spanish courts, accused of 'torture, terrorism and genocide'. He declared to the press: 'I wonder if General Pinochet would continue to read my books if he knew that their author was imprisoned three times during the Brazilian military regime and had many friends who were detained in or expelled from Chile during the Chilean military regime.' Some time later, when interviewed by the Caracas newspaper *El Universal*, the Venezuelan Miguel Sanabria, the ideological leader of an organization that supported President Hugo Chávez, revealed the bibliography used in his political degree course: Karl Marx, Simón Bolivar, José Carlos Mariátegui and Paulo Coelho. Books by Coelho appeared in the strangest hands and on the oddest bookshelves, such as those of the Tajik ex-major Victor Bout, who was captured at the beginning of 2008 in Thailand by American agents. In a rare interview, the retired KGB official, who was considered the biggest arms dealer in the world (and who inspired the film *Lord of War*, starring Nicolas Cage), candidly stated to *New York Times* reporter Peter Landesman that, when not selling anti-aircraft missiles, he would relax by reading Paulo Coelho. In the war launched by the United States against the Al Qaeda network, Coelho's books were read on both sides. According to the British *Sunday Times*, *The Alchemist* was the most borrowed book in the barracks library of the American soldiers of the 10th Mountain Division, who were hunting for Osama Bin Laden in the Afghan caves. And on visiting Number 4 concentration camp in Guantanamo Bay, where those suspected of having links with Bin Laden were imprisoned, the reporter Patrícia Campos Mello, of *O Estado de São Paulo*, discovered versions in Farsi of *The Pilgrimage* among the books offered to the prisoners by their American gaolers.

Coelho himself was surprised when he saw the film *Guantanamera*, directed by the Cuban Tomás Gutiérrez Alea, to see that, on the protagonist's long trip across the island in order to bury a relative, he was carrying a copy of *The Alchemist*. Since his books are not published in Cuba, he did some research and discovered that it was a Spanish copy, sold on the black market for an incredible US$40. 'I had no qualms about contacting the Cubans and giving up my rights as author, without getting a cent,' he later told newspapers, 'just so that the books could be published there at lower prices and more people could have access to them.' In an incident that shows that rudeness has no ideological colour, in 2007, Paulo was the victim of a gratuitous insult from the Cuban Minister of Culture, Abel Prieto, who was responsible for the organization of the Havana Book Fair. 'We have a problem with Paulo Coelho,' Prieto declared to a group of foreign journalists. 'Although he is a friend of Cuba and speaks out against the blockade, I could not invite him because that would lower the tone of the fair.' Not a man to take insults lying down, the author paid him back on his Internet blog with a six-paragraph article that was immediately reproduced in the daily *El Nuevo Herald*, the most important Spanish-language newspaper published in Miami, the heart of anti-Castroism. 'I am not at all surprised by this statement,' he wrote. 'Once bitten by the bug of power, those who have fought for liberty and justice become oppressors.'

His international prominence did not distance him from his country of origin. The choice of the Brazilian Academy of Letters for the launch of *The Devil and Miss Prym* in October 2000 was seen as a step towards his entry into the Brazilian Academy. This was not the first such step. When Anne Carrière had organized that dinner at the Carrousel du Louvre in 1998, all the members of the Brazilian delegation in Paris had been invited, but only three writers received personal telephone calls from Paulo reiterating the invitation – Nélida Piñon, Eduardo Portela and the senator and ex-president of the Republic José Sarney. Needless to say, all three were members of the Academy.

For the launch of *The Devil and Miss Prym* 4,000 invitations were sent out. The size of the crowd meant that the organizers of the event had to increase the security and support services. At the insistence of the author, one thousand plastic glasses of iced mineral water were distributed among those present, and he regretted that he could not do as he had in France, and serve French champagne.

To everyone's surprise, the Brazilian critics reacted well to *The Devil and Miss Prym*. 'At the age of fifty-three, Paulo Coelho has produced his most accomplished work yet, with a story that arouses the reader's curiosity and creates genuine tension,' wrote the reviewer in the magazine *Época*. One of the exceptions was the astrologist Bia Abramo, in the *Folha de São Paulo*, who was asked by the newspaper to write a review. 'Like his other books, *The Devil and Miss Prym* seems to be a well-worn parable,' she wrote, 'that could have been told in three paragraphs, like the various little anecdotes that tend to fill his narratives.'

Any careful observer of the author at this time would have realized that his energies were focused not on the critics but on being given a chair in the Brazilian Academy. Paulo had no illusions and he knew, from someone else who had been rejected as a candidate, that 'it's easier to be elected as a state governor than to enter the Academy'. It was well known that some of the thirty-nine academicians despised him and his work. 'I tried to read one of his books and couldn't get beyond page eight,' the author Rachel de Queiroz, a distant cousin, told newspapers, to which the author replied that none of his books even started on page eight. The respected Christian thinker Cândido Mendes, rector and owner of the Universidade Cândido Mendes (where Paulo had almost obtained a degree in law), gave an even harsher evaluation:

> I have read all his books from cover to cover, from back to front, which comes to the same thing. Paulo Coelho has already had more glory heaped on him in France than Santos Dumont. But he's not really from here: he's from the global world of facile thinking and of ignorance transformed into a kind of sub-magic. Our very pleasant little sorcerer serves this domesticated, toothless imagination. This subculture disguised as wealth has found its perfect author. It isn't a text but a product from a convenience store.

Convinced that these views were not shared by the majority of the other thirty-seven electors in the Academy, Paulo did not respond to these provocative comments and went ahead with his plan. He courted the leaders of the several groups and subgroups into which the house was divided, lunched and dined with academics, and never missed the launch of a book by one of the 'immortals', as the members of the Academy are known. At the launch of his novel *Saraminda*, José Sarney, who was also a favourite target of the critics, posed smiling for the photographers as he signed Paulo's copy, Paulo being the most sought-after by the hundreds of readers queuing to receive a dedication. The fact is that his objective had soon become an open secret. At the end of the year, the celebrated novelist Carlos Heitor Cony, who held seat 3 at the Academy, wrote in the *Folha do Sul*:

I wrote an article about the contempt with which the critics treat the singer Roberto Carlos and the writer Paulo Coelho. I think it's a miracle that the two have survived, because if they had been dependent on the media, they would be living under a bridge, begging and cursing the world. That isn't quite how it is. Each one has a faithful public, they take no notice of the critics, they simply get on with life, they don't retaliate and, when they can, they help others. I am a personal friend of Paulo Coelho, and he knows he can count on my vote at the Academy. I admire his character, his nobility in not attacking anyone and in making the most of the success he has achieved with dignity.

From the moment the idea of competing for a chair at the Academy entered his head, Coelho had nurtured a secret dream: to occupy chair number 23, whose first occupant had been Machado de Assis, the greatest of all Brazilian writers and founder of the Academy. The problem was that the occupant of this chair was the academic whom Paulo most loved, admired and praised, Jorge Amado. This meant that every time the matter came up he had to be careful what he said: 'Since the chair I want belongs to Jorge, I only hope to put myself forward when I am really old,' he would say, 'because I want him to live for many many more years.'

Already eighty-eight, Jorge Amado had suffered a heart attack in 1993 and, in the years that followed, he was admitted to hospital several times. In June 2001, he was taken into a hospital in Salvador with infections in the kidneys and right lung, but recovered sufficiently to be able to celebrate at home with his family the fortieth anniversary of his election to the Academy. However, only three weeks later, on the afternoon of 6 August, the family let it be known that Jorge Amado had just died. Chair number 23 was vacant. The news reached Coelho that night via a short phone call from the journalist and academic Murilo Melo Filho: 'Jorge Amado has died. Your time has come.'

Paulo was filled by strange and contradictory feelings: as well as feeling excited at the thought of standing as a candidate for the Academy, he was genuinely saddened by the death of someone who had been not only one of his idols but also both a friend and faithful ally. However, this was no time for sentimentality. Paulo realized that the race for a chair in the

Academy began even before the lilies had withered on the coffin of the deceased incumbent. His first campaign phone call met with disappointment, though. When he called the professor and journalist Arnaldo Niskier, who occupied chair number 18 and was one of the first to have learned, months earlier, of Paulo's intentions, Niskier poured cold water on the idea. 'I don't think it's the right moment,' Niskier told him. 'It looks as if Zélia is going to put herself forward, and if that happens the Academy is sure to vote in her favour.' Zélia was the writer Zélia Gattai, Jorge Amado's widow, who had decided to compete for her late husband's chair.

Alongside the many obituaries, the following morning, the newspapers announced the names of no fewer than five candidates: Zélia, Paulo, the astronomer Ronaldo Rogério de Freitas Mourão, the humourist Jô Soares and the journalist Joel Silveira. When taking his daily walk along the promenade above Copacabana beach, Coelho heard one of the few voices capable of convincing him to do – or not do – something: that of Chris. With her customary gentleness, she said that she had a bad feeling about the competition: 'Paulo, I don't think you're going to win.'

This was enough for him to give up the idea. His candidature, which had not even been formally registered, had lasted less than twelve hours. Paulo sent a fax to Zélia expressing his sorrow at her husband's death, packed his bags and left with Chris for the south of France. The couple were going to fulfil their old dream of spending part of the year in Europe, and the place they had chosen was a region near Lourdes. One of the reasons for the trip was to look for a house to buy. While they were still hunting, their address in France was the modest but welcoming Henri IV hotel in the small city of Tarbes.

On Tuesday, 9 October, the two were in Odos, a small village 5 kilometres from Saint-Martin, where some months later they would choose to settle. As though tempted by the Devil whom he had long ago driven away, Coelho had decided to add to his property portfolio something more suited to a rock star than to a man of almost monastic habits (a millionaire monk, that is): a castle. The castle the couple had their eye on was Château d'Odos, where Marguerite de Valois, or Margot, the wife of Henri IV, had lived and died. However, the whole affair came to nothing

– 'If I bought a castle,' he said to a journalist, 'I wouldn't possess it, it would possess me.' That afternoon, he left Chris in the hotel in Tarbes and took a train to Pau, where he boarded a flight to Monte Carlo, where he was to be a member of the film festival jury. In the evening, he was having a coffee with the director Sydney Pollack, when his mobile rang.

On the other end he heard the voice of Arnaldo Niskier: 'Roberto Campos has just died. May I give the secretary of the Academy the signed letter you left with me putting your name forward for the first position available?'

'If you think it's the right time, yes.'

On his return to France a few days later, he stopped off at the chapel of Notre Dame de Piétat, in the small town of Barbazan-Débat, and made a silent prayer: 'Help me get into the Brazilian Academy of Letters.'

A few hours later, in his hotel room in Tarbes, he gave a long interview over the telephone to the reporter Marcelo Camacho, of the *Jornal do Brasil*, an interview that began with the obvious question: 'Is it true that you're a candidate for the Brazilian Academy of Letters?'

He replied without hesitation: 'Absolutely.'

And the next day's *Jornal do Brasil* devoted the front page of its arts section to the scoop. In the interview, Coelho explained the reasons for his candidature ('a desire to be a colleague of such special people'); dismissed his critics ('if what I wrote wasn't any good my readers would have abandoned me a long time ago, all over the world'); and vehemently condemned George W. Bush's foreign policy ('What the United States is doing in Afghanistan is an act of terror, that's the only word for it, an act of terror'). The campaign for the vacant chair was official, but Coelho told the journalist that, because of a very full international programme, he would not be back in Brazil for another two months, in December, when he would carry out the ritual of visits to each of the thirty-nine electors. This delay was irrelevant, because the election had been set for March 2002, following the Academy's end-of-year recess.

In the weeks that followed, two other candidates appeared: the political scientist Hélio Jaguaribe and the ex-diplomat Mário Gibson

Barbosa. Both were octogenarians and each had his strong and weak points. The presence in the competition of one of the most widely read authors in the world attracted the kind of interest that the Academy rarely aroused. The foreign media mobilized their correspondents in Brazil to cover the contest. In a long, sardonic article published by the *New York Times*, the correspondent Larry Rother attributed to the Academy the power to 'transform obscure and aged essayists, poets and philosophers into celebrities who are almost as revered as soccer players, actors or pop stars'. Rother included statements from supporters of Coelho such as Arnaldo Niskier ('he is the Pelé of Brazilian literature'), and added:

> Mr Coelho's public image is not that of a staid academic who enjoys the pomp of the Thursday afternoon teas for which the Academy is famous. He began his career as a rock 'n' roll songwriter, has admitted that he was heavily into drugs at that time, spent brief periods in a mental institution as an adolescent and, perhaps worst of all, refuses to apologize for his overwhelming commercial success. Brazilian society 'demands excellence in this house', the novelist Nélida Piñon, a former president of the Academy, said in the newspaper *O Globo* in what was interpreted as a slap at Mr Coelho's popularity. 'We can't let the market dictate aesthetics.'

Ignoring all the intrigues, Paulo did what he had to do. He wrote letters, visited all the academicians (with the exception of Padre Fernando Ávila, who told him curtly that this would not be necessary) and received much spontaneous support, such as that of Carlos Heitor Cony and ex-president Sarney. On the day of the election, involving four successive ballots, none of the three candidates obtained the minimum nineteen votes required under the rules. As tradition directed, the president burned the votes in a bronze urn, announced that chair number 21 was still unoccupied and called for further elections to be held on 25 July.

That evening, some hours after the announcement of the result of the first round, a group of 'immortals' appeared at Paulo's house to offer the customary condolences. One of them – Coelho cannot remember precisely who – said:

> It was very good of you to put yourself forward as a candidate, and our short time together has been most enjoyable. Perhaps on another occasion you could try again.

Since he had received a modest ten votes as opposed to the sixteen given to Jaguaribe, the group was somewhat taken aback by their host's immediate reaction: 'I'm not going to wait for another opportunity. I'm going to register my candidature tomorrow. I'm going to stand again.'

It's likely that the date of the new election was of no significance to the majority of the academicians, but Coelho saw in it an unmistakable sign that he should put himself forward as a candidate: 25 July is the feast day of St James of Compostela, the patron saint of the pilgrimage that had changed his life. Nevertheless there was no harm in asking for confirmation from the old and, in his opinion, infallible I Ching. He threw the three coins of the oracle several times, but they always gave the same result: the hexagram of the cauldron, synonymous with certain victory. The I Ching had also made a strange recommendation: 'Go travelling and don't come back for a while.' He did as he was told.

Paulo flew to France, installed himself in the hotel in Tarbes and for the following three months conducted his campaign with mobile phone and notebook in hand. When he arrived, he saw on the Internet that he was only going to have one opponent in the contest: Hélio Jaguaribe. Christina recalls being surprised by Paulo's self-confidence: 'I discovered that Paulo had negotiating skills about which I knew nothing. His sangfroid in taking decisions and talking to people was a side of him I didn't know.'

Although many of Paulo's supporters thought it risky to run his campaign from a distance, the I Ching insisted: 'Do not return.' The pressure to return to Brazil grew stronger, but he remained immovable. 'My sixth sense was telling me not to go back,' the writer recalls, 'and faced by a choice between my sixth sense and the academicians, I chose the former.' But the campaign began to get serious when one of his supporters started canvassing votes during the Thursday afternoon teas using a seductive argument: 'I'm going to vote for Paulo Coelho because the corn is good.' In the jargon of the Academy, 'good corn' was a metaphor used to refer to candidates who, once elected, could bring both prestige and material benefits to the institution. From that point of view, the 'immortal' argued, the author of *The Alchemist* was very good corn indeed. There was not only his indisputable international fame, evidenced by the extraordinary interest in the election shown by the foreign media: what softened even the most hardened of hearts was the fact that the millionaire Paulo Coelho had no children, something which fuelled the hope that, on his death, he might choose the Academy as one of his heirs – as other childless academicians had in the past.

Unaware that there were people with an eye on the wealth it had cost him such effort and energy to accumulate, three weeks before the election, Coelho returned to Rio de Janeiro. There, contrary to what the oracles had been telling him, he was not greeted with good news. His opponent's campaign had gained ground during his absence and even some voters whom he had considered to be 'his' were threatening to change sides.

On the evening of 25 July 2002, the photographers, reporters and cameramen crowding round the door of the building in Avenida Atlântica in Copacabana were invited up to the ninth floor to drink a glass of French champagne with the owners of the apartment: Paulo had just been elected by twenty-two votes to fifteen. Jaguaribe appeared not to have taken in his defeat, and was not exactly magnanimous when expressing his dismay at the result. 'With the election of Paulo Coelho, the Academy is celebrating the success of marketing,' he moaned. 'His sole merit lies in his ability to sell books.' To one journalist who wanted to know whether he would be putting his name forward again, Jaguaribe was adamant: 'The Academy holds no interest for me any more.' Three years later, though, once he had got over the shock, he returned and was elected to the chair left vacant by the economist Celso Furtado. A year after that, it was the turn of Celso Lafer, the foreign minister, who took the chair left vacant by Miguel Reale.

If, in fact, any of the 'immortals' really had voted for Paulo Coelho in the hope that 'the corn' would be good, they would have been bitterly disappointed. In the first place, the international spotlight that followed him around never once lit up the Academy, for the simple reason that he has attended only six of the more than two hundred sessions held in the Academy since his election, which makes him the number one absentee. Those who dreamed that a percentage of his royalties would flow into the Academy's coffers were also in for a disappointment. In his will, which Paulo has amended three times since his election, there is no reference to the Academy.

Enjoying a honeymoon period following his victory, and being hailed by an article in the weekly American *Newsweek* as 'the first pop artist of Brazilian literature to enter the Academy, the house which, for the past 105 years, has been the bastion of the Portuguese language and a fortress of refined taste and intellectual hauteur', Coelho began to write his speech and prepare for his investiture, which was set for 28 October. He decided to go to Brasília in person to give President Fernando Henrique his invitation to his inauguration. He was cordially received at Planalto Palace, and was told that the President had appointments in his diary for that day, but would send a representative. While waiting for his plane at Brasília airport, he visited the bookshop there and saw several of his books on display – all of them produced by Editora Rocco and not one by Objetiva. At that moment, he began to consider leaving Objetiva and going back to his previous publisher.

At the inaugural ceremony, the guests wore black tie while the academicians wore the uniform of the house, an olive-green gold-embroidered cashmere jacket. To complete the outfit, the 'immortals' also wore a velvet hat adorned with white feathers and, at their waist, a golden sword. Valued at US$26,250, the uniform used by Paulo had been paid for, as tradition decreed, by the Prefecture of Rio, the city where he was born. Among the hundreds of guests invited to celebrate the new 'immortal' were Paulo's Brazilian publishers, Roberto Feith and Paulo Rocco. The polite remarks they exchanged gave no hint of the conflict to come. The episode in the bookshop at Brasília airport had brought to the surface concerns that had, in fact, been growing for a while. Something similar had occurred some months earlier, when Paulo's agent Mônica, on holiday with her husband Øyvind in Brazil, decided to extend their trip to Natal, in Rio Grande do Norte. Mônica discovered that there were no books by Coelho on sale anywhere in the capital of Rio Grande (which at the time had more than six hundred thousand inhabitants), not even in the bookshop in the city's international airport.

However, the author had far more substantial reasons to be concerned. According to his calculations, during the period between 1996 and 2000 (when Objetiva launched *The Fifth Mountain*, *Veronika* and *The Devil and Miss Prym*), he had lost no fewer than 100,000 readers. The book whose sales he used as a reference point for this conclusion was not his blockbuster *The Alchemist* but *By the River Piedra I Sat Down and Wept*, which was the last book published by Rocco before his move to Objetiva. What he really wanted to do was to leave Objetiva immediately and go back to Rocco; there was, however, a problem: the typescript of his next novel, *Eleven Minutes*, was already in the hands of Objetiva and Roberto Feith had already suggested small changes to which the author had agreed.

As so often before, though, Paulo let the I Ching have the last word. Four days after taking his place in the Academy, he posed two questions: 'What would happen if I published my next book, *Eleven Minutes*, with Editora Objetiva?' and 'What would happen if I published my next book and my entire backlist with Rocco?' When the three coins had been thrown, the answer didn't appear to be as precise as the questions: 'Preponderance of the small. Perseverance furthers. Small things may be done; great things should not be done. The flying bird brings the message: It is not well to strive upward, it is well to remain below. Great good fortune.' On reading this response, most people would probably have been as confused as ever, but for Paulo Coelho the oracle was as clear as day: after seven years and four books, the time had come to leave Objetiva and return to Rocco.

Annoyed by the news of the change, and particularly by the author's decision to take with him a book that was ready for printing, Roberto Feith decided that he would only release the typescript of *Eleven Minutes* if Objetiva were reimbursed for the production costs. Paulo saw this as a threat and unsheathed his sword: he took on a large law firm in Rio and prepared for a long and painful legal battle. He announced that he was going back to Rocco – the publisher who, he stated, would launch *Eleven Minutes* during the first few months of 2003 – and left for Tarbes with Chris, leaving the Brazilian publishing market seething with rumours. Some said that he had left Objetiva out of pique, because Luís Fernando Veríssimo was now their main author. Others said that Rocco had offered him US$350,000 to return.

Things only began to calm down when Chris, on her daily walk with Paulo, advised him to bring an end to the conflict with Feith. 'It looks as though you want a fight more than he does! What for? Why?' she asked. 'Do what you can to see that it ends amicably.' After some resistance, Paulo finally gave in. He stopped in front of a crucifix and asked God to remove the hatred from his heart. A few weeks later, after some discussion between representatives of the two parties, Feith not only released *Eleven Minutes* but also returned to Paulo the four titles in his backlist that Paulo wanted to go to Rocco. There was just one point on which the owner of Objetiva dug in his heels: he refused to allow the insertion of his suggestions in the Rocco edition and in any foreign versions. This obliged Mônica to take back the copies of the text that had already been sent to translators in several countries. The problem had been resolved, but Coelho and Feith haven't spoken to each other since.

The book that had caused the uproar had its origins some years earlier, in 1997, in Mantua, in the north of Italy, where Coelho had given a lecture. When he arrived at his hotel, he found an envelope that had been left by a Brazilian named Sônia, a reader and fan who had emigrated to Europe in order to work as a prostitute. The packet contained the typescript of a book in which she told her story. Although he normally never read such typescripts, Coelho read it, liked it and suggested it to Objectiva for publication. The publisher, however, wasn't interested. When Sônia met him again three years later in Zurich, where she was living at the time, she organized a book signing such as probably no other writer has ever experienced: she took him to Langstrasse, a street where, after ten at night, the pavement teems with prostitutes from all parts of the world. Told of Coelho's presence in the area, dozens of them appeared bearing dog-eared copies of his books in different languages, the majority of which, the author noted, came from countries that had been part of the former Soviet Union. Since she also worked in Geneva, Sônia suggested a repetition of this extraordinary event in the red light district there. That was where he met a Brazilian prostitute whom he called Maria and whose life story was to provide the narrative for *Eleven Minutes*: the story of a young girl from northeastern Brazil who is brought to Europe in order, she thinks, to be a nightclub dancer, but who, on arriving, discovers that she is to be a prostitute. For the author, this was 'not a book about prostitution or about the misfortunes of a prostitute, but about a person in search of her sexual identity. It is about the complicated relationship between feelings and physical pleasure.'

The title he chose for the 255-page book is a paraphrase of *Seven Minutes*, the 1969 best-seller in which Irving Wallace describes a court case involving an attempt to ban a novel about sex. Seven minutes, according to Wallace, was the average time taken to perform a sexual act. When *Eleven Minutes* was published in the United States, a reporter from *USA Today* asked Paulo why he had added four minutes. With a chuckle, he replied that the American's estimate reflected an Anglo-Saxon point of view and was therefore 'too conservative by Latin standards'.

Eleven Minutes was launched in Brazil during the first quarter of 2003 and was received by the media with their customary irony – so much so that a month before its launch the author predicted the critics' reaction in an interview given to *IstoÉ*: 'How do I know that the critics aren't going to like it? It's simple. You can't loathe an author for ten of his books and love him for the eleventh.' As well as not liking *Eleven Minutes*, many journalists predicted that it would be the author's first big flop. According to several critics, the risqué theme of the book, which talks of oral sex, clitoral and vaginal orgasms, and sadomasochistic practices, was too explosive a mixture for what they imagined to be Paulo Coelho's average reader. Exactly the opposite happened. Before the initial print run of 200,000 copies had even arrived in Brazilian bookshops in April 2003, Sant Jordi had sold the book to more than twenty foreign publishers after negotiations that earned the author US$6 million. Three weeks after its launch, *Eleven Minutes* was top of the best-seller lists in Brazil, Italy and Germany. The launch of the English edition attracted 2,000 people to Borders bookshop in London. As had been the case with the ten previous books, his readers in Brazil and the rest of the world gave unequivocal proof that they loved his eleventh book as well. *Eleven Minutes* went on to become Paulo Coelho's second-most-read book, with 10 million copies sold, losing out only to the unassailable *Alchemist*.

CHAPTER 29

The Zahir

PAULO AND CHRIS spent the first few months of 2004 working on making the old mill they had bought in Saint-Martin habitable. The plan to spend four months there, four in Brazil and four travelling had been scuppered by the suggested programme Mônica had sent at the beginning of the year. Sant Jordi had been overwhelmed by no fewer than 187 invitations for Paulo to present prizes and participate in events, signings, conferences and launches all over the world. If he were to agree to even half of those requests there would be no time for anything else – not even his next book, which was just beginning to preoccupy him.

He had been working on the story in his head during the second half of the year, at the end of which time just two weeks were enough for him to set down on paper the 318 pages of *O Zahir*, or *The Zahir*, the title of which had been inspired by a story by Jorge Luís Borges about something which, once touched or seen, would never be forgotten. The nameless main character, who is easily recognizable, is an ex-rock star turned world-famous writer, loathed by the critics and adored by his readers. He lives in Paris with a war correspondent, Esther. The narrative begins with the character's horror when he finds out that she has left him. Written at the end of 2004, in March of the following year, the book was ready to be launched in Brazil and several other countries.

However, before it was discovered by readers around the world, Brazilians included, *The Zahir* was to be the subject of a somewhat surprising operation: it was to be published first in, of all places, Tehran, capital of Iran, where Coelho was the most widely read foreign author. This was a tactic by the young publisher Arash Hejazi to defeat local piracy which, while not on the same alarming scale as in Egypt, was carried out with such impunity that twenty-seven different editions of *The Alchemist* alone had been identified, all of them pirate copies as far as the author was concerned, but none of them illegal, because Iran is not a signatory to the international agreements on the protection of authors' rights. The total absence of any legislation to suppress the clandestine book industry was due to a peculiarity in the law, which only protects works whose first edition is printed, published and launched in the country. In order to guarantee his publishing house, Caravan, the right to be the sole publisher of *The Zahir* in the country, Hejazi suggested that Mônica change the programme of international launches so that the first edition could appear in bookshops in Iran.

Some days after the book was published, it faced problems from the government. The bad news was conveyed in a telephone call from Hejazi to the author, who was with Mônica in the Hotel Gellert in Budapest. Speaking from a public call box in order to foil the censors who might be bugging his phone, the terrified thirty-five-year-old publisher told Coelho that the Caravan stand at the International Book Fair in Iran had just been invaded by a group from the Basejih, the regime's 'morality police'. The officers had confiscated 1,000 copies of *The Zahir*, announced that the book was banned and ordered him to appear two days later at the censor's office.

Both publisher and author were in agreement as to how best to confront such violence and ensure Hejazi's physical safety: they should tell the international public. Coelho made calls to two or three journalist friends, the first he could get hold of, and the BBC in London and France Presse immediately broadcast the news, which then travelled around the world. This reaction appears to have frightened off the authorities, because, a few days later, the books were returned without any explanation and the ban lifted. It was understandable that a repressive and moralistic state such as Iran should have a problem with a book that deals with adulterous relationships. What was surprising was that the hand of repression should touch someone as popular in the country as Paulo Coelho, who was publicly hailed as 'the first non-Muslim writer to visit Iran since the ayatollahs came to power' – that is, since 1979.

In fact, Coelho had visited the country in May 2000 as the guest of President Mohamed Khatami, who was masterminding a very tentative process of political liberalization. When they landed in Tehran, and even though it was three in the morning, Paulo and Chris (who was wearing a wedding ring on her left hand and had been duly informed of the strictures imposed on women in Islamic countries) were greeted by a crowd of more than a thousand readers who had learned of the arrival of the author of *The Alchemist* from the newspapers. It was just before the new government was about to take office and the political situation was tense. The streets of the capital were filled every day with student demonstrations in support of Khatami's reforms, which were facing strong opposition from the conservative clerics who hold the real power in the country. Although accompanied everywhere by a dozen or so Brazilian and foreign journalists, Coelho was never far from the watchful eyes of the six security guards armed with machine guns who had been assigned to him. After giving five lectures and various book signings for *Brida*, with an audience of never fewer than a thousand, he was honoured by the Minister of Culture, Ataolah Mohajerani, with a gala dinner where the place of honour was occupied by no less a person than President Khatami. When the seventy-year-old Iranian novelist Mahmoud Dolatabadi turned down an invitation to be present at the banquet given in honour of his Brazilian colleague, of whom he was a self-confessed admirer, he referred to the limitations and the fragility of Khatami's liberalization process. Hounded by the government, he refused to fraternize with its censors. 'I cannot be interrogated in the morning,' he told the reporters, 'and in the evening have coffee with the president.'

Some weeks after *The Zahir*'s publication in Iran, 8 million copies of the book, translated into forty-two languages, arrived in bookshops in eighty-three countries. When it was launched in Europe, the novel came to the attention of the newspapers – not in the political pages, as had been the case with the Iranian censorship, but in the gossip columns. In the spring of 2005, a question had been going round the press offices of the European media: who was the inspiration behind the book's main female character, Esther? The first suspect, put forward by the Moscow tabloid *Komsomólskaia Pravda*, was the beautiful Russian designer Anna Rossa, who was reported to have had a brief affair with the author. When he read the news, which was reproduced on an Italian literary website, Coelho was quick to send the newspaper a letter, which his friend the journalist Dmitry Voskoboynikov translated:

Dear readers of *Komsomólskaia Pravda*

I was most intrigued to learn from your newspaper that I had an affair with the designer Anna Rossa three years ago and that this woman is supposedly the main character in my new book, *The Zahir*. Happily or unhappily, we shall never know which, the information is simply not true.

When I was shown a photo of this young woman at my side, I remembered her at once. In fact, we were introduced at a reception at the Brazilian embassy. Now I am no saint, but there was not and probably never will be anything between the two of us.

The Zahir is perhaps one of my deepest books, and I have dedicated it to my partner Christina Oiticica, with whom I have lived for twenty-five years. I wish you and Anna Rossa love and success.

Yours

Paulo Coelho

In the face of this quick denial, the journalists' eyes turned to another beautiful woman, the Chilean Cecília Bolocco, Miss Universe 1987, who, at the time, was presenting *La Noche de Cecília*, a highly successful chat show in Chile. On her way to Madrid, where she was recording interviews for her programme, she burst out laughing when she learned that she was being named as the inspiration for Esther in *The Zahir*: 'Don't say that! Carlito gets very jealous ...' The jealous 'Carlito' was the former Argentine president, Carlos Menem, whom she had married in May 2000, when he was seventy and she was thirty-five. Cecília's reaction was understandable. Some years earlier, the press had informed readers that she had had an affair with Coelho between the beginning of 1999 and October 2000, when she was married to Menem. Both had vehemently denied the allegations. Suspicions also fell on the Italian actress Valeria Golino.

However, on 17 April 2005, a Sunday, the Portuguese newspaper *Correio da Manhã* announced on its front page that the woman on whom Paulo had based the character was the English journalist Christina Lamb, war correspondent for the *Sunday Times*. When she was phoned up in Harare, where she was doing an interview, she couldn't believe that the secret had been made public. She was the 'real-life Esther', the newspaper confirmed. 'All last week I fielded phone calls from newspapers in Spain, Portugal, Brazil, South Africa, even Britain, asking how I felt being "Paulo Coelho's muse",' she said in a full-page article in the *Sunday Times Review*, entitled 'He stole my soul' and with a curious subtitle: 'Christina Lamb has covered many foreign wars for the *Sunday Times*, but she had no defences when one of the world's bestselling novelists decided to hijack her life.'

In the article, the journalist says that she met Coelho two years earlier when she was chosen to interview him about the success of *Eleven Minutes*. At the time, the writer was still living in the Henri IV hotel. This was their only meeting. During the following months, they exchanged e-mails, he in the south of France and she in Kandahar and Kabul, in Afghanistan. Coelho so enjoyed Christina's *The Sewing Circles of Herat* that he included it in his 'Top Ten Reads' on the Barnes & Noble website. When she checked her e-mails in June 2004 she found, 'among the usual monotonous updates from the coalition forces in Kabul and junk offering penis enlargement', a message from Coelho with a huge attachment. It was the Portuguese typescript of his just completed book *The Zahir*, with a message saying: 'The female character was inspired by you.' He then explained that he had thought of trying to meet, but she was always away, so he had used her book and Internet research to create the character. In the article published in the *Sunday Times*, she describes what she felt as she read the e-mail:

I was part astonished, part flattered, part alarmed. He didn't know me. How could he have based a character on me? I felt almost naked. Like most people, I guess, there were things in my life I would not wish to see in print. [...]

So with some trepidation I downloaded the 304-page file and opened it. As I read the manuscript I recognized things I had told him in Tarbes, insights into my private world, as well as concerns I had discussed in my book.

The first paragraph began: 'Her name is Esther, she is a war correspondent who has just returned from Iraq because of the imminent invasion of that country; she is thirty years old, married, without children.'

At least he had made me younger.

What had at first seemed amusing ('I was starting to enjoy the idea that the heroine was based on me, and now here she was disappearing on page one,' Christina wrote) was becoming uncomfortable as she read on:

I was slightly concerned about his description of how Esther and her husband had met. 'One day, a journalist comes to interview me. She wants to know what it's like to have my work known all over the country but to be entirely unknown myself ... She's pretty, intelligent, quiet. We meet again at a party, where there's no pressure of work, and I manage to get her into bed that same night.'

Astonished by what she had read, Christina told her mother and her husband – a Portuguese lawyer named Paulo:

Far from sharing my feeling of flattery, he was highly suspicious about why another man should be writing a book on his wife. I told a few friends and they looked at me as though I was mad. I decided it was better not to mention it to anyone else.

If the *Correio da Manhã* had not revealed the secret, the matter would have ended there. The revelation would not, after all, have caused any further discomfort for the journalist, as she herself confessed in her article:

> Once I got used to it, I decided I quite liked being a muse. But I was not quite sure what muses do. [...] I asked Coelho how a muse should behave. 'Muses must be treated like fairies,' he replied, adding that he had never had a muse before. I thought being a muse probably involved lying on a couch with a large box of fancy chocolates, looking pensive. [...] But being a muse is not easy if you work full time and have a five-year-old. [...] In the meantime, I have learnt that going to interview celebrity authors can be more hazardous than covering wars. They might not shoot you but they can steal your soul.

The book seemed destined to cause controversy. Accustomed to the media's hostility towards Coelho's previous books, Brazilian readers had a surprise during the final week of March 2005. On all the news-stands in the country three of the four major weekly magazines had photos of Coelho on the cover and inside each were eight pages about the author and his life. This unusual situation led the journalist Marcelo Beraba, the ombudsman of the *Folha de São Paulo*, to dedicate the whole of his Sunday column to the subject.

The 'case of the three covers', as it became known, was deemed important only because it revealed a radical change in behaviour in a media which, with a few rare exceptions, had treated the author very badly. It was as though Brazil had just discovered a phenomenon that so many countries had been celebrating since the worldwide success of *The Alchemist*.

Whatever the critics might say, what distinguished Paulo from other best-sellers, such as John Grisham and Dan Brown, was the content of his books. Some of those authors might even sell more books, but they don't fill auditoriums around the world, as Paulo does. The impact his work has on his readers can be measured by the hundreds of e-mails that he receives daily from all corners of the earth, many of them from people telling him how reading his books has changed their lives. Ordinary letters posted from the most remote places, sometimes simply addressed to 'Paulo Coelho – Brazil', arrive by the sackload.

In February 2006 – as if in acknowledgement of his popularity – Coelho received an invitation from Buckingham Palace – from Sir James Hamilton, Duke of Abercorn and Lord Steward of the Household. This was for a state banquet to be given some weeks later for the President of Brazil, Luiz Inácio Lula da Silva, by Queen Elizabeth II and Prince Philip during the President's official visit to Britain. The invitation made clear that the occasion called for 'white tie with decorations'. As the date of the banquet approached, however, newspapers reported that, at the request of the Brazilian government, both President Lula and his seventy-strong delegation had been relieved of the obligation to wear tails. When he read this, Coelho (who had dusted off his tails, waistcoat and white tie) was confused as to what to do. Concerned that he might make a blunder, he decided to send a short e-mail to the Royal Household asking for instructions: 'I just read that President Lula vetoed the white tie for the Brazilian Delegation. Please let me know how to proceed – I don't want to be the only one with a white tie.'

The reply, signed by a member of the Royal Household, arrived two days later, also by e-mail:

Mr. Coelho:

Her Majesty The Queen Elizabeth II has agreed that President Lula and members of his official suite need not wear white tie to the State Banquet. However, that will be just a small number of people (less than 20). The remainder of the 170 guests will be in white tie, so I can reassure you that you will not be the only person wearing white tie. The Queen does expect her guests to wear white tie and you are officially a guest of Her Majesty The Queen, not President Lula.

CHAPTER 30

One hundred million copies sold

SOME WEEKS AFTER HANDING HIS PUBLISHERS the typescript of *The Witch of Portobello*, which he had finished a week prior to the banquet at Buckingham Palace, Coelho was preparing for a new test. Two decades had passed since 1986, when he had followed the Road to Santiago, the first and most important of the penances imposed by Jean. In the years that followed, the mysterious Master had, in agreement with Coelho, regularly ordered further trials. At least one of these the author has confessed to having fulfilled purely out of respect for the duty to find disciples to whom he should transmit the knowledge he had received from Jean and show them the route to spiritual enlightenment. 'I have disciples because I am obliged to, but I don't enjoy it,' he told journalists. 'I'm very lazy and have little patience.' In spite of this resistance, he has acted as guide to four new initiates as demanded by RAM.

Besides following the Routes, the name given by members of the order to the different pilgrimages, he was ordered by Jean to submit to various tests. Some of these did not require much willpower or physical strength, such as praying at least once a day with his hands held beneath a jet of flowing water, which could be from a tap or a stream. Coelho does, however, admit to having been given tasks that were not at all easy to perform, such as submitting to a vow of chastity for six months, during which time even masturbation was forbidden. In spite of this deprivation, he speaks with good humour about the experience, which happened in the late 1980s. 'I discovered that sexual abstinence is accompanied by a great deal of temptation,' he recalls. 'The penitent has the impression that every woman desires him, or, rather, that only the really pretty ones do.' Some of these tests were akin to rituals of self-flagellation. For three months, for example, he was obliged to walk for an hour a day, barefoot and without a shirt, through brushwood in thick scrubland until his chest and arms were scratched by thorns and the soles of his feet lacerated by stones. Compared with that, tasks such as fasting for three days or having to look at a tree for five minutes every day for months on end were as nothing.

The task Jean set his disciple in April 2006 may seem to a layman totally nonsensical. The time had come for him to take the External Road to Jerusalem, which meant spending four months (or, as the initiates prefer to say, 'three months plus one') wandering about the world, wherever he chose, without setting foot in either of his two homes – the house in France and his apartment in Rio de Janeiro. For him this meant spending all that time in hotels. Did this mean that only those with enough money to pay for such an extravagance could join the order? Coelho had been troubled by this very question twenty years earlier, just before setting off along the Road to Santiago, and he recalls Jean's encouraging reply: 'Travelling isn't always a question of money, but of courage. You spent a large part of your life travelling the world as a hippie. What money did you have then? None. Hardly enough to pay for your fare, and yet those were, I believe, some of the best years of your life – eating badly, sleeping in railway stations, unable to communicate because of the language, being forced to depend on others even for finding somewhere to spend the night.'

If the new Road to Jerusalem was unavoidable, the solution was to relax and put the time to good use. He devoted the first few weeks to carrying out a small number of the engagements that had accumulated in Sant Jordi's diary, among which was the London Book Fair. While there, he chanced to meet Yuri Smirnoff, the owner of Sophia, his publisher in Russia. Coelho told him that he was in the middle of a strange pilgrimage and that this might be the perfect opportunity to realize an old dream: to take the legendary Trans-Siberian Railway which crosses 9,289 kilometres and traverses 75 per cent of Russia, from Moscow to Vladivostok. Some weeks later, he received a phone call while he was touring in Catalonia, in northern Spain. It was Smirnoff calling to say that he had decided to make Coelho's dream come true and was offering him a fortnight on one of the longest railway journeys in the world.

Coelho assumed that the gift would be a compartment on the train. Much to his surprise, when he arrived in Moscow on 15 May, the agreed date for his departure, he discovered that Smirnoff had decided to turn the trip into a luxurious 'happening'. He had hired two entire coaches. Paulo would travel in a suite in the first, and the other two compartments would be occupied by Smirnoff, his wife and Eva, an admirer of Coelho's work, who would act as his interpreter during the two-week journey. He was also provided with a chef, two cooks and a waiter, as well as two bodyguards from the Russian government to ensure their guest's safety. The second coach was to be given over to thirty journalists from Russia and other European countries, who had been invited to accompany the author. Altogether, this kind gesture cost Smirnoff about US$200,000, and it proved to be a very poor investment indeed: some months later Coelho left Sophia for another publisher, Astrel.

It turned out to be an exhausting fortnight, not just because of the distance covered, but because he was constantly besieged by his readers. At every stop, the platforms were filled by hundreds and hundreds of readers wanting an autograph, a handshake, or even just a word. After crossing the provinces in the far east of Russia and skirting the frontiers of Mongolia and China, on a journey that crossed eight time zones, the group finally arrived in Vladivostok on the edge of the Sea of Japan on 30 May.

During the interviews he gave while on his Trans-Siberian journey Coelho made it clear that, in spite of the comfort in which he was travelling, it was not a tourist trip. 'This is not just a train journey,' he insisted several times, 'but a spiritual journey through space and time in order to complete a pilgrimage ordered by my Master.' Despite all these years of being a constant presence in newspapers and magazines across the world,

no journalist has ever been able to discover the true identity of the mysterious character to whom Paulo owes so much. Some months after the end
of the World Cup in 2006, someone calling himself simply a 'reader of
Paulo Coelho' sent a photo to the website set up for collecting information
for this book. It showed Coelho wearing a Brazilian flag draped over his
shoulders, Christina and a third person walking down a street. The third
person was a thin man, with grey hair, wearing faded jeans, a Brazilian
football shirt and a mobile phone hanging around his neck. It was hard to
identify him because he was wearing a cap and sunglasses and his right
hand was partly covering his face. The photograph bore a short caption
written by the anonymous contributor: 'This photo was taken by me in
Berlin during the 2006 World Cup. The man in the cap is Jean, Paulo
Coelho's Master in RAM.' When he saw the photo, the author was deliberately vague: 'What can I say?' he said. 'If it isn't him, it's very like him.'

Two months after the end of the World Cup, Brazilian bookshops
were receiving the first 100,000 copies of *The Witch of Portobello*. It was
a book full of new ideas. The first of these, to be found right at the beginning, is the method used by the author to relate the travails of Athena,
the book's protagonist. The story of the young Gypsy girl born in
Transylvania, in Romania, and abandoned by her biological mother is
narrated by fifteen different characters. This device brought eloquent
praise for his work in the *Folha de São Paulo*. 'One cannot deny that, in
literary terms, this is one of Paulo Coelho's most ambitious novels,' wrote
Marcelo Pen. The book is the story of Athena's life. Adopted by a
Lebanese couple and taken to Beirut, from where the family is driven out
by the civil war that raged in Lebanon from 1975 until 1990, she then
settles in London. She grows up in Britain, where she is educated, marries
and has a son. She works for a bank before leaving her husband and going
to Romania in order to find her biological mother. She then moves to the
Persian Gulf, where she becomes a successful estate agent in Dubai. On
her return to London, she develops and seeks to deepen her spirituality,
becoming, in the end, a priestess, who attracts hundreds of followers. As
a result of this, however, she becomes a victim of religious intolerance.

The second innovation was technological. The book appeared on the
author's website before the printed version reached the Brazilian and

Portuguese bookshops, and in just two days his web page received 29,000 hits, which took everyone, including the author, by surprise. 'It was just amazing, but it proved that the Internet has become an obligatory space for a writer to share his work with the readers,' he told newspapers. To those who feared that the initiative might rob bookshops of readers, he replied: 'In 1999, I discovered that the edition of *The Alchemist* published in Russia was available on the Internet. Then I decided to confront piracy on its own ground and I started putting my books on the web first. Instead of falling, sales in bookshops increased.'

As though wanting to reaffirm that these were not empty words, the site where he began to make his books available (www.piratecoelho.word press.com) has a photo of the author with a bandana on his head and a black eye patch, as though he were a real pirate. Convinced that someone only reads books on-screen if he has no other option, and that printing them out at home would cost more than buying them in the bookshops, Coelho began to make all his books available online. 'It has been proved that if people read the first chapters on the Internet and like it,' he states, 'they will go out and buy the book.'

Since the middle of 2006, he and Mônica and Chris, as well as some of his publishers, had been hoping that the number of books sold would pass the 100-million mark around the feast day of St Joseph, 19 March, the following year, when he had decided he would celebrate his sixtieth birthday. As it turned out, the 100-millionth book was not sold until five months later, in August, which was his real birthday. Although he had told the newspapers that being sixty was no more important than being thirty-five or forty-seven, in February, he decided that he would celebrate St Joseph's day in the Hotel El Peregrino, in Puente la Reina, a small Spanish town 20 kilometres from Pamplona, halfway along the Road to Santiago. That day he announced on his blog that he would be glad to welcome the first ten readers to reply in Puente la Reina. When the messages began to arrive – coming from places as far away as Brazil, Japan, England, Venezuela and Qatar – Paulo feared that those who replied might think that the invitation included air trips and accommodation, and hastened to clarify the situation. To his surprise, they had all understood what he meant and were prepared to bear the cost. On the actual day, there were five Spaniards (Luís Miguel, Clara, Rosa, Loli and Ramón), a Greek (Chrissa), an Englishman (Alex), a Venezuelan (Marian), a Japanese (Heiko) and an American who lived in northern Iraq (Nika), as well as the ex-football star Raí and Paulo's old friends, among them Nelson Liano, Jr, his partner on the *Manual do Vampirismo*, and Dana Goodyear, the American journalist. In his blog, Liano summed up the atmosphere at El Peregrino:

> It was a celebration in honour of St Joseph in four languages. Paulo adopted the feast day of the patron saint of workers to celebrate his birthday, following an old Spanish Christian tradition. While the party was going on, a snowfall left the Road to Santiago completely white. Salsa, French regional music, the bolero, tango, samba and the unforgettable hits that Paulo had written with Raul Seixas gave a panmusical note to the party, accompanied by the very best Rioja wine.

Five months later, as his real birthday was approaching, the team led by Mônica at Sant Jordi was working flat out on the preparation of a smart forty-page folder in English, the cover of which bore a photo of a beaming Paulo Coelho and the words 'PAULO COELHO – 100,000,000 COPIES'. The urgency was due to the fact that the folder had to be ready by the first week of October, for the Frankfurt Book Fair.

While the people at Sant Jordi were engaged on this, on 24 August, the man himself was, as usual, devoting himself to more spiritual matters. Anyone strolling along the narrow, sunny little streets in Barbazan-Debat, 10 kilometres from Saint-Martin, at three o'clock that afternoon, might not even have noticed the presence of the man with close-cropped white hair, wearing trainers, T-shirt and bermudas. Coelho had just come out of the small chapel of Notre Dame de Piétat and sat down on a wooden bench, where he placed a notebook on his lap and began to write. The few tourists who drove past would have found it hard to associate that slight, rather monk-like figure with the author courted by kings, emirs and Hollywood stars and acclaimed by readers all over the world. Christina, who was watching from a distance, went over to him and asked what he was writing.

'A letter,' he replied, without looking up.

'Who to?' she went on.

'To the author of my biography.'

Posted some hours later at Saint-Martin post office, the letter is reproduced in its entirety below.

Barbazan-Debat, 24 August 2007

Dear Fernando

I'm sitting here outside this small chapel and have just repeated the usual ritual: lighting three candles to Notre Dame de Piétat. The first asking for her protection, the second for my readers and the third asking that my work should continue undiminished and with dignity. It's sunny, but it's not an unbearably hot summer. There is no one in sight, except for Chris, who is looking at the mountains, the trees and the roses that the monks planted, while she waits for me to finish this letter.

We came on foot – 10 kilometres in two hours, which is reasonable. We shall have to go back on foot, and I've just realized that I didn't bring enough water. It doesn't matter; sometimes life gives you no choice, and I can't stay sitting here for ever. My dreams are waiting for me, and dreams mean work, and I need to get back home, even though I'm thirsty.

I turn sixty today. My plan was to do what I always do, and that's how it's been. Yesterday at 23.15 I went to Lourdes so that I would be there at 00.05 on the 24th, the moment when I was born, before the grotto of Our Lady, thank her for my life so far and ask for her protection for the future. It was a very moving moment, but while I was driving back to Saint-Martin, I felt terribly alone. I commented on this to Chris, who said: 'But you were the one who chose to spend the day like this!' Yes, I chose it, but I began to feel uncomfortable. There we were, the two of us alone on this immense planet.

I turned on my mobile. At the same moment, it rang – it was Mônica, my agent and friend. I got home and there were other messages waiting for me. I went to sleep happy, and in the morning I realized that there was no reason for last night's gloom. Flowers and presents, etc. began to arrive. People in Internet communities had created extraordinary things using my images and texts. Everything had been organized, for the most part, by people I had never seen in my life – with the exception of Márcia Nascimento, who created something really magical that made me glad to say 'I'm a writer who has a fan club (of which she is the world president)!'

Why am I writing to you? Because today, unlike other days, I have an immense desire to go back to the past, using not my own eyes, but those of someone who has had access to my diaries, my friends, my enemies, to everyone who has been a part of my life. I should like very much to be reading my biography right now, but it looks like I'm going to have to wait.

I don't know what my reaction will be when I read what you've written, but in the chapel, it says: 'You will know the truth, and the truth will set you free.' Truth is a complicated word – after all, many religious crimes have been committed in its name, many wars have been declared, many people have been banished by those who believed themselves to be just. But one thing is certain: when the truth is a liberating truth, there is nothing to fear. And that was basically why I agreed to a biography: so that I can discover another side to myself. And that will make me feel freer.

A plane's flying by overhead, the new Airbus 380, which has not yet been put into service and is being tested near here. I look at it and think: How long will it take for this new marvel of technology to become obsolete? Of course, my next thought is: How long before my books are forgotten? Best not to think about it. I didn't write them with one eye on eternity. I wrote them to discover what, given your training as a journalist and given your Marxist convictions, will not be in your book: my secret corners, sometimes dark and sometimes light, which I only began to be aware of when I set them down on paper.

Like any writer, I always flirted with the idea of an autobiography, but it's impossible to write about yourself without ending up justifying your mistakes and magnifying your successes – it's human nature. So that's why I accepted the idea of your book so readily, even though

I know I run the risk of having things revealed that I don't think need to be revealed. Because, if they're a part of my life, they need to see the light of day. That's why I decided – a decision I've often regretted over the past three years – to give you access to the diaries that I've been writing since I was an adolescent.

Even if I don't recognize myself in your book, I know that there will be a part of me there. While you were interviewing me and I was forced to look again at certain periods of my life, I kept thinking: What would have become of me if I hadn't experienced those things?

It's not worth going into that now: Chris says we should go back home, we have another two hours to walk, the sun's getting stronger and the ground is dry. I have asked her for another five minutes to finish this. Who shall I be in your biography? Although I haven't read it, I know the reply: I shall be the characters who crossed my path. I shall be the person who held out his hand, trusting that there would be another hand waiting to support me in difficult times.

I exist because I have friends. I have survived because they were there on my path. They taught me to give the best of myself, even when, at some stages in my life, I was not a good pupil. But I think that I have learned something about generosity.

Chris says that my five minutes are up, but I've asked for a little more time so that I can write here, in this letter, the words that Khalil Gibran wrote more than a hundred years ago. They're probably not in the right order, because I learned them by heart on a distant, sad and gloomy night when I was listening to Simon & Garfunkel on that machine we used to call a 'gramophone', which has now been superseded (just as, one day, the Airbus 380 will and, eventually, my books). They are words that speak about the importance of giving:

'It is only when you give of yourself that you truly give. Therefore give now, that the season of giving may be yours and not your inheritors.

'People often say: "I would give, but only to the deserving." The trees in your orchard say not so. They give that they may live, for to withhold is to perish.

'Therefore, when you share something out, do not think of your-
selves as generous people. The truth is, it is life that divides things up
and shares them out, and we human beings are mere witnesses to
our own existence.'

I'm going to get up now and go home. A witness to my own existence, that is what I have been every day of the sixty years I am celebrating today.

May Our Lady of Piétat bless you.

Paulo

When this biography was completed, in February 2008, the A380 was in
commercial operation. Given how fast new technology becomes obsolete, it is highly likely that manufacture of the A380 will have ceased long
before the hundreds of millions of copies of Paulo Coelho's books disappear and, with them – despite what the literary critics may think – the
profound effect they have had on readers in even the most far-flung
corners of the planet.

FACTS ABOUT
PAULO COELHO

BOOKS PUBLISHED

	English title
Teatro na Educação (1973)	
Arquivos do Inferno (1982)	
Manual Prático do Vampirismo (1985)	
O Diário de um Mago (1987)	*The Pilgrimage*
O Alquimista (1988)	*The Alchemist*
Brida (1990)	*Brida*
O Dom Supremo (1991)	
As Valkírias (1992)	*The Valkyries*
Na Margem do Rio Piedra eu Sentei e Chorei (1994)	*By the River Piedra I Sat Down and Wept*
Maktub (1994)	
O Monte Cinco (1996)	*The Fifth Mountain*
Manual do Guerreiro da Luz (1997)	*Manual of the Warrior of Light*
Cartas de Amor do Profeta (1997)	
Veronika Decide Morrer (1998)	*Veronika Decides to Die*
Palavras Essenciais (1999)	
O Demônio e a Srta. Prym (2000)	*The Devil and Miss Prym*
Histórias para Pais, Filhos e Netos (2001)	
Onze Minutos (2003)	*Eleven Minutes*
O Gênio e as Rosas (2004)	
O Zahir (2005)	*The Zahir*

Ser como o Rio que Flui (2006)   *Like the Flowing River*
A Bruxa de Portobello (2006)   *The Witch of Portobello*
O Vencedor está só (2008)   *The Winner Stands Alone*

Excluding pirate editions, his books have sold over 100 million copies in 455 translations, published in 66 languages and 160 countries.

MAIN PRIZES AND DECORATIONS

Golden Book – Yugoslavia, 1995, 1996, 1997, 1998, 1999, 2000 and 2004
Grand Prix Littéraire Elle – France, 1995
Guinness Book of Records – Brazil, 1995/1996
Chevalier des Arts et des Lettres – France, 1996
Livre d'Or – France, 1996
ABERT Prize, Formador de Opinião – Brazil, 1996
Premio Internazionale Flaiano – Italy, 1996
Super Grinzane Cavour Literary Prize – Italy, 1996
Finalist in the International IMPAC Literary Award – Eire, 1997 and
    2000
Protector de Honor – Spain, 1997
Comendador da Ordem do Rio Branco – Brazil, 1998
Diploma da Ordem Fraternal do Cruzeiro do Sul – Brazil, 1998
Fiera Del Libro per i Ragazzi – Italy, 1998
Flutuat Nec Mergitur – France, 1998
Libro de Oro for *La Quinta Montaña* – Argentina, 1998
Medaille de la Ville de Paris – France, 1998
Senaki Museum – Greece, 1998
Sara Kubitschek Prize – Brazil, 1998
Top Performance Nacional – Argentina, 1998
Chevalier de l'Ordre National de la Légion d'Honneur – France, 1999
Huésped Distinguido de la Ciudad de Nuestra Señora de la Paz –
    Bolívia, 1999
Książka Zagraniczna – Poland, 1999
Libro de Oro for *Guerrero de la Luz* – Argentina, 1999

Libro de Oro for *Veronika Decide Morir* – Argentina, 1999

Libro de Platina for *El Alquimista* – Argentina, 1999

Medalla de Oro de Galicia – Spain, 1999

Crystal Prize of the World Economic Forum – Switzerland, 1999

Crystal Mirror Prize – Poland, 2000

Member of the Pen Club Brazil – Brazil, 2001

Bambi Prize for Cultural Personality of the Year – Germany, 2001

Ville de Tarbes – France, 2001

XXIII Premio Internazionale Fregene – Italy, 2001

Diploma of the Academia Brasileira de Letras – Brazil, 2002

Miembro de Honor – Bolivia, 2002

Club of Budapest Planetary Arts Award in recognition of his literary
    work – Germany, 2002

International Corine prize for the best work of fiction for *The Alchemist*
    – Germany, 2002

Prix de la Littérature Consciente de la Planète – France, 2002

Ville d'Orthez – France, 2002

Médaille des Officiers des Arts et des Lettres – France, 2003

Medal from the Lviv Book Fair – Ukraine, 2004

Nielsen Gold Book Award for *The Alchemist* – United Kingdom, 2004

Order of Honour of Ukraine – Ukraine, 2004

Order of Saint Sophia for contribution to knowledge and culture –
    Ukraine, 2004

Premio Giovanni Verga – Italy, 2004

Golden Book award from the newspaper *Vecernje Novosti* – Serbia, 2004

Budapest Award – Hungary, 2005

Ex Libris award for *Eleven Minutes* – Serbia, 2005

Goldene Feder Award – Germany, 2005

International Author's Award from DirectGroup Bertelsmann –
    Germany, 2005

8th Annual International Latino Book Award for *The Zahir* – United
    States, 2006

I Premio Álava en el Corazón – Spain, 2006

Kiklop Award for *The Zahir* in the Best-Seller of the Year Category –
    Croatia, 2006

ARTICLES

Weekly articles written by Paulo Coelho are published in 109 publications in 60 countries: Albania, Argentina, Armenia, Austria, Bolivia, Bosnia and Herzegovina, Brazil, Bulgaria, Canada, Chile, China, Colombia, Costa Rica, Croatia, Czech Republic, Dominican Republic, Ecuador, Egypt, Eire, El Salvador, Estonia, Finland, France, Georgia, Germany, Greece, Guatemala, Honduras, Hungary, India, Indonesia, Iceland, Italy, Japan, Lithuania, Mexico, Netherlands, Nicaragua, Norway, Oman, Panama, Peru, Poland, Portugal, Puerto Rico, Romania, Russia, Serbia, Slovakia, Slovenia, South Africa, South Korea, Spain, Sweden, Switzerland, Taiwan, Ukraine, United Arab Emirates, United Kingdom and Venezuela.

CINEMA

The film rights for four of his books have been negotiated with the following American studios:

The Alchemist (Warner Brothers)
The Fifth Mountain (Capistrano Productions)
Eleven Minutes (Hollywood Gang Productions)
Veronika Decides to Die (Muse Productions)

INTERNET

Apart from his website, www.paulocoelho.com, which is available in sixteen languages, the author has a blog, www.paulocoelhoblog.com, and a Myspace page, www.myspace.com/paulocoelho.

PAULO COELHO INSTITUTE

The Paulo Coelho Institute is a non-profit organization financed entirely from the writer's royalties and managed by Belina Antunes, the mother of his agent, Mônica. From time to time, Paulo makes large contributions from his other activities. The Institute's main aim is to give opportunities to underprivileged and excluded members of Brazilian society, particularly children and the elderly. The Solar Meninos da Luz, founded in 1996, is co-sponsored by the Paulo Coelho Institute, which makes an annual contribution of US$400,000. The school offers entirely free education to 430 needy children in the Pavão-Pavãozinho e Cantagalo *favela* in Rio de Janeiro.

ACKNOWLEDGEMENTS

AUTHOR'S NOTE

This book started life at the beginning of 2005 at Saint-Exupéry airport, in Lyons, in the south of France, when I met Paulo Coelho for the first time. As a journalist, I was used to accompanying international names and stars and imagined I would find him surrounded by bodyguards, secretaries and assistants. To my surprise, the man with whom I would spend much of the following three years turned up alone, with a rucksack on his back and dragging a small suitcase on wheels. It was there that the excavation began that would reveal one of the most extraordinary individuals I have ever worked with.

After six weeks at his side, I returned to Brazil. Since the entire course of his life has revolved around Rio, I moved there and spent eight months following the trails left by the writer. I looked for Paulo Coelho everywhere and probed behind the events that had left so many scars. I searched for him in the dark alleys of the roughest areas of Copacabana, among the records of the insane and the ruins of what had once been Dr Eiras's clinic, in the dangerous world of drugs, in files dating from the years of political repression in Brazil, in satanism, in mysterious secret societies, in his partnership with Raul Seixas, in his family and his genealogy. I talked to friends and those who had fallen out with him, interviewed many of his ex-lovers and spent some time with his present – and, he vows, his last – partner, the artist Christina Oiticica. I rummaged through his life, dug deep into his private affairs, read his will, studied his medications, read his bank statements, felt in his pockets and searched for the children I imagined must have resulted from his various relationships and love affairs.

I won a bet with him that gave me access to a treasure that he had decided was to be burnt after his death: a trunk that held forty years of diaries, many of them recorded on cassette tapes. I spent weeks closeted in the Paulo Coelho Institute scanning documents, photos, old diaries and letters both received and sent. Once my time in Rio was over, I again accompanied him on trips to various corners of the earth with a recorder slung over my shoulder, listening to his nasal voice and to his comments, and watching that strange tic he has of flicking away non-existent flies from his eyes. I went with him on the road to Santiago de Compostela, I saw how moved he was on meeting a group of ordinary readers in Oñati, in the Spanish Basque country and in Cairo, and I watched him being acclaimed by men in black ties and women in long dresses at banquets held in his honour in Paris and Hamburg.

I put together the pieces left behind by Paulo Coelho throughout his sixty years, and the result is this book. Although the responsibility for everything written here is mine alone, I must acknowledge the help of the dozens of people who helped me along the way. Firstly, my old friend Wagner Homem. I asked him to apply his expertise to organizing the vast quantity of data, interviews and documents that I accumulated during three years of research. He ended up moving into my house, where for ten uninterrupted months he worked on that, as well as reading and re-reading the final text and making valuable suggestions for improving it. My gratitude must also go to two brothers: one putative, Ricardo Setti, who has long been in charge of quality control with regard to my books and whose talent has saved me at the most difficult moments, and one real, Reinaldo Morais, who moved heaven and earth to make sure that the book reached its final destination safely.

I must also thank all those who generously collaborated on this book, the many people I interviewed and the researchers, journalists, trainees and stringers who found and interviewed the individuals who have given life, colour and human warmth to this story. These are: Adriana Negreiros, Afonso Borges, Aldo Bocchini Neto, Alfonso Molinero, Ana Carolina da

Motta, Ana Paula Granello, Antônio Carlos Monteiro de Castro, Armando Antenore, Armando Perigo, The Association of Old Boys of the St Ignatius College, Áurea Soares de Oliveira, Áureo Sato, Beatriz de Medeiros de Souza, Belina Antunes, Carina Gomes, Carlos Augusto Setti, Carlos Heitor Cony, Carlos Lima, Célia Valente, Cláudio Humberto Rosa e Silva, César Polcino Milies, Dasha Balashova, Denis Kuck, Devanir Barbosa Paes, Diego de Souza Martins, Eliane Lobato, Eric Nepomuceno, Evanise dos Santos, Fernando Eichenberg, Firmeza Ribeiro dos Santos, Francisco Cordeiro, Frédéric Bonomelli, Gemma Capdevila, Herve Louit, Hugo Carlo Batista Ramos, Ibarê Dantas, Inês Garçoni, Instituto Paulo Coelho and Sant Jordi Associados, Ivan Luiz de Oliveira, Ivone Kassu, Joaquim Ferreira dos Santos, Joca do Som, José Antonio Martinuzzo, Juliana Perigo, Klecius Henrique, Leonardo Oiticica, Lourival Sant'Anna, Lúcia Haddad, Luciana Amorim, Luciana Franzolin, Luiz Cordeiro Mergulhão, Lyra Netto, Marcio José Domingues Pacheco, Marcio Valente, Marilia Cajaíba, Mário Magalhães, Mário Prata, Marisilda Valente, Mariza Romero, Marizilda de Castro Figueiredo, Pascoal Soto, Raphael Cardoso, Ricardo Hofstetter, Ricardo Schwab, Roberto Viana, Rodrigo Pereira Freire, Samantha Quadrat, Silvia Ebens, Silvio Essinger, Sylvio Passos, Talles Rodrigues Alves, Tatiana Marinho, Tatiane Rangel, Véronique Surrel, Vicente Paim and Wilson Moherdaui.

Finally, I would like to thank the hundreds of people from more than thirty countries who sent data, documents and photos to the website http://www.cpc.com.br/paulocoelho/, which was created in order to receive such contributions, some of whom supplied important information that I have used in this book.

Fernando Morais
Ilhabela, March 2008

THOSE INTERVIEWED FOR THIS BOOK

Acácio Paz
Afonso Galvão
Alan Clarke
Amapola Rios
André Midani
Andréa Cals
Antonio Carlos Austregésilo de
    Athayde
Antonio Carlos 'Kakiko' Dias
Antonio Cláudio de Lima Vieira
Antônio Ovídio Clement Fajardo
Antônio Walter Sena, Jr. ('Toninho
    Buda')
Arash Hejazi
Ariovaldo Bonas
Arnaldo Niskier
Arnold Bruver, Jr.
Artur da Távola
Basia Stepien
Beatriz Vallandro
Cecilia Bolocco
Cecília Mac Dowell
Chico Castro Silva
Christina Oiticica
Cristina Lacerda
Darc Costa
Dedê Conte
Eduardo Jardim de Moraes
Élide 'Dedê' Conte
Ernesto Emanuelle Mandarino
Eugênio Mohallen
Fabíola Fracarolli

Fernando Bicudo
Frédéric Beigbeder
Frédéric Morel
Geneviève Phalipou
Gilles Haeri
Glória Albues
Guy Jorge Ruffier
Hélio Campos Mello
Henrique Caban
Hildegard Angel
Hildebrando Goes Filho
Ilma Fontes
Índio do Brasil Lemes
Isabela Maltarolli
Ivan Junqueira
Jerry Adriani
Joel Macedo
Jorge Luiz Costa Ramos
Jorge Mourão
José Antonio Mendonça Neto
José Antonio 'Pepe' Domínguez
José Mário Pereira
José Reinaldo Rios de Magalhães
José Wilker
Julles Haeri
Kika Seixas
Leda Vieira de Azevedo
Lizia Azevedo
Marcelo Nova
Márcia Faria Lima
Márcia Nascimento
Marcos Medeiros Bastos

Marcos Mutti

Marcos Paraguassu Arruda Câmara

Maria Cecília Duarte Arraes de Alencar

Maria Eugênia Stein

Marie Christine Espagnac

Marilu Carvalho

Mário Sabino

Maristela Bairros

Maurício Mandarino

Michele Conte

Milton Temer

Mônica Antunes

Nelly Canellas Branco

Nelson Liano, Jr

Nelson Motta

Orietta Paz

Patrice Hoffman

Patricia Martín

Paula Braconnot

Paulo Roberto Rocco

Pedro Queima Coelho de Souza

Regina Bilac Pinto

Renato Menescal

Renato Pacca

Ricardo Sabanes

Rita Lee

Roberto Menescal

Rodrigo Meinberg

Rosana Fiengo

Serge Phalipou

Sidney Magal

Silvio Ferraz

Soizik Molkhou

Sônia Maria Coelho de Souza

Stella Paula Costa

Vera Prnjatovic Richter

Zé Rodrix

Zeca Araújo

Zuenir Ventura

PHOTOGRAPHIC ACKNOWLEDGEMENTS

Every effort has been made to ensure the origin and ownership of the photos used in this book. This was not always possible, particularly in the case of photos obtained from family collections or those of friends of Paulo Coelho. I should be happy to give credit to the photographers should they come forward.